Age *of* Iron

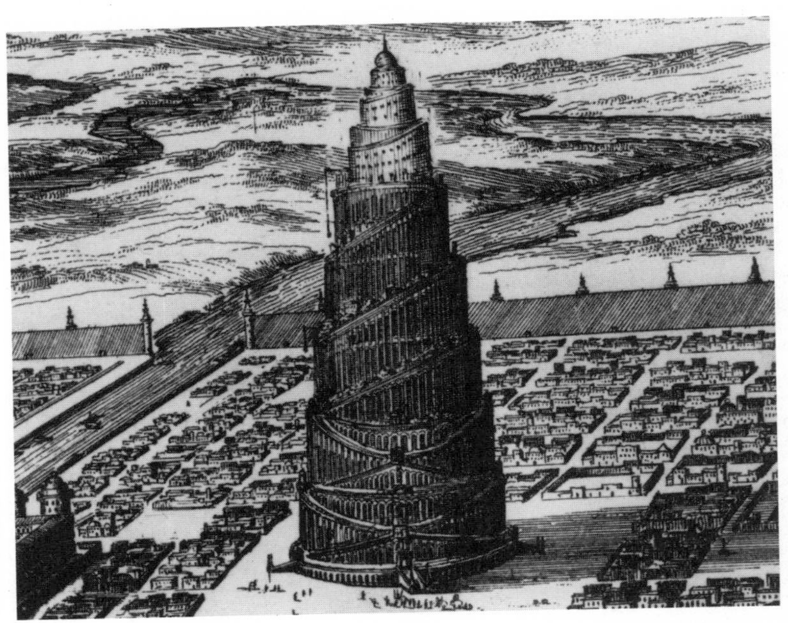

AGE *of* IRON

English Renaissance Tropologies of Love and Power

GALE H. CARRITHERS, JR.,
and JAMES D. HARDY, JR.

LOUISIANA STATE UNIVERSITY PRESS *Baton Rouge*

Manufactured in the United States of America
First printing
07 06 05 04 03 02 01 00 99 98 5 4 3 2 1

Designer: Michele Myatt Quinn
Typeface: Adobe Garamond
Typesetter: Wilsted & Taylor Publishing Services
Printer and binder: Thomson-Shore, Inc.

The frontispiece image of the Tower of Babel is reproduced courtesy of the Philip Mills Arnold Semeiology Collection, Washington University Libraries, St. Louis, Missouri.

Library of Congress Cataloging-in-Publication Data
Carrithers, Gale H., 1932–
Age of iron : English renaissance tropologies of love and power / Gale H. Carrithers, Jr. and James D. Hardy, Jr.
p. cm.
Includes index.
ISBN 0-8071-2246-7 (cloth : alk. paper)
1. English literature—Early modern, 1500–1700—History and criticism. 2. Literature and history—Great Britain—History—16th century. 3. Literature and history—Great Britain—History—17th century. 4. Christianity and literature—England—History. 5. Power (Social sciences) in literature. 6. Renaissance—England. 7. Love in literature. I. Hardy, James D. (James Daniel), 1934– . II. Title.
PR428.H57C37 1998
820.9′3823—dc21 98-13800
CIP

The paper in this book meets the guidelines for permanence and durability of the Committee on Production Guidelines for Book Longevity of the Council on Library Resources. ♾

To our children

This is the race of iron. Neither day nor night will give them rest as they waste away with toil and pain. Growing cares will be given them by the gods, and their lot will be a blend of good and bad.

—Hesiod

Then came the age of iron
And from it poured the very blood of evil:
Piety, Faith, Love and Truth changed to Deceit,
Violence, the Tricks of the Trade, Usury, Profit.

—Ovid

We are fallen, I do not only say, into an iron age, but into an age whose very iron hath gathered rust.

—Thomas Pierce

. . . our age was Iron, and rusty too.

—John Donne

Iron Age presents itself, calling forth the evils.

—Ben Jonson

Contents

Preface

Scholars largely agree that western European, certainly English, Renaissance culture was "religious"; and they agree that relative to it, eighteenth-century culture was "secular." This book is animated by the idea that the culture of Renaissance England was fundamentally, profoundly, and obviously centered on religion, for the most part Protestant but also Roman Catholic, or animist, with an occasional whiff of witchcraft and magic. We understand religion as the ocean, so to say, while economics, court politics, law, even literature were the currents, the waves, the whitecaps, even sometimes the foam, always to be known within the underlying religious context. We argue that the Renaissance English saw their lives and society and civilization in religious terms and in particular within the context of four dominant tropes: journey toward ultimate justice and mercy; the differentiating and defining moment; calling, as a Pauline ambassador of the good; and theater, with its manifold permutations (including the true remnant awash in a sea of theatrical pretense). We argue that the Renaissance English understood their lives primarily in terms of "faith and fear" and / or "the sure and certain hope." Religion, therefore, is not merely a topic to be studied, like Parliament, the Jacobean stage, colonization, or the draining of the fens, but is the matrix within which all the others occurred and within which contemporaries understood subjects now seen as essentially secular.

This study focuses primarily on literary texts and on their (more or less proleptic) criticism, *especially by trope,* of that change-in-progress. Thus we foreground what one in an Aristotelian moment might call material causes, whereas much recent scholarship (cited appreciatively below) has foregrounded formal causes, specifically institutional changes (including those in the production, status, or rhetoric of literary discourse). But it is not only to supplement the remarkable past generation of Renaissance scholarship that we emphasize trope. Historically, the more theocentric culture depended on trope in ways that the later, immanentist, or secular, culture did not. Philosophically, it is a commonplace to observe that symbol precedes idea, yet the tropes and their powers of cultural critique have been occluded in current scholarship.

As the foregoing clearly indicates, we are in some ways sharply divided from those new historicists who have emphasized, among other things, a genuine (though not always clear) cultural division between the orthodoxy of the powerful and a heterodoxy of the marginalized, the oppressed, and those "despised and rejected of men." This preoccupation with elites and those oppressed has two corollaries, one critical and the other political. The critical corollary involves a laudable effort to see texts within their social and historical context rather than as isolated and deracinated artifacts. The political corollary, however, is a constant and intense preoccupation with power, and texts are seen as reflecting the division of life between elites, patriarchal or otherwise vile but certainly oppressive, and virtuous victims who have been held long in social, even legal, servitude. Thus the text—whether the *Book of Common Prayer,* one Donnean, Shakespearean, or Miltonic, or a court opinion such as *Rex* v. *Hampden*—contains a hidden code that must be cracked to reveal the contents of righteous resentment, culturally dominant thought control, or subverted subversion.

We applaud the emphasis on historical context, as will appear. We dissent, however, from the preoccupation with the invidious nature of power, which may reflect more of the twentieth century than of the seventeenth. Of course we are in several senses *interested* in history, without, in any sense entailing determinism, being historicists. We try to attend to the historical constraints and conditionings of our writers and ourselves. We are reflecting upon the Renaissance and on the interrelationships of text to context during that period. We are hermeneutic students interested in those somewhat imprecise, successively illuminating interrelationships rather than in linear ideologies of alleged cause and effect, historicist or other.

Again, in a sort of coda recapitulating earlier themes, we return to a new historicist favorite concept, power. Again, we are in dissent. Our construal of *power* implies not social cleavage or class consciousness and hostility but instead an attitudinal / theological polarity. We use *power* as the usual (though not universal) opposite of *love.* Power here has a tropic reference, especially in connection with theatricality. In general, accordingly, power signifies the fraudulent promises of salvific change. This might involve technological *hubris,* supported by Francis Bacon and exposed as hollow by John Milton in Books VI, VIII, and XII of *Paradise Lost.* It might be the mythic representation of masque in which the state seems to be changed from tragic to beneficial. It might be the political mask of power presented as order or God's will. Always it involved seeming and appearance, what the Italians call *bella figura.*

The implications of this are clear enough. We aspire to be past-minded, to use an old term from historiographic critical theory. We are examining how the Renaissance English conceived themselves, and we ordinarily attempt to use contemporary terms with their contemporary meanings. We are not writing about modern politics using Renaissance examples. We attempt to examine a religiously centered symbolic and analogical public culture in something close to its signifiers and signifieds.

In reflecting upon the culture of Renaissance England and construing it, we have employed some few specialized terms and have had to make choices when multiple names were available. We have settled on *trope,* as opposed, say, to *theme* or *motif,* as the proper name for the four dominant parsings of divinely ordained but fallen human reality, transcendantly conceived but immanently recognized. When we employ the term *trope,* it will always be in this general sense of language turned by and with regard to transcendence rather than as a specific, rhetorical term (as when one says "the trope of chiasmus").

We also ponder the labels for various religious groups in Renaissance England. While the larger distinctions, such as Protestant and Catholic, are satisfactorily clear and conventional, the same cannot be said for smaller but absolutely essential distinctions. Keeping in mind the useful comments by Donna Hamilton in *Shakespeare and the Politics of Protestant England,* we nonetheless have decided to use the traditional terms *Anglican* and *Puritan* and to use them as indicators of mutual differentiation. Although *Anglican* is of Victorian origin as a term, it is still more accurately descriptive, if anachronistic, than any other term in ordinary usage. Confining the term *Church of England* to meaning the church as a public and legal institution rather than a faith contributed clarity to political discussion but eliminated a synonym for *Anglican. Conformist* made sense, at least under Elizabeth I, when a broad spectrum of Puritan life and thought remained formally within the Church of England, but less and less sense under the Stuarts. *Nonconformist* made little sense for any part of the Renaissance, as it hid the variety of Calvinist conventicles and groups and congregations. *Puritan,* however, already generally understood as meaning some form of Calvinist divergence (ecclesiological or theological) from the royal settlement, had a broad general use, comparable to *Anglican.* Although Puritanism also contained a large number of incompatible, even conflicting, opinions, the term still illuminated the fundamental fact of some dissent in a particular (Calvinist) direction, whether carried as far as separation or not. Finally, both *Anglican* and *Puritan* were (and are) sufficiently broad and inclusive terms to allow us to examine the Renaissance English religious scene *as a whole,* our aim. So we have accepted some anachronicity ("Anglican") and some imprecision ("Puritan").

Our attempt to scrutinize English religious culture as a whole has also influenced our choice of texts. It would have been possible to choose any number of pamphleteers, minor poets, lesser sermonizers, or authors of religious tracts, and this has been done by serious scholars in writing important books, which then provide invaluable checks and balances. But we wished to canvass some of the "commanding heights" of English letters, from drama and poetry to sermon and liturgy, for if here could be found the dominant religious tropes of Renaissance self-conception, elegantly and imaginatively expressed and generally free from cant and the "rank odor of sanctity," then this fact alone would help illuminate the whole culture. Thus, we chose from among the written texts those of general, rather than narrowly polemical, interest. Ben Jonson, John Donne, Andrew Marvell, John Milton, and the *Book of Common Prayer* have been the focus of our attention, with William Shakespeare a presence nearby.

While we are, like all scholars, uncomfortably aware that the best is far different from the rest, we recognize that both brilliant and ephemeral participated in the same general culture, though with widely different degrees of intellectual power and reflective critical independence with regard to what Alfred North Whitehead called "inert ideas." And it is the critical independence that shows both the heart and the limits of the general culture. So we chose from among the most prominent, confident that they would show more facets of English Renaissance self-understanding and "self-fashioning" than would the troops in the trenches of partisan doctrinal conflict.

A word about our conventions of presentation is also needed. A literary critic will often say, "At this point Mosca overreaches," or the like. That convention of critical discourse acknowledges that a poem or play unfolds to our eyes in the present tense. Here, we normally use a past tense in order to keep in play the other side of the equation: one reads Jonson now, but he wrote at an earlier stage (which we seek to understand) of the cultural transformation still raging around us (which we also seek to understand). A lesser matter: *we,* consistently, we hope, means Hardy and Carrithers; suppositions about commonalities are indicated by constructions such as "all of us," "who among us?," "one," and the like.

Our joint and several work on this book has been aided in ways we are delighted to acknowledge with thanks here. Our university provided a sabbatical semester, and its Graduate Research Council provided a summer grant to Carrithers. Dean Billy Seay of the Honors College sponsored the team-taught seminar crucial to our thoughtful interaction on Renaissance matters and provided clerical help in the person of the splendid Karen Powell. Readers for the Press have been anonymous to us but very present in their approbation and their strictures. To some of the latter we have responded with positive efforts, to others with hearts hardened. We deeply appreciate the professionalism of Catherine Kadair and the Louisiana State University Press staff, most immediately the exemplary care of Christine Cowan, our copy editor. We should probably have taken more of her expert advice. The dedication page acknowledges another kind of presence and another kind of joy and hope.

Age *of* Iron

I

Dominant Tropes of Renaissance Life

This book is a series of reflections on what once was called the "World Picture" and has more recently and usefully been called "habits of thought"—basic habits of thought of the English from the third edition of the *Book of Common Prayer* to the poetry of Andrew Marvell and those valedictories of "stupendious force," *Paradise Regain'd, Samson Agonistes,* and *Paradise Lost,* the second edition of which appeared in 1674. Between the two terms, we are more comfortable with associations of daily living (including dynamic and unsystematic assumption) that arise from Debora Shuger's happy usage "habits of thought" than we are with the taxonomic spatiality of "world view." In our analysis of what articulates and animates these habits of thought, we have examined works that are formal in structure, content, and purpose but have tried to do so within a wider context of the assumptive, almost intuitive, general English culture. We have sought to cross the changing and semipermeable boundaries between high literacy and (much more common) semiliteracy, or secondary orality, and the large terrain of oral culture. Although texts alone, the normative medium of criticism, including our own, cannot easily cast so inclusive a net, the concept of broad cultural habits of thought can. Accordingly, in considering that general culture, we agree with Shuger and many previous critics that "Renaissance habits of thought were by and large religious."[1]

But we differ from much current criticism, both in approach and conclusion, in exactly what these English Renaissance habits of thought might be. Rather than in issues of social power and cultural dominance or in pejorative and invidious language or in the psychology of exclusion, we find the orga-

1. Debora Shuger, *Habits of Thought in the English Renaissance: Religion, Politics, and the*

nizing nexuses of English thought in four cultural tropes of religious expression and existential understanding during the period. That Renaissance folk, from celebrated writers to the nonliterate, understood life as, in, and through tropes no literary scholar would deny. The identity, pervasiveness, and significance of those tropes, however, remains a matter for argument and can

---

Dominant Culture (Berkeley, 1990), 9. This important book is critical of much previous new historicist work, while retaining the new historicist approach. A quite different view of the Renaissance and Baroque "habits of thought" can be found in Anthony Raspa, *The Emotive Image: Jesuit Poetics and the English Renaissance* (Fort Worth, 1983), esp. Chaps. 1 and 2. Raspa presents an aesthetic, "affective" version of the Baroque world view, which he sees as composed of the following: "The universe was presumably meaningful. . . . its forces could best be represented by mythological figures. . . . these mythic forces were emotive. . . . man's faculties controlled his contact with the universe" (11). We find this view only narrowly useful, since it omits almost completely time, either human or eternal, and concentrates entirely on vicissitude within what our artists deemed to be this level of the great chain of being. A particular aesthetic seems to us to be too small a foundation upon which to build a notion of a Baroque world view. A third post-Tillyard book on the general world view of Renaissance England is Stephen L. Collins, *From Divine Cosmos to Sovereign State: An Intellectual History of Consciousness and the Idea of Order in Renaissance England* (New York, 1989); it features learned analyses of both the process and the content of the changes in the contemporary conceptions of social order that occurred between 1559 and 1642. Using literary examples as well as conventionally historical ones, Collins traces changes in consciousness ("history as order") and self-consciousness ("defining order as history") (p. 5 and last chap.). We find the social psychoanalysis and the critical theory to be seriously anachronistic and ahistorical and a serious impediment in an otherwise very strong book about the diminishing devotional, pietistic, and generally religious content in the contemporary ideas of public order and responsibility. Furthermore, a general and analytic conception of public order, whether in the form of history as order or order as history, does not, we suggest, allow sufficient room for religion qua religion or for either more or less divinized love. Moreover, Collins moves the tilt toward secularism back three generations (from 1670), and we dissent. Finally, in a time when most people were not in direct contact with the Crown and were in direct contact with the local church, we urge that Bible, Prayer Book, and sermon counted for much in notions of public order.

For relations of all this to private life, see, by Nancy Armstrong and Leonard Tennenhouse, the important, intensely engaging *The Imaginary Puritan: Literature, Intellectual Labor, and the Origins of Personal Life* (Berkeley, 1992). Their argument for the growing inclusiveness and significance of "personal life" in Milton's life, Milton's writings, and the modern Western world since seems to us cogent (and their canvass of much criticism of Milton or related culture, expertly discriminating). Their argument would be enriched and reinforced by the work of Walter Ong, M. T. Clanchy, Jesse Gellrich, and Brian Stock (whom they do not cite) on the orality / literacy continuum. They would not call the "culture that sought to differentiate the individual's rights from those of both God and king" exactly *new* (28) if they had kept in mind the common-law tradition from Magna Carta through Coke. And they seem to collapse

provide a discursive common ground for historians and cultural or literary critics. The tropes we descry as habitual to English thought in the seventeenth century are part of the shared medium *interactively* linking the more conventionally literary texts we consider with conventionally historical documents and with the variously powerful or literate writers and citizens.

Four tropes seem dominant: the defining (ideally the salvific) moment of illumination or choice; the world as God's theater, with humanity as actors, scriptors, or presumptuous directors; the world as way and life as journey, wherein one travels willfully, if vicissitudinally, toward God, or perhaps away; and, finally, life as ambassadorship, in which one exhibits virtue (or vice) to mediate, advocate, and foster a transcendent (or merely absolutist) reign, *caritas* for Augustine of Hippo, *Dei gloriam* for Ignatius of Loyola.[2] Moment as trope manifests the metonymic (as when the sinner may "turn from his wick-

---

(as Milton did not) "all the charities" into that "wedded love" that Milton did hail as their source. Yet if their Milton is less a poet of exile than merely the poet who went home, he nonetheless *moved,* and that, we agree, cannot be overemphasized.

With regard to grander homes (mostly), and a counterhistoricism, see C. H. George, "Parnassus Restored, Saints Confounded: The Secular Challenge to the Age of the Godly, 1560–1660," *Albion,* XXXIII (1991), 409–37. He insists on the dominance *everywhere* in his learned range of examples, of a pagan secularism, *pace* the "fog . . . of Protestant culture" in seventeenth-century England and twentieth-century scholarship, the latter too often intent on "often inappreciable differences" in revolutionary Christian factionalism; but it was the age of religious, not classical humanist, wars and persecutions. We would highlight the theatricality of his artistic examples; and more generally we differentiate between folk animism, classicism (both more and less assimilated to Christianity), and incipient cultural materialism.

For a spectrum of new historicist examinations of Renaissance literature from the less to the more useful, see Jonathan Dollimore, *Radical Tragedy: Religion, Ideology, and Power in the Drama of Shakespeare and His Contemporaries* (Chicago, 1984); Jonathan Dollimore and Alan Sinfield, eds., *Political Shakespeare: New Essays in Cultural Materialism* (Ithaca, 1985); Margaret Ferguson, Maureen Quilligan, and Nancy Vickers, eds., *Rewriting the Renaissance: The Discourse of Sexual Difference in Early Modern Europe* (Chicago, 1986). Compare Kenneth Burke, *A Grammar of Motives* (New York, 1969), "four master tropes," 503–507. Burke, like Hayden White after him, meant metaphor, metonymy, synecdoche, and irony. We address these elements of discourse mainly as variations of our four tropes—variations in mode or degree of presence.

2. *Ad regnem caritatis* ("toward the reign of love") is Augustine's prescriptive guide for resolving (by choosing between) alternative readings of ambiguous scriptural passages: *De doctrina Christiana,* Bk. 4 in J. P. Migne, ed., *Patrologiae cursus completus . . . series Latina* (Paris, 1844–64), XXXIV, col. 60; this central Augustinian work is so important for literary and cultural studies that modern translations are widely available). *Ad majorem Dei gloriam* ("to the greater glory of God") is the motto of the Society of Jesus.

edness and live") becoming synecdochic. It defines a condition of discontinuity, in which the present suddenly, in "the twinkling of an eye," becomes ontologically different from the past and in which the present will inform the future. We include within the general category of trope of moment the Renaissance (and medieval) understanding of the finality, permanence, and commitment implied in personal honor or word as bond or oath, in which the swearer is in an instant changed profoundly in his relationships to the rest of humanity.[3] *Theatrum mundi,* intrinsically metaphoric (theater stands in the place of life, as an imitation of an action), seems always in a fallen world at least incipiently ironic. The human false always hides within the human truth, and theater both reveals and masks. But the trope was itself turned through more than the axis of faithful-to-deceitful representation. There was the axis of power: Who shall produce theater? God? Hamlet or Claudius? Octavius or Cleopatra? Oberon or Theseus or Bottom? Related to that, the axis twists from the immanently knowable or makable to the dreamily imponderable in space or unpredictable in time to the transcendently mysterious. Primary reality may be seen unified in the action and dramatis personae who perform it (as in liturgy, and ostensibly in masque) or divided, questioned by a character (as by Macbeth), or questioned everywhere on this great stage of fools but in anguish (*e.g.,* the scene concluding *King Lear*). Allied to the axis of truth-mask-deceit, theater is a trope of discovery both onstage and off, as in *All's Well That Ends Well, Hamlet,* or *The Revenger's Tragedy.* Theater as

3. See J. Douglas Canfield, *Word as Bond in English Literature from the Middle Ages to the Restoration* (Philadelphia, 1989), esp. Foreword and Afterword for the context; but his richly provocative book should be consulted at length. Similarly, see Georges Van Den Abbeele, *Travel as Metaphor: From Montaigne to Rousseau* (Minneapolis, 1992), in which Descartes and Montesquieu are treated along with the title figures, and the focus is not inappropriately, for them and for the dawning age, secular. See, as a methodological model, Caroline Walker Bynum, *The Resurrection of the Body in Western Christendom, 200–1336* (New York, 1995). She lucidly explicates tropes—primarily the tropes of seed, statue, and clothing—as animating and shaping theological argument about body, self, and resurrection at critical moments over eleven centuries and longer. Timothy Hampton, in *Writing from History: The Rhetoric of Exemplarity in Renaissance Literature* (Ithaca, 1990), makes a convincing case for the cultural significance of the historical exemplar from Desiderius Erasmus and Guillaume Budé to Shakespeare and Corneille and for the disintegration of the figure in the culture of rising power and historical awareness. Above all, see Anthony Low, *The Reinvention of Love: Poetry, Politics, and Culture from Sidney to Milton* (Cambridge, Eng., 1993), "the Biblical marriage trope" as frequently and powerfully significant.

trope seems to have been, outside the liturgy, poorly suited to animating any form of love other than narcissism. It seems better suited to power.[4] Court life was peculiarly the province of such theatricality, with its emphasis on show, on power, on "containment of subversion," on the use of theater as a supplement for law, bureaucracy, money, and "honors" in the art of ruling. In Re-

4. No reader of Renaissance literature has altogether overlooked *theatrum mundi.* We urge renewed consultations of: Ernst Curtius, in the context of his polymathic mapping of *European Literature and the Latin Middle Ages,* trans. Willard Trask (New York, 1953), 138–44; Herbert Weisinger, in his ambivalent reflections on myth and the passions of literary-cultural study in *The Agony and the Triumph: Papers on the Use and Abuse of Myth* (East Lansing, 1964), 58–70; and, most imperatively, Howard D. Pearce, "A Phenomenological Approach to the *Theatrum Mundi* Metaphor," *PMLA,* XCV (1980), 42–57, and Bruce Wilshire, *Role Playing and Identity: The Limits of Theatre as Metaphor* (Bloomington, 1982), esp. 237–57. For a useful recent study of Continental power-shows as festivities, or as dumb-shows in the graphic arts, see Marie Tanner, *The Last Descendant of Aeneas: The Hapsburgs and the Mythic Image of the Emperor* (New Haven, 1993); R. J. W. Evans, reviewing her (*New York Review of Books,* February 17, 1994, pp. 25–27), appositely demurs at her exclusivity and some overreading of evidence; but neither he nor she seems to have considered the factor of love, so vital to the differing currency of an Elizabeth's or a James's representings. See, in this connection and with regard to Chap. 2, below, Alvin Kernan's *Shakespeare, the King's Playwright: Theater in the Stuart Court, 1603–1613* (New Haven, 1995), to hand as this book was substantially complete: a carefully regiocentric and court-centered canvass of Shakespeare as very much the King's man, "somewhat boldly" locating "theater among the major institutions of the state" and in "the ultimate theater of the court" (201, 23). We identify ultimacy elsewhere, think Kernan a bit premature in proclaiming "the Leviathan State" (1–23), and think Jonson *more* the King's man, but the formal causes and partial case are superbly argued. Implicitly, Evans, Tanner, Kernan, and even their royal subjects are benign compared to the theatrical tropism as narcissistic black hole, in Michel Foucault's DeLeuzian "Theatrum Philosophicum," in *Language, Counter-Memory, Practice: Selected Essays and Interviews,* ed. Donald F. Bouchard (Ithaca, 1977), 165–96, a kind of boundary (to these matters) as extreme as the theatricalism Milton assigned to Satan.

Thus, theater, and less conspicuously moment and ambassadorship, foreground issues heavily engaged in recent years, issues of history, historicism, and freedom. This early note seems the place to sketch our belief, manifest in the text to follow; and we do so with gratitude to Jonathan Crewe for his clarification of the issues in his introductory chapters to both *Hidden Designs: The Critical Profession and Renaissance Literature* (New York, 1986) and *Trials of Authorship: Anterior Form and Poetic Reconstruction from Wyatt to Shakespeare* (Berkeley, 1990). Briefly: we believe in both historicity and historiography; that Queen Elizabeth I and King Charles I died in 1603 and 1649 must be acknowledged with minimum construal (Crewe's modest word in preference to *interpretation*), whereas the significance of those deaths and, a fortiori, the degree to which each monarch was effectively moribund five years before physical death, or a living force ten years after, are matters of *inevitable* construal. It is much the same,

naissance England, theater was viewed as political in origin and nature and was the quintessential power trope—the trope that identified the ways of government, *including divine government.*

The third trope, carrying moment and theater beyond tychastic (from *tuchē,* chance) time into the realm of extended, even metaphysical, time, was the idea of the journey of life. Commonly literal and easily metaphoric, it could subsume the synecdochic and even the ironic (as in Donne's "Good Friday 1613, Riding Westward," concluding "burn off my rusts and I'll turn my face"). A lifetime of prayerful hope and thanksgiving (trying to ride eastward) lay at the core of a Christian view of life. The final trope that informed all of Renaissance life, irrespective of class or faith, was calling, the doctrine of ambassadorship, which, like journey, offered rich permutations: from the metonymy of everyday encounter to the metaphor of business transaction to the synecdochic and ironic pretense of power charade. It also justified building the city on a hill and letting "your light so shine." Ambassadorship may, in socioreligious terms, be described as especially the "Puritan trope."

---

we contend, with the range of elements in the particular iconographic and printed texts we consider as counterparts to quasi-panoramic historical settings, elements from etymology to genre to cultural indisposition. In construing, we agree with Crewe that "close reading is not only rigorously entailed in the consideration of form, but that the passage through close reading is not really avoidable even in the most expansively cosmopolitan discourse of the Renaissance" (*Trials of Authorship,* 16). The ideological naïveté or cultural myopia sometimes attendant on close reading we would distinguish as failure of critical discernment or responsibility, and we as historical creatures are not immune. Responsibility: of course the language and culture of the time (with its ambiguous presencings of the past) both enabled and restrained artists of that time, as our time does of any of us. But "culture" or "discourse" does not produce or even imply the *Book of Common Prayer* or *The Alchemist* or "Upon Appleton House," say, or this essay, which was altogether unpredictable to us when we first began teaching a seminar together some years ago; we deplore careless quasi-Foucauldianism. With that, we affirm the pastness of the past; it is myth that repeats itself (or the mini-myths of allegory, romance, or ideology), never history. We cannot rewrite the Renaissance; it can only be ourselves that we remake. But we can reexamine Renaissance matters (not the same as "*the* Renaissance"). In doing so we necessarily engage metaphor and engage in metaphor, but we try to avoid, as we believe our main chosen writers did, totalizing metaphor, which is to say, myth. Katharine Eisaman Maus writes, with a narrower focus but in similar spirit, of modes of disjunction "between an unexpressed interior and a theatricalized exterior" in *Inwardness and Theater in the English Renaissance* (Chicago, 1995). Certainly there was interiority, as she shows. Readers of the Bible, the *Book of Common Prayer,* and St. Augustine should always have seen this. Readers of the scholarship of Walter Ong and followers would have recognized that literacy has always fostered, whereas primary orality inhibits, the sense of interiority.

In all of these tropes, the dominant themes and images were expressed in terms of the relative positions and relationships of competitiveness and power and gain and bargain, on the one hand, to those of love and giving and affirmation and trust, on the other. The language of love and power had always an implied sense of ambivalence, of the partial and the shared, of the human condition consisting, in the same act and at the same time, of both giving and getting, of both the human and the divine. The term *trope* also preserves the dynamism of *turning,* as well as its association with Augustinian *retorqueo* and its implications of movement in general, and dynamism is in several ways more important to our argument than taxonomy. We also mean very large senses of *turn:* broadly cultural and indeed ontological, as in representation by some variation. The variation can range from the minimum for accommodating divine truth to fallen perception, to amendment by total substitution, from personal change to broad cultural shifts.

Obviously the tropes of moment, theatricality, journey, and ambassadorship do not exhaust the list of ideas and images animating Renaissance life. The familiar term *master-trope* is a provocative notion, but it obscures the *competition* for mastery, which we see expressed and dramatized, as underlying those conflicts peculiarly illuminated in major literary texts. Scholars have also discussed the idea of social hierarchy more or less sanctified or mystified by the scale of rank.[5] William Shakespeare famously enunciated it in *Troilus and Cressida:*

> Take but degree away, untune that string,
> And hark what discord follows. Each thing meets
> In mere oppugnancy.
>
> (I, iii, 109–11)

5. With regard to the scale of being, the founding document for modern scholarship has been Arthur Lovejoy's *The Great Chain of Being* (Cambridge, Mass., 1936). The existential status of the chain has of course been contested ("an advanced condition of rust by the end of the sixteenth century") by J. W. Lever and his reintroducer Jonathan Dollimore in *The Tragedy of State: A Study of Jacobean Drama* (London, 1987), vii–xviii, 5. The ideological status of the chain has been reaffirmed, in notably sophisticated fashion, by Joel Fineman, *e.g.,* in "The Turn of the Shrew," in *The Subjectivity Effect in Western Literary Tradition: Essays Toward the Release of Shakespeare and the Question of Theory,* ed. Patricia Parker and Geoffrey Hartman (New York, 1985), 120–42. We grant the obvious, that questioning and contention increasingly occurred in the exclusively human ontological niche as authority and even law might increasingly assert hierarchies within that niche, of monarch to subject, say, or man to woman. But our concern is binocularly with the contestability our authors affirm within that niche and their

Yet this ideal had already deteriorated, as the irony of the words Shakespeare puts in the mouth of his wily Ulysses, in so dark a play, indicates. "Degree" as self-interested confusion of ontological difference with social status was contested by radical religion, with its priesthood of all believers, and was victim of the multiplication of purchased titles and offices, victim of literacy, and victim of the rising power of kings. So we judge this and other figures and images to be of somewhat lesser status, not minimizing their currency, but arguing that their declining correspondence with reality made them less engrossing and consequential than were theater, moment, journey, and ambassadorship.

Moreover, we choose and emphasize these four tropes because of their religious resonance. In an age of intense, even strident and fearful belief, no general cultural idea or figure or image that failed to aim beyond the purely human level of the great chain of being could embrace all varieties of rank, "condicion," "qualitie," or private belief. For the Renaissance citizen all human things, and thus all ideas about things, came from God and led properly back to God. The divine judge, "from whom no secrets are hid," both supplemented and complemented human judgment. The tropes were the way in which the Renaissance citizenry imagined action, order, and being and in which they longed for all things human finally to be put right.

Accordingly, we are more interested in religion as the basis for general cultural habits of thought than we are in politics or systematic theology. We are somewhat removed from the conflict about the nature of English Protestantism. Charles and Katherine George postulated a general English Protestant mind, whereas John New argued for theological differences between Anglican and Puritan.[6] We tend to agree with the Georges about large grounds of simi-

---

persisting conviction of radical ontological difference between the human level and animal-vegetable-mineral levels below and angelic and divine levels transcendently above. The displacement of convictions of transcendence by phantasms of human power is a major concern of our writers.

6. We basically agree with John F. H. New, *Anglican and Puritan: The Basis of Their Opposition, 1558–1640* (Palo Alto, 1964): there are substantial theological differences between the two. We diverge from Charles and Katherine George, *The Protestant Mind of the English Reformation, 1570–1640* (Princeton, 1961), when they argue that serious theological differences between Puritan and Anglican did not exist and thus could not be a cause of revolution, though we do agree that a "Protestant mind," inclusive of both groups, did exist. See also Patrick McGrath, *Papists and Puritans Under Elizabeth I* (London, 1967), and, more recently, J. Sears McGee, *The Godly Man in Stuart England: Anglicans, Puritans, and the Two Tables, 1620–1670* (New Haven,

larity but acknowledge the power of small religious differences to divide, which is New's point. The four dominant tropes of Renaissance life, we argue, were intrinsic to the perception and understanding of all the English, and we attribute the differences in emphasis and expression to idiosyncratic personal experience and literary ability as well as to theological doctrine. While they

---

1976), an excellent book that inclines, it seems, more to New than to the Georges. In this connection one must not neglect the important works of Nicholas Tyacke, especially "Puritanism, Arminianism and Counter-Revolution," in *The Origins of the English Civil War,* ed. Conrad Russell (London, 1973), 119–43, an extremely important article in the development of a current view that a new group of bishops, tainted with Arminianism and an affection for liturgical ritual, emerged to disrupt a Church of England that was essentially dominated by preaching and tended toward Calvinist predestination orthodoxy. See also Nicholas Tyacke, *Anti-Calvinists: The Rise of English Arminianism, c. 1590–1640* (Oxford, 1987). This view has not gone without comment and challenge, particularly in *Past and Present.* See Peter White, "The Rise of Arminianism Reconsidered," *Past and Present,* No. 101 (1983), 34–54; Nicholas Tyacke and Peter White, "Arminianism Reconsidered," *Past and Present,* No. 115 (1987), 201–29; and P. Lake, "Calvinism and the English Church, 1570–1635," *Past and Present,* No. 114 (1987), 32–76. See also Peter White, *Predestination, Policy and Polemic: Conflict and Consensus in the English Church from the Reformation to the Civil War* (Cambridge, Mass., 1992). We cannot agree with the pure Tyacke thesis, particularly as it implies a rapid and radical change in Anglican directions after 1630. We are, however, in complete agreement with Tyacke's emphasis on liturgy and systematic theology as expressed in preaching and with Tyacke's view of the importance of religion in Stuart England. We agree as well with the view of H. R. Trevor-Roper that England cannot be considered in isolation, as if there were no connection with the continent. See H. R. Trevor-Roper, *Catholics, Anglicans and Puritans: Seventeenth Century Essays* (London, 1987). For a careful examination of the Catholic Church, see the indispensible work of Kevin Sharpe, *The Personal Rule of Charles I* (New Haven, 1992), Chap. VI. But see and heed Anthony Low's review article on David Cressy's *Bonfires and Bells: National Memory and the Protestant Calendar in Elizabethan and Stuart England* (Berkeley, 1989), in *Ben Jonson Journal,* I (1994), 231–37. Low praises Cressy and others for countering "the continuing or increasing exclusion of things Roman Catholic from the mainstream of literary studies." Two important corrective works: J. T. Rhodes, "Continuities: The Ongoing English Catholic Tradition from the 1570s to the 1630s," *John Donne Journal,* XII (1993), 139–51, and, with reference to the sixteenth century, Dennis Flynn, *John Donne and the Ancient Catholic Nobility* (Bloomington, 1995). See also Julian Davies, *The Caroline Captivity of the Church: Charles I and the Remoulding of Anglicanism, 1625–1641* (Oxford, 1992). Davies is one of the critics of the Arminianism thesis advanced by Tyacke and supported generally by "revisionist" historians. In this context "revisionism" means a rejection of the importance of ideology and principle, whether religious or political, and an acceptance of the separation of religion and politics into two discrete categories. Davies suggests that religious and constitutional principles were "at the heart of the debate and struggle" (2) and that politics and religion described parts of the same issues. He argues that the church of

defined variations within the Protestant habits of thought, the dominant tropes belonged to both Anglican and Puritan and in great measure meant the same things to both.

Yet if the areas of agreement within English Protestantism were broad, the points of contention were sharp. Differences in emphasis, journey for Anglicans and ambassadorship and moment for Puritans, were, for many contemporaries, decisive.[7] The differences between Anglican and Puritan, however described as "mixture," so decried by Puritans, on the role and office of bishops or the nature of the sacraments (especially the Eucharist) were impossible to compose. Differences in tropic emphasis, discord over the form of the ritual, disagreement over things others declared as adiaphora: these were precisely what could not possibly be compromised. Existential experience of the faithful demanded a certain form for satisfactory worship, a particular emphasis within the tropes for a resonant explanation of life and grace. The sharpness of division could abate only with the discovery of religious liberty (compromise or victory alike unnecessary). In a culture whose habits of thought, belief, and religious attachment were largely symbolic and analogic, the right religion was embodied in the familiar details. Thus, understanding in terms of the tropes resided in but also fostered and exceeded texts and connected the texts to life and to religious inclination.

We also argue that the major tropes held their position not merely for universality of experience but also from ontological urgency. Even ostensibly bold and linear description, seemingly the very (metaphorical) heart of literacy and historiography, lacks the multiple impressions of trope. It is not merely a question of a picture being worth a thousand words; it is the problem of the prejudicial limitations of linearity. As description and as main-line history, linearity tends to privilege metonymy: part-part-whole, that and that

Charles I, particularly after 1630, was a departure sharper in theory than practice from the Elizabethan or Jacobean church. We generally agree with the moderate thesis and careful research of Davies, and we suggest that the discounting of principle and the putative separation of (tendentiously defined) religion and politics are appropriate for a crypto-religious twentieth-century materialist world view, not for the Christian and tropic cultural framework of late medieval / Renaissance England.

7. McGee, *The Godly Man,* esp. Chaps. 3, 4, and 5. Chapter 3 deals with divergent emphases between Anglicans and Puritans concerning the Ten Commandments, whereas 4 and 5 deal with the divergent emphases concerning the fruits of conversion. McGee's view that the common ground between Anglican and Puritan was broad while the differences were sharp is compelling.

and that, this and then this and then this. Contiguity relationships foster and reinforce themselves, formally leaving out at the beginning (while seeming to explain away) similarity or other relationships. But contiguity and similarity relationships regularly entail and implicate one another. The historian selects details because they are significant, which is to say emblematic or synecdochic (or else pursuant of the power phantasm of "completeness"). The Renaissance citizen, eager to situate the self in relation to community and divinity, regularly engaged the wider range of tropes, sensing that secular disorder both could and could not lead by steps to a radically different yet not utterly dissimilar transcendent order.[8]

In this context, we consider the painting of "The Battle of Lepanto," by Paolo Veronese. Here the Christian Armada was arrayed in all its triumphant glory. The defeated Turks were crushed by both man and God, for above the battle was the light of salvation, the Church Triumphant, the miraculous intervention of God in favor of his people, and the apotheosis of crusading heroes, particularly Don John of Austria. But there was more to the painting than was painted. The Papacy, frightened of Spanish political power, nonetheless contributed scarce cash to the enterprise. Venice, battered by the shift of trade routes to the Atlantic and shaken by fiscal crisis, nonetheless mobilized once again as the paladin and shield of Christendom against the Turk. The *arsenali* turned out the galleys on their assembly line in what many felt was a losing cause and a foolhardy venture. After all, under Turkish threat,

8. Christianity has *always* been radical: "He hath put down the mighty from their seats, and exalted them of low degree" (Luke 1:52). For the dynamics of that literally radical tendency during the period in question, see especially George H. Williams, *The Radical Reformation* (Philadelphia, 1962); John Gee and George Hardy, *Anabaptist Beginnings (1523–1533): A Source Book,* Bibliotheca Humanistica et Reformatorica, Vol. XVI (Nieuwkoop, 1976); Lawrence Stone, *The Causes of the English Revolution, 1529–1642* (New York, 1972); Norman R. C. Cohn, *The Pursuit of the Millenium* (Rev. ed.; New York, 1970). The point about the mutual implication of similarity and contiguity is often acknowledged but nowhere more decisively than by Maria Ruegg in "Metaphor and Metonymy: The Logic of Structuralist Rhetoric," *Glyph,* VI (1979), 141–57. That point, and the related point about historical details selected *in* history and *by* historians, is used and illustrated helpfully by: Stephen Kogan, *The Hieroglyphic King: Wisdom and Idolatry in the Seventeenth-Century Masque* (Rutherford, N.J., 1986); J. G. A. Pocock, *The Ancient Constitution and the Feudal Law: A Study of English Historical Thought in the Seventeenth Century: A Reissue with a Retrospect* (Cambridge, Eng., 1987); McGee, *The Godly Man,* 144–49. See, still, J. H. Hexter, *Reappraisals in History: New Views on History and Society in Early Modern Europe* (London, 1961).

Venice had recently been forced to cancel the annual celebration of the marriage of the city to the sea. The Turks, whose navy had controlled the Mediterranean Sea since the fall of Rhodes in 1522 and whose naval power was merely checked at the siege of Malta, seemed invincible. Nonetheless, the increasingly supine Italian subjects of imperial Spain had built a fleet, while Spain herself, threatened on every front by war, bankruptcy, revolt, and heresy, led the enterprise. Out of fear and pessimism came deliverance, palpably a miracle, painted as a shining moment of the Church Militant and Triumphant. The whole of the *theatrum mundi,* with God as Producer, was arrayed in one canvas in a rare *moment* of apparent reconciliation with the *theatrum coeli.* The reality, as was to be expected in a fallen world, fell far short of the ideal; nevertheless, the ideal shimmered brightly and seriously, else it would not have occurred to anyone to commission the painting. Nor would the painter have known how to paint it. The crucial point is the centrality of concurrent universality and particularity of image. A conception, if it is to have the cultural power to define society, the individual in it, and the heaven that awaits, cannot be imageless. "We would see a sign," say the people.[9]

The people would also hear of the witness expressed by signs, testified to by others, and written into the record. We thus situate this study in regard to the matter of orality and textuality. The conventionally *literary* texts constitute the clearest element of textuality on which we focus, for the general reasons of their historical importance and continuing (we do not say universal) human interest. These texts were obviously part of the society of high literacy, which was centered on the town and country house. Of these centers of literacy the most important in terms of political and cultural power was the interconnected world of court and capital. It is a commonplace that London dominated England, that London's religious climate of opinions was vital for the success of Henry VIII's national Anglican church in the sixteenth century, and that London's Puritan cast meant victory for Parliament and Cromwell a century later. Nonetheless, we remember Rebecca West's dictum that people forget truths that are simple and resist learning truths that are com-

9. The biblical and omnipresent *cri de coeur* may be self-explanatory. For much entailment that is not self-explanatory, see, of course, Angus Fletcher's seductively argued *Allegory: The Theory of a Symbolic Mode* (Ithaca, 1964). However, we find his taxonomically neat distinction between *trope* as a play on single words and *figure* as a play on groups of words, even paragraphs, practically and historically untenable.

plex, and the predominance of London seems to warrant reiterations on both grounds.[10]

We have also considered at length a written text that deeply echoed the oral culture, the *Book of Common Prayer,* which stood at the center of a national, not merely court / capital, religious experience. The Prayer Book was addressed to "all sorts and condicions" of people and addressed them in the form of literacy and the mode and norms of orality, the vocalization of various written texts compiled by superbly literate men, such as Archbishop Thomas Cranmer, for the use of people some of whom could not themselves read or read well but who knew people who could. The copious reiterativeness of the text and the mode of the text's normal usage and apprehension were oral-aural. Repetition of the services would teach them to the least literate. The Prayer Book's cadences became the rhythm of worship; its language, already incipiently archaic by 1600, became the sound of the sacred; its prayers and collects and lessons, the collective vocabulary of faith, while the sermons it framed were the words of the Word, and its sacraments, the fount of grace. It was the formal expression of "all the charities" and of the four major tropes of life. Sometimes called the "nation of the Book," referring to the "King James" Bible of 1611, the England of our long century from 1559 to 1674 was at least equally the corporate reader, speaker, and auditor of the *Book of Common Prayer.*

An important element of the relationships between the presence of voice and the persistence of script was the impact of a constantly increasing English literacy and semiliteracy in the four generations between Edward VI and the Popish Plot. Literacy and semiliteracy altered not only the relationship of people to text but also the relationships of the written texts to each other. We have in mind the concept of intertextuality: at its simplest a mutual inter-referentiality of individual texts to each other. At a more complex level, intertextuality was a growing cultural world of thousands of mutually complementary works in which the reader was led from text to text in an endless continuum, in which thought was nudged from the aggregative toward the analytic, and in which conventions of writing powerfully shaped discourse (though never so deterministically, we insist, that genius cannot do something brilliant for the first time). The textual cultural world was a seamless

10. Rebecca West, *The Meaning of Treason* (New York, 1945), Epilogue.

web of written word and general memory. The *Book of Common Prayer* was the primary vehicle for bringing that intertextual continuum into the culture of primary orality and of rudimentary literacy. This phenomenon of oral referentiality to a written text known by all and to voices heard therein we shall call "interorality," and we judge that it is similar in mode and function to the intertextuality of the literate.[11] Transcending local lore and legend, the Prayer Book linked the auditor to a general interoral continuum, as well as to the world of texts, specifically the Bible. If the Prayer Book was in the (oral) language "understanded of the people," that language, in turn, reflected constant hearing of the liturgy, in the slightly archaic language as if of grandparents and in the (translated) language of forefathers, as in a prayer "of Chrysostom" or a psalm "of David." It is precisely this general phenomenon of interorality that we believe to have been implied by Keith Thomas in his magisterial book *Religion and the Decline of Magic: Studies in Popular Beliefs in Sixteenth- and Seventeenth-Century England.*[12] The steady pressure of a centrally imposed religion, conducted in English and accompanied by growing semiliteracy and genuine literacy, we believe, gave rise to an interoral culture above the level of lore and within the realm of tropic expression.

We argue further that the tropes of defining moment, journey, *theatrum mundi,* and ambassadorship become so implicated, so mutually reflexive and interactive, that they can only be separated artificially. The reality is multiplex. For example, the physical and historical reality of the Battle of Lepanto, which was fought in countless individual actions, was painted as a theatrical panorama of a shining moment on the general journey of grace for both society and the individuals whom love has called to be ambassadors. "Let your light so shine" says Scripture, and the literary and religious tropes that variously described that light described the same thing. We seem not so far here from the scholastic four-level mode of interpreting texts, and Carl Becker, in *The Heavenly City of the Eighteenth Century Philosophers,* long ago warned against mistaking a change in style for a change in substance, against seeing a change in language as a change in ideas, even as New Critics and more or less poststructuralist new new critics have repeatedly warned us to do exactly

11. We rely on Walter Ong, particularly his *Orality and Literacy: The Technologizing of the Word* (London, 1982).

12. Keith Thomas, *Religion and the Decline of Magic: Studies in Popular Beliefs in Sixteenth- and Seventeenth-Century England* (London, 1971), an essential book for understanding Tudor and Stuart England.

that.[13] Of course, there are differences as well as similarities between the scholastic levels of literal, allegorical, moral, and anagogic meaning and the Renaissance tropes of moment, journey, theater, and ambassadorship. While both taxonomies are multiple and interrelated sets of definitions, the Renaissance tropes involve movement, change, dynamism, and creativity, whereas the scholastic levels of meaning are a relatively static taxonomy.[14] The scholastic levels of meaning are hierarchical, and the Renaissance tropes are not. The scholastic levels describe texts, and the Renaissance tropes are organizations of experience exceeding textuality. Both obviously share, however, the pre-Socratic insistence on the unity of nature and thus knowledge that includes all surface diversity.[15]

13. Carl Becker, *The Heavenly City of the Eighteenth Century Philosophers* (New Haven, 1932), esp. Chap. 1. The alternating preponderance, over time, of views that a change in what passes for style is (or is not) a change in what passes for ideas or substance may be a special case of what George Kubler argues as all artistic fashions wearing out; see his *The Shape of Time: Remarks on the History of Things* (New Haven, 1962). We make no such general assumption but try to examine each exhibit in our series for its similarities and differences in regard to other exhibits. Accordingly, we will attend somewhat more to aspects of cultural code or preoccupation and ideology than to style in the limited sense of individual idiosyncrasy but will not deny or exclude that last. Of course, the New Criticism at best was far from blind to stylistic and thematic (to include the tendentious notion of the ideological, but far more than that) continuities and discontinuities over historical time. See, for notable examples, the first dozen or more chapters in W. K. Wimsatt and Cleanth Brooks's *A Short History of Literary Criticism* (New York, 1957) and the essays on Longinus, Poe, and the southern literary imagination by the unfortunately neglected Allen Tate; for trenchant recent parsing of these issues, see Howard Felperin's *The Uses of the Canon* (Oxford, 1990). With regard to historiography, see Hans Kellner, *Language and Historical Representation: Getting the Story Crooked* (Madison, Wisc., 1989), esp. Pts. 3 and 4, for a keen analysis of the issues.

14. As static taxonomy, the scholastic levels are akin to Aristotle's four causes; thus Fletcher (*Allegory,* 313 n. 11): literal-material, allegorical-formal, tropological-efficient, anagogical-final.

15. See Charles H. Kahn, *Anaximander and the Origins of Greek Cosmology* (New York, 1960), and R. D. Hicks, trans. and ed., *Diogenes Laertius: Lives of the Eminent Philosophers* (2 vols.; Cambridge, Mass., 1970–72), Bk. II, 1 (Anaximander), I, 131–33, Bk. IX, 6–8 (Heraclitus), II, 415–17, Bk. VIII, 25–27 (Pythagoras) II, 341–43; see also, for a convenient source of fragments and introduction, Milton C. Nahm, ed., *Selections from Early Greek Philosophy* (New York, 1947). See also Malcolm Schofield, *An Essay on Anaxagoras* (Cambridge, Eng., 1980), for an analysis of Anaxagoras' theory (from fragment 12, pp. 3–5) that "in everything there is a portion of everything" (3) and the implications of unity of matter and perhaps origin arising therefrom. But see the debated fragment (fragment 10), which includes the question "For how will opposites coexist with opposites?" (136). Nonetheless, if one looks at the fragments assembled

Yet further, the Renaissance tropes implicitly accepted the Great Chain of Being as a useful and valid (albeit necessarily sketchy) description of reality, and not merely as a quaint though interesting idea.[16] It is a scholarly commonplace that heaven and hell were psychologically real enough in an era of witch hunts, autos de fé, the Inquisition, established churches, and dissenters with cropped ears.[17] We also suggest that the contemporary sense of the intimate connection between heaven and earth included a lively sense of both the constant communication and the ontological difference between God and humanity and of the importance of both.[18] This sense of the gulf between the divine and the human was a central provision of orthodox Calvinism, as the Canons of the Synod of Dort showed, whereas the interest of heaven in human affairs underlay the rogation festivals, the cults of saints, and the multiplicity of holy objects within Catholicism, even the English variety.[19] In both major forms of religion, the importance of public worship and the efficacy of prayer went unquestioned. We assume (with Arthur Lovejoy) that the Great Chain of Being realistically and satisfactorily, for virtually all citizens, indicated both the fact of difference and the fact of connection between heaven

by Nahm as a whole, not concentrating on the quite substantial difference between the "schools" of philosophy, one of the things that most clearly emerges is that the pre-Socratics, excepting only the Sophists, were all agreed on the essential unity of the cosmos, however that unity might be described.

16. The conceptual utility of the Great Chain when *not* oversimplified or overelaborated within major ontological levels (as it often was by authority-agents) is a truth of Renaissance life so simple as to be sometimes neglected in the dialectics of modern scholarship. See nn. 4 and 5, above. Despite its focus on Italy, Paul Oskar Kristeller's *Renaissance Thought and Its Sources: The Classic, Scholastic, and Humanist Strains* (New York, 1979), incorporating *The Classics and Renaissance Thought* from 1955, remains a model of massive learning clarified but not oversimplified.

17. See, especially, Thomas, *Religion and the Decline of Magic,* Chaps. 7–9 on magic and Chaps. 14–18 on witchcraft.

18. Milton, the most prominent case, is considered in terms of this recirculatory communication about and because of the differences between human and divine, in our *Milton and the Hermeneutic Journey* (Baton Rouge, 1994).

19. For elaboration, see Steven Ozment, *The Reformation in the Cities: The Appeal of Protestantism to Sixteenth and Seventeenth Century Germany and Switzerland* (New Haven, 1975); see also John T. McNeill, *The History and Character of Calvinism* (London, 1954), 265, on the Synod of Dort. Calvinism and its antecedents are discussed more fully in Chap. 5, below; see esp. nn. 22–31. For the importance of the laity in the Protestant Reformation, see Paul A. Russell, *Lay Theology in the Reformation: Popular Pamphleteers in Southwest Germany, 1521–1525* (Cambridge, Eng., 1986).

and earth; and we are convinced that the Renaissance tropes participated in this general cultural understanding, else both their universality and their particularity would have been compromised.

If we are correct in viewing the major Renaissance tropes of theater, journey, ambassadorship, and moment as linguistic parsings, expressive understandings in general images, of a comprehensive view of life extending all along the Great Chain of Being, then we cannot ignore particular expressions of these tropes and their implications within culture. The metalanguage that embraces them all is that of the dialectic of love and power. The absolute and total opposites, such as all power and no love, no power and all love, all of both, and neither of both, exist only in the metaphors of theology. In *Paradise Lost,* Milton described the interface between the allness and nothingness of love in terms of a single defining and damning moment as the Son routs Satan and the rebellious angels:

> he . . . as a herd
> of goats or timorous flock together thronged
> Drove them before him thunderstruck, pursued
> With terrors and with furies to the bounds
> And crystal wall of heav'n, which op'ning wide,
> Rolled inward, and a spacious gap disclosed
> Into the wasteful deep; the monstrous sight
> Struck them with horror backward, but far
> Worse urged them behind; headlong themselves they
> Threw down from the verge of heaven. . . .
>
> (VI, 856–65)

When faced with the totality of love and power, described as the "chariot of Paternal Deity" and "count'nance too serene to be beheld," Satan and his horde gave themselves into "unsufferable noise" and "rout."[20]

In terms of the absolute, the divine level of the Chain of Being, love and

20. We are here and throughout quoting from the edition of John Shawcross, *The Complete Poetry of John Milton* (Rev. ed.; Garden City, N.Y., 1971). There is of course much more to be said about the extensive and complexly metaphoric "war in Heaven," and much of it has for the current generation been said by Stella Revard in *The War in Heaven: "Paradise Lost" and the Tradition of Satan's Rebellion* (Ithaca, 1980). Christopher Hill, *Milton and the English Revolution* (London, 1979), 372, virtually reduces the war in heaven to the Battle of Edgehill. On Milton and wars see James A. Freeman, *Milton and the Martial Muses: "Paradise Lost" and European Traditions of War* (Princeton, 1980), esp. Chap. 3.

power are totally reconcilable, albeit in a reconciliation inexpressible by the impoverished, fallen human language. In the ordinary course of events, viewed from the human level of the Great Chain, however, the language and the reality of love and power, of gift and gain, are mixed and dialectical. In *The Merchant of Venice,* the casket of lead that contains Portia's picture has the legend: "Who chooseth me must give and hazard all he hath" (II, vi, 9). And love certainly means a free gift and a certain hazard, but there is gain as well: for Bassanio, in wedded love and repaired fortune; for Portia, in wedded love and protection; and for Antonio, in life itself. It is not for nothing that we are told to "cast our bread upon the waters," and it is equally important and true that it will return to us "after many days." In the language and reality of fallen love and power, the dialectic of connection is as important as the dialectic of opposition.

Connection might be acknowledged as philosophically important and existentially essential, but it was opposition that increasingly shaped and turned the Renaissance mind. This can be seen clearly enough in a number of ways, the anti-Machiavel tracts for one, *King Lear* for another, Renaissance love poetry for a third. Love poetry, particularly with the *carpe diem* topos, seems to us as clear an illustration of the elements of opposition in love and power as one may find. Swainish exhorters, from Christopher Marlowe's shepherd to Marvell's death-haunted syllogist to (most reductively) Milton's Satan regarding unfallen Adam and Eve, declared love as the route to power as well as the instrument of power. Here love was presented as offering or seeming to offer a show or a journey while in reality promising only a (decidedly nonsalvific) moment. Love was also seen as a bribe, requiring, like theater, the willing suspension of disbelief in return for entertainment. *Carpe diem* love poetry was an endlessly repeated *coup de théâtre,* with theater defined in the essentially Augustinian terms of sin as the failure of reason and will. Finally, the essential element of *carpe diem,* as well as of its fraternal twin, the pastoral, is simplicity, the seizure of a fraction of time and / or space to circumvent the vast unmanageability of both, or (to vary the images from hand to ear) the constant replay of a single tone. It is the simplicity, we suppose, that natural ally of nostalgia and longing generally, that gives the theatrical moment its tempting verisimilitude.

The *carpe diem* motif within the tension of love and power, had another, more theological side. As the man wooed the maid, the lyrical language of enticement tended to invoke a metaphor of the fall, of the journey into sin.

Hence Ben Jonson, for another instance, adverted to stolen fruit, in "Come, My Celia." We are also reminded of the excruciatingly lengthy *Roman de la Rose,* not exactly a *carpe diem* poem, though close, not precisely a pastoral, though almost, not quite a theological treatise, though nearly so. In the *Roman,* the dreamer / lover did personify characteristics of both Adam and Satan, precisely as did the importunate wooer in the *carpe diem* lyrics. The pursued maiden was the eternal Eve, cozened by "glozing lies" into believing that love was the same as desire. Her fall was always brought about by another. The man both delivered the false promise (Satan) and was himself deceived by it (Adam), for, as Donne pointed out: "Love is a growing, or full constant light / And his first minute, after noone, is night" ("A Lecture Upon the Shadow"). Augustine, in sterner terms, had the same message: what one does not love for God's sake is loved for oneself, and generations of Renaissance poets averred that that always falls short of anticipated satisfaction.[21] For both the man and maid, the anticipated journey is merely theater.

Of course, there were ways to be caught other than the swift delumination from "noone" to night, from lust and hope to recrimination. Donne, in "The Baite," played off Marlowe's passionate "shepherd": the courtly lover has fallen in love with his intended victim, who was transformed from a possible Eve into a prospective Laura. Whether this emotional *volte-face* will turn exotic-dream, marine-piscatory pastoral theater into journey is left to conjecture, but the change of trope is clear enough.[22]

However resolved, in wit, in ironic or surprised reversal, or in fraud, the tension between love and power that appeared in the *carpe diem* lyrics was emblematic of the wider Renaissance bearing and thought. The love / power dialectic showed life on both levels of being and both arenas of judgment and gave mundane, even quotidian, expression to the dominant tropes of

21. Augustine's *Enchiridion . . . de Fide, Spe et Caritate* may be found in Migne, ed., *Patrologia Latina,* XL, 231–90; a convenient English version is J. R. Shaw, trans., *The Enchiridion Addressed to Laurentius; Being a Treatise on Faith, Hope and Love,* in *A Select Library of the Nicene and Post-Nicene Fathers of the Christian Church,* ed. Philip Schaff (14 vols.; Buffalo, 1886–90), III, 229–76.

22. Ralegh's wiser but not sadder "Nymph" replies precisely with a rejection of the atemporality and reliability in the "shepherd's" scenario, in that respect echoed by Miss Lorelei Lee: "Days grow cold, and knights grow old." For a thorough and sensitive canvass of the many-faceted polymodality of pastoral, see Sukanta Chaudhuri, *Renaissance Pastoral and Its English Developments* (Oxford, 1989), esp. Chaps. 1 and 8–11; see also Andrew V. Ettin, *Literature and the Pastoral* (New Haven, 1984).

Renaissance life. Providing a stereophonic / stereoptic language of self-understanding, love and power, with their interrelationship of connection and opposition, gave the tropes their transcendence and their commonality. In recurring to love and power again and again in what follows, we are not subscribing to any Jungian notion of primordial archetype and derivative archetypal imagery. Rather, we are closer to Julia Kristeva's construal of psychic functioning, with love as semiotic, power as symbolic (developmentally subsequent and potentially either complementary or opposed), and the four tropes as serving in Renaissance church and *polis* some central functions both syntactic and lexical (*i.e.,* as both articulators and vocabulary).[23]

The society that so largely understood itself through journey, moment, ambassadorship, and theater was made unquiet by religious, civil, and social change, perturbed by the imminent but imponderable dangers of witchcraft, disturbed by foreign menace, dearth, and a doubtful future in either world. Society was less and less satisfied to rely on the familiar and proverbial verities (literally constituted in proverbs) from the past of primary or residual orality and equally unable to trust the modern promises of money and political power.[24] These tensions and troubles of the years between 1540 and 1640 have been described by Lawrence Stone as "a seismic upheaval of unprecedented magnitude" and thus different in kind as well as degree from English social conflict before Henry VII or after Queen Anne.[25] This seismic upheaval,

23. See the following by Julia Kristeva: *In the Beginning Was Love* (New York, 1987); *Tales of Love* (New York, 1987); *Powers of Horror: An Essay on Abjection* (New York, 1982); *Dark Sun: Depression and Melancholia* (New York, 1989), esp. Chaps. 4, 5, 7; *Revolution in Poetic Language* (New York, 1984), esp. 13–106; *Desire in Language* (New York, 1980), esp. Chaps. 6, 8, 9.

24. Stone, *The Causes of the English Revolution,* esp. Chaps. 2 and 3.

25. Lawrence Stone, "Social Mobility in England, 1500–1700," *Past and Present,* XXXIII (1966), 16–55. On the entire issue of the gentry, which is at the core of this judgment, see Stone, *The Causes of the English Revolution,* Chap. 1. See also the article which began the gentry dispute, R. H. Tawney, "The Rise of the Gentry, 1558–1640," *Economic History Review,* XI (1941), 1–38, and the blistering repudiation of Tawney's Marxist ideology by H. R. Trevor-Roper, "The Elizabethan Aristocracy, an Anatomy Anatomized," *Economic History Review,* 2nd ser., III (1951), 279–97, which was aimed directly at Lawrence Stone, "The Anatomy of the Elizabethan Aristocracy," *Economic History Review,* XVIII (1948), 1–53, and hit both Stone and Tawney. From these three articles, spread over more than a decade, came the huge gentry debate. The debate in general is beyond the scope of this work, though the English social history it covers

however, occurred within clear limits: "In fact, relatively little structural change took place in English society between the fourteenth and nineteenth centuries: what altered was the role of the various social classes within a fairly static framework."[26] Although the contents *were* substantially shaken over a long period of time, the container generally held its shape, and the metaphor of new wine and old bottles seems appropriate here. Stone's insight into the stability of English social structure in the face of massive internal social change constitutes an entry for examination of Renaissance English reaction to a world they both retained *en gros* and were losing *en détail.*

The very limits imposed by a constant general social structure made even more disturbing the social changes, the religious dissent, the political disputes, the personal sense that times were getting worse, and the suspicion that a moral regeneration of person and society was required if the commonwealth were to be saved, but remote. Because social, economic, and religious changes were so disturbing, they were also very visible and invited comment by all authors and vigilance by all authorities. Social commentary appeared in several varieties, with theater being the most visible; but whether in polemic, dramatic, or poetical guise, social commentary usually involved complaint. This might take the form of ridicule, with Thomas Nashe or Jonson, or the sober worry of John Stubbes or sermonic exhortations to duty and calling, but the tone of all was, at a minimum, cautionary. Religious commentary, predictably, was more varied, with Puritans calling for purification against the (often reluctant) supporters of the establishment, who, like the judicious Richard Hooker, generally advised letting well enough alone. Consequently, the public was peppered with minor tendentious doctrinal tracts of all types, to the evident perturbation of the public repose. The authorities did what they could,

---

is not. On the connection between social movement, government, and revolution, see Perez Zagorin, *The Court and the Country: The Beginning of the English Revolution* (New York, 1970). Also important on the interrelationships between society and government is Conrad Russell, *The Fall of the British Monarchy, 1637–1642* (Oxford, 1991). This is a post-gentry book, concentrating on the facts of politics. We agree with Russell's assessment that "England in 1637 was a country in working order, and was not on the edge of revolution" (1). We are generally unpersuaded by Marxist schemas that reduce everything to economics and the English revolution to a contest between the feudality and bourgeoisie. We acknowledge such schemas may persuade those for whom no other factors are real. We deny, with Christopher Pye, that even *circulation* is a universal solvent; see his "The Theater, the Market, and the Subject of History," *English Literary History,* LXI (1994), 501–22.

26. Lawrence Stone, *The Crisis of the Aristocracy, 1558–1641* (Oxford, 1965), 5.

but doctrinal zeal could not be stopped. The sense of social disturbance and the attendant need for regeneration lay at the heart of public discourse and formed the matter of social and religious commentary.

All of the tracts, efforts at suppression, theater both official (masques) and public, and sermons were aimed at a society that must be reformed or preserved, because it could not be escaped. There was not, to anything like the imaginative and practical degree of nineteenth-century America, a frontier to "light out for." Radical change within a limited social context had the paradoxical effect of increasing unquiet and foreboding and decreasing the assurance that everything was under control—control that contemporaries knew they lacked and ardently wished to find. The evolving society was less and less well represented by the old stratigraphy of names: gentlefolk, the goodman, and the tradesman were still called the same thing, but often they appeared in a different stance one to another. Men were vexed and troubled, as Carl Bridenbaugh wrote, and one need only notice the vast increase in lawyers and lawsuits from 1560 to 1640 to know he was right.[27] Accordingly, we include a glimpse at the society and religious doctrines over which there was so much contention.

Vexations, troubles, and chagrins began, in the nature of things, as immediate and personal problems and reactions to personal problems. They were always the same yet varied infinitely. But they also went beyond the individual and immediate, as did the dominant tropes, to connect the personal with the general. A disobedient son was a daily vexation but was also representative of a general moral complaint concerning defective calling or journey and the want of a salvific moment. Ills, being both personal and more than personal, were part of the continuous social fabric that ran from local lives seen and intimately understood to lives socially and geographically remote but still com-

27. The old wineskins in the biblical citation were expected to break, a lamentable spillage, but one may think of the comic and the dangerous possibilities for effervescent beverages heated in their sealed containers; *cf.*, less figuratively, the characterization of Dienbienphu as "hell in a very small place." See, in this connection, the outstanding book by Carl Bridenbaugh, *Vexed and Troubled Englishmen, 1590–1642* (New York, 1968), and Thomas Nashe's *Christ's Teares over Jerusalem* (London, 1593), in *The Works of Thomas Nashe,* ed. R. B. McKerrow (5 vols.; London, 1904–10), II, 85, 134–35. See also, on social classes, the classic book by Peter Laslett, *The World We Have Lost: England Before the Industrial Age* (New York, 1971), esp. Chaps. 1–3. Vexation, however, was not restricted to England and to the generations living between the Armada and the Civil Wars. See, for example, Gerald Strauss, trans. and ed., *Manifestation of Discontent in Germany on the Eve of the Reformation* (Bloomington, Ind., 1971), esp. Chaps. 4–7.

prehensible. Each vexation was, if fully understood, a part of the general journey and a part "of this worlds Theater in which we stay" (in Edmund Spenser's words), not quite necessarily "this great stage of fools" (in Lear's). This sea of troubles (in Hamlet's equally conventional image), however, was not merely the vicissitude and progression of the "thousand natural shocks that flesh is heir to," immediately and powerfully felt as those things were. Vexation and suffering also had a religious meaning. God, it was believed, sanctified suffering (for the believer) by using it as the occasion for bringing the sufferer closer to him. Suffering was not senseless, not random, not inexplicable, nor even untoward or evil, but instead offered the opportunity for understanding life in all its dimensions of journey and the calling to God. Pain, personal, physical, social, might become the occasion of a salvific moment. The Puritan John Winthrop in his famous diary wrote that he never had such "sweet communion" with God as when he was ill. Nor was this exclusively a Puritan experience. John Donne expressed in his *Devotions Upon Emergent Occasions* a similar attitude toward suffering (in this case near unto death). In "Meditation XVII," primarily known for its disquisition on the parish bell, Donne expressed the theology of suffering in terms of treasure, resonant of Matthew 6:19–21: "For affliction is a treasure, and scarce any man hath enough of it. No man hath affliction enough that is not matured and ripened by it and made fit for God by that affliction."[28] Donne thus explained suffering and afflictions in terms of the theology of redemption and sanctification, as well as in terms of the pastoral psychology of understanding affliction as appropriate to increase and confirm faith rather than degrade it. Such theology was a nonprescription pain transformer, not a pain-killer. Apparent evil betokened genuine good at least in the sense of good opportunity. The tropes formed the mode for understanding the transformation from the *civitas terrena* into the *civitas Dei,* from the momentary into the eternal, to be effected by suffering.

Fortunately for all concerned, "God is English," as John Aylmer exuberantly informed his readers, who might suppose from this that England enjoyed a unique divine favor.[29] The queasy notion that God might be Spanish was impossible to entertain after the Armada. God's undoubted Englishry did

28. John Donne, "Meditation XVII," *Devotions* (1623). See also McGee, *The Godly Man,* Chap. 2, for a careful and clear explanation of the theology of suffering.

29. John Aylmer, *An Harborowe for Faithfull and Trewe Subjects* (1558), in Bridenbaugh, *Vexed and Troubled Englishmen,* 13. See also William Haller, *The Elect Nation* (New York, 1964), 87–88.

not, of itself, solve all problems; indeed, it made them seem worse. Granted English, but was he Anglican? And if he did subscribe to the established church, did he incline to the Puritan party thereof? Wherein was the anxious believer—was there any other kind?—to find the clear statement and direction of God's will? In good morals and a pious devotion to one's calling, certainly, but one might still be led away from right doctrine and the pure word by improper church governance or from a lack of "the word of God . . . plentifully preached." God's obvious and fortunate nationality alone was not enough. C. V. Wedgwood has succinctly observed: "Theological controversy became the habitual reading of all classes, sermons directed their politics and moral tracts beguiled their leisure. . . . Fear of witchcraft grew among the educated and devil-worship spread among the populace."[30]

Just so. Not only did the Reformation produce a diversity of cults; it also produced an increased intensity of feeling within them. Recognized denominations participated in the steady growth of religious fervor in the century after 1550, but their intensity of fear and hope was clouded by witchcraft and magic, which were part of common apprehension in England and the Continent in the decades after the Council of Trent.[31] It was clear to men and women of the generations from 1550 to 1670 that they desperately needed salvation, and correct doctrine in all matters theological and ecclesiastical was necessary to this end. Devotional books by the score, attendance at sermons, religious bills and broadsides, traveling preachers, relics and cults of saints, persecution, and the covert resort to magic all testified to the gnawing need for religious certainty during the Elizabethan and early Stuart efforts to fix the nature of the established church. And if a rectified church were not rector to the realm, what then? If such were even thinkable . . .

In England, religious opinions between 1540 and 1640 firmly settled into a dispute between Anglicans of somewhat puritanic and low-church position and those Puritans whose zeal for reform was such that they gradually veered toward Separatism or were cited for nonconformity. Roman Catholicism, like High Church Anglicanism, survived but did not grow, while the demand for good and vigorous preaching and a ritual comfortable to the commonalty grew steadily from its beginnings in Lollardry.[32] A plain practice adminis-

30. C. V. Wedgewood, *The Thirty Years War* (1938; rpr. New York, 1961), 20.

31. Thomas, *Religion and the Decline of Magic,* Chaps. 7–9 on magic, Chap. 22 on the decline of magic, and Chaps. 14–18 on witchcraft.

32. This has been noted by scholars studying late medieval and Renaissance religion. See the most eminent of the early English historians, George Macauley Trevelyan, *Illustrated En-*

tered with the fierce exhortations of a "hot gospeller" fit much English taste. The Service of the Word was paramount; indeed the Word was all that many desired. The witty and strenuously literate styles of Donne and Lancelot Andrewes were much admired but less frequently copied; a more rural "coo and bellow" against sin and popery was the provincial style.[33] Eminent divines with a Puritan leaning, such as Thomas Cotton, John White, or John Davenport, moved huge followings with sermons that easily lasted from two to three hours. A people gaining literacy but *raised* in orality listened in rapt attention and remembered what they had heard.[34] Few slept; this was not yet the eigh-

---

glish Social History (4 vols.; London, 1949–52), I, 37–51, in many ways the summative work of a distinguished career. See also Trevelyan, *England in the Age of Wycliffe* (London, 1909), and Gerald R. Owst, *Preaching in Medieval England: An Introduction to Sermon Manuscripts of the Period c. 1350–1450* (Cambridge, Eng., 1926). We have used these older works partly because of their excellence and partly because they helped set out the parameters of the social history of English history. Two modern books of great use are Sharpe, *The Personal Rule of Charles I,* Chap. 6, and D. Underdown, *Revel, Riot and Rebellion: Popular Politics and Culture in England, 1603–1660* (Oxford, 1985). In general, we would argue that it is possible, absent the gentry controversy, to make valuable and lasting contributions to the social history of early modern England. It is not possible, however, absent the gentry controversy, to establish a Marxist schema for explaining the social history of early modern England. Hence, we suppose, comes the peculiar ferocity and longevity of the arguments over the gentry.

33. The phrase is H. L. Mencken's, from "In Memorium: W. J. B.," in *Prejudices: Fifth Series* (New York, 1926); its aptness seems to us to reach into any society where moderately literate authority figures exhort audiences who are quite modestly and often first-generationally literate. In any case, note the boiler-plate prose of *Certain Sermons or Homilies* . . . (1570). Still useful, despite predating Walter Ong's work on orality and literacy, are William Fraser Mitchell, *English Pulpit Oratory, from Andrewes to Tillotson* (London, 1932), and Gerald Robert Owst, *Literature and Pulpit in Medieval England: A Neglected Chapter in the History of English Letters and of the English People* (Rev. ed.; Oxford, 1961). The defining contrasts of hyperliterates like Andrewes and Donne preaching to hyperliterate auditories should be kept in mind and will receive attention in Chap. 4, below.

34. The discernment (and exhumation) of the issues (and facts) of orality and literacy has been one of the ongoing, far-from-complete, yet insufficiently assimilated, triumphs of current scholarship. See virtually the entire oeuvre of Walter Ong, perhaps most conveniently introduced by *Orality and Literacy.* For thoughtful cultural survey, see Elizabeth Eisenstein, *The Printing Press as an Agent of Change in Early Modern Europe* (Cambridge, Eng., 1979), or her illustrated abridgement: *The Printing Revolution in Early Modern Europe* (Cambridge, Eng., 1983). For brilliant detective work on the formidably resistant matters of the cultural dynamics of literacy in particular settings (where one needs but usually lacks statistics), see: M. T. Clanchy, *From Memory to Written Record: England, 1066–1307* (Cambridge, Mass., 1979); David Cressy, *Literacy and the Social Order: Reading and Writing in Tudor and Stuart England* (Cambridge, Eng., 1980); Franz H. Bäuml, "Medieval Literacy and Illiteracy," *Speculum,* LV (1980),

teenth century, and many came more than once a week or once a Sunday. There was a hunger for the Word that cut across urban and rural habitation, across the overlapping boundaries of literacy and the oral culture, and extended even to those "of meane respect, qualitie and condicion." Such craving for the Word could never be satisfied merely by the word and must eventually be transformed into an attempt to found the city on a hill.[35] One recalls the trope of ambassadorship in such an enterprise.

So, from the time of Geoffrey Chaucer, English religious opinion had drifted, swirled, and eddied, though at different speeds in different parts of the realm, toward a Puritan position. Early in the serious modern study of this social history, George Macauley Trevelyan asserted:

> If we seek the origins of some of the distinctive traits of English Puritanism, of its asceticism, of its war on sin, its sabbatarian rigor, its fear of hell, its attacks on the Bishops and wealthy clergy, its crude denunciation of opponents, its vigorous and soul-stirring sermons, its tendency to unctious sentiment, its lapses into hypocrisy, its equalitarian appeal to the poor and lowly, they are all to be found in the mediaeval Church, and particularly in the work of the friars. But not of the friars alone; clerk Langland was Bunyan's forerunner.

In this regard, the Reformation changed almost nothing. We have no trouble seeing the Franciscan shadow in Thomas Hooker or John Davenport.[36]

Moreover, and this distinguished England from the Continent, the Puritan tendencies did not lead immediately and automatically to separation and nonconformity. The initial English impulse was to reform from within. The work of the Puritan Feoffees for Impropriations from 1626 to 1632 illustrated this tactic. The lay Feoffees, an essentially secret group, attempted to gain

---

233–65; Brian Stock, *The Implications of Literacy: Writing Language and Models of Interpretation in the Eleventh and Twelfth Centuries* (Princeton, 1983). See also, for their rich suggestiveness (and extensive bibliographies), Jesse M. Gellrich's *The Idea of the Book in the Middle Ages: Language Theory, Mythology, and Fiction* (Ithaca, 1985) and *Discourse and Dominion in the Fourteenth Century: Oral Contexts of Writing in Philosophy, Politics, and Poetry* (Princeton, 1995). Finally, for London, the excellent book by Tessa Watt, *Cheap Print and Popular Piety, 1550–1640* (Cambridge, Eng., 1991), is essential not only for the issues of literacy but also for the development of Protestant religious opinion.

35. Perry Miller, *The New England Mind: The Seventeenth Century* (1939; rpr. Boston, 1961).

36. Trevelyan, *Illustrated English Social History*, I, 43; Bridenbaugh, *Vexed and Troubled Englishmen*, 297–306.

control through the purchase of all lectureships, lay ecclesiastical revenues, and lands of the Church of England that they could get and the filling of these positions with Puritan preachers. This "pious design" could not remain a secret forever, and in 1632 Archbishop William Laud launched a successful suit against the Feoffees in the Court of Exchequer alleging that they were usurping royal prerogative and "introducing many Novelties of dangerous consequence, both in Church and Commonwealth."[37] But this did not diminish the popularity of religious lectureships, nor did it stanch the flow of Anglican religious opinion toward Puritanism, nor did it even drive out of the church all of those who had been involved. The suit against the Feoffees was like the weather; the opinion the Feoffees represented was like the climate.

Accordingly, the chasm between Anglican and Puritan, in the end, could not be bridged, certainly not by the squalid and disgraceful High Church persecution set in motion by Charles I and his creatures, nor even by the quasitoleration that both preceded and followed it. The Puritan persuasion was fiercely and permanently wedded to the service of the Word, in particular to the preaching of sermons. The Anglican church was, fundamentally, a sacramental church, and its basic service was the Eucharist, whatever sort of ceremony might accompany it. Anglican worship centered on the "full perfect and sufficient sacrifice oblation and satisfaction for the sins of the whole world," no matter how that might be interpreted, rather than on pervasive efforts to "laud and magnify his holy name." Anglicans regularly did and do pray aloud for a dual ministry: that their priests might "preach the true and lively word" and "rightly and duly administer the sacraments." Some things are more equal than others, however, and for the liturgically minded, opposite the Puritan, these were not the same things.[38]

37. See Bridenbaugh, *Vexed and Troubled Englishmen,* 293–309. See also the important book by Isobel M. Calder, *The Activities of the Puritan Faction of the Church of England, 1625–1633* (New York, 1957), which includes documents concerning the suit and dissolution of the Feoffees, and Paul S. Seaver, *The Puritan Lectureships: The Politics of Religious Dissent, 1560–1662* (Stanford, 1970). Sharpe, *The Personal Rule of Charles I,* 308–12, casts the activities of the Feoffees within the context of the economic problems of the English church. On that issue, see Christopher Hill, *Economic Problems of the Church from Archbishop Whitgift to the Long Parliament* (Oxford, 1968).

38. McGee, *The Godly Man,* Chap. 1, gives a brief and convenient summary of the context of the liturgical dispute. Of course, the scholar must have recourse to Richard Hooker. For the impact of Calvinism on English poetry, see James D. Boulger, *The Calvinist Temper in English Poetry* (The Hague, 1980). For our purposes parts I and II were useful.

These differences, though they lay at the heart of doctrinal definition and liturgical experience, in the years from 1580 to the revolution frequently appeared to be less serious than they really were, and they appeared to contemporaries to be quite serious indeed. Anglicans and Puritans had no trouble recognizing each other when they met in person or in print, though, as Sears McGee so deftly puts it, there was also "broad agreement among Anglicans and Puritans about the sinfulness of many sins and the graciousness of many graces."[39] In weekly liturgical practice the Anglicans and separatists might seem to be more similar than different. Both participated in a general Protestant religious culture. The early seventeenth century was the golden age of Anglican pulpit oratory. The sermons were roughly as long as the entire preceding and following elements of the service combined, from matins through the Eucharist. Moreover, there were sermons every Sunday, and communion only a few times a year in most parishes of the established church. Beyond that, the Anglicans, like the Puritans, held preaching in high regard since it "saveth because it maketh wise to salvation." In his defense of the Anglican church and the Prayer Book, Richard Hooker gave the established position on sermons, in terms of both theory and practice: "So worthy a part of diuine seruice we should greatly wrong, if we did not esteeme preaching as the blessed ordinance of God, Sermons as keyes to the kingdome of heauen, as wings to the soule, as spurres to the good affections of man, unto the sound and healthie as foode, as phisicke unto diseased mindes." The importance and general usefulness of preaching thus affirmed, and in terms not too high for a rhetorical age that greatly valued the well-made sermon, Hooker could also assert that "Sermons are not the only preaching which doth save soules." He had more than the "rich treasures" of the Scripture in mind. Hooker also regarded the sacraments as instructional, though to a lesser degree than the Word or preaching, and the instructional element of the sacraments was the smaller part of their worth. Nonetheless, the sacraments did serve as "bonds of obedience to God, strict obligations to the mutuall exercise of Christian charitie, prouocations to godlines, preseruations from sinne, memorials of the principall benefit of Christ."[40] In these particular benefits, they did not differ

39. McGee, *The Godly Man,* 69.

40. Richard Hooker, *Of the Lawes of Ecclesiasticall Politie,* Books I–V (1594–97) Facsimile Edition (Menston, Eng., 1969), V, ¶ 22, p. 39; V, ¶ 21, p. 38; V, ¶ 57, p. 127. The book and paragraph numbers are given first, followed by the facsimile page number. We have eliminated the idiosyncrasies of Renaissance printing, while retaining the original spelling. But see the edition definitive for most scholarly purposes, W. Speed Hill, ed., *The Folger Library Edition of the*

materially from sermons or the reading of the Word. They showed the path of right and duty, to the benefit of the individual and the commonwealth.

The sacraments went beyond mere example, beyond a demonstration of "holinesse" that would complement exhortation. In Hooker, and for the Anglican communion, the sacraments had "therefore, undoubtedly some other more excellent and heavenly use." This was seen in the "mixt nature" of the sacraments, secondarily as "markes of distinction to separate Gods owne from strangers" and crucially and primarily as the "saving grace of Christ unto all that are capable thereof." In the sacraments, of which God was the author, grace was the "consequent," through "entering into the souls of man we are not able to apprehend or expresse how."[41] This was true of all the sacraments, and Hooker examined them one by one, devoting to their explication a quarter of the long fifth book of his *Of the Lawes of Ecclesiasticall Politie.*

The sacrament of the Eucharist, which was the most disputed among the various major Christian denominations, received the greatest attention. Hooker discussed the central focus of the Eucharist:

> [In it] we so receive the gift of God, that we know by grace what the grace is which God giveth us, the degrees of our own increase in holinesse and vertue wee see and can iudge of them, we understand that the strength of our life begun in Christ is Christ, that his flesh is meate and his bloud drinke, not by surmised imagination but truely, even so truely that through faith wee perceiue in the body and bloud sacramentally presented the very tast of eternall life, the grace of the Sacrament is here as the foode which we eate and drinke.

Works of Richard Hooker (Cambridge, Mass., 1976–92). On Hooker, see also the illuminating article by Brendan Bradshaw, "Richard Hooker's Ecclesiastical Polity," *Journal of Ecclesiastical History,* XXXIV (1983), 438–44, and also Richard Bauckham, "Richard Hooker and John Calvin: A Comment," *Journal of Ecclesiastical History,* XXXII (1981), 29–33, esp. 32–33, where Bauckham argues that Hooker "displayed a massively uncritical loyalty to the Elizabethan ecclesiastical *status quo*" (33). We disagree with the comment "massively uncritical" in *both* of its two clear implications: that Hooker wrote as an uncritical political toady and that the imprecise and somewhat murky ecclesiology of the Church of England could only be correctly described in a critical way. For a shrewdly more sympathetic reading of the ambiguity of Hooker, see Shuger, *Habits of Thought.* See, as alternative to what we are trying to do, both Leo F. Solt, *Church and State in Early Modern England, 1509–1604* (New York, 1990), which narrativizes institutional history largely in terms of *potestas jurisdictionis* and *potestas ordinis,* and the review of Solt's book by Margo Todd in *Albion,* XXIII (1991), 734–36, demanding more "to do with the people of England" by narrativizing more recent scholarship of sectarian difference.

41. Hooker, *Lawes,* V, ¶ 57, p. 127.

Hooker took cognizance of the heated doctrinal arguments concerning the exact nature of the Eucharist, from Huldrych Zwingli to John Oecolampadius, from consubstantiation to transubstantiation, but he argued that the hairs split by theologians were things about which "we neede not greatly to care nor inquire." He warned, "Take therefore that wherein we all agree, and then consider by it selfe what cause why the rest in question should not rather be left as superfluous then urged as necessarie."[42] It was an Anglican sentiment, reasonable, moderate, willing to assuage rather than exacerbate differences, and it had no chance of acceptance in a time of angry theological debate that tended toward polemical and quasiprecise definitions of the unknowable. Therefore, even though these things "wherein we all agree" were numerous and important, reflecting common participation in the Protestant culture, the things that divided Anglican from Puritan, though fewer, stood, as contemporaries clearly understood, at the very heart of the faith and the liturgy.

For the established church, accordingly, the ministry was dual, with liturgical experience perhaps occasionally weighted in favor of the Word (with a Donne or Andrewes); but the sacrament and the grace it was adjudged to provide remained at the core of Anglican self-conception. When the Puritans demanded more and better preaching, the Anglicans agreed with them; when the Puritans demanded a desacramentalization of the church, the Anglicans stood against them. The similarity of actual services in Anglican and dissenter churches, particularly in the more Puritan of the Anglican parishes, might be substantial, but the real presence (albeit of imprecise definition) in the Eucharist, and the bishops that this demanded, was a difference that ultimately could not be bridged. For Puritans, the sermon was the core of the service and its reason for being; for the Anglicans the sermon was supposed to be part of the preparation for a real presence communion. And Anglican priests, at least in the syntax of prayer ("both by their life and doctrine"), were to instruct as much by example as by sermon.

Thus the *Book of Common Prayer,* with its sacramental bias and its presumption of bishops, defined the growing chasm between Anglican and Puritan. And everyone knew it. From the years of exile under Mary I, when the more radical reformers attempted to get the Geneva service substituted for the 1552 Prayer Book, through the Puritan Waldegrave / Middleburg liturgy of 1584 / 1586, through the moderate Hampton Court revision in 1604, the more

42. *Ibid.,* V, ¶ 67, pp. 174, 177.

radical brethren tried to get the *Book of Common Prayer* set aside. They did not succeed. Royal authority, regarding the bishops as stout support of the throne, clung to the substance of the 1559 *Book of Common Prayer* and even went on the offensive with a new Bible, the Authorized or "King James" Version of 1611. Both were surely works of love for many, but they were undeniably works of power (royal, ecclesiastical, and parliamentary) for all and surely offensive to the severely Puritan.

The *Book of Common Prayer,* therefore, stood at the juncture of the permanent tension between the Service of the Word and the Service of the Sacrament (Eucharist). These two had been linked together at least since the time of Hippolytus, and there had never been general agreement on where the greater emphasis should lie.[43] They provided two different views of the people's work, of how the pure love of God might be most easily embraced. We cannot say why Puritans, in general, preferred the Word or Anglicans, in general, retained the sacramental Eucharist. We can only note that the two sides made serious efforts to avoid a formal break. The Anglicans so far enhanced preaching that the sermon dominated the service and the faithful had to be enjoined by law to communicate at least three times a year. Puritans tried to reform the established church from within, abolishing the bishops and with them sacramental worship, writing their own prayer book, and endowing preacherships. The *Book of Common Prayer* survived, however, and with its survival there came an ecclesiological, theological, and liturgical chasm that would not be closed. Aidan Kavanagh's conception that liturgy is "primary theology" certainly describes the reality of practice in England from 1560 to 1640, for Puritans and Anglicans alike.[44] The "people's work" became the emblem of the people's faith and the realm's division.

The people's faith during the sixteenth and seventeenth centuries extended far beyond theology, liturgy, or ecclesiology, broad though these concerns might be construed to be. "With us society is both church and commonwealth," wrote Richard Hooker, and that was presumed to include the whole of this world.[45] It certainly included the hierarchical social structure, divided generally into the nobility and the commons, and subdivided much more

43. See Bard Thompson, *Liturgies of the Western Church* (Cleveland, 1961), Chap. 2 on Hippolytus, including the text of the liturgy. See, of course, Dom Gregory Dix, *The Shape of the Liturgy* (2nd ed.; Westminster, 1945), a monument of Anglican scholarship.

44. Aidan Kavanagh, *On Liturgical Theology* (New York, 1984), esp. Chap. 5.

45. Hooker, *Lawes,* V.

elaborately. If most agreed on hierarchy as the organizing principle for European society, all else was in doubt or in flux. The social hierarchy suffered from a rapid inflation of honors after 1603, which coincided with some rises and some falls among propertied families but a decline in the prestige of the nobility. At the same time, the growing wealth of the substantial urban merchants, particularly in London, combined with the endemic penuriousness of the Crown, inexorably made money into the high road to honor. Money also altered the relationships between both lord and tenant and lord and land, as capitalization of the countryside, from drainage projects to mining to enclosure, altered forever the medieval rural society of self-sufficiency and local welfare. Beyond all this, as the towns, particularly London, grew in the century after Henry VII, they became an exciting and mobile babble of dialects and accents and a kaleidoscope of costume and attitude, which once clearly identified class but could no longer be relied on to do so. Present confusion—of appearance, of values, of rank, of birth—replaced a supposed past of stability, and it seemed to all more difficult to recognize and do God's good pleasure.

Most disconcerting of all, because in a sense most intrusively immediate, was the confusion created by novelties in appearance and accent. When prosperous bumpkins came to town and purchased coats of arms or knighthoods and swaggered about in sword and fur addressing in outlandish accents the well-bred, the staid and sober were scandalized. In so oral a time, when most could not read easily and many could not read at all, class and station and hierarchy were fixed by long acquaintance or marked by dress and by accent (the more important, the more dominant the orality of the audience.)[46] When servant girls went to town or market dressed in ribbons and purses, all "welbeseene," when esquires sounded like louts and shopkeepers boasted coats of arms, society had become fit grist both for lament and for comedy. Of course there were laws. The Sumptuary Act of 1533 prescribed accoutrements of dress allowable by social rank, and it was repromulgated ten times by Elizabeth I, but it finally had to be abandoned in 1603 as impossible to enforce.[47] The Act of Precedence of 1539 regulated who stood where in the hierarchy of formal status, but interminable quarrels and the fixed practice of purchase of honors

46. Hence (at least in part) the fact, so opaque to modern readers, that in literature from Chaucer to Fielding, characters with north country or other distinguishing accents seem automatically to be butts for hilarity.

47. See Stone, *The Crisis of the Aristocracy,* 29.

after 1603 managed to assert the value, prestige, and status of rank while at the same time undermining it.[48] Philip Stubbes complained that the commingling of base rank and costly and noble apparel made it "verie hard to knowe who is noble, who is worshipfull, who is a gentleman, who is not; for you shall have those . . . go daylie in silkes, velvets, satins, damasks, taffeties and suchlike, notwithstanding that they be both base in byrthe, meane by estate, and servyle by calling."[49] Such social overweening and arrogance, the well-born were convinced, must lead to the "high displeasure of God" and the undermining of the Commonwealth. The laughter invited by the comic playwright depended on a share in such concern, however light the touch, however ambivalent the laughter.[50]

All of these conditions were much more pronounced and visible in London than anywhere else. The capital, home to near a tenth of the population of England during the Renaissance, was also a metropolis too large to be governed by the social conventions that were common in the shire and that most English had been brought up to respect. London's size, wealth, hideous conditions of life for most, trades and professions, and amount of crime made the capital a great stew of social change and personal freedom: "In London, the ritch disdayne the poor. The Courtier the Citizen. The Citizen the Countriman. One Occupation disdayneth another. The merchant the Retayler. The Retayler the Craftsman. The better sort of Craftsman the baser. The Shoomaker the Cobler. The Cobler the Carman. One nyce Dame disdaynes her next neighbor shoulde have that furniture to her house, or dainty dishe or devise, which she wants. She will not goe to Church, because shee disdaines to mixe herselfe with base company, and cannot have her close Pue by herself."[51]

This was not, of course, an exact description of Tudor London. There was in this passage much of the "o tempora, o mores" complaint common to all cultures since ancient Sumer. There was also the accustomed disparagement

48. A restating of Tawney's famous law on the relationships among the availability and desirability of honors.

49. Philip Stubbes, *Anatomy of Abuses in Shakespeare's Youth* (1583; rpr. London, 1877–79), quoted in Stone, *The Crisis of the Aristocracy,* 28.

50. See Frank Whigham, who is little concerned with comedy but who elaborates on the structures and tropings of class anxiety throughout his valuable *Ambition and Privilege: The Social Tropes of Elizabethan Courtesy Theory* (Berkeley, 1984).

51. Nashe, *Christ's Tears Over Jerusalem,* in *The Works of Thomas Nashe,* ed. McKerrow, II, 134–35.

of the capital, such as was exemplified by the satires of Juvenal. Beyond that, the Nashe plaint echoed the theme of pastorals, from (at least) Vergil on, that simple moral virtue was to be found in the country. Nonetheless, the catalog of disdain went beyond the conventional. In addition to the common literary models that might reassure the learned, the Nashe catalog had psychological resonance for Tudor men and women sensitive to invidious and unjust social distinctions. Disdain was the breastplate of the anxious. Only in a society longing to believe that somewhere or somewhen the proper respect was shown for genuine rank and merit, only there could such a catalog have its full resonance. But the rank-consciousness and anxiety that lay behind Nashe's prose were to find no social or political solution, and the sense that much was amiss continued to grow, as did the identification of that unease with religious dissent and social pretensions.

While these attitudes pullulated in provincial towns as well as London, in the capital such social tensions were rubbed raw by the suspicion, indeed the obvious evidence, that many were getting ahead; tensions were made even worse by the knowledge that no one could really tell who these people were because of confusion of dress, manners, accents, and attitudes. London had come to embody the trope of theatricality monstrously allied to human depravity. The artificiality and the "seeming," so associated (disparagingly) with theater, stood out in London as fundamental characteristics of life. Thus was the Christian commonwealth undermined, as the church and the judicious Hooker understood. For Jonson, and perhaps for Donne, London connected the trope of the *theatrum mundi* with sin and sanctimoniousness and also with the triumph of power over love. Sir Thomas Wyatt's identification of honesty with (a country) retreat in "Mine Own John Poyns" came to be a constant undercurrent in Renaissance moral assessment of life in the court and capital. Theater, whether in Prince Hamlet's or Nashe's moralizing, was regularly the Renaissance trope for describing the falsity of mere appearance, of mere concern with power.[52]

52. Middleton and Dekker's *The Roaring Girl* is the unavoidable illustration, somewhat in the nature of a brilliant cartoon, of the cross-dressing, hoydenish (and historical) Moll Frith, of thieves' cant, and gender and class stereotypings and pretensions. See also John L. McMullan, *The Canting Crew: London's Criminal Underworld, 1550–1700* (New Brunswick, N.J., 1984); and see J. A. Sharpe, *Crime in Early Modern England, 1550–1750* (London, 1984), an informative treatise in the social-scientific mode; and see Anthony Fletcher and John Stevenson, eds., *Order and Disorder in Early Modern England* (Cambridge, Eng., 1985). We found the editors' introductory essay to be especially useful.

Personal appearance, an individual form of the inflation of honors, only reflected what was going on officially. The distribution of honors, held down for a generation by Elizabeth I's reluctance to award rank, broke out in a flood with the accession of the impoverished James I. On a single day, July 23, 1603, at the coronation of the king, 432 knights were dubbed, and in that year alone 934 were so raised. In 1611 an entirely new noble order was created, the baronet, a hereditary knighthood whose members were supposed to pay £1,095 for the honor, and all of whom did pay something. Even more, courtiers were given the right to prefer to honor, and thus the value of a knighthood or a baronetcy was quoted on an informal curb market as courtiers strove to dispose of the preferments at a profit. This activity does not include the sale of peerages under the first two Stuarts, nor the bribes and favors paid at the lower end of the scale for coats of arms or titles of esquire.[53] It was precisely this extended process of hawking dignity that later formed the essential background to Ben Jonson's *The Devil Is an Ass,* written in 1631, but was in place as early as *Eastward Ho!,* by Jonson, George Chapman, and Thomas Dekker (for which Jonson was briefly jailed, in 1605).

The obvious reaction to the demoralizing auction of honor was a disgust with the process, along with a hardening of opinion (a Jonsonian theme) in favor of hierarchy and inequality, thus paradoxically increasing the general value of rank since so many wanted it while diminishing the value of most of the rungs as the arrivistes arrived.[54] Sumptuary legislation faded, but universities resolved into two classes of students, and projects developed for excluding the commoners from the Inns of Court. Treatises bemoaned both the false appearance of nobility and the increasing arrogance of the great (with matching insecurity) toward their social subordinates, but the unabating drive for rank and privilege by yeomen and merchants and their sons continued. It was not just servant girls who wished to go about in the world all "welbeseene."

Our emphasis on the inflation and the sale of honors stems from vast contemporary complaint over these practices, which in turn arose from the fact that, increasingly, honor was available only from the king, who genuinely was the "fount of honour." In spite of the ridicule that often attended the newly honored, kings were supposed to dispense honors. With the *officium* of royalty, which both James I and Charles I took seriously, came the responsibility

53. Stone, *The Crisis of the Aristocracy,* Chap. III, esp. 76, 82–119.

54. Tawney's law again, and see Jonson's comedies, such as *The Alchemist* and *The Devil Is an Ass,* both discussed in Chap. 5, below.

to distribute honor and recognition to subjects, a monarchical monopoly given the king by God and denied to anyone else.[55] Properly, honor from the king was analogous to grace from God; at least that is how the Stuarts (and probably Elizabeth I as well) saw it. Disgruntled subjects, and their numbers grew rapidly after 1603, increasingly denied the grace, seeing in its place a racket, and came to regard the king as the patron of toadies and time-servers. Whether or not one completely accepts the thesis of Mary Douglas that the Renaissance patron had become the local "Big Man," with all the dubious associations of illegitimacy that concept may engender (the *basileus / tyrannos* dialectic at a minimum), it remains true that monarchical approval was the single most important element in social standing. Werner Gundersheimer is surely correct when he asserts that patronage, especially and overwhelmingly royal patronage, was the pervasive cement of political, artistic, and social relationships during the Renaissance, and, we add, during the Baroque period as well.[56]

Although James I created knights, baronets, and peers by the hundred, the king, who did what he could do, could not do enough. There was the sheer pressure of numbers. "Policy required the distribution of patronage to conciliate the politically preëminent; lack of resources prevented its realization."[57] Although the influence peddling around the king made the distribution of honors seem tawdry and the bribes made the system seem corrupt and the unworthy choice drew disrepute on all involved, the actual numbers were hardly excessive. A thousand baronets and fewer than twice that many knights in a population of over three million were not the sustained royal assault on the established social order that some contemporaries imagined. Even allowing for fevered social exaggerations, the number of royal preferments fell short of social revolution and was, instead, substantially inadequate to satisfy the legitimate aspirations created by Elizabethan withholding and a half-century

55. James I, *Basilikon Doron,* in *The Political Works of James I,* ed. Charles H. McIlwain (Cambridge, Mass., 1918), esp. Book V. See also by James I, *The Trew Law of Free Monarchies: Or The Reciprock and Mutuall Duetie Betwixt A Free King and His Naturall Subjects,* in *The Political Works of James I,* ed. McIlwain, 53–70, dealing primarily with the idea of justice.

56. Mary Douglas, *Natural Symbols* (London, 1973), esp. 89–90, 156–71; Werner Gundersheimer, "Patronage in the Renaissance: An Exploratory Approach," in *Patronage in the Renaissance,* ed. Guy Fitch Lytle and Stephen Orgel (Princeton, 1981), 3–23, esp. 13–16.

57. Linda Levy Peck, "Court Patronage and Government Policy: The Jacobean Dilemma," in *Patronage in the Renaissance,* ed. Lytle and Orgel, 45.

of inflation, population growth, prosperity, urbanization, and increased trade.

Those who did succeed in obtaining honor and rank created a visible and continuing social and political presence in Jacobean England. But the new families were, in some way, also competitors with the already established. The Duke of Buckingham and his numberless relatives may be seen as an example. The duke did the best he could for them, but not all received as much as was desired. And the preferment some did get was keenly resented by those who also judged themselves deserving but who were overlooked. A genuine shortage of promotions meant a surplus of rancor, and James's casual indifference to who and what should be honored meant that favorites increasingly turned honor into debauched desire and power serum. If honor could no longer be considered honorable, mere money and influence and "projectors" and politicians would replace the ancient social values of justice, hierarchy, and community and would diminish the political gain and social stability that patronage was supposed to ensure. By James I, patronage was a thing done so ineptly that the king propped himself up with one hand and knocked himself down with the other.

Thus, patronage had more than a psychological and familial dimension: it was an important element in royal administration. Fiscal patronage may be considered as an effort by the crown to obtain money from the locally successful, which it certainly was; but it was also a way to command a subject's performance of duty commensurate with real rank in society. The ubiquitous Tudor and Stuart Justices of the Peace occupied positions of prestige and power within the county, while extending royal power on a sustained basis to every corner of the realm.[58] So James's extensive sale and distribution of honor was a serious act of policy to tie the subject to the crown and to encourage the more substantial subjects to do their duty as the king thought it should be done.

Honors or duty, however, availed nothing against the overwhelming disability of insufficient estate or engulfing personal debt. From the Elizabethan

58. James S. Cockburn, *A History of English Assizes, 1558–1714* (Cambridge, Eng., 1972); for a single shire, see Thomas G. Barnes, ed., *Somerset Assize Orders, 1629–1640* (Somerset, 1959). See also J. H. Gleason, *The Justices of the Peace in England, 1558 to 1640* (Oxford, 1969), and Joel Hurstfield, *Freedom, Corruption and Government in Elizabethan England* (London, 1973), for a broader view of judicial government, as well as A. H. Smith, *County and Court: Government and Politics in Norfolk, 1588–1603* (Oxford, 1974), a more limited and detailed view.

peers, whose summons to the House of Lords was quietly ended because of poverty, to the falling gentry so much discussed, a lack of money made it impossible for a subject to support formal honors. While only a modern Marxist would have the myopia publicly to assert that all that honors honored was wealth, it was nonetheless true that a substantial estate was the fundamental base upon which rested honorific recognition. That James I could be perceived to make wealth a *sufficient* cause of elevation and be damned for it does not mean that wealth was not generally acknowledged to be a *necessary* cause. This did not, of course, mean that it was necessary for the same families to be always wealthy or to be wealthy always to the same degree. Hence the extended, acidulous, and anguished debate over whether the gentry was rising, falling, both, or neither. Hence, too, the wise comment by Lawrence Stone, previously quoted, to the effect that while the personal upheaval might have been substantial, there was "relatively little structural change" in English society during the Renaissance. Hence, historically, the angry and growing contrast between a "vexed and troubled" people and a monarch, Charles I, who declared himself to be the happiest monarch in Christendom and advertised his reign to be a time of peace.[59]

Such a judgment of smug satisfaction was not completely unrealistic, if the observer took care to look only in the right places for confirmation. The formal workings of politics and the law were the salient right places, for here Charles was doing pretty well during the decade of his personal rule. An expansive application of "feudal" fiscality brought precarious stability to royal finances, a process aided by the ship money levy, which brought in over £100,000 a year from 1635 to 1638. Complaint against this innovation culminated in the "ship money" case, *Rex* v. *Hampden,* which ended in royal victory in 1638 when the Star Chamber decided that *rex* and *lex* were indissoluable and that the will of the king was law. The victory pleased Charles enormously, and the general disregard of it in the country, along with an increasing refusal to pay, did not warn the king that what he had thought a permanent tax was only a deteriorating expedient.

There were other areas of success as well. Animated by a concern for the poor and a fear of social unrest, Charles had infused local government with a purpose and an energy it had lacked under his father. In 1631 the Privy Coun-

59. Stone, *The Crisis of the Aristocracy,* 5; Kevin Sharpe, *The Personal Rule of Charles I,* 276–84, 608–11, 770, 880.

cil issued the Book of Orders concerning how local government ought to run. Thomas G. Barnes has stated it succinctly: "What was novel about the Book of Orders was the inclusiveness of the program contained in it, the intensity with which the program was executed subsequently, and the duration of that intensity."[60] Beyond that, Parliament, that quarrelsome, unreliable, and inefficient body, had not met since the stormy dissolution in 1629 and seemed not greatly to be missed. As Kevin Sharpe reminded us, however, "The problems of the early seventeenth century were problems for the king *and* parliament, rather than one of inevitable conflict between them."[61] Still, most Stuart government was local, carried by Justices of the Peace and Lords Lieutenant and in Quarter Sessions and the Assize Courts. Charles I had cause to regard himself as all "welbeseene."

But the King would have done well to heed Richard Hooker's aforementioned comment: "With us society is both Church and commonwealth." Political success in Caroline England was more than countered by problems with religion. The efforts by Archbishop Laud to increase the power and influence of the episcopacy were, and more importantly were seen to be, a departure from the days of Good Queen Bess. Laud's efforts to promote uniformity in practice provoked violence in Scotland by 1637, the *event* that led directly to the collapse of royal personal rule. His efforts to tighten up the procedure of the ecclesiastical courts made these institutions a local nuisance and a threat to everyone in the parish, as no one was immune from the suspicion of improper conduct or the denunciation of enemies. Moreover, by his emphasis on the sacraments, Laud appeared to be hostile to preaching, an im-

60. Thomas G. Barnes, *Somerset, 1625–1640: A County's Government During the "Personal Rule"* (Cambridge, Mass., 1961), 179. On the impact of the Stuart rule on local government, see Valerie Pearl, *London and the Outbreak of the Puritan Revolution: City Government and Natural Politics, 1625–1643* (Oxford, 1961), an important book on the most important local government of them all. On the connections between local and central government, see G. E. Aylmer, *The King's Servants: The Civil Service of Charles I, 1625–1642* (London, 1961); and, for an earlier period, see Derek Hirst, "Court, Country and Politics Before 1629," in *Faction and Parliament: Essays in Early Stuart History,* ed. Kevin Sharpe (Oxford, 1978), 105–37. See also Kevin Sharpe, *The Personal Rule of Charles I,* Chap. 7. Finally, see the general and essential treatise on English government carried from Crown to laborer by Anthony Fletcher, *Reform in the Provinces: The Government of Stuart England* (New Haven, 1986), esp. Pts. I and II.

61. Kevin Sharpe, *The Personal Rule of Charles I,* xvi. See also, for a similar position on government, Conrad Russell, Introduction, 14–16, and "Parliament and the King's Finances," 91–116, esp. 92–94, in *The Origins of the English Civil War,* ed. Conrad Russell (New York, 1973).

pression he confirmed by his actions on impropriations. Keith Thomas has amply demonstrated that one basic thread of the Protestant Reformation was hostility to symbolism, magic, superstition, and ignorance of the word of God. An ambivalence toward preaching and his fondness for the mysteries of the sacraments were sufficient to convict Laud in the minds of many of doing violence to the true religion. In a society where religion was the guarantee of right order in this world and of good entry into the next, Charles and Laud were treading a dangerous path for Protestant potentates.

There remains still the matter of the king, who, even after Hull had closed its gates against him, wistfully inquired, "Are the hazards and miseries of civil war in the bowels of my most flourishing kingdom the fruits I must now reap after seventeen years of living and forgiving among them with such a measure of justice, peace, plenty and religion as all nations about either admired or envied?" In thus invoking the political message of the Peter Paul Rubens ceiling of the Whitehall Banqueting House, Charles was not simply illustrating his profound isolation from the real opinion of many of his subjects. As Raymond Anselment so astutely reminds us about Charles and his followers, "Central to their experience is a pervasive sense of loss." What was gone, primarily, was peace, "once possessed and then lost."[62]

The loss of that peace, however, which Charles felt to be one of the chief glories of his reign, came from the king's own fatal imprudence in pushing the Prayer Book controversy with the Scots. The triumph of peace, which the king and his court had celebrated in the masque *Albion's Triumph* in 1632 or in *Coelum Britannicum* in 1634, had already been lost in fact by the time it was again celebrated in masque in *Britannia Triumphans* in 1638.[63] Contemporaries knew how fragile peace might be, as their constant praise of it in prayer book, art, and masque indicated. We are reminded of *A Midsummer Night's Dream,* the closest thing to a court masque Shakespeare ever wrote, in which unbending time itself is made malleable to support right political order.[64] But the magic of Titania and Oberon was not available to the bureaucratic dull-

62. Charles I, *Eikon Basilikon,* ed. Philip Knachel (Ithaca, 1966), 39; Raymond Anselment, *Loyalist Resolve: Patient Fortitude in the English Civil War* (Newark, Del., 1988), 22 and *passim.*

63. See Stephen Orgel and Roy Strong, *Inigo Jones: The Theatre of the Stuart Court* (2 vols.; London, 1973), II, 660–703, for text, costumes, and staging of *Britannia Triumphans.*

64. We have treated Milton's supracourtly *Mask* and his anticourtly, supra-antimasque *Samson Agonistes* in our *Milton and the Hermeneutic Journey,* Chaps. 6 and 7, and have glanced at Shakespeare, Chap. 2, appended Note, and *passim.*

ness of Laud nor to the political and religious unwisdom of the Bishops' War. In mourning the loss of peace, whose "blessings could but enable, not compel, us to be happy," those nostalgic for the years of Charles' triumphs were mourning what they themselves had carelessly thrown away.[65]

Still, the loss of peace abroad was only one of the sorrows which came "not as single spies, but in battalions." At home, the religion of which Charles had boasted stood increasingly apart from the religion of the nation. The English favored the bluff and vigorous sermon, the king, the symbolic, allegorical, artistic, and complex mysteries of the liturgy and sacraments, which were rich in suggestion and psychodrama. Forceful linearity on one side and elegant synecdoche on the other, these were two tendencies that even the sonorities of the Prayer Book could only contiguate, not conjoin. In religious terms, then, whether treating of the mysteries of the faith or of kingship, Charles I appropriated as his own the trope of the *theatrum mundi.* But in so doing, in stating his case in the form of symbol, allegory, classical myth, personification of peace, plenty, or justice, or mock-heroic role and pose, Charles I confused the earthly seeming of symbol with the reality of the *theatrum coeli.* It was the latter that interested his subjects, and they did not see it in the shallow posing of any king and court. As William Prynne declared in his *Histrio-Mastix* in 1633, an immense and intemperate assault on the theater, attendance at plays was the "cause of untimely ends in Princes."[66] The *theatrum mundi* was also almost a byword for the false, the politic, the hypocritical, the masked, and, by definition, the unworthy. When the king presented himself in artful pose, in masque or in painting, he embraced the mode of the fraudulent. With journey thus abandoned, ambassadorship was lost as well, and the successive formal royal moments were of brass, not gold. The king could not be believed to represent his people to God, no matter how elegantly he played the role. To profess royal happiness in such suspect circumstances was worse than a blun-

65. Anselment, *Loyalist Resolve,* 23, taken from Edward Hyde, Earl of Clarendon, *The History of the Rebellion and Civil Wars in England Begun in the Year 1641,* ed. W. Dunn Macray (6 vols.; Oxford, 1992), I, 96.

66. As quoted in Stephen Orgel, *The Illusion of Power: Political Theatre in the English Renaissance* (Berkeley, 1975), 44. And see, for his very full and thoughtful treatment, Jonas Barish, *The Antitheatrical Prejudice* (Berkeley, 1981). See further, Timothy Murray, *Theatrical Legitimation: Allegories of Genius in Seventeenth Century England and France* (New York, 1987), the antitheatrical bias discussed with reference to Bacon and Derrida and a cultural "crisis of transference" (Chap. 2).

der; it was a crime, and a crime understood as sin.[67] Charles was seen in a sinister light, as a king failing in his duty toward God. It was not a problem of a callow and satisfied king ruling a sullen and mutinous mob; it was rather a king representing concerned and serious subjects to God in a style and manner they did not believe could mediate the Almighty's favor.

In stating that he was the happiest monarch in Christendom, Charles I was expressing his feeling that he was doing his religious duty, outwardly expressed as image in marriage, parentage, painting, and masque and as policy in the Prayer Book, prerogative, and episcopal supremacy. Five years later, bewilderment at God's judgment of ruin and civil war on his pious efforts informed his queries: Was he the Job of kings? Had he not lived and ruled so as to embody the Word, the right order for which he knew his subjects hungered? But their judgment went against him. In the minds of many, the royal ostentation of ambassadorship was construed as posturing theater.

Clearly, by all that has gone before, we dissent sharply from the modern mode of fixing historical causality for the Civil War in matters of economics or in the movement of the gentry or in social oppression or in constitutional issues of parliament and prerogative. We find the explanation of the king's fall, his wistful confusion in that event, and his satisfaction with his state before 1640 to lie essentially in religion. The other matters gave formal or material reinforcement to that primary cause. We also suggest that while the gap between the literary / theological self-conception embodied in the tropes of journey, movement, ambassadorship, and theater and the tangible and stressful daily realities may appear large, the too-casually-historical notion that the central cultural metaphoric self-conceptions of a people are significantly divorced from the daily rounds of life within that culture must be rejected. We cannot suppose that the realities of general cultural self-conception are unreal, that how people judge their lives is unrelated to how they live them. We argue instead that the general cultural tropes of self-conception were psychologically antecedent to the choices of daily life and communal history, were the standards by which life and history were judged and understood, and were, finally, the intellectual matrix through which the future was anticipated. It is not cause and effect that we advance here, that linear progression so beloved by historians, but rather a more generally hermeneutic analysis of

67. The allusion here is to Talleyrand's comment that Napoleon's judicial murder of the duc d'Enghein was worse than a crime; it was a blunder.

continual recirculation and reciprocation between life as it was lived and trope as it was understood and interpreted. The Shakespearean formula from Lear that "nothing shall come of nothing" is here reversed to the notion that all must come from all, not only once but continuously, in a system in which the distinct categories of cause and effect are subsumed into a general matrix of circumstance and successive approximation that embraces the hard facts of phenomenal history as well as the tropic interpretations with which contemporaries engaged their world.[68] So we suggest that a hermeneutic historical method of general cultural circumstance and recirculatory, incremental understanding will allow us to move conveniently from trope to event and back, analogous to the idea of the Great Chain of Being, but with more fidelity to experience.

We therefore return to our original position that the major Renaissance tropes of moment, journey, theater, and ambassadorship carried for contemporaries two important and complementary meanings: they explained the nature of life "here below" and at the same time connected that life to the eternal life above, which was thus never out of mind nor altogether beyond sight or hearing. From processions to sermons to marriages and funerals to common expressions of language (*e.g., zounds*), the two worlds were physically close. We follow Johan H. Huizinga in noting that "one sound rose ceaselessly above the noises of busy life and lifted all things unto a space of order and serenity: the sound of bells."[69] Life was lived in two realms simultaneously. The greater infused and stood in judgment of the lesser. Life had about it a character of synchronicity, of experience having two meanings at the same time, one known by perception, the other by faith and trope. This synchronicity did not, of course, result in a world where everyone habitually undertook continuing internal moral dialog concerning daily activity. The racked

68. For "circumstance" and reinforcement to our sense of hermeneutic reapproximation, we draw on José Ortega y Gasset, *Meditations on Quixote,* trans. Evelyn Rugg and Diego Marin (New York, 1961), both the introduction and notes by Julian Marias. In the vein of tropic interpretation, we are appreciatively mindful of the trail-blazing thought of Hayden White, notably in *Tropics of Discourse* (Baltimore, 1978).

69. Johan H. Huizinga, *The Waning of the Middle Ages: A Study of the Forms of Life, Thought and Art in France and the Netherlands in the XIVth and XVth Centuries* (London, 1924), 10. For a wealth of particulars, see Cressy, *Bonfire and Bells,* esp. Chap. 5; his larger argument, that there was a widespread historicizing and secularizing of the calendar by the later seventeenth century, is harmonious with our own.

rent, the legal fix, the arrogance of office, great place unjustly pressed, all noticed by Hamlet, were the very stuff of life. A sense of daily connection to God did not obliterate sin, Pelagius to the contrary notwithstanding. Instead, such a sense defined sin. It gave a name and meaning to the frequently vile and (literally) disgraceful activities that went on "in all times and in all places." But the connection with God did create a second dimension by which to measure life—a dimension beyond transient prestige, power, wealth, or rank. All of these things, delectable as they were, had still to be measured in the *longue duré* against the laws of God, and very few doubted what they were, though many made the choice of power over love. The four dominant tropes were the chief media and modes of that constant measurement. They were the way Renaissance Englishmen defined the crucial difference between seeming, which Hamlet disclaimed, and what really was, surpassing the shows of merely human signifying. That is, albeit without perfect concordance or exhaustiveness, the tropes did articulate truths about disparate levels of reality, truths in which people reposed their ultimate trust.[70]

70. Maus's *Inwardness and Theater* begins with Hamlet's speech and elaborates searchingly on "shows" as variously concealing or revealing; but she does not consider many other possibilities of the trope or the other three tropes.

2

Masque and Bergamasque: The Universe in Emblem and Allegory

The area of politics most precisely illuminated by the chief tropes of the Renaissance was political and royal iconology. The Renaissance was an age that believed art had the power to transform ordinary and mundane reality into an emblem of the ideal or the heroic or the mythic.[1] Thus, if one were sufficiently secure to *be* aesthetic (admittedly a minority status), then the ordinary and secular reality was invested with beauty and meaning that connected the sad world of humanity to the divine and the perfect. This put a great burden upon art, imputing to it the imaginative task and (more or less) effect of depicting the unseen and ineffable in an image. But there was more. The literal and the allegorical elements of the painting, building, poem, or spectacle could be combined to make manifest the officially appropriate theological and political program. Thus art was quintessentially persuasive, transforming

1. On this crucial point see Stephen Orgel, *The Illusion of Power: Political Theatre in the English Renaissance* (Berkeley, 1975), 40; see also A. Katzenellenbogen, *Allegories of the Virtues and Vices in Medieval Art* (New York, 1964). See also the important book by Roy Strong, *Splendor at Court, Renaissance Spectacle, and the Theatre of Power* (Boston, 1973), 16–21. For a specifically English application of this phenomenon of art as instruction in both power and truth, see the important book by R. M. Smuts, *Court Culture and the Origins of a Royalist Tradition in Early Stuart England* (Philadelphia, 1987). Charles I, like Elizabeth I, had a firm belief in both the didactic power and political usefulness of art. On the general role of language in political discourse, see the important book by J. G. A. Pocock, *Politics, Language and Time: Essays on Political Thought and History* (New York, 1973). See especially "Languages and Their Implications: The Transformation of the Study of Political Thought," 3–41, and "Time, Institutions and Action: An Essay on Traditions and Their Understanding," 233–72.

the ordinary into the emblematic so that the viewers or auditors understood the essential grace and goodness of the ideal shown wherein all was rightly ordered.

Such art was, in the general opinion of Renaissance princes and politicians, essential to the public prosecution of statecraft; indeed, statecraft in its absence was reduced to the shadow realm and *disjecta membra* of conspiracy, murder, court intrigue, and spies. Grandeur and magnificence were the essential, virtually the only, conceivable public face of power and policy. A showing forth of rank was of the very essence of rank; mere birth or title held in obscurity soon faded into family memory and local jokes, as Petrucchio so clearly knew. More than simple rank (if such could even be imagined) was displayed; approved social posture and attitudes were also presented. The presentation of virtue or triumph rivaled rank in importance, for the great were also the guarantors of right order. In the Renaissance, art alone possessed this potentiality to display triumphant virtue, so conspicuously lacking in mere political and theological polemic. It is hardly surprising then, as Jakob Burkhardt told the nineteenth century in *The Civilization of the Renaissance in Italy,* that Renaissance men and women manipulated fashion, attitude, home, garden, and language to create an artistic and theatrical stage on which to present their lives and their meaning. Baldassare Castiglione's *The Courtier* was a manual on this practice. Art was both observed and lived, as Charles I and his court recognized by being both observers and participants in the masques presented at court.[2]

Programmatic art of this sort, whether its public purpose was the glorification of king, patron, or God, appeared in three general forms. There were, in the first place, relatively static and staged *mise-en-scènes:* gardens, interior decor, sculpture, painting, or architecture. These materialized as the art of setting and included some of the most stupendous work of the Renaissance: the Sistine Chapel, Palladian villas, or the *Ecstasy of St. Theresa* come readily to

2. Jakob Burkhardt, *The Civilization of the Renaissance in Italy* (2 vols.; New York, 1958), I, Pt. 2; II, Pt. 5. See also, of course, Baldassare Castiglione, *The Book of the Courtier* (Sir Thomas Hoby translation of 1621), ed. J. H. Whitfield (London, 1974). See Stephen Orgel and Roy Strong, *Inigo Jones: The Theatre of the Stuart Court* (2 vols.; London, 1973), I, 15–49, II, 537–98, 661–704. See Stephen Greenblatt's *Renaissance Self-Fashioning* (Berkeley, 1979), but self-fashioning was not new behavior for those with the requisite wealth and leisure *or* with the Christian commitment to being reborn or to "put on" Christ. Greenblatt's preoccupation with power and exteriority, to the neglect of interiority, love, calling, and journey, seems one-sided.

mind. The second variety of Renaissance public art was literary, in particular emblem books and poems of praise. Finally, there were the three types of spectacle, all inherited from the Middle Ages and reworked to variously sacral or secular purpose by Renaissance monarchs. These were the formal entry, chivalric tilts of arms, and interior entertainment from masque to opera to ballet. These spectacles, beginning with the Burgundian pageants of Philip the Good, were costly, impressive, and rich in symbolism.[3] In fifteenth-century Burgundy, these were rich occasional pieces staged on rare occasions. They retained that aesthetic character in the sixteenth and seventeenth centuries but became very frequent as spectacle assumed the primary role in the presentation of statecraft. As Roy Strong has remarked, "romantic dramatization was a perfectly normal means of expressing a brutal political reality."[4]

One of the fundamental shifts from medieval to Renaissance public art was, quite apart from changes in form or function, in the *object* of adoration. The glory of God was increasingly replaced by the apotheosis of sovereign and dynasty. The cult of kingship, borrowing liberally from the cults of the Virgin or of the saints, established the monarch as the fount of all honors, the center of public life, the visible and psychosocial link with the Almighty. Royal life was transformed into a continuous public religious and political ceremony, with spectacle at its center. Recall the famous comment of James I in the *Basilikon Doron:* "A King is as one set on a stage, whose smallest actions and gestures, all the people gazingly doe behold."[5]

3. Johan Huizinga, *The Waning of the Middle Ages: A Study of the Forms of Life, Thought and Art in France and the Netherlands in the XIVth and XVth Centuries* (London, 1924), esp. Chaps. 6, 7, and 19, though the entire book deals with the public aesthetic of fifteenth-century Burgundy. We and others will in the future prefer the restored text, *The Autumn of the Middle Ages,* trans. Rodney J. Payton and Ulrich Mammitzsch (Chicago, 1996).

4. Strong, *Splendor at Court,* 16.

5. James I, *Basilikon Doron,* in *The Political Works of James I,* ed. Charles H. McIlwaine (Cambridge, Mass., 1918), Bk. III, 43. An interesting examination of English political thought from the standpoint of the civil rather than the common law is Brian P. Levack, "Law and Ideology: The Civil Law and Theories of Absolutism in Elizabethan and Jacobean England," in *The Historical Renaissance: New Essays on Tudor and Stuart Literature and Culture,* ed. Heather Dubrow and Richard Strier (Chicago, 1988), 220–41. On the politics of James's works, see Jonathan Goldberg, *James I and the Politics of Literature* (Baltimore, 1983), in which the king's works are, of course rightly, considered as symbolic acts of royal power, as absolutism in action. It does not necessarily follow that James I was able, through his writing, to play a central role in Jacobean culture. See also the perceptive review by Annabel Patterson, "Talking About Power,"

Because the *theatrum mundi* had unfortunate connotations of the false, the king had to call on the undoubted power of art and play his role and set his stage with the proper and convincing metaphors and emblems. The *theatrum mundi* had to reflect persuasively the *theatrum coeli.* Art had to succeed where physical force or polemical argument could not: to convince the nation that the king and nobility possessed the mandate of heaven. Of course, royally sponsored art tended to be not an act of love or even gift to the people but rather a narcissistic gift by royalty and aristocracy to themselves. Its essentials reflected the generally agreed-upon socioreligious hierarchy established by heaven (often, albeit paradoxically, metaphorized in classical rather than Christian terms) through emblematic depiction of king and courtier in idealized roles of antique virtue, Roman triumph, appropriate religious attitude, mythical heroism, or symbolic control over nature. Hierarchical artistic idealization was "both Platonic and Machiavellian; Platonic because it presents images of the good to which the participants aspire and may ascend; Machiavellian because its idealizations are designed to justify the power they celebrate."[6] The power of art lay partly in the fact that it was the art of power.

English monarchs, like their Valois and Habsburg rivals on the Continent, utilized every extant art form to exalt the state and the role of monarchy and to achieve that apotheosis of the sovereign needed to keep social order. The English Crown possessed a chivalric order, the Garter; the English nobility had coats of arms and emblems; there were Accession Day tilts (November 17 for Elizabeth I); Elizabeth I went on progresses and had processions; there were portraits of the monarch, masques and plays for entertainment, and the royal decor was consciously dynastic (roses) and imperial. In all of these things England was like the Continent.

But there were also differences, both of taste and of purse. The English Crown was never able to build palaces on the continental scale, nor were royal entries a prominent part of the English *politique de spectacle.* Emblem books began on the Continent in the 1530s but did not circulate in England until the 1580s. Elizabeth I, however, utilized the tilt to greater effect than her continental contemporaries. In England, interior entertainment moved toward the

---

John Donne Journal, II (1983), 91–106, esp. 97–100. For the "level of" or manifestation as idea (complementary to iconography and trope) of liberty and governance, see, for notable examples, J. H. Hexter, ed., *Parliament and Liberty from the Reign of Elizabeth to the English Civil War* (Stanford, 1992), and Mark Nicholls, *Investigating the Gunpowder Plot* (Manchester, 1991).

6. Orgel, *The Illusion of Power,* 40.

masque, while on the Continent, influenced by the genius of Claudio Monteverdi, opera became the standard form (and, in turn, fashionable in England, but scarcely before the eighteenth century).

The greatest difference between England and the Continent, however, lay in the matter of artistic motifs and style. In England the public artistic style and motifs were consciously archaic, while on the continent the motifs were humanist (that is, classical in inspiration) and the style was high Renaissance, merging into the international Baroque of Peter Paul Rubens and Giovanni Bernini. The liturgy of royal apotheosis looked different in England, though in function it was still power in another form, taking on the task of visual and figural propaganda, reaching persons and emotions untouched by mere text, teaching values by imposing concreteness on allegorical dramatization. Art was in the business of demonstrating, not remonstrating. If we may be permitted a momentary descent from the aesthetically excellent to the cynically tawdry, art in the Renaissance and the Baroque period was an early form of network television. A thirty-second negative political commercial differs from the Rubens Whitehall Banqueting House ceiling in most respects but not in all.

In an article on Titian's *Allegory of Prudence,* Erwin Panofsky remarked that this was Titian's only work that "may be called 'emblematic' rather than merely 'allegorical': a philosophical maxim illustrated by a visual image rather than a visual image invested with philosophical connotations." This is a neat definition, conforming to the Aristotelian method (from the *Posterior Analytics*) of defining by dividing, thus laying bare the essential differences in the two categories of didactic art.[7] But the differences in emphasis implied by Panofsky's distinction between "emblematic" and "allegorical" cannot be construed to exhaust the definition of Renaissance emblem. The initial Renaissance description of an emblem came from Andrea Alciati, whose *Emblemata* appeared in 1531.[8] Alciati's book was the first important work in a genre that

7. Erwin Panofsky, "Titian's 'Allegory of Prudence': A Postscript," in his *Meaning in the Visual Arts: Papers in and on Art History* (Garden City, N.Y., 1955), 147; Aristotle, *Posterior Analytics* (Cambridge, Mass., 1960), 227–31, Vol. II of Loeb Classical Library *Aristotle,* 23 vols.

8. Andrea Alciati, *Emblemata cum commentariis,* ed. Stephen Orgel (New York, 1976), a Garland reprint of the 1621 Padua edition, with the 1571 Claudius Minos commentary and let-

would grow to a tremendous population in the next several generations. By the middle of the eighteenth century, when the interest in iconology waned, over 1,000 emblem books had been published, most obscure, but some, like Alciati's, translated into several European languages and enjoying multiple editions. The importance of Alciati's *Emblemata* was not merely that it was first but also that it laid down the basic definition of an emblem as consisting of three distinct parts: the picture, the motto, and the epigram. Emblems were thus a mixed mode of thought, both linguistically and pictorially symbolic, both word and picture.[9] This definition, while too rigid to fit all of the emblems and emblem books that would follow, did provide a base from which contemporaries could improvise and to which they could add.

Thus, while Panofsky's somewhat two-dimensional distinction in emphasis between emblem and allegory did not anatomize entirely the relevant Renaissance issues, it will prove a valuable point of departure for an examination of the implications of political use of emblems as means of visual propaganda. For English monarchs of the Renaissance, elegant philosophical messages, though satisfying to the *cognoscenti,* were much less important than a simple, even crude message. Emblem and allegory were, for royal political purposes,

---

ter. On emblems, see especially Peter Daly, *Literature in the Light of the Emblem: Structural Parallels Between the Emblem and Literature in the Sixteenth and Seventeenth Centuries* (Toronto, 1979). For a systematic examination of the spread and influence of Alciati's work through several languages over a century, see the major work, part of the *Index Emblematicus,* by Peter Daly and Simon Cuttler, *Andreas Alciatus, Emblems in Translation* (Toronto, 1985), and Peter Daly, *et al., The English Emblem Tradition, Vol. II* (Toronto, 1993). In connection with the relationship between emblem and literature, see Anthony Raspa, *The Emotive Image: Jesuit Poetics and the English Renaissance* (Fort Worth, 1983), Chap. 1. On emblems in general, the pioneering work of Mario Praz, *Studies in Seventeenth Century Imagery* (London, 1939), continues to repay study. On emblems in England, see Rosamund Tuve, *Elizabethan and Metaphysical Imagery* (Chicago, 1947), and Rosemary Freeman, *English Emblem Books* (New York, 1966). On image books in England, see Stephen Orgel's edition of Samuel Daniel, *The Worthy Tract of Jovius* (1585; rpr. New York, 1979); Daniel's translation was of Paolo Giovio, *Dialogo dell' Imprese Militari et Amorose* (1574), one of the most influential of the emblem books. See also Otto Vaenius [van Veen], *Armorum Emblemata,* ed. Stephen Orgel (1608; rpr. New York, 1979). And see Peter Daly, ed., *The English Emblem and the Continental Tradition* (New York, 1989).

9. Daly, *Literature in the Light of the Emblem,* 3–53, esp. 6–9; see also Peter Daly, Leslie Duer, and Anthony Raspa, eds., *The English Emblem Tradition* (Toronto, 1988), esp. viii–xi. For a well-documented example of "syncretism," see Elizabeth See Watson, *Achille Bocchi and the Emblem Book as Symbolic Form* (Cambridge, Eng., 1993), esp. 37–40 and associated illustrations.

the same thing, and Alciati's tripartite definition was only as good as the purpose it served. Thus emblems were judged not on their internal consistency or their distinctions but on their clarity, inclusiveness, and insistence.

We find the same situation to exist with regard to the fundamental philosophical differences between the iconology within the Aristotelian tradition, which emphasized taxonomic characterization of various emblems, and the iconology from the Neoplatonic tradition, which used emblems as an entry to speculative meditation. Within the Aristotelian school the most important book was Cesare Ripa's *Iconologia,* published in 1592, which rapidly became the standard text for visual personification, being frequently reprinted and translated into four languages. It utilized the Aristotelian method of definition by division into classification based on essential, not contingent, characteristics. Hence, for example, he dealt with Friendship (*Amicitia*) generally, rather than with a specific friendship between two people or even with that of some middling degree of specificity, such as friendship between relatives.[10] It was, of course, a reflection of the Aristotelian distinction between genus and species.

Neoplatonic iconology, illustrated by Christophoro Giarda, whose *Bibliothecae Alexandrianae Icones Symbolicae* appeared in 1626, rejected classification in favor of illumination. Emblem ought to lead the viewer up toward God, in terms of both emotions and reason, because the images seen had some element within them that was redolent of the Divine.[11] That element was, of course, love: the love that led to recognition / understanding—an understanding that went beyond both language itself and images in general. E. H. Gombrich has quoted the important passage in the Pseudo-Dionysius: "The higher we rise, the more concise our language becomes, for the Intelligibles present themselves in increasingly condensed fashion."[12] Condensation opposed diffusion because sin (*contra Manichaeae*) was nothing. This conjunctive idea, of elevation, compression, and illumination engendered by

10. Cesare Ripa, *Iconologia,* ed. Stephen Orgel (New York, 1976), 16–18 (from the Padua edition of 1611). See Daly, *Literature in the Light of the Emblem,* 59–60, for Ripa's importance for Ben Jonson. On this, see also Allan Gilbert, *The Symbolic Persons in the Masques of Ben Jonson* (1948; rpr. New York, 1969), 3.

11. Christophoro Giarda, *Bibliothecae Alexandrianae Icones Symbolicae,* ed. Stephen Orgel (New York, 1979), from the Milan edition of 1628.

12. E. H. Gombrich, *Symbolic Images: Studies in the Art of the Renaissance* (Chicago, 1972), 168.

love, implicit in emblems was a long way from the prosaic and rational / disjunctive classification of Aristotelian iconology. The bias here, however (in ideals of conclusion and condensation), is toward the visual and palpable. In political art, with its emphasis on the *efficacy* of the message, the distinction between Aristotelian and Neoplatonic essentially vanished. The idea behind political art was that it should be both.

So, too, with distinctions drawn by Aristotelian iconographers between emblems and *imprese;* though they were clear enough philosophically, politics acted to render those distinctions unimportant. For Ripa, icons presented static, general, or generic categories, whereas *imprese* intended movement via "propositions which 'assert or deny.'"[13] Such movement, involving contingent characteristics, was accordingly of a lower order than the generic essentials of the emblem. Such movement to "assert or deny" was secondary to the Neoplatonists, who were concerned with the movement toward the One attained by the viewer, not that implicit in the image. In politics, it was the Neoplatonic view that prevailed in this matter; the political patrons were essentially receptionist in their theology of emblem and device.

Further, the contemporary division over the role of formal learning in the interpretations of art was also blunted by the imperatives of political iconology. The need for substantial ancient learning was accentuated by the first of the emblem books, Alciati's *Emblemata.*[14] Panofsky summarized elegantly: "A set of symbols surrounded with the halo of remote antiquity and constituting an ideographic vocabulary independent of linguistic differences, expansible *ad libitum* and intelligible only to an international élite, could not help but capture the imagination of the humanists."[15] This was certainly true enough in the beginning, yet Ripa, and even Giarda, moved in the opposite direction, trying to clarify the "ideographic vocabulary," the one by rational and ordered classification, the other by indicating the mode and direction of movement. Ripa was classically descriptive and clear in his descriptions. *Abondanza* (Plenty) was a barefoot "gracious woman," with garlands in her hair, dressed in green and gold, holding a cornucopia in her right hand and grain in her left. Every detail was clearly and meticulously described, and anyone familiar with the text could never fail to recognize and understand the ap-

13. Gombrich, *Symbolic Images,* 139–45, esp. 142.

14. Panofsky suggests a knowledge of Macrobius' *Saturnalia.*

15. Panofsky, *Meaning in the Visual Arts,* 159.

pearance and meaning of *Abondanza.* Giarda was less physically descriptive in his analysis of *Poesis, Lex Canonica, Historica,* or *Philosophia Moralis,* concentrating instead on moral and philosophical characteristics, thus less on recognition, *i.e.,* categorical control, and more on understanding and movement.[16] In both cases, the unmistakable effort was away from the obscurity penetrable only by the learned initiate toward a common cultural meaning.

Politics, as usual, had things both ways. Some of the individual emblems and devices used by Renaissance artists, in painting, in tournaments, and in masques, were certainly obscure and only the learned could penetrate the fog of allusion. At the same time, in the same work of art, the general political program was utterly obvious. Still further, we find the inclusiveness of politics affecting even the modern distinctions between iconology, the identification of the ideological program of a work of art, and iconography, the tracing of that program in a particular text. Although different things, in the realm of political art that distinction was virtually without a difference. It is only a slight exaggeration to say that all political art can be traced to the same text: "Render unto Caesar that which is Caesar's, and render unto God that which is God's," the latter clause an unintentionally ironic afterthought in this context (unlike the biblical). During the late Renaissance and the Baroque period, when politics had the pungent odor of divine-right absolutism as a surrogate for sanctity, everything aside from private prayer belonged to Caesar at least in part, as the program of political art, no matter how obscure the emblem, tried to make clear. At the level of the metatext, both the program and the origin of the work of art were the same, and the two modern disciplines could be seen virtually to coincide.

The didactic and emblematic art of the Renaissance, so intensely political in nature, was accordingly eclectic and inclusive of competing philosophies. Obscure images were juxtaposed to obvious ones, classical mythic figures mingled with Christian heroes and saints, medieval and ancient images mingled together, pagan personification passed through Christian gloss to political image, Platonic ascension stitched to Aristotelian category, *imprese* rendered as emblem. Such eclecticism, we infer, was the result of extra-artistic purpose, of a deliberate political effort to harness the undoubted power of art through the artfulness of the powerful. Or, if the reader construes most *discretionary* making and doing as partaking of art (as we do), then "artfulness"

16. Ripa, *Iconologia,* ed. Orgel, 1–2.

above is not an ironic term, and "extra-artistic purpose" may well be amended to "extra-occasional purpose."

Moreover, Neoplatonic love might be proclaimed, but the function of the emblem books was to articulate, buttress, and organize the exercise of power. This was inevitable. Today, when economics and sociology are powerful, the political and social elite are interested in statistics. In an age when art was seen as uniquely powerful, the politically and socially powerful were concerned about art. Thus, the emblem books entered the dominant tropes from the portal of power and played a role in secularizing society, in leading both king and subject away from *agape* toward something less humane and more instrumental.

There is a certain irony in this. The old images of Virgin and Child, of church and saint, of Christianized mythology, of personified virtues remained the same. But in the political art that the emblem books served, the older images came increasingly to have newer meanings, even though the older ones were never completely lost or even meant to be lost.[17] The love of God was not opposed by political art; it was instead to be understood as operating through the divine right of the king, to be mediated by royal power.[18] Such tendentious mediation came to dominate all other characteristics of emblem books and emblem usage, leading to the emblematic eclecticism of royal art, to the sense of theater found in the art of politics, and to the constant invocation of themes and images of the divine, the ideal, the heroic, the beneficent and virtuous.[19] Insofar as monarchy is conceived and felt as intrinsically the nexus of such symbology, maladroitness or ineptitude in any royal person

17. Roy Strong, *The Cult of Elizabeth: Elizabethan Portraiture and Pageantry* (Berkeley, 1986), esp. Chaps. 1 and 6. See also George Kubler, *The Shape of Time: Remarks on the History of Things* (New Haven, 1962), esp. 77–83.

18. See Katzenellenbogen, *Allegories of the Virtues and Vices,* Pt. 2, on static representation; but see, on movement, Kubler, *The Shape of Time,* esp. Chaps. 3 and 4.

19. Strong, *Splendor at Court,* esp. Chaps. 2 and 7; Strong, *The Cult of Elizabeth,* esp. Chaps. 1, 5, and the conclusion (on Henry, Prince of Wales) to Chap. 6; Mark Breitenberg, "'. . . the hole matter opened': Iconic Representation and Interpretation in 'The Quenes Majesties Passage,'" *Criticism,* XXVIII (1986), 1–25. See also Goldberg, *James I and the Politics of Literature,* for an analysis of James's entry pageant. See Sara van den Berg, "The Passing of the Elizabethan Court," *Ben Jonson Journal,* I (1994), 31–61, for sensitive reading of Elizabeth's entry ceremonies as foregrounding *her* role, her funeral ceremonies as foregrounding monarchy, and James's entry arches and ceremonies as foregrounding metropolitan London (with Jonsonian and Dekkerian subtexts). We agree but see all three framed within tropologies of journey, theater, moment, and calling. For a rich deciphering of political-imagistic eclecticism, earlier

will be insufficient to discredit that mediatorial scheme (which indeed seems to remain the articulated horizon for some of the English to this day).

The connection of emblem to power had a further element: a pretense to completeness. The emblems implied that they exhausted all that might be communicated by that particular figure or category or genus. Thus, the description by Ripa and the accompanying illustration carried within itself a "complete" idea, which might be combined with others but could also stand alone. Neoplatonists pretended to the same exhaustiveness, with the icon as a sufficient cause for the mind's journey to the One. This pretense to completeness was, of course, reductive in its very nature, if for no other reason than by its implication that only the icon was sufficient for understanding. In this reductive claim of completeness, all irony of the picture on the page or of the relationship of word to image was occluded. Disjunction of any sort was denied. The emblem, including all variations of picture, motto, epigram, explanation, poetic elaboration, and attribution to antiquity or noble house, and quotation from authority, was ostensibly therefore a symbolic universe unto itself. Such pretense can only be the language of power, and of fallen power at that.

The pretense to completeness and self-sufficiency that the emblem exhibited came from both picture and text. The emblem was, like heraldic devices it so much resembled, visual recognition and propaganda, and it also performed the same task textually. For the Aristotelian categories and classification of Ripa, the emblem as a whole, texts and picture combined, was an analog to a proverb. It presented, in elaborate and ornate form, commonplace wisdom, ordinary ideas, received notions. The words *mors, et vita,* appearing along the hem of *Amicitia*'s skirt, meaning that true friendship existed in life and transcended death, certainly indicated a notion that fit proverbial wisdom.[20] As for the Neoplatonic texts, they were an analogue to popular devotionals, as they were an invitation to meditation on the divine elements in the ordinary. We are reminded of the contemporary *Introduction to the Devout Life* by Francis de Sales, a manual designed, like the Neoplatonic emblem books, for ordinary and accustomed usage by literate folk.[21] Emblem books, which had begun life as a genre with Alciati's scholarly, difficult, and even ob-

---

but characteristic, see Margaret Aston, *The King's Bedpost: Reformation and Iconography in a Tudor Group Portrait* (Cambridge, Eng., 1993), and see Marie Tanner, *The Last Descendant of Aeneas: The Hapsburgs and the Mythic Image of the Emperor* (New Haven, 1993).

20. Ripa, "Amicitia," in *Iconologia,* ed. Orgel, 16–18.

21. On Francis de Sales, see Imbrie Buffum, *Studies in the Baroque from Montaigne to Rotrou*

scure collection of antique mythology, rapidly became more popular and more accessible. Given the cultural ubiquity of commonplace books and manuals of devotion, these were predictable directions for the evolution of emblems. The political user of this mixed textual and graphic genre was dependent on its analogy to already established, understood, and accepted forms. Politics is, after all, the manipulation of the utterly familiar to give it temporal and public general meaning, since the unfamiliar will tend to provoke fear and loathing.

Having begun with a single painting, Titian's *Allegory of Prudence,* as a point of entry, we emerge with a more general view. Again Panofsky:

> The emblem . . . as defined by one who ought to know, partakes of the nature of the symbol (only that it is particular rather than universal), the puzzle (only that it is not quite so difficult), the apophthegm (only that it is visual rather than verbal), and the proverb (only that it is erudite rather than commonplace).[22]

More might be added. The emblem also partook of heraldry, only that it could be more complicated and nuanced. It was a special case of metaphor, tending toward the taxonomic variety of that inexhaustibly rich figure. In a general way, an emblem was a mini-allegory, too small and particular to fit a larger general purpose, as did the *Roman de la Rose,* but still large enough to allude both to a contemporary meaning and an ancient myth. In an appropriately Aristotelian proportion with an appropriately theological referent, one might say that the emblem was to a major allegory as a passing single sin was to Original Sin itself. Nonetheless, size notwithstanding, the emblem partook of the allegorical frame of reference and habit of thought that was characteristic of Renaissance imagination.[23]

(New Haven, 1957), Chap. 2. The *Introduction à la vie dévote* may be found in the *Oeuvres* (Annecy, 1893), conveniently available as *Introduction to the Devout Life,* trans. and ed. John K. Ryan (Garden City, N.Y., 1961).

22. Panofsky, *Meaning in the Visual Arts,* 148.

23. Daly, *Literature in the Light of the Emblem,* esp. 27–35, 54–71, and Chap. 5; see also Strong, *The Cult of Elizabeth,* Chap. 1. "Renaissance imagination": the portmanteau notion is intractable yet irresistible to others as to us. Recall Debora Shuger on habits of thought, and Walter Ong and Elizabeth Eisenstein on effects of literacy and printing (cited in Chap. 1), and see Michel Foucault at his best, in Chap. 2 (on analogy), in *The Order of Things* (New York, 1971), Basil Willey, *Seventeenth Century Background* (Oxford, 1934), Molly M. Mahood, *Poetry*

Finally, we suggest that the emblems were also eminently suitable to illustrate in short form the four major tropes of Renaissance life. Illustration with textual additions of the appropriate virtues and attitudes, along with an invitation to consider them more deeply, both materialized and reinforced the tropes of moment, journey, theater, and ambassadorship; they were thus both cause and effect. Theater and ambassadorship were physically present in the emblem, making the images instantly accessible to everyone, moment symbolically present in the brevity, and journey often explicitly or by allusion present in the content (as throughout the culture). So emblems, which were a common cultural experience, at least in town, helped give a concreteness to the Renaissance tropic habits of thought and were part of the artistic connection between daily life and its religious justification and context.

We properly begin this examination of the artistic representation of Renaissance tropes with the cult of Queen Elizabeth I, who was consistently and self-consciously attached to the "politie" of the realm through the mythic and iconic representations of the royal person.[24] Roy Strong has parsed the phenomenon of secular iconology decisively:

> The cult of Gloriana was skillfully created to buttress public order and, even more, deliberately to replace the pre-Reformation externals of religion, the cult of the Virgin and saints with their attendant images, processions, ceremonies

---

and Humanism (New Haven, 1950), Harold Fisch, *Jerusalem and Albion* (New York, 1964), Harry Berger, Jr., *Second World and Green World: Studies in Renaissance Fiction Making* (Berkeley, 1988). Sophisticated in regard to theory and generously comprehensive is Jean Howard, "The New Historicism in Renaissance Studies," in *Renaissance Historicism: Selections from "English Literary Renaissance"* (Amherst, 1987), 3–33; our emphasis on omnipresent tropes may respond to Howard's call for deparochializing Renaissance studies.

24. See Roy Strong, *Gloriana: The Portraits of Queen Elizabeth I* (London, 1987), esp. 34–44; Roy Strong, *Tudor and Jacobean Portraits* (2 vols.; London, 1969), I, 99–112, esp. the section on iconography, 109–12, and II, plates 184–220; Strong, *The Cult of Elizabeth,* 14–16. See also Elkin Calhoun Wilson, *England's Eliza* (Cambridge, Mass., 1939), an older book that repays examination; Frances A. Yates, *Astraea: The Imperial Theme in the Sixteenth Century* (London, 1975), one of the central studies in the Elizabethan iconology of power; Roy Strong, *Splendor at Court,* esp. Chaps. 1 and 2, for a discussion of the general functions played by show and spectacle on the Renaissance political stage; Breitenberg, " 'the hole matter opened,' " 3–4, 13–20.

> and secular rejoicing. So instead of the many aspects of the cult of Our Lady, we have the "several loves" of the Virgin Queen; instead of the rituals and festivities of Corpus Christi, Easter or Ascensiontide, we have the new fêtes of Elizabeth's Accession Day and birthday.[25]

It is a bit ironic that Puritans, with their detestation of images for a transcendental faith, should have participated in the same phenomenon with regard to a secular faith. Yet that is what happened. The whole realm joined in celebrating the cult of Gloriana, of Astraea, of *Eliza Triumphans,* the "unspotted lily" whose multiple images stood as the symbol of her age. These individual images themselves were thrown together from both the Christian and classical past with little regard for origin or former meaning. The allegorical meanings outlined by Fulgentius in the sixth century were forgotten.[26] The heavy weight of multiple levels of medieval allegory was basically discarded.[27]

25. Strong, *The Cult of Elizabeth,* 16. Pageantry and royal iconology were not the only things comprising the local drift of opinion. See G. B. Harrison, *The Elizabethan Journals, Being a Record of Those Things Most Talked of During the Years 1591–1603* (Ann Arbor, 1955). For an Accession Day reference, see iii, 51–52. See Christopher Marlowe's fictive examples of tourney-emblems in *Edward II,* II, ii, 11–46, glossed by the characters Lancaster and Mortimer, and the latter's condemnation of "idle triumphs, masques, lascivious shows . . . bestowed on Gaveston" (ll. 156–57).

26. The only modern edition of Fulgentius is the 1898 work by Rudolph W. O. Helm, ed., *Fabii Planciadis Fulgentii V. C. Opera* (rpr. Stuttgart, 1970) in *Bibliotheca Scriptorum Graecorum et Romanorum Teubneriana.* This edition has been used by Leslie George Whitbread, ed., *Fulgentius, the Mythographer* (Columbus, Ohio, 1971). Both contain the treatise concerning an allegorical reading of classical myth, *Mitologiarum Libri Tres.*

27. Emile Mâle, *The Gothic Image: Religious Art in France of the Thirteenth Century,* trans. Dora Nussey (New York, 1958), esp. Introduction and Bk. IV, Chaps. 1, 5. For a complementary movement in the allegorical content of public art, see Erwin Panofsky, *Studies in Iconology* (New York, 1962), esp. Introduction and Chaps. 5 and 6 on Neoplatonism. The humanistic content in official Elizabethan iconology was certainly present, though thoroughly mixed with the medieval.

On the relationship of humanism to the general religious culture of Reformation England, see Hugh Richmond, *Puritans and Libertines: Anglo-French Literary Relations in the Reformation* (Berkeley, 1981). "Humanism became elitist, backward looking and conformist, while Reform became popular, radical, and iconoclastic" (112). This dictum is absolutely right, and it is of great use in understanding both emblems and the masque. See also Horton Davies, "Calvinism and Literary Culture," *John Donne Journal,* III (1984), 105–12. For "a tradition of principled acts of desecration" restored to view, see Richard S. Peterson, "In from the Cold: An Englishman at Rome, 1595," *American Notes and Queries,* V (1992), 115–19.

The past was pillaged for present use and thrown into a rich *pot au feu* of adulatory praise, both in written compliment and in visual image. Elizabeth I was, at the same time and with no apparent embarrassment, Venus, the Virgin, Astraea, Cynthia, Belphoebe, the Child of Vergil's Fourth Eclogue, Gloriana, the wise virgin, *Eliza Triumphans,* the Queen of Pleasure, of Love, of Justice, of Beauty, and "Our glorious English court's divine image / As it should be in this our Golden Age."[28] Elizabethan artist and Elizabethan audience, alike anxious about the health of the Commonwealth, understood the general patriotic message well enough.

The meaning of the particular images must thus be ascertained anew, in terms not of past reference but of present employment. Tudor royal iconology involved partially renaming and "refiguring" the visual and literary elements of past allegory and applying the collected motifs in a new series of compliments. Sources as diverse as the *Roman de la Rose,* the Bible, the Matter of Britain, and Francesco Colonna's *Hypnerotamachia Poliphili,* an architectural dream vision and romance from 1499 about ancient architectural motifs, were put to use in constructing symbols for royal spectacle. The form remained the same: the purpose of iconological representation was fixed and constant, but the individual details and elements were often cut loose from their traditional meanings. The whole made sense, though individual details sometimes did not, and the whole was the idea of Elizabeth as the real and necessary guardian of the Commonwealth.

All of these themes came together in the "Rainbow Portrait" of Queen Elizabeth I, commissioned after 1600 by Robert Cecil. It fitted neatly into the imagery and compliment found in the *Hymnes to Astraea* of 1599 by the lawyer-poet Sir John Davies, as well as the major themes of royal portraiture since 1579: imperial ambitions, the victory over the Armada and the "abominations" of the "bishop of Rome," and the image of youth and beauty in which Elizabeth was shown not as she was in body but as she was in symbolic and iconic imagination.[29] These general programmatic themes were pre-

28. Quoted in Strong, *The Cult of Elizabeth,* 54. Valeria Finucci would seem to imply that Elizabeth's status was special only in *degree,* that "The Female Masquerade" was and is universal (Finucci and Regina Schwartz, eds., *Psychoanalysis and Literature* [Princeton, 1994], 61–88): *Gender* self-fashioning? Perhaps, and what of sufficiently leisured *men?*

29. See Strong, *Tudor and Jacobean Portraits,* II, plate 215, for a black-and-white reproduction of most of the "Rainbow Portrait"; see particularly Strong, *Gloriana,* 156–61, for an extended discussion of the various iconological themes informing this portrait.

sented in specific visual symbols, all common enough during the Renaissance and all essentially independent of each other, their mutual interrelationships coming from the iconology of the entire painting. The rainbow, which Elizabeth held in her right hand, accompanied by the motto "Non Sine Sole Iris," was the dominant motif of the painting, a metaphor for peace and tranquility with obvious biblical references (to Noah) as well as royal ones. The rainbow was held by the queen, almost as she would a chair back, rather than appearing from behind and above the queen, as if it were something in which she merely participated but did not control. This element of the painting heightened the compliment to the queen by associating her with the powers of heaven. It was Gloriana as Queen, not the royal office alone, that domesticated the rainbow and, by clear implication from the motto, the sun itself. The theatricality, both of the world and of heaven, and the ambassadorship of such a painting were obvious.

The other iconological elements in the painting also emphasized personal excellence and virtue as contributory to royal *auctoritas.* These have been described by Strong: a gauntlet representing chivalry, a serpent depicting wisdom, a heart indicating reason and mercy and an armillary sphere alluding to empire. Another iconological element in the painting, a golden cloak enfolding the royal person, was embroidered with a repeated motif of lidded eyes and ears. By this visual device all are brought into the painting, are intimately associated with Gloriana herself. The eyes and ears, watching and listening are our own, mobilized to the protection and sustenance of the Crown against the dangers of domestic subversion and foreign menace. Mouths, less conspicuous among the details, are supplemented by the painting as a whole, which tells forth the praise of Astraea. These latter points, though interesting, are of minor importance. The rainbow emblem carried the essential message, while the details restated the general program in a series of motifs that collectively reinforced the theme, making the whole greater than the sum of its parts.[30]

A single portrait fell short of establishing royal policy. Indeed, from the first "Sieve Portrait" in 1579, royal portraiture in general came to be increasingly symbolic and programmatic. The Renaissance canons of proportion, perspective, representation, and psychological realism were modified both by an English quasi-medieval emphasis on line and color and by the political program.

30. Strong, *Gloriana,* 156, 161, and the color detail in plate 4.

Imperial policy and ambition dominated the "Armada Portrait," *ca.* 1588. *Eliza Triumphans* rested her hand on a globe, and the two background panels flanking the royal portrait depicted the defeat of the Spanish fleet. A second iconic theme, that of eternal youth and beauty, the *imago juventutis* dominated most portraits after 1590. With this theme two factors seem to have been at work. As the queen aged, her ministers wished to keep this fact in the background, since the queen's survival was believed to be the foundation on which the Commonwealth rested. Beyond that, we sense a sort of sympathetic magic, as if the youthful portraits would themselves prolong youth, as if appearance, the *theatrum mundi,* could not merely mimic but also alter reality. For late Elizabethan royal portraiture, the image of youth pointed away from an invocation of the king's second and eternal body, which was the theme of royal funerals and coronations. Here, the emphasis was on the person of Elizabeth I herself; the longer she lived, the better it would be for everyone, and the portraits' presentation of a still-youthful queen was a magical effort to that end.[31]

Both the magical image of youth and the accoutrements of imperialism appeared in the "Ditchley Portrait," *ca.* 1592. The queen's features are recognizable and certainly middle-aged; her characteristic angularity and prominent chin, nose, and cheek bones show clearly. But the ravages of age have been softened and arrested, though the iconic youth of the last portraits was still to come. She was depicted standing on a map of England, dressed in a white

31. On this continuing theme of medieval and Renaissance thought concerning the combined mortality of the king with the immortality of the *officium* of kingship, see Ernst Kantorowicz, *The King's Two Bodies: A Study in Mediaeval Political Theology* (Princeton, 1957), and Ralph E. Giesey, *The Royal Funeral Ceremony in Renaissance France* (Geneva, 1960). Note the persistence of the theme in Handel's Coronation Anthem from "Zadok the Priest": "Long live the King. May the King live forever." See Strong, *Gloriana,* 146–87, for a discussion of the theme of youth in connection with the work of Nicholas Hilliard. Recent comments on portraits of Elizabeth include Richard Helgerson, in *Forms of Nationhood: The Elizabethan Writing of England* (Chicago, 1992), and Albert Labriola, "Painting and Poetry of the Cult of Elizabeth I: The Ditchley Portrait and Donne's 'Elegie: Going to Bed,'" *Studies in Philology,* XCII (1996), 42–63. See Christopher Pye, *The Regal Phantasm: Shakespeare and the Politics of Spectacle* (New York, 1990), 43–81; Pye considers the portraits of Elizabeth, the frontispiece to *Leviathan,* and "Theatricality and Power" in a meditative and provocative conflation of Elizabethan, Hobbesian, Kantorowiczian, and (problematical) Lacanian imagery. Lacan is especially unsatisfactory in this context, for he seems to have supposed that no one ever loved anything. And what of liturgy?

brocaded gown with ropes of pearls, while behind her head the heavens were divided into night and storm and day and light, with the storm giving way to dawn. She thus combined person and realm with the cosmic images of goodness and the true faith in conflict with, and soon to triumph over, evil. The depiction of *Eliza Triumphans* standing on England with her head reaching to the heavens also was a direct repudiation of the papal excommunication of the queen in 1570. In the "Ditchley Portrait," Elizabeth I stood framed by England and heaven, uniting both into a single cosmological system, precisely as Roman Catholic theology held that the pope was the intersection point between heaven and earth that united the two through the power to bind and loose.[32] Here *Eliza Triumphans* visually took the papal role, of justice connected to God, of power that has a divine origin, of the *ecclesia triumphans.* The painting was an affirmation of the Church of England and a statement that Elizabeth I was the Defender of the Faith and the visible head of the church. The ships near the port cities around her feet would presumably carry forth the faith, as well as further commerce. While the ecclesiology of the Anglican church and the representative traditions of English government might deny to Elizabeth I what was implied by the *plenitudo potestatis* that the theology of papal power claimed, still the queen did govern and represent both church and Commonwealth. The "Ditchley Portrait" thus referred to both Moses and Aaron. Because the program of the painting so powerfully com-

32. On the papal theology of power see Walter Ullmann, *Principles of Government and Politics in the Middle Ages* (New York, 1961), esp. the Introduction, Pt. I, Chap. 3, and Pt. II, Chaps. 1 and 2. This superb book may be complemented by Michael Wilks, *The Problem of Sovereignty in the Later Middle Ages* (Cambridge, Eng., 1963), esp. Pts. 1 and 5. And see Walter Ullmann, *Medieval Papalism: The Political Theories of the Medieval Canonists* (London, 1949), esp. Chaps. 3 and 4, and his *The Origins of the Great Schism: A Study in Fourteenth-Century Ecclesiastical History* (1948; rpr. London, 1967), 143–60, and Brian Tierney, *Foundations of Conciliar Theory* (Cambridge, Eng., 1955). For the Renaissance Roman Catholic view that the pope was not an absolute theocratic monarch in secular affairs but did have an indirect control over the secular arm, see Cardinal Robert Bellarmine, *De potestate summi pontificis,* trans. George Moore (Chevy Chase, Md., 1950). On Bellarmine, a standard Roman Catholic work is James Broderick, S. J., *The Life and Work of Blessed Robert Francis Cardinal Bellarmine, S. J., 1542–1621* (2 vols.; London, 1928); on the "Ditchley Portrait" itself, see Strong, *Tudor and Jacobean Portraiture,* I, 104–105, and color plate facing p. 104; Strong, *Gloriana,* 134–41. Timothy Murray argues that LaCalprenèdde's prose portrait of Cardinal Richelieu, in comparison "compels the beholder to speak, to re-present, an infinity of praises" (*Theatrical Legitimation: Allegories of Genius in Seventeenth Century England and France* [New York, 1987], 137–40).

bined the religious and political legitimacy of Elizabeth I, the customary iconologic details of the last twenty years of her reign, those involving empire, beauty, youth, chivalry, virginity, wisdom, and love were subordinated to the main themes or merely implied. The program, however, was clear, and religion was at its heart. As Hooker said: "With us society is both church and commonwealth."

Portraiture was not the only mode for the official depiction of the queen to take. There was also public festival, the most important instance of which was November 17, *Eliza Triumphans'* Accession Day. Here the usual popular expressions of joy, ringing bells, bonfires, public feasts, and games, complemented the Accession Day tilts. These celebrations gradually increased in number and extravagance, so that by the nineties they were expected everywhere in the realm, even the north, and provided a national accompaniment for the central event, the royal tilt at Whitehall. These fabulous tournaments were held virtually every year in the last quarter-century of Gloriana's reign, and records survive, with a few exceptions, from 1581 to 1602.[33] Strong has sifted these records meticulously for what they tell about the psychology of the Elizabethan court and the cult of Elizabeth I. The theme and image he has described present a picture of feudal, chivalric, courtly pageants whose basic artistic inspiration came from a chaotic merging of classical mythology and medieval romance. The tournament itself was an exercise in archaic chivalric knighthood, no longer having any serious connections with warfare. The knights rode against each other, separated by a wooden barrier. It was still dangerous sport; in 1559 Henry II of France had been killed by the Comte de Montgomery in such a tilt. But the pass at arms was only a small part of the festival. More to the point than the actual tilt were the costumes. The various knights scheduled to ride appeared in costume as Philisides, the Shepherd Knight (often played by the Earl of Essex), or the Wild Knight or the Discontented Knight or the Knight of Pendragon Castle or the Unknown Knight or the Enchanted Knight or the Blind Knight or the Black Knight and so on until the inventions of myth and romance ran out, which they never did nor could. The knights themselves, accompanied by squires sometimes running into the dozens, also richly costumed, paraded around the tiltyard. A squire

33. Strong, *The Cult of Elizabeth,* Chaps. 4 and 5; in connection with the pageantry of Elizabeth I, see John Nichols, *Progresses and Public Processions of Queen Elizabeth* (1823; rpr. New York, 1966).

presented the queen with gifts and a pasteboard shield emblazoned with the knight's device and accompanied this with poems and speeches in honor of the queen. Elizabeth I herself took a role in this pageant. Seated with her ladies in a long gallery overlooking the tiltyard, she was variously Gloriana, the Faerie Queen, Astraea, the Virgin who saved the realm, Queen Helen of Corinth, the Goddess of the Moon and Sea, *Eliza Triumphans,* Belphoebe, the Goddess of Love and Beauty, and always the object of the courtly love of the assembled chivalry.

The devices, *imprese,* emblems, mottoes, poems, speeches, colors, and courtly names all had an individual purpose, a compliment to Gloriana that could advance personal careers. The Earl of Essex used the occasion of the Accession Day tilt to declare his love for the queen and thus ask her pardon for having married the widow of Sir Philip Sidney without royal permission. The Earl of Cumberland, having failed to gain the governorship of the Isle of Wight, appeared as the Discontented Knight in the tilt of 1600, and his squire's speech to the queen complained that favor had fallen on those who had not so faithfully served the Crown.[34] Here the iconology and allegory were both serious and self-consciously ironic, making the tilts, at the same time, a genuine expression of support for the Crown and love for the queen and their own parody. The politicians tilting on Accession Day were, after all, hard-bitten careerists who clearly knew the difference between romance and reality. One is not dealing here with Don Quixote, who is still a decade in the future as of the middle nineties. The image might be from *Orlando Furioso, Amadis de Gaule,* or Ovid's works, but the underlying, granite subtext was institutional continuity, loyalty to the queen, and personal favor and advancement. More *sub* than *text,* we judge: a semiotic concert of desires and loves for stability and self and more or less philadelphic affection for her yet conjoined with an *assemblage* from the symbolic order.

This complexity can also be seen in the literature that complemented the pageant, whether written for the event, as was much of the work of Sir John Davies or the *Polyhymnia* of George Peele from 1590, or written within the romance tradition, as much of the poetry by Spenser or the *New Arcadia* of Sir Philip Sidney. Again, a serious subtext was covered by an almost rococo elaboration of neomedieval adornment. The accoutrements provided charm and

34. Strong, *The Cult of Elizabeth,* Chap. 5; see p. 140 for Cumberland's expression of disappointment.

poetic suggestiveness, as well as hidden allusions whose details may, on occasion, be problematical but whose general theme was clear. Behind the artificiality of a familiar and deliberately archaic mode lay the serious theme that the reign of *Eliza Triumphans* was moving England to "this our Golden Age," for which Arcadian pastoral and romance were appropriate metaphors. This attempt to unify Arcadian longing for social and human perfectibility, both anticipatory and nostalgic, with current political reality embodied by Astraea certainly had a hard political core as well as a (perhaps paradoxical) sense of ironic distance. It was a political effort to bring together love and power.

This self-deprecatory wit and distance in the public political display of Gloriana's Accession Day can be further seen in the deliberate humor that was part of these tilts. "The Queen and her ladies expected eulogy and amusement, and it is the humour which is most difficult to discern four hundred years later."[35] If the wit often escapes most readers now, one must always remember that once it was clever and that humor and gentle self-ridicule were a sanctioned part of this public political theater. Had this been a fearful or even merely solemn occasion without a sanctioned leaven of humor, the result of Cumberland's appearance as the Discontented Knight complaining of royal favor due but not given could only have been attainder and trial. The environment of the deliberate archaism of romance and chivalry transformed the complaint by lightening its style. A year later a Hermit spoke on behalf of a Clownish Knight who was accompanied by a crowd of rustics asking in a long narrative speech that they might be permitted to joust, the likes of Bottom, Snout, and Snug again. Here also, was a more solemn meaning: "How Protestant chivalry in its religious aspects lends itself to pastoral allegory."[36] But the broad humor stood out and set the tone for the whole affair. Even more important, the rude mechanicals, though the butt of some gentle humor by their betters and by Londoners, still were able, at least symbolically, to approach the queen. Such good humor was one of the things that tied the queen to her people; only genuine affection could animate such an occasion. Elizabeth I, who approved the staging of the tilts, clearly understood the essential truth of political propaganda: To have enough self-confidence to laugh genially at oneself is to induce others to take one favorably and confidently and seriously.

35. *Ibid.*, 139.

36. Yates, *Astraea*, 101. See Catherine Bates, *The Rhetoric of Courtship in Elizabethan Language and Literature* (Cambridge, Eng., 1992), especially for practices of gift-giving and -receiving as ambiguously and ambivalently mediatorial between love and power.

It is a lesson that, in our own time, was understood by Franklin D. Roosevelt but not by totalitarians of any variety. One reads of it being urged on current political figures by their "handlers," with uneven results.

It is a tribute to the confidence that queen and subject had in each other that the tilts could be both compliment and parody together. And Elizabeth I did it every year in the most perilous times of her reign. By appearing as courtly knights, the leading nobles of the realm could join in the game, saluting the queen by mocking themselves, at the same time that all affirmed their currency in antique manners and mores. So deft a touch was one of the political characteristics absent in her Stuart successors.

An archaic, none-too-solemn style fit the then-prevailing English idea of decorum, of the proper style with which to address the sovereign. The continental baroque style did not come to England until near the end of the reign of James I and would seem foreign, solemn, and suspect. The psychopolitical comfort engendered by Elizabethan tilts and paintings went beyond a general appeal to the traditional and the normative, strong as that was in preindustrial England. Nostalgia was also involved, longing for a partially remembered past tinged with a sense that the past was the true location of hope, virtue, and right, as well as comfort.

Nostalgia fit well into a basic notion of the common (English) law: that it was custom immemorial and traditional, had arisen from the people, and was the guide to public right as well as individual rights.[37] Thus nostalgia complemented the general cultural idea that the age of gold did truly exist in the past, never mind how distant. In a traditional and largely oral society, the sense of historical time was not particularly precise.[38] Finally, nostalgia had a personal dimension. Remembrance of the past was also a reminder of challenges surmounted, of a safety the uncertain future could not provide.

Nostalgia was the path to secular understanding and comprehension, as well as a reminder of love, for individuals. All can be seen in the evocative modern poem "Moraga Avenue" by Thomas D'Evelyn:

37. Sir Edward Coke, *Institutes,* esp. Pt. 2 on ancient laws and statutes.

38. But see the Venerable Bede, *Ecclesiastical History of the English Nation,* trans. J. King (2 vols.; London, 1930), Bk. IV, Chap. 2. "Neither was there ever since the English first came to Britain any time more happy than that present; when they both had most valiant and Christian kings . . . and the desires of all were wholly bent to the late joyful tidings of the kingdom of heaven, and if any desired to be instructed in the reading of Holy Scripture there lacked not masters ready to teach them."

Then, this firestorm
in the hills! A form
takes on the street where
my grandpa would stare
down traffic while
grandma, her smile
hid by the steering wheel,
backed out. Oh seal
off the avenue!
I see it all as a few
red maple leaves
drift from the eaves.[39]

But the nostalgia complex has a communal aspect as well. Collective recognition was of the right social order, glimpsed as traditional and wherein "ancient" law was applied or long-approved duty performed. The archaic form, costume, and banter of the tilts enabled the Renaissance spectator, like the modern poet, to "see it all."

So the romantic, Arcadian, and chivalric public theater of the Accession Day tilts was, like the entire reign of Elizabeth I, a delicate and constantly adjusted balance of ambiguous and contradictory elements: sharp Renaissance statecraft; an effective secret service; a church compromise that was neither Calvinist nor Roman Catholic, called Protestant; an elaborate iconology and public theater couched in nostalgic and neomedieval terms to make a familiar contemporary impression; the use of humor and wit to suggest seriousness; and a deliberate archaism to indicate modernity. Ambiguity is the key here. The various iconologic elements of Gloriana's portraiture and political theater were deliberately left in mutual opposition, in an almost Heraclitean dialectical tension.

And so we are brought back to our original premise: that Elizabethan iconology, whether in portrait or in performance, with its essentially medieval technique of conflating time, space, and idea into a single multidimensional

39. Thomas D'Evelyn, "Moraga Avenue Anniversary Ode, Oakland Fire," *Bostonia* (Winter, 1992–93), 16. See also Harry Levin, *The Myth of the Golden Age in the Renaissance* (Bloomington, 1969); especially in Chap. 3, on geography, he catalogs some who in "this Iron Age" were nostalgic or apprehensive about more iron to come: Hakluyt, Montaigne, Spenser's Talus, Thomas Bastard on artillery, Thomas Heywood, Robert Burton (66–148).

image in which Renaissance artistic canons of perspective, proportion, realism, representation, and chiaroscuro were subordinate to allegory, comfortably included the deliberate archaism of romance, Arcadia, and chivalry and both sacred and secular theme, ignored contradictions or ambiguities, was not dependent on superb artistic talent, and all for the single reason that it asserted a genuine affection and romance between sovereign and people. The queen really was Gloriana, *Eliza Triumphans* and the "unspotted lily" whose virtue and wisdom were believed (not without cause) to safeguard the realm. These were not *just* names; they were names given to express the national sense that Elizabeth I was the primary factor in the safety of the Commonwealth. The cause being iconologically represented and "puffed" must seem right and just, and Elizabethan images were as if Platonically real. As the Stuarts were to discover, power had its uses, but it could not replace love, nor was image everything.

After Elizabeth's death on March 24, 1603 (New Style), the custom of royal iconology continued, in both portraiture and masque, though sonnets addressed to James I never became a popular genre. But if the custom continued, something was missing. Gloriana inspired a devotion that her successors never could. Jacobean or Caroline England, either during the first run or the reprise, was rarely called a golden age and was usually considered to be a time of troubles and an age of iron. However stylized the image of the queen presented by Elizabethan iconographers might have been, many courtiers and commoners alike genuinely loved the queen, and their praise was heartily meant. We find it difficult to convince ourselves that the same was true of those who paid (and were paid for) compliments to James and Charles (of either number). One must wait until the time of Henry Purcell and John Dryden before something of the old spirit of genuine support for the reigning sovereign appeared.

Of course, that is a modern judgment. At the time, both the monarchs and artists assumed that iconic and allegorical presentations of the royal political programs could continue, though perhaps not exactly as before. Perhaps there would even be improvements, but the really phenomenal success of Elizabethan iconology, they believed, would certainly continue. Thus, in the new reign the Accession Day tilts continued, the king remained sovereign of the Garter, and the portraits continued to carry a political program. In part, therefore, it was the mixture as before.

But the old mixture no longer worked very well. The tilts continued, but

James I could never fill the role played by Gloriana. He was debarred primarily by gender but also by foreignness, by character, and by temperament from filling the role of courtly beloved, even in the most abstract or displaced manifestation, such as the image of King Arthur. So the tournaments and jousts made less and less sense to both monarch and subjects. A final effort to pump some meaning into the accustomed ceremony came between 1610, when James's elder son Henry Frederick was created Prince of Wales and given his own household, and 1612, when the young prince died of typhoid fever. He was designated as the chosen chivalric heir to Astraea, becoming in his person the revival of Protestant knightly virtue of the Arthurian mold.[40] This theme first appeared upon the young prince's initial appearance bearing arms, but even then the theme was carried primarily through masque, specifically in *Prince Henry's Barriers,* by Ben Jonson and Inigo Jones, presented on Twelfth Night, 1610. The Accession Day tilt was secondary. When the young Arthurian hero died two years later, the tilts receded even further. Their death blow came in 1620 when Prince Charles' costume, accoutrements, entourage, and appearance cost nearly £6,500. This sum, enough for a country gentleman to live comfortably for a lifetime, reached beyond royal *grandeur* into monstrous greed. Such gross expenditure, of course, entirely changed the nature of the

40. On Prince Henry, see Elkin C. Wilson, *Prince Henry and English Literature* (Ithaca, 1946), and, more recently, Roy Strong, *Henry Prince of Wales and England's Lost Renaissance* (New York, 1986). The sharply personal sense of loss such as the D'Evelyn poem illustrates was part of the mourning for Prince Henry. The funeral procession was a mile long as London paid farewell to a prince who, in popular imagination, would have been a valiant and Christian king who would champion the Protestant cause. In this case the nostalgia was for an imagined chivalric past that had never happened, and the sadness, for a heroic and Protestant future that could never be. For a clear and detailed chronological account, see Graham Parry's "The Politics of the Jacobean Masque," in *Theatre and Government Under the Early Stuarts,* ed. J. B. Mulryne and Margaret Shewring (Cambridge, Eng., 1993), 87–117, which emphasizes the fact and aim of magnificence and minimizes any ambiguity in Johnson's panegyric, though the latter's insistence on the golden age *restored* protests much. Referentiality is explicated (especially with regard to the Overbury murder) by Martin Butler and David Lindley, "Restoring Astraea: Jonson's Masque for the Fall of Somerset," *ELH,* LXI (1994), 807–27; they rightly note the irony of Astraea's reign being *concretely* golden (823) but occlude the master issue of love versus power. See also Martin Butler, "Reform or Reverence? The Politics of the Caroline Masque," in *Theatre and Government,* ed. Mulryne and Shewring, 118–56: a richly detailed exposition of the ambiguities, the elisions of (for example) distinctions between power and goodness, and finally the failure of the late masques. Although attentive to anti-Puritan elements, this, too, is less attentive to concerns of love, especially in religious modalities.

joust, eliminating utterly the element of self-deprecatory humor as well as the entire element of a free gift of loyalty and affection from subject to sovereign. At this level of expense and magnificence, the subject was no longer a participant but only a passive and excluded spectator at what once had been, still within living memory, a happy act of love and loyalty. Still, James I, with his legendary tastelessness, planned more tilts, but the last, in 1622, fell victim to bad weather.[41]

The problem with the Accession Day tilts, from the viewpoint of the monarch, was that they no longer expressed the subject's appropriate love and loyalty in an effective way. Jerzy Limon has expressed this pithily: "What was true, say in 1600, was not true . . . in 1620. 'Political' texts of the past always lose their original political character as time goes on."[42] The tilts had simply outlived their contemporary cultural resonance, if not for the entire realm, then at least for court and capital. A generation earlier, they had been a successful vehicle for expressing popular as well as aristocratic loyalty. Then they gradually became quaint, though cherished as long as Astraea lived, and finally an embarrassment. Cultural taste had moved to something different. The international baroque style, handsomely represented by Rubens and Andrea Palladio, was coming finally to England by 1620. The tilt, as cultural power-theater, lost its place as representative of current taste and style and faded into unimportance.

As the tilts faded, the importance of masques grew, for they represented the new courtly style. Like the tilts, the masques were theater of power, with impact variously immediate, mediate, and subliminal in their mobilization of multiple sensory modes and multiple modes of artistic expression.[43] Like the

41. Roy Strong, *The Cult of Elizabeth,* 138. For the text of *Prince Henry's Barriers,* see Stephen Orgel, ed., *Ben Jonson: The Complete Masques* (New Haven, 1969), 142–58; see also Orgel and Strong, *Inigo Jones,* I, 159–75.

42. Jerzy Limon, *The Masque of Stuart Culture* (Newark, Del., 1990), 8.

43. On theatricality, see *Ibid.,* Pt. 2, esp. Chap. 4. See also Clifford Geertz, "Centers, Kings, and Charisma: Reflections on the Symbolics of Power," in *Culture and Its Creators: Essays in Honor of Edward Shils,* ed. Joseph Ben-David and Jerry N. Clark (Chicago, 1977), 150–71, 309–14, for provocative synchronic assemblage. See Jean Howard, "Scripts and / versus Playhouses: Ideological Production and the Renaissance Public Stage," in *The Matter of Difference: Materi-*

tilts, the masques commingled contemporary and mythic allusions, though masques were usually far more careful to make the parts fit together into a coherent whole.[44] Again, like the tilts, the masques were occasions for the demonstration of love and loyalty to the Crown, though they were more cameral and exclusive in participation. As with the tilts, the audience was part of the show, in marked contrast to the sharp modern playhouse distinction between player and observer / auditor. Francis Beaumont and John Fletcher indicated in *The Maid's Tragedy* what the masques, like the tilts must do: "[Masques] must commend their King, and / speake in praise of the assembly. . . . in person of some God, they'r / tied to rules of flatterie."[45] And, like the tilts, masque engaged in a religious, mythic, and political dialogue, involving the sovereign in relationship to the past, to the people, to God, to right order.

---

alist Feminist Criticism of Shakespeare, ed. Valerie Wayne (Ithaca, 1991), 221–36. Howard is highly intriguing in her consideration both of *play-house* attendance as frighteningly *commercial* (framing objections to play content or ambience) and of Althusserian "ideology" as what we would call a secularized version of the trope of calling. This essay first appeared in *Renaissance Drama,* XX (1989), and since in Howard's *The Stage and Social Struggle in Early Modern England* (London, 1994). Consider also such faint derivations as "throwing out the first ball" and the "Americas Cup [sailboat] Race."

44. On the general topic of myth and its referentiality, see the important book by Stephen Kogan, *The Hieroglyphic King: Wisdom and Idolatry in the Seventeenth-Century Masque* (Rutherford, N.J., 1986); on the connection with the entire subject of emblems, see Daly, *Literature in the Light of the Emblem;* see also Karl Josef Holtgen, *Aspects of the Emblem: Studies in the English Emblem Tradition and the European Context* (Kassel, Germany, 1986), esp. Chap. 1, on Francis Quarles, *Emblemes* (1635). Both the early Stuart kings moved around a great deal, as can be seen in John Nichols, *The Progresses, Processions and Magnificent Festivities of King James I* (London, 1828), and Kevin Sharpe, *The Personal Rule of Charles I* (New Haven, 1992), 630–31. We suspect that the fiscal burden of these royal visits was not less than it had been under Elizabeth I, but the love that softened the blow before 1603 was increasingly absent after. On the court opinion diversely manifested by and under James I, see Linda Levy Peck, ed., *The Mental World of the Jacobean Court* (Cambridge, Eng., 1991). For rational (or rationalized) aspects of contemporary mentation in general and historiography in particular, see Daniel R. Woolf, *The Idea of History in Early Stuart England: Erudition, Ideology, and "The Light of Truth" from the Accession of James I to the Civil War* (Toronto, 1990). See the notably suggestive review of Sharpe, *The Personal Rule,* by Thomas Cogswell in *Albion,* XXV (1993), 688–91. For an appropriately full account of the complexity of James's personal politics and emphasis on divine-right absolutism (favorable to James), see Maurice Lee, Jr., *Great Britain's Solomon: James VI and I in His Three Kingdoms* (Urbana, 1990).

45. This famous passage is quoted everywhere. See, for example, Stephen Orgel, *The Jonsonian Masque* (Cambridge, Mass., 1967), 105.

There were, of course, differences. Time passes. Things change. Among the changes are always the meanings of the words, emblems, and symbols used in public display, as well as the implicit political assumptions that underlie all social theater.[46] Tilts, that perfectly clear albeit imprecise political theater, rested, as we have seen, on a medieval style of courtly love combined with a mirror for princes, imbued with chivalric loyalty to the Crown. By the time of the new century, these attitudes, though still comprehensible, had less and less resonance in the mode of tilts, though they seemed entirely appropriate and unexceptional to (at least) a court circle when displayed in a masque. The Stuart masques presented the same ideals, used the same icons and symbols, but meant something slightly different, less bellicose, more urbane (not least so when pastoral), more attuned to the emerging political culture of divine *right* of kings, as opposed to the divine *protection* and *approval* regularly attributed to Gloriana. The tilts were transformed from physical event into symbolic one as in the Jonson and Jones masque *Prince Henry's Barriers.* The courtly mode was now domestic, not public, though it ultimately was supposed to carry a similar political message. The imperial motif returned, as with the Jones and Sir William Davenant masque *Britannia Triumphans,* performed in 1637, though the symbols looked a far distance from the Armada portrait. And the empire itself had new meaning, changing from distant and glorious destiny to a dream now being fulfilled. Even Nature, so conspicuously artificialized in spectacle, betokened royal power. So the stage changed, and the props, players, and roles adjusted, but toward a constant denouement, as the orienting figure of *auxesis,* honorific enhancement, ostensibly of royal nobility, but failing that, of royal power, materialized.

Newness and sameness merged to change the constant message in an effort to keep the power and resonance, to hit the moving target of public belief. It was not easy for the masque to do that. Viewed today with some distaste, they were also suspected by contemporaries. Called "toyes" by Sir Francis Bacon, they were more roundly attacked by Puritans.[47] While Charles I regarded the masque as an appropriate vehicle for presenting his "policie," his opponents with more success pointed to the same body of work as evidence for the king

46. On this point see J. G. A. Pocock, "Working on Ideas in Time," in *The Historian's Workshop,* ed. L. P. Curtis (New York, 1970). See also Elizabeth D. Harvey and Katharine Eisaman Maus, eds., *Soliciting Interpretation: Literary Theory and Seventeenth-Century English Poetry,* (Chicago, 1990), esp. ix–xxiii.

47. Francis Bacon, "Of Masques and Triumphs" (1625): "These things are but toyes." See also Kogan, *The Hieroglyphic King,* 11.

as a spendthrift tyrant. As the political assumptions slowly changed during the personal rule of Charles I, the frozen political theater of the masque became a liability.

Nonetheless, in spite of these caveats and comments, we still must address Bacon's observation that kings liked and wanted masques.[48] Why? In the first place, masques attempted to undo and reverse the fixed and lengthy theatrical heritage of the state as tragic (a cultural heritage to which "Eliza" had seemed, especially after 1588, a providential exception). The masque seized and enlarged and embellished the notion that the king and monarchy were forces for good and even salvation. The *res publica* in the masque was to be the deliverer (at last) of peace and abundance and contentment that seemed always beyond reach. The state would lose its tragic look. The king would surpass the heretofore unsurpassable (albeit declined and fallen) Romans, and statecraft, stripped of its Machiavellian technique, would embark upon the Neoplatonic path to virtue.[49]

Allied to this was the notion of the king and the state as minister and guide in times of suffering. The theology of suffering (as noted earlier) was one of the most pervasive and important ideas in Renaissance Christian living. It was, basically, an attempt to explain why the rain fell on the just and unjust

48. Bacon, "Of Masques and Triumphs": "Since princes will have such things, it is better they should be graced with elegancy, than daubed with cost. Dancing with song, is a thing of great state and pleasure."

49. On the notion of the Jacobean state as an instrument of political and thus moral tragedy, rather than a mirroring instrument of a God-centered divine order, see J. W. Lever, *The Tragedy of State: A Study of Jacobean Drama* (London, 1987), esp. the Preface, Introduction by Jonathan Dollimore, and Chap. 1. This book was part of the "new left" criticism, concerned with Marxist ideology, power as the only important factor in social or interpersonal relationships, the West as a society of oppression, and literature as a key to unlocking the web of power / oppression relationships. There is a great deal of Renaissance criticism reflecting these general positions, and a good sample, from Marxist to new historicist to feminist, can be found in the footnotes to Dollimore's introduction. We regard this intrusion of a latter-day political ideology into Renaissance criticism as productive of occasional insight but as usually overdrawn in its conclusions and theoretically inappropriate by virtue of insistent presentmindedness. But see Jonathan V. Crewe, "The Hegemonic Theater of George Puttenham," in *Renaissance Historicism: Selections from "English Literary Renaissance,"* ed. Arthur F. Kinney and Dan S. Collins (Amherst, 1987), 93–107. Beyond its focus on part of *The Arte of English Poesie* (1589), Crewe's essay superbly canvasses the issues, earning in its own terms its conclusion that stagings of transgression "to subversive effect" can "only . . . reinstate the law that is transgressed." But Crewe does not address the ambiguity of mere *positive* or else (higher) *normative* law being reinstated, much less the theater of liturgy (see Chap. 3, below).

alike, why Job was tested, and to do so in terms of God's loving admonition and correction, of God's grace constantly seeking people out and nudging them toward virtue, prayer, and worship. God, the theology of suffering held, sent affliction in mind, body, or estate as a chastisement to remind the sufferer of the hideous nature of sin and the saving nature of grace. Sears McGee quotes the moderate Anglican from Lord Falkland's Great Tew Circle, Anthony Favindom: "It cannot consist with the wisdom of God, that Christ should suffer and die, and that we might live as we please, and then reign with him."[50] Thus affliction was the appropriate admonition for all, and that meant *all* who lapsed into sin (no Pelagius here), whether or not they had in their hearts a sense of assurance of salvation and grace. The difference was, therefore, in the individual heart, not the external problem. Those who had experienced grace and felt themselves to be saved tried constantly to understand their affliction as a Godly and gracious reminder of the trope of journey and its salvific destination, while for the stony-hearted, affliction was a dreadful foretaste of hell.[51] Thus sin was the *ultimate* cause of suffering, though not necessarily the proximate cause.

On this all Protestants, Anglican and Puritan alike, were agreed. On this, but not on every implication to be drawn from this. The Puritans, who were rigorous Augustinians (theirs the later, anti-Pelagian Augustine), emphasized the utter fallenness of humanity, the radical impairment of the human will, the constant failures of human reason, the even more constant human lapse into sin, the narrowness of the way and the straitness of the gate to heaven, and the absolute need for exceptional and "saving" grace from God. The Anglicans emphasized the "comfortable words" and the yoke that was easy and

50. Quoted in J. Sears McGee, *The Godly Man in Stuart England: Anglicans, Puritans, and the Two Tables, 1620–1670* (New Haven, 1976), 52.

51. *Ibid.*, Chap. 1. See also the important book by John Stachniewski, *The Persecutory Imagination: English Puritanism and the Literature of Religious Despair* (Oxford, 1991), esp. Chaps. 1 and 4. For an individual example of this aspect of Calvinist psychology, see Paul R. Seaver, *Wallington's World: A Puritan Artisan in Seventeenth-Century London* (Stanford, 1985). These are essential to understanding the psychological and pastoral reality of hell and "lostness." Among older books, see Geoffrey F. Nuttall, *The Holy Spirit in Puritan Faith and Experience* (Oxford, 1946), and his *Visible Saints: The Congregational Way, 1640–1660* (Oxford, 1957), which identify a less despairing segment of English Calvinism. See also, on conversion, Norman Pettit, *The Heart Prepared: Grace and Conversion in Puritan Spiritual Life* (New Haven, 1966). Although this study deals with America, the phenomenon of spiritual preparation and regeneration is transatlantic, at least.

the burden that was light (Matthew 11:30), and thus the need was for "common" grace and a human, not "above heroic," scale of effort to avoid sin. Ironically, and cultural history is nothing if not ironic, it was the Puritan John Milton who most powerfully enunciated the Anglican opinion, in *Paradise Lost* and (notwithstanding the echo just above) in *Paradise Regain'd.*

It was at this point of differing emphasis on the way of suffering that the masque became important. The true and lively sign of personal sanctification was the Godly life, and the masque presented the king as the most sanctified man of all, leading the essence of the Godly public life and, indeed, leading the whole people to Christ. Just as a right understanding of affliction led directly to an appreciation of God's love and grace and relieved suffering and brought hope and prosperity, so too did a right understanding of politics and the king, who was bestowing the secular blessings of peace, justice, and empire on the nation. The appropriate understanding of royal governance would bring the same sense of grace as did the right understanding of God's divine plan. The masques, Jacobean as well as Caroline, emphasized the connections between sovereign and God, and divine right of kings provided one of the models, the theology of suffering and benefit being another, for understanding that connection. One ought to welcome the king's role with gratitude because the royal yoke was akin to Christ's yoke. The masque presented royal rule, much as theological treatises did suffering and affliction, in a triumphant and joyous mode as the beneficent rule of a kind and loving father. This central element of masque and its relationship to tragedy have been decisively expressed by Dolora Cunningham: "The virtue of princes is to masque as the fall of princes is to tragedy."[52] Nothing better epitomizes the function of the masque in relation to sin, suffering, the king, and the salvific role of the polity than this concise remark. We call the state tragic partly because in the state's own terms, princes always fall. We see as an implication of this tenet that masque of its nature would, for anyone minded like Jonson or Thomas Campion, aim toward reconciliation of humanity with God.

Masque, like its successful continental rival opera, presented its message in what today would be called a multimedia format, with the addition, in the work of Inigo Jones, of special effects. Being built, like opera and *intermezzi,*

52. Dolora Cunningham, "The Jonsonian Masque as a Literary Form," *ELH,* XXII (1955), 123. Stephen Orgel has recognized the continuing significance of this article in his essential *The Jonsonian Masque.*

on the foundation of processions, pageants, and court revels and dancing, masques were an agglutination of essentially discrete elements, from dance and music to *mise-en-scène* and script, into an entity that was not dramatic but didactic.[53] Indeed, it is only a slight exaggeration to say that masques were the iconology of paintings brought to occasional life with dance, music, scene, costume, and text, and they thus anticipate the Clausewitzian definition of a continuation of politics by other (artistic) means.[54] Within the modern world, the stage for masques has been reduced from the political to the parochially *socio*political, as in the Mardi Gras balls in New Orleans. Here mythical theme, costume, music, dance, stage decor, pantomime, and the calling out of spectators to participate in the dance are all brought together in a powerful and concordantly expensive display of social force. Good social order is defined in terms not of God or king but rather of the aggrandizement of the social elite. Salvation has been attenuated to social prophecy and retrospection, albeit in a residually Catholic and vestigially European subculture.

Mardi Gras balls and masques retain, in common with the Stuart masques,

53. See Orgel, *The Jonsonian Masque*, 6–7. On the political implications of the didactic nature of the masque and of theater in general, see Richard Dutton, *Mastering the Revels: The Regulation and Censorship of English Renaissance Drama* (Iowa City, 1991), for masques, esp. Chap. 9. On masque and politics, see also Kevin Sharpe, *Criticism and Compliment: The Politics of Literature in the England of Charles I* (Cambridge, Eng., 1987), esp. Chap. 1. See also, on masque, Douglas Brooks-Davies, *The Mercurian Monarch: Magical Politics from Spenser to Pope* (Manchester, 1983), Chap. 2 on the court masque. We are in general agreement with the notion of the king as magician in the masques.

54. On examples of the use and limits of the politics of masque, see Orgel, *The Jonsonian Masque*, Chaps. 4 and 5. See also (the long standard) Enid Welsford, *The Court Masque* (Cambridge, Eng., 1927), and Allardyce Nicoll, *Stuart Masques and the Renaissance Stage* (London, 1937); but see, necessarily, the modern examination of the politics of masque, Kevin Sharpe, *Criticism and Compliment.* The most complete examination of both the texts and *mise-en-scène* of masques is in Orgel and Strong, *Inigo Jones.* For the Clausewitz reference, see Carl von Clausewitz, *On War*, ed. and trans. Michael Howard and Peter Paret (Princeton, 1976), Bk. I, Chaps. 23 and 24, pp. 86–87. "War is merely the continuation of policy by other means" (Chap. 24).

Consider, though: George V and Queen Mary attended a showy, confected-for-the-occasion *durbar* in India. George VI and his queen went in showy progress to America and to Franklin and Eleanor Roosevelt in 1939 (partly in successful riposte to the Duke of Windsor's embarrassing visit to Hitler's Germany). Jacqueline Kennedy presumably knew some history of royal display and reportedly consulted histories of presidential funerals in devising the remarkable national experience of her husband's funeral.

the relation of time to text. The dancing, music, and display of costume took, and in Mardi Gras balls still take, hours, but the written text was only a few pages. In the Stuart masque the essential message of princely virtue required the written text and could not be carried by the staging, costume, dancing, and music alone. Jonson was right. The artistic difficulty in the Stuart masque was integrating the various elements into a unity, something that opera had been able to do. But with opera the audience was not part of the performance, the praise of royal virtue was not the point of the work, and the king was not the central figure of the presentation. Even with the superior abilities of Ben Jonson and Inigo Jones put to the task, the masque rarely achieved the artistic coherence that is a hallmark of great opera. Masques, particularly in unskillful hands, were often so disjointed that their scripts could seem to reflect the comment by Lord Thurlow on a parliamentary amendment: they were needed "to connect the nonsense of one part of the Bill, with the nonsense of the other."[55]

The heart of the difficulty in making a masque was the king. Both in the masque and in the audience, he must be praised and, in effect, praise himself and do so in terms that were neither impossible nor parodic, not an easy task for the first two Stuarts. While Inigo Jones in his stagecraft could rely on arches, movable scenes, fabulous costumes, lighting, and curtains to achieve an effect, the poet had only two sources of theme, an occasion, such as Prince Charles' 1623 return (happily unmarried) from Spain, or a mythic representation of a royal virtue or general desirable condition, such as that in *The Masque of Queens* in 1609. In both cases, the poetics of compliment were sufficiently difficult to require allegory.

Jonson's initial effort was the twin production of *The Masque of Blacknesse*, presented on Twelfth Night, 1605, and *The Masque of Beautie*, designed to follow it but not played until the Sunday after Twelfth Night in 1608.[56] These

55. "The Lord Chancellor presumed that the wish of their lordships was to pass some bill of regulation [of the slave trade]; but as the bill stood, it was nonsense. He therefore concluded that some amendments would be proposed to connect the nonsense of one part of the Bill, with the nonsense of the other" (*The Parliamentary History of England from the Earliest Period to the Year 1803*, XXVII (1788–89) (London, 1816), Col. 641. We are indebted to our colleague Patrick C. Lipscomb, III, for bringing to our attention this delicious comment, so tempting a description of all but the finest masque. See Patrick Lipscomb, "William Pitt and the Abolition of the Slave Trade" (2 vols.; Ph.D. dissertation, University of Texas, 1960), I, 250–51.

56. For the texts of the two masques, see Orgel, ed., *Ben Jonson*, 47–74. For the texts and

possessed a single common theme: the "bright nymphs," after a year's obedience to "Great Aethiopia, goddess of our [Niger's] shore" would, in consideration of their virtue, be revealed in beauty. The queen, Anne of Denmark, danced in both masques, and in her person carried the theme of virtue, obedience, and beauty from the formal presentation of text, stage, costume, music, and dance into the reality of the polity. Her person identified the king as the one figure powerful enough to cause virtue to reign and beauty to show forth.

In these two early masques Jonson set the general pattern he would follow throughout his court career. Jonsonian masques would be part of the *speculum principis* tradition of moral instruction. Virtues were imputed to the prince in the hope that he would emulate them and rule rightly. Failing that, guilt might be induced when the prince fell short, or failing that, shame over failure. Virtue pretended, the triumph of duty over inclination, was perhaps all that could be hoped and indeed all that was needed. In the fallen world the trope of ambassadorship was the one appropriate for princes, for their virtue in many a case might consist only of justice, not goodness, of representation, not the thing itself.

The Jonson masque was thus a double instrument of policy. It was, of course, a piece of royal propaganda, a depiction of the king as he thought his subjects ought to see *and* understand him. Here was the familiar Renaissance apotheosis of kingship. But there was also a message from the Commonwealth to the king. Implied, not directly stated, but still serious and direct, Jonson told James I that the political nation expected good and loving government and that it was the king's obligation to provide it. Unlike all other masques, those by Jonson dwelt more on what the king owed his people than on what they owed him. They were lessons not merely in royal grandeur but also in royal duty. It was this dimension that made the Jonson masques unique.

All of these characteristics could be seen in the Twelfth Night masque for

---

the Inigo Jones drawings for costume and staging, see Orgel and Strong, *Inigo Jones,* I, 88–99. On these two masques, see D. J. Gordon, "The Imagery of Ben Jonson's *The Masque of Blacknesse* and the *Masque of Beautie,*" *Journal of the Warburg and Courtauld Institutes,* VI (1943), 101–21. Since this early and important article, see Richard S. Peterson, "Icon and Mystery in Jonson's *Masque of Beautie,*" *John Donne Journal,* V (1986), 169–200. On the Jonson theater, including masque, see Robert Wittenburg, *Ben Jonson and Self-Love: The Subtlest Maze of All* (Columbia, Mo., 1990). All masque performance dates are given in New Style.

1618, *Pleasure Reconciled to Virtue.*[57] The moral of the masque, which honored Charles, Prince of Wales, was evident in its title; the pleasure was not merely sensual but also of and in virtue. This view of the pleasure of the good, instantly recognizable from Aristotle's *Nichomachaean Ethics,* served the function of denying the Puritans' assertion that all earthly pleasures were vices and must be avoided by the truly virtuous (whom detractors like Jonson took as either the truly guilt-ridden and religiously obsessed or the hypocritical), by claiming that virtue itself was an earthly pleasure. It was also implied that the king and the Prince of Wales took pleasure in doing justice, that they were the true ambassadors of right rule.

The theme of right rule appeared in the context of nature rather than human morality in the masque *Mercury Vindicated from the Alchemists at Court.*[58] In this masque Mercury, a natural element, was being pursued by Vulcan, the alchemists, and a Cyclops, all intent on capturing him, heating him, adulterating him, and transforming him into something artificial and unnatural. The Cyclops proclaimed the virtue of "subtile fire, thou soul of art" to transform weak "Nature, that through age is lamed." Mercury has been unwillingly conscripted "in the reign of the Cyclops . . . become alchemists since their trade of armor-making failed them . . . as if the title of philosopher . . . were to be fetched out of a furnace" (35–37, 42–44). The alchemists as androids, who actually appear and dance as "imperfect creatures, with helms of limbecks on their heads" (161–62), are those who, in the elements of their concoction, suggest the unloving new men of power and technique whom we see in the plays (and in projects for impositions or indeed in the Overbury murder): "Scales of the globe, filings of figures . . . title-bane, niter of clients, tartar of false conveyance" (144–48).

Mercury was made to defend himself vigorously, denouncing the scheme of alchemy as impious and fraudulent and invoking the aid of the king: "That are both the Sol and Jupiter of this sphere, Mercury invokes your majesty against the sooty tribe here; for in your favor only I grow recovered and warm" (96–98). The efforts of Vulcan and the alchemists to catch Mercury fell short, and Nature, now refreshed, appeared with a subordinate Prometheus to cele-

57. For text and costumes for this masque, see Orgel and Strong, *Inigo Jones,* I, 277–93; for text alone, see Orgel, ed., *Ben Jonson,* 263–76.

58. The text is in Orgel, ed., *Ben Jonson,* 213–23. This masque can be read as pointed notes to *The Alchemist* (which is not to deny its simultaneous applicability to court factionalism).

brate right order in both nature and society: the royal reign of love as opposed to that of projectors, technology, and power.

A third example of the general theme of right order on an ostensibly cosmic scale was *The Golden Age Restored,* presented in January, 1615.[59] The title, the fact of "Pallas in her chariot descending," the personified antimasquer Iron Age, and generic accompaniments of music, dances, settings by Inigo Jones ("yond cave," "The scene of light"), all suggest an expansive, vaguely Ovidian trifle. Such masques were reproached as extravagant frivolity and defended as instruction by praising, *laudando praecipere.* That mode appeared through the personified Golden Age and Astraea, jointly *ex machina,* who were associated through Pallas Athena's power with love, faith, joys, light, poetry, and the "age of better metal" (which is equally "mettle"). A personified Iron Age was announced by "A tumult and clashing" as though "all the Iron Age were up in arms!" The Iron Age now emerged, calling up vice to bring her companions:

Avarice,
Bring with thee Fraud and Slander,
Corruption with the golden hands
Or any subtler ill that stands
To be a more commander.
Thy boys, Ambition, Pride and Scorn
Force, Rapine and thy babe last born,
Smooth Treachery, call hither
Arm Folly forth, and Ignorance.
(40–48)

Clearly this was more an existential platoon of baneful dispositions and actions than a strictly orthodox procession of the seven deadly sins with Pride in the lead. Scorn is noteworthy as adversive to Love. The similarly notable tendency of several figures to emphasize material gain accorded with the framing antimasque action of "pyrrhic dance" and of projected final assault on Jove to "let him feel / The Iron Age is turned to steel" (59, 63–64). The reference here was to military technology. Mining, metallurgy, and calls for better artillery projectiles reinforced one another; harquebus became musket, with more precisely produced parts and ball ammunition; garments became uniforms as one of the first results of mass production. All stood as an apt fig-

59. The text is in Orgel, ed., *Ben Jonson,* 224–32.

ure for mercantilist materialism. This catalog of the nature of the age of iron, an age of dis-grace and unlove, was followed by predictions of victory over Jove, since now "malice is far greater."[60]

The scene then changed from the antemasque to the return of Pallas Athena and the appearance of the twin goddesses, Golden Age and Astraea (Justice). Not merely would the new reign of God be established from on high, as an act of unmerited grace; it would also be supported on earth by the poets. The poets Geoffrey Chaucer, John Gower, John Lydgate, and Edmund Spenser were named to assist in this victory of peace, love, faith, and joy and the rout of strife, hate, fear, and pain. "As of old, all now be gold" sang the choir, a result that could only come from the influence of the Jove who "is present here." James I would never receive a higher compliment, nor a greater task. Even Astraea, whose still-green memory was invoked, had not been able to do so much. *The Golden Age Restored* was a measure of how cosmic and how tropic were the mythic and religious expectations of Renaissance state-craft. It was a measure also of the gap between political expectations and the means available to achieve them. Jonson placed the later *Mercury Vindicated* before *Golden Age* in his 1616 Folio, the more triumphant image of James / Jove tactfully and cautionarily last.

The Caroline masques continued many of the same themes as did those Jonson wrote for James I, though toward the end of the personal rule, the moral lessons turned blatantly political with the mythology only the ostensible occasion for the political message. A second change involved the king, who was now often a masquer instead of a spectator, thus giving greater psychological and artistic focus to these productions, since there was no need to invent a method of tying the masque to a passive viewer. But these were details in the great scheme of the masque, which retained the function of showing

60. See *The Golden Age Restored,* ll. 59, 60–64, where Jove is to be made to feel "The Iron Age is turned to steel." For an instance of more limited and topical reference, see Martin Butler on Jonsonian adjustments for different audiences in successive performance: " 'We are one mans all': *The Gypsies Metamorphosed,*" in *Patronage, Politics, and Literary Traditions in England, 1558–1658,* ed. Cedric C. Brown (Detroit, 1991), 247–67. For telling detail about some Jonsonian adjustments for publication, see David Lindley, "Embarrassing Ben: The Masques for Frances Howard," in *Renaissance Historicism,* ed. Kinney and Collins, 248–64. With regard to the first masque, *Hymenaei* (1606), Russ Mc Donald wrote, "Evil is vanquished but not destroyed" (*Shakespeare and Jonson: Jonson and Shakespeare* [Lincoln, 1988], 148). For the most far-reaching brief for Jonson managing his text to rebut in folio the "cozenings" of [secular] theater, see Murray, *Theatrical Legitimation,* Chaps. 3 and 4.

the royal beauty bright. One of the constant examples of royal grace and virtue during the personal reign was peace and tranquillity, a not-inconsiderable blessing during the publicized horrors of the Thirty Years War.

One of these masques in celebration of, or possibly in instruction about, peace was *The Triumph of Peace,* presented on February 3, 1634. Written by James Shirley, with staging by Jones, the masque was played and danced by the gentlemen of the Inns of Court, who also paid for the production. Ostensibly *The Triumph of Peace* was an expression of loyalty from the Inns of Court on the occasion of the birth of James, the Duke of York, but there was more involved than that. Bulstrode Whitelocke had a great deal to say about Archbishop Laud's persecution of the intemperate and incautious William Prynne, a gentleman of Lincoln's Inn, whose *Histrio-Mastix,* an excess of Puritan crankiness, attacked the theater in general and "women actors, notorious whores" in particular, while also claiming that the habit of watching plays was a cause of the fall of princes.[61] This last was alleged to be an insult to the king and queen. All in all, it seemed like a good time for the barristers to show the flag and present an expensive masque.

The Triumph of Peace began with the now-customary antimasque of disorder, involving "projectors" (*The Staple of News* comes to mind here, to say nothing of *The Alchemist* and *Mercury Vindicated*), one of whom had a perpetual motion machine to thresh wheat while another had invented a hollow iron bridle that would emit a cooling vapor to refresh a horse. The projectors played a secondary role to Confidence, Opinion, Fancy, Novelty, Admiration—all characters again implying the capacity of people to be deceived and

61. Orgel, *The Illusion of Power;* Orgel and Strong, *Inigo Jones,* II, 539–45; Kevin Sharpe, *The Personal Rule of Charles I,* 647–52, and for the trial, 670–82. On the role of Queen Henrietta Maria in the court entertainments in general and the masque in particular, see Erica Veevers, *Images of Love and Religion: Queen Henrietta Maria and Court Entertainments* (Cambridge, Eng., 1989), esp. Chaps. 2 and 5. This important book emphasizes the religious role played by court masque, along with the importance of Platonic love and Platonic kingship. See, however, Barbara Lewalski, "Anne of Denmark and the Subversions of Masquing," *Criticism,* XXXV (1993), 341–55, where she expertly anatomizes how the Queen's quasiseparate court and its several masques were evidently intended to aggrandize Anne and womanly counsel from Pallas Athena to Elizabeth to Anne herself. But her court could never succeed James's, as Prince Henry's could for a shining moment be anticipated to do, and James was the effective *heir* of Elizabeth and patron of the masques. If they could not aggrandize (or even instruct) him, then whom, in all their tiny audience? These masques apparently do not make the truly subversive reference: to Mary.

led astray. When the antimasque was cleared off, Irene, Eunoma, and Dice (*i.e.,* Peace, Goodrepute, and Justice) appeared and began their tribute to the king and queen: "To you great King and Queen, whose smile / Doth scatter blessings through this isle, / To make it best" (608–10) were presented the "Sons of Peace, who tender you, by me / Their joy-exalted heart" (819–20).[62] What exactly was meant by peace, whether politically and religiously at home or militarily abroad, was not stated. Nor did it need to be. The fact of the masque in itself showed the hopes of the capital and the political nation.

By 1637, as the political and religious difficulties of the personal reign grew in insistence, the masque *Britannia Triumphans,* created by Jones and Davenant, presented the king's position on the general course of affairs.[63] The basic theme of the masque was that Britanocles "the glory of the western world, hath by his own wisdom, valor, and piety not only vindicated his own, but far distant seas infested with pirates, and reduced the land, by his example, to a real knowledge of all good arts and sciences" (19–23). But though his fame was known in heaven and abroad, at home it was different. Fame was enjoined: "If there can be any maliciously insensible, awake them from their pretended sleep, that ever they with the large yet still increasing number of the good and loyal may mutually admire and rejoice" (27–30). The accomplishment of clearing the seas of pirates was, we judge, a not-too-subtle reference to the good use made of ship money. The king was the classic case of the prophet without honor in his own country, and his subjects were gravely at fault for not recognizing the king's wisdom and virtue, his concern for their welfare, and their own good fortune in having so noble a king. Action and Imposture began the debate over the intention of Fame to assert the glory of the king. It was the standard debate between right order and (potentially) chaotic disorder, always, of course, to be settled in favor of the former. But this time a new tone was heard, a tone of complaint against injustice rather than the usual smug assertion of triumph. The masque ended in the justification, even the apotheosis, of the king, but the road to that end showed a lack of confidence that this must inevitably occur. This note of uncertainty would reappear three years later in *Salmacida Spolia.* These two masques presented a curiously modern attitude, the combination of triumph with insecurity. They were the oddest of Renaissance royal spectacles, the masques of plaint.

62. Texts of masque and drawings are in Orgel and Strong, *Inigo Jones,* II, 546–65.

63. Orgel and Strong, *Inigo Jones,* II, 662, for masque and drawings, II, 660–703.

Salmacida Spolia was the last of the Caroline masques, again the joint work of Inigo Jones and Sir William Davenant. It was presented on January 21, 1640, at a time when English government was seriously troubled and Charles I was about to be forced to call his first Parliament since 1629.[64] The masque reflected these troubles and was part of Charles' response to the "brutal political reality" he faced. The written work began with exposition: "Discord, a malicious Fury, appears in a storm . . . having already put most of the world into disorder, endeavours to disturb these parts, envying the blessings of tranquility we have long enjoyed" (1–5). England was described as an "over-lucky, too-much-happy isle" (134), whose peace could "never altered be / But by thy surfeits of felicity" (136–37). But that would happen. The "people's vice" was to hold in contempt "every blessing they possess." Still, there was hope. England was ruled by a "secret wisdom, in the person of the King . . . under the name of Philogenes or Lover of his People" (13–14). In the masque this was enough to bring order from chaos and repel Discord. The text concluded with a song to Charles and Henrietta Maria:

> That we may wish your sceptres ruling here
> Loved even by those who should your justice fear.
> (481–82)

But the brutal political reality had gone beyond the power of art and symbol to heal the breach. It no longer mattered if the king loved his people; large numbers of them did not love him and that had become the more important fact. The king, many thought, was not the cure but the cause of discord. The image of a king unjustly attacked and wrongly accused of standing apart from his people and patiently enduring contumely and working on behalf of his benighted flock inspired only disdain. Masque had always had only a courtly audience; far from tying the king to his people it had, unlike the Elizabethan tilts, only served to separate them further. Whatever its general artistic merit, the masque failed in its fundamental political task, which was to present to the political nation the royal person as he ought to appear, the symbol and image of right rule and public graciousness.

64. Text, plans, scenery, and costumes are in Orgel and Strong, *Inigo Jones,* II, 728–85; a convenient text edition is David Lindley, ed., *The Court Masque* (New York, 1995), 200–13. On the times, see Kevin Sharpe, *The Personal Rule of Charles I,* Chaps. 15 and 16; on the place of the queen, see Veevers, *Images of Love and Religion,* 112–13, 118, 121.

To turn from masque to Stuart royal portraiture is to honor the French maxim that the more things change, the more they stay the same. The mode of presentation changed from movement and tumult to the stilled instant of time, but the political program and the allegorical symbols remained the same. Absolutely superb artists, Rubens and Sir Anthony Van Dyck, were used to depict Charles I and Henrietta Maria, but the artistic superiority of their work was politically unconvincing, leading us to suppose that if the masques had been "better," it would not have mattered. Portrait could be what masque was not, artistically stupendous and permanent, but it could not do what masque could not, foster domestic tranquillity. Art, no matter the visible and extensive faith of contemporaries, had not that power. The *theatrum mundi* was, after all, the sort of symbol and seeming, behind which (Heraclitus had been right after all) lurked a dark and intractable reality.

Statecraft, which often is only a refusal to accept or even acknowledge that reality, chose pretense (today called "image") on the illogical but nonetheless empirically verifiable grounds that such reality can be created (a "good" marriage, for example, or Winston Churchill in 1940). So James I continued the iconographical program that he inherited from Elizabeth I, though he gave it far less attention and invested little imagination in his political appearance. Portraiture was the poor step-child to masque. James added no new iconographical elements to his portraits; indeed, there was retreat rather than advance on the ideas that had been presented in the portraits of Elizabeth I. Gone was the "mask of youth" that dramatically transformed Elizabeth I from an angular middle-aged spinster into a Cynthia or Belphoebe of ageless beauty. James also neglected to fill Elizabeth's role as the patron of chivalry, except in the formal sense of the Garter. Even the imperial emblems were relegated to a secondary role, except for the Whitehall Banqueting House ceiling, which was commissioned abroad. Finally, again excepting the Banqueting House ceiling, the portraits of James I had few allusions to the king's connection to God, a sharp departure from the practice of Astraea. James I appeared as he was, portly, dull, complacent, and uninspiring, an ordinary man rather than the core of a cult. Part of this was certainly due to the king's notorious dislike of sitting for his portrait, and part was due also to the royal interest in the masque. Whatever the ultimate reasons for the conventionality of Jacobean royal portraiture, the result was a series that could hardly be either the inspiration for or the reflection of the apotheosis of royalty.

A representative example of a portrait from early in the reign was a full-length painting, probably by John de Critz, probably around 1606 or 1607. It shows the king dressed as a nobleman, with jeweled cape, sword, and jewels, and the Garter around his calf. Aside from the Garter, the figure here could have been any peer, an indication of the paucity of royal symbolism or iconic program. A second painting, from 1618, showed the king in a black suit and hose, the suit ballooning out so alarmingly around the hips that James I looked like an eggplant. Again he wore the Garter, and the king's left hand rested on a table on which were collected the symbols of office, his crown, scepter, and orb. Below the right foot the painter included some royal armor. Here one sees James I as both gentleman and king, though no advance on the general iconography had been made since Elizabeth I. The portrait had no particular political theme, nor did it appear to celebrate any special idea or triumph. It appeared to be merely a new portrait, in which the king, unfortunately, was rather realistically depicted. A third portrait, again full length, this by Daniel Mytens from 1621, showed the king seated, wearing his Garter robes. A plumed hat rested on a table to the king's left, and above his head, though definitely in the background, was a Tudor rose, above which was inscribed *"Beati Pacifici."* This portrait presented a political message, peace, an important and welcome statement during the early years of the Thirty Years War, when the king's son-in-law was being dispossessed of his Rhenish Palatinate by the Catholic League. Again, one saw the unmistakable face of the king, and in this portrait he showed serious signs of age. A tired king sat for this portrait and gave the unfortunate impression that he had not imposed peace but merely accepted it.[65]

These paintings, and others as well, were, of course, widely reproduced, with variations in costume and setting and also in the skills of the artist. Royal portraits, while serving as likenesses of the sovereign and emblems of public policy, were also templates for dissemination throughout the realm and beyond. Uninspired portraits, therefore, were not merely a matter between patron and painter. They were an element of policy—an element that James I seemed to take lightly.

His son and successor, Charles I, did not follow the paternal example in

65. Strong, *Tudor and Jacobean Portraits,* II, plates 346 (Critz), 352 (Sower), 354 (Mytens).

this matter. Charles I took artistic representation of royalty very seriously indeed, and he paid a great deal of attention to the iconic program of official painting. He was also concerned about the painters, and with Rubens and Van Dyck the English Crown employed its best artists since Hans Holbein the Younger. But technical talent is not the same as psychological and political success. The court of Charles I, though the locus of superior painting, was not an effective agent of communicating royal values and programs to the realm, representing instead "a courtly civilization with few native roots." Indeed, the Caroline court's "cosmopolitanism and baroque styles aroused little sympathy within a realm still suspicious of French and Italian culture on religious grounds, where a taste for Renaissance art had scarcely penetrated beyond the Court."[66] Excellence in art and in political iconography did not and do not always have the same appearance.

Caroline political mythology found its most complete and detailed representation in the nine Rubens panels in the new Inigo Jones Banqueting House at Whitehall. The building itself, a product of the reign of James I, was substantially finished, though not completely so, by January 6, 1622, when a Twelfth Night masque, *The Masque of Augurs* by Ben Jonson, was presented there. The iconographic program of the Rubens ceiling paintings was also the "invention" of Inigo Jones and was designed to celebrate James I, not his son Charles, though the general depiction of the Stuart idea of royalty fit the son better than it had the father. The ceiling panels were not actually commissioned until after 1630 and were complete (probably) by 1634. In 1635, the nine

66. Malcolm Smuts, "The Political Failure of Stuart Cultural Patronage," in *Patronage in the Renaissance,* ed. Guy Fitch Lytle and Stephen Orgel (Princeton, 1981), 166, 165. In this connection, see Peter Thomas, "Two Cultures? Court and Country Under Charles I," in *The Origins of the English Civil War,* ed. Conrad Russell (New York, 1973), 168–93. Thomas presents the extreme view of the hostility between Charles' court and the country: "There were, it seems, two warring cultures. But it is more accurate to talk of a breakdown of the national culture" (184). See Martin Butler, "Politics and the Masque: *Salmacida Spolia,*" in *Literature and the English Civil War,* ed. Thomas Healy and Jonathan Sawday (Cambridge, Eng., 1990), 59–74, for a detailed and persuasive gloss of it as a masque of compromised accommodation and suspect conciliation. For better poetry, and superb criticism of far greater reach than her title suggests, see Ann Baynes Coiro, *Robert Herrick's "Hesperides" and the Epigram Book Tradition* (Baltimore, 1988); she notes Jonson modulating flattery with praise and correction (95–101), observes Herrick following Jonson in "epigrams of advice" to the king (200–206), and brilliantly identifies *Hesperides* as metamasque of "disillusionment" and "wrenching . . . irony" (2–42, 107, and *passim*), not plaint.

panels by Rubens arrived in England and were hoisted into place by 1637. Charles I (actually) paid Rubens £3,000 for the panels, a bargain by today's standards, though how much of one is unclear because they are unlikely to be put on the market. The ceiling consists of a large rectangle at both the north and south ends, each flanked by two smaller ovals. The center is a large oval, the artistic and iconographic focus of the work, flanked by two long, narrow rectangular panels. The ensemble reflected Renaissance ideals of alternating balance and symmetry, celebrated from Leon Battista Alberti through the Enlightenment.

The general program has been persuasively described by Roy Strong, in the Walter Neurath Memorial Lecture of 1980, as one of politics and religion combined, of the king as both the triumphant ruler of Great Britain and the glorious personification of Solomon.[67] In the Rubens ceiling, the religious motif of James I as the antipapal Protestant champion was as important as the idea of James as the successor to the Trojan Brutus and the restorer of the British empire. Such a mingling of religious and political imagery was appropriate for the Baroque period, when politics had a religious core and was articulated in religious terms.

The large oval panel, positionally central to the iconologic program, carried the clearest exposition of the political / religious triumphalism that characterized the baroque image of statecraft. It depicted the apotheosis of James I, as he was carried triumphantly to heaven. He was guided in this journey by Justice, on whom his gaze is unwaveringly fixed. At the king's side were also Faith, with a Bible, and Religion, carrying a lighted altar. These three iconic figures represented the virtues that Charles I thought personified his father's reign and the duties both owed to God. In the top half of the oval, this theme was repeated, with Minerva, representing wisdom and justice, and a winged victory (Nike figure) receiving the king and offering him a crown of laurel. Surrounding the two mythic women were putti / seraphs, holding crowns and roses and, by obvious implication, praising the king. James I here was allied iconographically both to Solomon and to Christ, whose representative on earth he claimed to be. James *triumphans* was emblematic of *iusticia triumphans* and the true *ecclesia triumphans,* as church, state, king, type of Christ, and Christ all appear as the painting is read at different levels.

67. Roy Strong, *Britannia Triumphans: Inigo Jones, Rubens and Whitehall Palace* (London, 1980). This is a study of the architecture and iconology of the Banqueting House and its role in Charles' political program.

Moving to the central rectangle at the south end of the hall one saw the same religious and political themes repeated, though in a more specific context. Here was James I representing the golden age, both in his own reign and person and as Solomon. Below the king, Mercury and Minerva vanquished Mars and the hydra-headed depiction of Satan in a victory of justice, peace, and the true church over evil, war, and popery. The king gestured toward two female figures representing Peace and Abundance. Above the king, winged figures held the king's crown of victory. The painting has aptly been entitled the *Benefits of the Government of James I,* though this slighted the strong ecclesiological themes of the true (Anglican) church triumphant in the person of the Defender of the Faith. Flanking the central panel were two smaller ovals, one showing Liberality vanquishing Avarice and the other the victory of Temperance over Excess.

At the north end, the central rectangle depicted the king seated on his throne, in an attitude evoking the judgment of Solomon. The baby, Great Britain, sat between two female figures representing England and Scotland, while under their feet were the now useless weapons of war and above the scene putti / seraphs supported the royal arms and the Tudor roses. Although the union of the kingdoms was, in practical if not legal fact, dead by 1608, not to be accomplished for another century, the royal political representation here depicted the union as complete and perfected.[68] To reinforce both the imperial and Christian message, standing next to the king was a male figure in antique dress, perhaps the mythical Brut or the first Christian king, Lucius. The two flanking ovals again contained virtues supplanting vice, with Hercules clubbing Envy into submission while Minerva stood triumphant over a nude female Ignorance.

The themes here, which were depicted in such masques as *The Golden Age Restored,* the *Coelum Britannicum,* or *Britannia Triumphans,* involved a vision of the king that was fairly close to the beatific vision of Theresa of Avila.[69] The king, though not the author of grace, was nonetheless one of the channels through which the benefits of divine grace, in the form of the true church, peace, plenty, justice, and good government, flowed to his people. The connection between priest and king, reiterated in the Coronation Anthem by George Frideric Handel in *Zadok the Priest,* was suggested in this ceiling. Fi-

68. *Ibid.,* 16–34.

69. See *The Life of Theresa of Jesus: The Autobiography of Theresa of Avila,* trans. and ed. E. Allison Peers (Garden City, N.Y., 1960).

nally, the ceiling insisted on the virtue of obedience, never specifically personified but everywhere implied in the program of the nine panels.

Beyond the Banqueting House ceiling in Whitehall, Charles I commissioned one other body of work, less apocalyptic and more human, that carried the program of royal right and virtue. That was the series of paintings by Van Dyck of Charles I, both with horses and with his wife, Henrietta Maria of France. Strong has succinctly described the object of this body of work: "The philosophy which governed the arts at the Cavalier court was to make manifest and articulate the lustre and influence of the king."[70]

Charles I was adopting here an artistic and political tradition already old by the apogee of the baroque international style. Mediterranean in origin, the Renaissance standard personifications of polity as virtue and greatness underwent an alternation from the abstract to the personal, first in Renaissance despotisms and later in the transalpine kingdoms: the ruler replaced the state as the repository of the public good. The political program increasingly reflected the basic psychological tenet of divine-right monarchy, that the king was a "little god." The deification of royalty, commonplace on the continent during the first half of the seventeenth century, meant that the royal virtues of justice, wisdom, chastity, prudence, and piety, which were emphasized with Elizabeth I and in the early years of James, shared the iconic stage with bold assertions of apotheosis as seen in the Whitehall Banqueting House ceiling. The three Van Dyck portraits fell about halfway along this spectrum; the virtues were still thematically recognizable while the deification of the king was implied rather than trumpeted. The political program thus had to be inferred as well as recognized.

The Van Dyck portrait of Charles and Henrietta Maria, *ca.* 1632, fit into

70. Roy Strong, *Van Dyck: Charles I on Horseback* (New York, 1972), 92. The luster and influence of the king certainly, indeed primarily, included religion. For this aspect of the work of Anthony Van Dyck, see John Rupert Martin and Gail Feigenbaum, *Van Dyck as Religious Artist* (Princeton, 1979). Martin and Feigenbaum wrote: "Portraiture, even in its most sober form, has always been associated with religious art. . . . Van Dyck takes this tradition for granted. His greatest portraits . . . all begin with the assumption that man was made in God's image and that the portraitist has every right to assume that he confronts a *particello divina* in each of his sitters" (11). On Van Dyck at the court of Charles I, see also Christopher Brown, *Van Dyck* (Oxford, 1982), Chap. 4; see also the recent book of essays on Van Dyck: Arthur Wheelock, Jr., Susan Barnes, and Julius Held, eds., *Anthony Van Dyck* (New York, 1990), particularly the essay by Oliver Miller, "Van Dyck in London," 53–58. This volume also catalogs the works at the National Gallery exhibition of 1990–91.

this middle register. Against a conventional background, Charles received the victor's laurels from his wife and queen. The scene Charles looked at included those viewing the painting. On a table in the shadows behind the king rested the crown, orb, and scepter, but the king's humanity was emphasized rather than his royalty.[71] This was a domestic, even intimate moment, and the king received the laurels in his capacity as a husband and gentleman as well as a king. Private virtue was in the foreground, royal symbols retired to the side of the scene. The viewer was invited to assume that the private happiness and virtue on the small domestic scene transferred to the larger domestic stage of the Commonwealth.

A similar image of Charles I as private perfection was the Van Dyck painting "Charles I at the Chase" from 1635. Here the king was again depicted as the ideal gentleman and courtier, standing at ease, leaning on a staff, sword at his side, perfectly dressed in informal attire, looking at the viewer in an attitude of polite but coolly detached interest. Behind the king a groom attended a horse, and all three figures were framed by a large tree.[72] The king here was what every noble would wish to be, could it have been so. For Charles, as all could see, it was so, and, again, private virtues assumed the role of political characteristics. Again, the audience itself must tie together public and private spheres and must also believe that virtue in one was safety and prosperity in the other.

A third portrait of Charles I by Van Dyck, from 1638, Charles I on horseback, showed the king in his public *officium* as king of Great Britain. The title appeared on a sign hanging from the trunk of the tree that shaded the mounted king and his groom. The groom held the king's helmet, appropriate since the monarch was dressed in armor and held in his right hand the marshal's wand of command. He gazed into the middle distance, symbolically taking the entire Commonwealth into his view and care. The three-quarter face has been frequently described as sad-eyed, which we interpret as meaning that the exalted *officium* of divine-right kingship involved more of the melancholy burden of responsibility and duty than it did the satisfaction of elegance. Although the most celebrated, this was not the only painting by Van Dyck showing Charles I as emperor and vicegerent of God. Five years earlier, in 1633, the Flemish master had painted the king riding through a triumphal

71. Strong, *Van Dyck,* 73.

72. Strong, *Van Dyck,* 55, plate 25; Brown, *Van Dyck,* 171, plate 170 (color).

arch, flanked to the left by a groom carrying his helmet and to the right by crown and coat of arms.[73] Again, though full-face, the gaze is thoughtful, and we are reminded of the plaintive theme of the *Salmacida Spolia.*

In both of the paintings of Charles I astride, the message of divine right of kings dominated the work, while the king as husband or gentleman was subsumed into the *officium* of Charles I as king and the embodiment of the Commonwealth. But the paintings stopped well short of the essential deification of the *officium* of kingship found in the Rubens Banqueting House ceiling. There was, in the restrained work of Van Dyck, none of the lush detail of apotheosis seen in the work of Rubens. The final step of seeing God in the king must here come from the viewer of the painting. This was, we believe, a matter of the religious and political resonance the viewer brought to the painting. In the works of Van Dyck, the specifically religious symbolism was implied rather than stated and invited the viewer to fill in an entirely personal interpretation of the king as husband, gentleman, and warrior / emperor. In the Whitehall Banqueting House, the king became the successor to Solomon, who was a conventional type for Christ, and thus all of the allegorical symbols had about them the effulgence of divinity. But the question always, in the psychopolitical arena, was how successful an impression the image made on the nation.

Taken as a whole, the royal political program, whether presented by work, painting, or performance, had, from Elizabeth I through Charles I, centered on making "manifest . . . the lustre and influence" of the Crown. In the different reigns this meant a different emphasis, and this goal was pursued in various ways and through different artistic styles. The neomedieval work done for Elizabeth I, with its deliberate archaism, differed dramatically from the triumphalist neoclassicism of Inigo Jones or the elaborate and suave international baroque style of Rubens and Van Dyck. Gloriana was celebrated as the courtly lover's ideal of beauty, honor, and love, while the Stuarts favored iconology that emphasized divine-right monarchy. The means of expression also

73. Strong, *Van Dyck,* 15, 21, plates 1, 5, and 24–25, plate 8; Brown, *Van Dyck,* 170, plate 169 (color), and 166–67, plate 166 (color).

differed. Tilts and tournaments dominated Elizabethan obeisance, but the Stuart style was the masque, with its complex mythological allusions, its formal and stately pattern of royal compliment, and its merely courtly audience. The often-jocular, outdoor, Tudor amateur muddle gave way to the private and professional Stuart pageant. It was a fateful political decision and it was artistically ironic. The political effectiveness of royal programmatic art declined as the artistic talent employed improved. Good art was not synonymous with good politics.

The annual progresses of Queen Elizabeth I were legendary in their time.[74] They were a trying occasion, rich in opportunities to lose royal favor and even richer in chances for vast personal and municipal expenditure. Most towns and peers, while honored by a royal visit, were also vastly relieved when the queen and her entourage departed and the huge exceptional expenditures ceased. In spite of the real burdens, however, the royal visits, after a few years and when the fiscal shock had worn off, were fondly remembered as occasions that tied sovereign and subject together in a single Commonwealth: The progresses "did represent in lively show / Our glorious English court's divine image / As it should be in this our Golden Age."[75] Politically, both progress and tilt were exercises in common sympathy.

We turn to the Stuarts. Here the household and the court, an emphasis on interiority, replaced the essentially outdoor displays of Elizabeth I. What Elizabeth showed forth, the Stuarts drew behind palace walls. The choice of masque as a favored form of royal political depiction both manifested and reinforced a privatism—as if an interiority of the soul—of the Stuarts. Both of the early Stuarts looked to the continent, particularly the Roman Catholic part, for their artistic and political culture, and that political culture was centered on the court. Whether one considers the punctilious and hidden ceremonial of the Escorial or the elegant and artistically superb courts of the north Italian duchies, the cameralist mentality steadily increased the distance between the subject's gaze and the prince's person. It was a political trend that

74. See Nichols, *Progresses and Public Processions,* for the details of the progresses and visit of Astraea. It was not, of course, a single progress, such as Louis XIV's journey to Bayonne in 1659 to meet his Spanish bride, that made the lasting impression but rather the constant (and expensive for the subject) repetition that impressed contemporaries. These progresses ended in time for the Accession Day (November 17) festivities that marked the queen's return to London.

75. John Davies, as quoted by Strong, *The Cult of Elizabeth,* 54.

led toward increasingly elaborate ceremony and court etiquette, and it culminated in the world of Versailles.[76] Consider Cardinal de Retz's comment concerning the Fronde: "The people entered the sanctuary and raised the veil which ought always to hide all that can be said or believed about the rights of peoples and kings, who never agree so well as in a relationship of silence."[77] The cardinal would have approved of the early Stuart court, where the veil, both physically and psychologically, was being steadily lowered to close off the royal entourage. The masque, with its elaborate ritual tableaus, its formal dancing and music, its ornate scenery, its arcane mythic allusions, was the perfect vehicle for the royal retreat behind the walls.

All of this royal emphasis on what occurred *in camera* had, as a necessary corollary in an impecunious state, a corresponding neglect of public spectacle. In spite of careful and elaborate iconographic royal programs in both masque and painting, the Stuart kings were unwilling to make any consistent effort to take the message to the country. We are struck by the same phenomenon that caught the attention of Malcolm Smuts: "An art-loving king attuned to the values of early baroque culture, with its emphasis upon the didactic functions of art and literature, nevertheless failed to launch a program of cultural propaganda and ceremonial display remotely comparable to those of several Continental courts."[78] As James I and his son failed to stage to the eyes of subjects their iconographic program, which was not altogether different from that of Elizabeth, it never became the normative English experience in political theater. One must not forget that the largest spontaneous London celebration between 1603 and 1641 came when Charles returned from Spain *without* a Spanish bride.

We have noted the irony: Even as the artistic talent at the royal disposal increased, the effectiveness of royalist iconography declined. We can only speculate as to the cause, but we think it is rooted in religion and in the personal distance of the Stuart monarchs. We suggest that the Stuarts, particularly Charles I, were not seen as *loving* defenders of the Protestant cause, no matter what the iconologic references in their paintings or masques. The Stuarts also

76. Louis de Rouvroy, duc de St. Simon, *Memoires,* ed. A. de Boislisle (41 vols.; Paris, 1879–1928). The period of the last years of Louis XIV is covered in the first twenty-eight volumes, and details of court etiquette are scattered throughout.

77. A. Feillet, J. Gourdault, R. Chantelauze, eds., *Oeuvres du Cardinal de Retz* (11 vols.; Paris, 1870–1920), I, 193–94.

78. Smuts, "The Political Failure," in *Patronage in the Renaissance,* ed. Lytle and Orgel, 173.

seemed less sympathetic, more foreign, more distant than Gloriana had been. Perhaps it was only nostalgia that gave Elizabeth I such a golden posthumous glow, but allegiance to a better past was one of the powerful sentiments in an age that regarded itself as composed of iron. A fondly remembered Gloriana diminished the current Stuarts, whose real and iconic shortcomings seemed worse than they were or should have been. All of this posed too heavy a burden to be carried by a sporadic and poorly managed iconologic political program. Thus the iconology lost most of its political, though not artistic, effectiveness, and with this loss came a sense that something essential was wrong in the Commonwealth. It is bad enough for those in power when the official symbols and icons can no longer be understood by a disaffected populace; it is much worse when they can be read but are disbelieved.

Artistic excellence, therefore, became innocently implicated in the growing unpopularity, both in intensity and extent, of the regime. Stuart political art, at least at its best, was characterized by beauty, elegance, and imagination, but that alone did not create a sympathetic audience. We agree with George Kubler that human sensibility "is our only channel to the universe," whether this universe is religious, social, or political: "The channel may of course be augmented by many useful (artistic) inventions; ultimately, however, every rational structure can be razed by adverse feeling."[79] And so it was. The passions of revolution razed the entire structure of English Renaissance political iconology.

Finally, it seems to us that the varying degrees of iconologic and psychological success of the Tudor and Stuart monarchs were rooted in the four dominant tropes of Renaissance life. The apotheosis of James I, far from being (as it so easily seems today) a silly affectation, was the defining, salvific moment in the central theme of James's reign, the journeylike *renovatio* of imperial Britain. It was the general and public equivalent of individual baptism by the Holy Ghost and hence overwhelmingly appropriate for a society becoming ever more religiously radical. Charles I as the perfect husband and the ideal courtier and Elizabeth I as the queen of love and beauty presented the sovereign in the role of ambassador to the whole Commonwealth (and Corpus Christi) of important and necessary public virtues. The masques were a *theatrum mundi* ambiguously correspondent to the even larger *theatrum coeli.* So

79. George Kubler, *The Shape of Time: Remarks on the History of Things* (New Haven, 1962), 66.

were the Accession Day tilts of Elizabeth I, where costume, symbol, and ritual successfully showed the subjects their queen as friend, protector, and lover of her people and as *called* to be so. The willing suspension of disbelief at the archaic jousts furthered a far more important willing affirmation of belief that their queen stood for good and grace and God. The trope of journey was also implicit everywhere: James I rising toward heaven; Charles I, astride the steed of empire, caught in an instant of stillness gazing into the middle distance of destiny; Elizabeth I with orb, crown, and rainbow—all were depicted within an illuminating movement that was not seen but understood. It was movement of faithfulness to calling, understood in three ways, to the future, to the people, and to God, and it gave the journey its salvific *telos.* In tilt and masque and painting the *Hagia Pneuma* wafted all to God.

Or at least it should have. The royal icon, however completely it caught the dominant Renaissance tropes during "this our Golden Age" of Elizabeth I, stood increasingly apart from the mythic culture during the two generations of the early Stuarts. What was the essential cultural nature of this failure? Today, it might be said that the regime simply promised far more than it could deliver, that it stood for ideals so grand that the grubby give-and-take of politics could never take us to the vision. That explanation might be adequate in discussing the Great Society, but it falls far short when applied to the Renaissance. In the profoundly Christian society of the northern Renaissance, the fundamental cultural issue did not concern inadequately funded government programs but, rather, involved love. Elizabeth I based her entire iconologic program on love, whether courtly, chivalric, religious, or divine. It was one of the canniest and subtlest political decisions made by that remarkable woman. For love was precisely what Renaissance society believed in and wished to see as a fundamental public virtue. The love of God for his people, the love of the queen for hers, the love of the subject for the sovereign and of the sovereign for justice and the good, the love of the whole Commonwealth for the true religion, all of these loves were caught in sonnets, tilts, and portraits of Gloriana. A society shaped by love, contemporaries believed, would be one in which power would not be misused and justice would prevail.

The Stuarts, by contrast, spoke to their subjects in the language of power—the power of divine-right absolutism. The royal prerogative was ever their concern when dealing with Parliament, and both masque and painting depicted the king in a role of power. The Christian imagination of the late northern Renaissance did not accord the same odor of grace to power that it did to love. Power, as we have indicated previously, was the progenitor of oppression, not of justice, and an iconography founded in power could hardly strike the same responsive social and religious note as did a program that had its referentiality in love. Love connected people and the Commonwealth to God, while power separated them. The seventeenth century is often called by historians the age of power. It was also the age of revolution and of pervasive political mistrust and unease. The failure to inscribe politics with love also divorced the regime from the dominant tropes that made sense of life. To treat love as only a private condition of diminished capacity or of heightened fervor and no longer as the image and language of public journey meant that the Crown abandoned tropic moment and ambassadorship and prostituted theater to a renascent phantasm of power. But public policy must work, and kings must have the power and control (the technology) to make it work. For some of the best minds in England, this fact defined an age of iron.

3

The True and Lively Theater: Love Reconciled to Power

Until well after World War II, it was not unusual for English scholars in Renaissance studies to allude casually to the *Book of Common Prayer,* confident they would be understood. Dame Helen Gardner and Evelyn Simpson come to mind as critics who presumably came to intellectual awareness within the ambit of the Church of England and may well have supposed that their audience was similarly situated within the common culture. "But, if not . . . ," a British officer wrote in a dispatch from Dunkirk, confident that those who received it would recognize the allusion to Daniel (3:18) and understand that the troops would fight on; all belonged to a common cultural tradition. For us the experience has been different. Our primary audience has been American, and our combined years of teaching and learning through eye and voice from scholarly professional venues to university seminars all together suggest the increasing truth of the following: Few are intimately familiar with the *Book of Common Prayer;* few writing for American audiences do so from long immersion in the American version of the Church of England; and few have been moved from other lines of religious or secular belief to a patiently imaginative examination of the Anglican liturgy. So we shall offer, with the analysis we propose, more recapitulation of the *Book of Common Prayer* than we include in connection with Shakespearean or Jonsonian drama. It seems to us irresponsible not to foreground, in a treatise on a general cultural horizon, a work that was once partially memorized by the majority of the English people and that they encountered weekly at a minimum and daily in many cases. It was so influential that the victorious Puritans in 1645 banned its use as subversive.

Renaissance literary and historiographic scholarship has inappropriately occluded the *Book of Common Prayer* in favor of controversial writings, which have been seized upon like splintery planks in a shipwreck. Someone has wisely observed that the controversialists, certainly the extremists, had to be believed to be read, in their coldly decisive logic and murderously hot passions. Religion, however, remained the sea. As the passions cooled in desuetude, despair, or death, the logic sank to dust. It is now impossible to ascertain how many even of the true believers read the typical pamphlet. But what church and state *meant* to by far the greatest number of people, high and low, was the *Book of Common Prayer.* That was true whatever their degree of literacy and was true over a wide range (not exhaustively wide) of attitudes toward the church and state. Matthew Arnold heard in the mid-nineteenth century the "long, withdrawing roar" of the "sea of faith," but the four tropes we discuss endure, albeit with change, and Prayer Book likewise.

Although the language and the idea of love and the language and idea of power were conventionally supposed in the Renaissance to be moral opposites, almost in Heraclitian tension with each other, we have argued that they could only be conventional, linguistic opposites. In a cosmos described by the *principium unitatis* of Pseudo-Dionysius, an idea one can find antecedent to Plato in the Milesian physicists and entailed in Judaeo-Christian theology, opposition must ultimately become reconciliation, and multiplicity must ultimately become unity.[1] The reality, as opposed to the mere appearance of things, could only be characteristic of the One, however variously described by middle Platonists, church fathers or Renaissance theologians, or by power fetishists.[2]

1. For Heraclitus and the Milesian physicists, see Milton C. Nahm, ed., *Selections from Early Greek Philosophy* (New York, 1947), 55–68, 84–98; see also Malcolm Schofield, *An Essay on Anaxagoras* (Cambridge, Eng., 1980), 3–5; on the Pseudo-Dionysius, see Walter Ullmann, *Principles of Government and Politics in the Middle Ages* (New York, 1961), 46–48. The basic text by Pseudo-Dionysius on this issue is *De coelesti hierarchia,* in J. P. Migne, ed., *Patrologiae cursus completus . . . Series Graeca* (166 vols.; Paris, 1857–66), III, 119–370, esp. caputs I, II, III, cols. 119–78; see also *De divinis nominibus,* in *Patrologia graeca,* III, caput I, cols. 585–636, esp. cols. 587, 588 (*unitas effectrix universae unitatis*).

2. For "the many and the one" as central, see James Smith, "Metaphysical Poetry," in *Determinations,* ed. F. R. Leavis (London, 1934). Errol E. Harris in *The Reality of Time* (Albany, 1988) has argued that defensible ideas of process presuppose both the reality and accessibility to human understanding of (what we here call) the One in at least the sense of eternal structural ground. See also George Allan, Review of *The Reality of Time,* by Errol Harris, in *History and Theory,* XXVIII (1989), 348–56, demurring at Harris' meliorist evolution.

The dark side, the collapse into quasi-Manichaean fallenness, was an occurrence familiar to our authors, who knew that "love is not love" (as Arthur Marotti and others have decisively argued) when the lingo of Eros was marshalled for power maneuvers.[3] But it is useful to begin with the positive, and we think it realistic; there is, after all, a significantly shared and somewhat orderly world we all inhabit rather than mere existential chaos or nothingness. For contemporaries, the Great Chain of Being provided a metaphoric mode of describing and understanding cosmic unity, while the ontological proof of God's existence provided a synecdochic mode and the Canons of the Synod of Dort, a metonymic.[4] In *Paradise Lost,* Milton described cosmic unity in terms of God-given natural creativity and its spiritual counterpart, essential freedom and natural right of choice. Both sinning angels and humans were partly "authors to themselves," enlargers over time of divine works of love. This ultimately means for all an increase in the general good, as with Satan who

> might
> Heap on himself damnation, while he sought
> Evil to others, and enraged might see
> How all his malice served but to bring forth
> Infinite goodness, grace and mercy. . . .
> (I, 214–18)

The clear implication of the Miltonic passage, inherent in the concept of the *principium unitatis,* is that the *motus ad formam* within Christian theology works essentially *ex opere operato,* in and through and of itself, as a function of the general rule, as they say in law.[5] Thus the centrality of the unity is

3. Particularly notable, on this much-hammered point: Arthur Marotti, *John Donne: Coterie Poet* (Madison, Wisc., 1986); Frank Whigham, *Ambition and Privilege: The Social Tropes of Elizabethan Courtesy Theory* (Berkeley, 1984); Linda Levy Peck, *Court Patronage and Corruption in Early Stuart England* (New York, 1990), notable for her judicious refusal to exaggerate patronage or faction; Catherine Bates, *The Rhetoric of Courtship in Elizabethan Language and Literature* (Cambridge, Eng., 1992).

4. On the Synod of Dort, see John T. McNeill, *The History and Character of Calvinism* (London, 1954), 265, and Chap. 5, n 24, below.

5. *Ex opere operato,* the theological formula used to describe transubstantiation, did not become formal doctrine until the Fourth Lateran Council, in November, 1215, in the first constitution "De fide catholica": "In qua idem ipse sacerdos et sacrificium Iesus Christus, cuius corpus et sanguis in sacramento altaris sub speciebus panis et vini veraciter continentur,

affirmed at the most fundamental cultural and theological level, that of the definition of God and the operation of grace. Almost as important, the general cultural relevance of the doctrine of unity rendered nominalist criticism, whether linguistic or epistemological, unimportant.[6]

Nonetheless, if virtually every Renaissance figure either affirmed or at least did not dispute the notion of the unity of the cosmos, the vast disparity between love and power on the human and microcosmic scale loomed large on imaginative horizons. It was easy to see one or the other, but difficult to see both together. While all things might in St. Paul's words "work together for good," the good that would come from, say, Iago's treachery, remained hidden, and the insolence of office and the law's delay were familiar to all. Moreover, things had always already been that way, or had been since the Fall, an alternative way of understanding the matter. Thus, there opened a cultural and phenomenological gap between the overarching, necessary, theological truth of the unity of the cosmos in God and the mundane, but equally compelling, truth about the moral diversity and disconnectedness of the world.

This seeming contradiction within a larger and ultimately significant pat-

---

transsubstantiatis pare in corpus et vino in sanguinem potestate divina." This doctrine was renewed at the Council of Constance (1414–18) in Session 15, on July 6, 1415, in the condemnation of 206 propositions of John Wycliffe, articles 1–5, 50; renewed again at the Council of Basel-Ferrara-Florence-Rome (1431–45), in Session 8, on November 22, 1439, and in Session 11, on February 4, 1442; and received final definition (for the Renaissance) at the Council of Trent in Session 13, on October 11, 1551 (second sitting of the council), in "Decretum de sanctissimo eucharistiae sacramento," Chap. 4, "De transsubstantiatione." At Trent (first sitting), in Session 7, on March 3, 1547, in "Decretum primum [De sacramentis], Chap. 1, no. 8, the concept of independent function without external cause, other than God, was spelled out. "Si quis dixerit, per ipsa novae legis sacramenta ex opere operato non conferri gratiam sed solum fidem divinae promissionis ad gratiam consequendam sufficere." All of these citations may be found most conveniently in Norman P. Tanner, S. J., *Decrees of the Ecumenical Councils* (2 vols.; London, 1990), I, 230, 422, 426, 546, 547, 581, 695, 697, and II, 685, 695, 697.

6. See Hans Blumenberg, *The Legitimacy of the Modern Age,* trans. Robert M. Wallace (Cambridge, Mass., 1983); see also Debora Shuger, *Habits of Thought in the English Renaissance: Religion, Politics, and the Dominant Culture* (Berkeley, 1990), Chap. 4. On the whole debate of the religious or secular content of modernity and its relationship to the Renaissance and to political theology and the idea of the sacred state in general, see Karl Löwith, *Meaning in History: The Theological Implications of the Philosophy of History* (Chicago, 1949), a book that is in fundamental disagreement with Blumenberg. A cogent brief discussion of this may be found in Stephen A. McKnight, *Sacralizing the Secular: The Renaissance Origins of Modernity* (Baton Rouge, 1989), esp. the Introduction. With respect to Shuger, we deny that "With the royal

tern of unity gave urgency to the dominant tropes of Renaissance life. The *theatrum mundi* seemed, within this system of thought, a corrupt and debased shadow of the *theatrum coeli.* On the one hand, seeming, on the other, reality; here, pretense, power, and unreliability, there, validity, love, and ultimate certitude: It all made a haunting contrast that supported both tragedy and comedy. Within this seeming contradiction ambassadorship might well be tragic, a possibility broached by Shakespeare's Henry V, Milton's Samson, and Henrik Ibsen's protagonist in *An Enemy of the People,* a drama written so recently that it has generally been considered social rather than theological in content. Beyond their superficial disparity, journey and defining moment could reinforce and even combine in a range and depth of meanings that almost inexhaustibly enlarged their suggestiveness.

But the chasm between chaotic diversity and teleological unity demanded bridging as well as illustration. It was that function of bringing the two perspectives of God and humanity together that was filled, at least for those in the established church, by the *Book of Common Prayer.* Here, in institutionally approved services addressing crucial human occasions from birth to death, the two levels of perception and of the Great Chain of Being were brought together into a single system in which both levels could be held in the mind at one time, responded to, and even enacted. Thus, reconciliation was a primary function of the *Book of Common Prayer:* reconciliation of the sinner with God, reconciliation of the whole Commonwealth with the divine plan for humanity, thereby reconciling love and power, and reconciliation of the believers with themselves and with the higher meaning of the dominant Renaissance tropes. Luigi Pirandello's "Six Characters" are "in Search of an Author" to complete their joint and several meanings; every Anglican congregation in England, every Sunday, every year, was in concert with priest / director enacting confrontation with the Author / Director, in the work of completing individual and corporate selves, characters who (formally, at least) had found their author.[7]

The first essential theme expressed in the *Book of Common Prayer,* reconciliation with God and community within the liturgy of the Church of England,

---

headship, the Church of England forfeited the Augustinian vision of the pilgrim church" (126). Unimaginative timeservers probably did. But Donne did not; and the Book of Common Prayer (far more powerful and pervasive than the Homily on Obedience) invited otherwise.

7. On Pirandello, see Howard D. Pearce, "A Phenomenological Approach to the *Theatrum Mundi* Metaphor," *PMLA,* XCV (1980), 53.

was not expected to be so much the work of an illuminating moment of grace as of the longer duration of an Augustinian journey entailing *conversio* and *agape.* This movement, impossible without the agency of God's grace, was put constantly before the worshipper by the liturgy. Thus, while the movement through the liturgy might not in itself be analogous to movement through life, both were headed in the same direction (it was to be hoped), which was grace and conversion. Certainly, absent grace in both life and liturgy, stasis was disaster. Donne would explicitly condemn *lethargy*—lethargy, opposite both movement and saving reflection or remembrance—in his sermons, which is to say, in a Prayer Book context. Milton, in the bardic liturgy of *Paradise Lost* and *Paradise Regain'd,* would imply that not to move toward God was in a fallen and falling world to move away, except for the very special case of a graced *stand* (of which more in Chapter 6).

We also see the *Book of Common Prayer* as embodying for Renaissance congregations true and lively theater, the authentic theater of self-realization and corporate reality animated by God's love, as opposed to the *theatrum mundi* of masking, power-mongering, and emptiness. The progression through the service was, in part, a psychodrama that distinguished sacred time from secular time and that defined the nature of the sacred for the participant. It is here in the drama that the progression from matins (sometimes through litany) to Eucharist has its meaning and importance. As the theater of and for the soul, the form of the liturgy as well as its content reminded believers of what was truly important and schooled and rehearsed them in embracing that, to the devaluing of the feckless and ephemeral.

We focus on Prayer Book worship as it would have been experienced in the century and a half after the first *Book of Common Prayer* of King Edward VI in 1549. This first Prayer Book was revised quite substantially in a Protestant direction in 1552, most notably in the rearrangement of elements of the previous communion service. In 1552 the pregnant phrase "having in remembrance his blessed passion, mightie ressurreccyon and gloryous ascencion" disappeared for more than three centuries. The phrases

> Drinke this in remembrance that Christes bloude was shed for thee and be thankefull

and

> Take and eate this, in remembrance that Christ dyed for thee, and feede on him in thy hearte by faythe, with thanks gevinge

were substituted for words explicitly indicative of a real-presence theology:

> The body (bloude) of our Lorde Jesus Christe whiche was geven for thee, preserve thy bodye and soule unto everlasting lyfe.

This substitution within the Canon of the Mass moved the service toward the basic Protestant views of justification by faith and eucharistic receptionism.[8] The Prayer Book of 1552 moved Anglican worship theologically toward the Calvinist communion services of Geneva, composed in 1542, or of Strasbourg, written in 1545, toward Martin Bucer's Strasbourg liturgy of 1539, and toward the Lutheran services of 1523 and 1526.[9] The emphasis on faith and "remembrance," while not actually denying the real presence (of some unexplained sort) helped give Anglican eucharistic worship its characteristic and distinct definition of being undeniably sacramental but not exclusively so.

This broad ground, which attempted to embrace both the sacramental theology of the Mass and the pastoral psychology of the communicant, whose heart was to be "lifted up," was further defined in the 1559 (Elizabethan) revision of the Prayer Book. The 1549 real-presence formulae ("The body . . . Take and eat. . . . The Blood . . . Drink this") were restored in 1559. The "Black Rubric" denying any "real or essential presence" in the eucharistic bread and wine was deleted. In 1562 a metrical version of the Psalter with a few hymns was authorized, thus moving the Service of the Word in a Protestant direction. In 1604, private baptism was limited to authorized ministers.[10] After

8. See Bard Thompson, *Liturgies of the Western Church* (Cleveland, 1961), 240–44; see Dom Gregory Dix, *The Shape of the Liturgy* (Westminster, 1945), for a view that Cranmer was Zwinglian in his Eucharistic theology. See also John Booty, "Communion and Commonweal: The Book of Common Prayer," *The Godly Kingdom of Tudor England: Great Books of the English Reformation,* ed. John Booty, David Siegenthaler, and John N. Wall, Jr. (Wilton, Conn., 1981), 139–216, esp. 143–47, 158–61. See also Peter Brooks, *Thomas Cranmer's Doctrine of the Eucharist: An Essay in Historical Development* (New York, 1965), and Horton Davies, *Worship and Theology in England: From Cranmer to Hooker, 1543–1603* (Princeton, 1970).

9. See Thompson, *Liturgies of the Western Church,* 95–227, for the two liturgies of Luther, the two of Calvin, the Bucer liturgy, and Zwingli and Farel.

10. For convenient summaries, see D. E. W. Harrison and Michael C. Sansom, *Worship in the Church of England* (London, 1982), esp. 51–62, 79–122; R. C. D. Jasper, *The Development of*

1604, however, the changes of three and a half centuries amounted to little more than tinkering with the established diction.

Although the changes wrought between 1549 and 1662 were theologically and eucharistically substantial, they were all *local* within the Prayer Book. The Prayer Book always included elements from five late medieval books of worship. From the Breviary had come morning prayer, evensong, and the lectionary; from the Missal came the communion service, collect, and Gospel and Epistle readings; from the Processional came the Litany; from the Manual, specific services, including baptism, marriage, burial, communion of the sick, and so forth; and from the Pontifical, confirmation.[11] The details of these Prayer Book elements changed, and some not included in 1549 were added in 1552, but the general framework stayed the same. The Prayer Book remained as it was designed: a compendium in one place of all the elements necessary for full Anglican worship.

At the level of the parish service, of course, any alteration, however slight, was always noticed and usually condemned. There were difficulties in establishing the 1549 book, fewer troubles in 1552, and almost none thereafter (this, obviously, apart from Protestants radical enough to reject the very notion of any prescribed common prayer beyond the Lord's Prayer). Worshippers would certainly have noticed real liturgical differences between 1549 and 1552. After 1559 the worshippers would have noticed almost no change because there were almost no changes. A word or phrase here and there could be altered, but the essential function of the Prayer Book and the basic form, tone, rhythm, and order of service remained constant. It is our considered and confident judgment that any worshipper, accustomed to the "order for morning prayer dayly" or evening prayer, Holy Communion, or marriage, baptism, or burial, according to the 1559 version, could have walked into a service conducted according to the texts of 1604 or 1662 (or 1789 in America), or indeed 1928, with no perplexity as to what was going on or what to do and with only a minimal sense of irregularity.[12] The substantial reconsiderations that occurred in the

---

the Anglican Liturgy, 1662–1980 (London, 1989), esp. 1–7; and Marion J. Hatchett, "Prayer Books," in *The Study of Anglicanism,* ed. Stephen Sykes and John Booty (Philadelphia, 1988), 121–33 (with bibliography).

11. Harrison and Sansom, *Worship in the Church of England,* 28–50. See, for more magisterial treatment, Dix, *The Shape of the Liturgy,* and Booty, "Communion and Commonweal," 161–63.

12. Put another way: Discontinuities in Anglican practice must have been minor for Angli-

realm of eucharistic theology did not, after 1559, cross seriously over into liturgics. What impresses, in general, is not change but continuity.

Over the centuries, though, no change is inevitably a kind of change. The Book's unchanging diction and syntax eventuated in its language, which in 1559 had been quite normal for serious, public, and formal discourse, coming to sound a bit elevated in eighteenth-century England, unmistakably churchy in the nineteenth century, and quaint to some (not all) Americans in the twentieth. But the liturgical stability that seemed to some in our time to be a sign of antipastoral rigidity or religious error or irrelevance seemed in the Renaissance and Baroque England to be an absolutely fundamental mark of political stability and religious truth.[13] Once the Prayer Book was published, it was presented to the "King's liege people" as the true and right way to hear the pure word of God and to worship to one's "soule's health." Therefore it was changed only under compelling political pressure and was changed as little as possible so that the liturgical continuity might increasingly satisfy the faithful that the Prayer Book was both "understanded" and inspired. Of course, *the truly great changes had been built into the Prayer Book from the very first:* vernacularity, universality, textuality, and dramaturgy. These were increasingly assimilated into the core Anglican formal religious experience, and it was the general satisfaction with these things among Anglicans that gave the Prayer Book its fundamental stability.

Protestant reformers everywhere, not just in England, wanted liturgies and Bibles "understanded of the people." The point is so antique and simple that its gravity may be overlooked. It involved confidence in the *adequacy* of the vernacular to bear the weight of translation from the sacred languages of biblical Hebrew or Greek or problematically inspired patristic Latin. Vernacular worship also meant an elevation of the whole people, who were declared capable of understanding the liturgy. Such popular understanding was explicitly

---

can sensibilities compared to the sense of oddity felt by Separatists in the presence of Anglican worship. One of the present writers caught a twinge of that sense of oddity upon venturing (as a college sophomore, with Presbyterian and Congregational conditioning) into Bruton Parish Church in Williamsburg in the 1950s.

13. An ideological reinforcement to this spirit is well noted by Jonathan Crewe: "Not only [Stoic] resistance to radical change and dissolution . . . but a discounting of them, accompanied by a complex problematic of relative immobility, bondage, repetition, and pain, is as characteristic of the Renaissance as its quasi-revolutionary enterprises and representations" (*Trials of Authorship: Anterior Form and Poetic Reconstruction from Wyatt to Shakespeare* [Berkeley, 1990], 9).

proclaimed important to the Commonwealth and pleasing to God. The vernacular liturgy also gave a new elevation to the individual. Theologically, it gave daily support for the radical notion of the priesthood of all believers, each one of whom was now able to judge the "people's work" for herself or himself (whereas Latin had been almost a puberty rite for upper- and middle-class males).[14]

Psychologically, the vernacular liturgy encouraged receptionism, the notion that the true transformation of the Eucharist occurred within and because of the ready heart of the believer, since the believer must now participate individually in divine services. Spiritually, vernacular worship meant that the worshipper could undertake individual mediation between God's self-revelation in Scripture and his will for the individual now; he or she could (perhaps) avoid confusion from Scripture's admitted difficulties, more by grace than by any dependence on an ordained priest. It contended against the spectatorial model of worship as properly and adequately conducted by clergy, with the laity standing by as mere visual observers. In large church buildings, the laity stood at an existentially considerable distance down the nave from a Eucharist celebrated behind a rood screen at the very top of the sanctuary. The English reformers, though inheritors of some large church buildings, programmatically aimed for parishes of no more than twelve hundred souls, with any new churches constructed to be sized accordingly.[15]

This vernacular, like *this* order of worship, became universal throughout England, adapting in its Cranmerian cadences and order the "greate diversitye" of "uses" of the past, Latin or vernacular. Cranmer wrote in the Preface:

> Nowe, from hence furthe, all the hole relme shall have but one use. And yf any woulde judge thys way more painfull, because that all thynges muste be read upon the booke where as before by the reason of so often repeticion, they could saye many thynges by heart; yf those men wyl weygh their laboure, with the profyte and knowledge, which dayly they shal obtayne by readying upon the boke, they wyl not refuse the payne, in consideration of the greate profite that shal ensue therof.

14. For Latin as puberty rite, see Walter Ong, *Rhetoric, Romance, and Technology: Studies in the Interaction of Expression and Culture* (Ithaca, 1971), Chap. 5; and his *Fighting for Life: Contest, Sexuality, and Consciousness* (Ithaca, 1981), Chap. 4.

15. John Addleshaw and Frederick Etchells, *The Architectural Setting of Anglican Worship* (London, 1948), Chap. 1; recently and more expansively, Nigel Yates, *Buildings, Faith, and Worship: The Liturgical Arrangement of Anglican Churches, 1600–1900* (New York, 1991).

Printing and the very fact of a book ordained by Parliament standardized the observances and constraints through the "hole relme." Thus, as remarked earlier, England became a nation of the Book, with reference to the 1611 version of the Bible and the *Book of Common Prayer.* The latter was the *context* of most public Bible reading as well as the context of most preaching.

Dramaturgy, opposed to spectatorship, was a matter not only of verbal metaphors of theatricality but of metonymic and synecdochic performance. It needs illustration at length to indicate what the worshipper would be doing in the 'people's work' of the *leitourgos,* thus showing the emphatic Prayer Book reinforcements to worshippers' internalization of all four tropes.

Would the worshipper enter church, certainly a "consecrated" place, conceiving it to be holy ground? Less so if inclined toward Puritanism, more so if inclined toward Catholicism. All would agree that the people's work for which the architecturally separate place was provided must be vital and momentous. Individuals might mutter to pew-mates their distaste for the theology of the sermon; city gallants might (it was complained) use services for social meetings at St. Paul's or even more social meetings elsewhere; but nearly all agreed that the liturgy was serious and that the inevitable secular irreverences were enormities, to be discouraged and condemned both by clerical censure and community disapproval.

Since going to church was a matter for most serious attention, both morning and evening prayer "dayly throughout the yeare" appropriately began with something like a clap of thunder. The priest was directed by the rubric, the red-letter guide akin to a stage direction, to "reade with a *loud* voyce some *one*" (our emphases) of the following Bible verses. Any one of the "Sentences," as these verses came to be called (for their sententiousness), would emphasize the individual hearer's need for the worshipful work to follow. The first emphasized the possible moment:

> At what time soever a synner doeth repente hym of hys synne from the bottome of hys heart: I wyl put all his wickedness oute of my remembraunce, sayth the Lorde.
>
> (Ezek. 28)

Since *repent* implied re-penitence, there was a suggestion here of the Augustinian journey with its reorientation from *aversio* to *conversio.* But in this sentence, the emphasis fell on an Old Testament foreshadowing of the Good News, looking toward the moment that articulated an ontological transformation of the penitent's understanding of the power of relationship to God.

The second option for the priest's loud voice initiated the interior drama of the *psychomachia:*

> I do know mine owne wickednes, and my synne is alway against me.
>
> (Ps. 51)

The theatricality here was that of spiritual combat, because "my synne" in this emphatically non-Manichaean book could not be a *thing* but must rather be an alternative version or orientation of the self, a matter of self-miscasting (albeit compelling) in the absence of grace, in this anti-Pelagian book.

The third text, also from Psalm 51, shifted the emphasis away from penitence to petition, presenting a plea for a dramatically climactic divine turning, a re-editing of the Book of Life:

> Turn thy face away from our sinnes (O Lorde) and blot out all our offences.

Theologically very similar, from near the end of the same psalm, the fourth sentence occluded the moment in preference for the petitionary scripting of a penitential scenario that combined the pastoral emphasis of the previous two sentences, as if in acknowledgment of the necessity of the liturgy following:

> A sorowfull spyryt is a Sacrifice to God: despise not (O Lord) humble and contrite hearts.

Here appeared a suggestion of ambassadorship. The sorrowful spirit or contrite heart was a mediator (but not an advocate) for the erring flesh or for elements of the spirit vulnerable to "assaults of the devil" or the snares of the world.

The fifth Sentence, designated in post-seventeenth-century editions of the Prayer Book as one particular to the season of Lent, was richly pregnant of journey:

> Rente your heartes, and not your garmentes, and turne to the lord your God: because he is gentle and mercyful, he is pacient and of muche mercy, and suche a one that is sory for your afflictions.
>
> (Joel 2)

There are the closely linked decisive moments, of the Augustinian turning not *toward* but *to* (*unto* in the Authorized Version) and the divinely responsive turn into compassion. There was also a cultural critique shifting the drama of protagonist-antagonist-spectator within the embassage to God rather than only to neighbors. Journey was given precedence over ambassadorship, and moment was preferred to theater, but all were implied within the Sentence.

The sixth (Dan. 9), pre-eminently of the eleven Sentences, foregrounded the Augustinian turn not so much as moment but rather as the journey of life with the omnipresent possibility of misdirection. The seventh resembled some others in inviting the priest to speak as Everyman and completed the petition of several of the previous Sentences:

> Correct us, O Lord, and yet in thy judgemente, not in thy furie, lest we should be consumed and broughte to nothinge.
>
> (Jer. 2)

But it asked for an extended judgment in preference to a moment of apocalypse, illustrating again the Anglican preference for considering time as extended rather than telescoped. Prayer Book worship, and literature congenial to it, honored decisive moments but always emphasized going on from them in "the acceptable year of the Lord" (Luke 4:19), because apocalypse belongs so mysteriously and unpredictably to God. So, too, in the eighth Sentence; there the priest spoke not as Everyman but as herald and ambassador from God and spoke in completion of the pastoral theology of petition, amendment, and judgment, apparent in the two previous Sentences:

> Amende your lyves, for the kingdom of God is at hand. (Matt. 3)

The Kingdom of God was at hand not only in the unpredictable apocalyptic sense but also in the predictable sense of individual state of grace and attendant *civitas Dei.*

The ninth Sentence, casting the priest momentarily as Every Prodigal, offered, like the sixth and seventh, a negation:

> I wyl goe to my father and saye to hym: father, I have synned agaynst heaven, and against thee, I am no more worthy to be called thy son.
>
> (Luke 15)

Here it was not the negating moment of divine retribution but rather the to-be-repented and repeated negativity of false or faithless ambassadorship. It was another step on the journey, and it was a rehearsal of truest, liveliest theater. The tenth again posited the priest as agent or ambassador for every person, petitioning for mercy:

> Enter not into judgemente with thy servaunts, O Lord, for no fleshe is righteous in thy syghte.
>
> (Ps. 143)

Such an opening would not only accord with the season of Lent but also serve as a prelude to the conjointly vocalized confession following shortly thereafter. In this, the tenth Sentence was similar to the sixth, ninth, and eleventh, again both a confession and a recognition that God's justice was mercy.

The eleventh Sentence offered a New Testament alternative of some rough equivalence with the others in terms of recognition of sin, of interior bad drama, and the need for repentence and the dependence upon grace.

> Yf we saye that we have no synne, we deceyve ourselves, and there is no trueth in us.
>
> (1 John 1)

The emphasis, however, has moved as if typologically from flesh to spirit and, in Protestant fashion, to the priesthood of all believers and to individual responsibility for penitence.

All of these opening Sentences were designed to separate sacred from secular time and did so by reminding the worshipper of the tropes that explained life here and aspired to higher being. In this function the Sentences were reminiscent of their origins in the medieval canonical hours, matins and lauds for the morning and vespers and compline for the end of the Christian devotional day. The Sentences thus marked the temporary (and metaphorical) end of the people's work in the world and the prayerfully permanent (and real) beginning of the people's work of the soul: from repentence to conversion, regeneration, and redemption. Resonant of the four basic tropes, the opening Sentences reminded the Renaissance English that they lived their whole lives (now and hereafter) in the very words of the Word.

The opening Sentence, in the priest's loud voice, would be followed immediately by attention given to the primary concern of the parishioners, sin and forgiveness. The priest read an exhortation to confession, and then came the general confession of sin, spoken by all while kneeling, followed by the absolution. These three elements unfolded with intimations of a certain equivalence, even leveling, of all society before "the throne of the heavenly grace."

Such intimations were expressed both by textuality and by the copiousness characteristic of orality: "Confess [manifold synnes and wickedness] with an humble, lowely, penitent and obedient heart." The copiousness here and throughout the Prayer Book, especially in doubletons, suggests the equivalence before God of the Anglo-Saxon colloquial word and those who used it with the Latinate or French-derived word and its more schooled users. Thus the worshippers would be urged to "not dissemble nor cloke" their sins; were reminded that "we assemble and mete together," having "erred and strayed" (the Augustinian and biblical exhortation's "unto the throne" and the absolution's "turne from . . . wickedness"); and then were assured that the priest speaking for the Lord did "declare and pronounce . . . absolution and remission . . . pardoneth and absolveth."

The exhortation to the general confession included an inventorial argument of the whole service to follow: to confess sin, "to rendre thanks . . . to set foorth . . . prayse, to hear his most holy word, and to aske those things which be requisite and necessary." The absolution recapitulated in its petition that "those thinges may please him, which we *do* at this present" (our emphasis). All of these actions of the service included powerful suggestions of the world-transforming significance of what was properly going on: "Accompany me . . . unto the throne of . . . grace," as "there is no health in us" (a significant alternative metaphor for sin), but "spare . . . restore . . . graunt . . . that we may herafter live a godly, righteous, and sobre life." The absolution's assurances "that . . . life hereafter may be pure and holy . . . that at the last we may *come to* hys eternall joye" (our emphasis) were designed to change the worshippers' orientation toward an always new and always-needing-to-be-new life-world. The things done "at this present" will necessarily be repeated "dayly throughout the yeare" by the clergy and more than once a week, every week, by most in England in the century from the inception of, to the (temporary) outlawing of, the Prayer Book.

The way of the faithful worshipper was (and is) a hermeneutic journey. It is precisely not a hermeneutic *circle* (that medieval and Renaissance image of perfection and recent image of futility) but rather an ongoing journey of successive approximation, recasting the future in consideration of the past, considering the hoped-for end by the salvific beginning known to faith, knowing the whole necessarily yet incompletely by the part and by "a glass darkly" because wholeness and completion are by definition to the human state (fallen or not) an unimaginable perfection.[16] Here there was contingency. The priest's very absolution was conditional, meant for God's "people, *being penitent,*" that is, "all them *which truely* repent and *unfeynedly believe*" his holy Gospel (our emphases). Thus, the congregation would "beseche him to graunt us true repentaunce," a prayer that would need repetition all life long, as both human endeavor and grace were combined in the continuous journey of repentance and forgiveness. Early Anglican clergy did not have the word *hermeneutic,* but they had the concept of paradox, the logic of contingency, and abhorrence of Pelagianism (*i.e.,* salvation through self-improvement).[17] The new life, to be "godly, righteous and sobre," was always begun, always granted by grace, but never completed by action. Conditionality was theologically insistent; Anglican worship was always about becoming, not about celebrating a gracious condition of being.

After the people answered "Amen" to that carefully unarrogant absolution, the priest would "begin the Lordes Prayer wyth a loude voyce." Some congregations joined in; certainly all were commanded to speak it together later, at the conclusion of the service, a Protestant innovation. Here, the final clause ("for thine is the kingdom") was omitted in favor of petitionary dialogue and the Gloria:

Minister: O Lord, open thou our lyppes.
People: And our mouth shal shewe forth thy prayse.
Minister: O God, make spede to save us.
People: O Lord, make haste to help us.
Minister: Glory be to the father, and to the sonne, and to the holy ghost. As it was in the beginning, is now and ever shal be: worlde wythout ende. Amen.

Thereupon the people would say or sing Psalm 95 as a celebrative continuation of the formally antiphonal nature of the service. Psalm 95, sung (most likely) and punctuated with a Gloria, would be followed by a ministerial reading of the psalm or psalms appointed for that day in the calendar of the Prayer Book. These were individually punctuated with Glorias and followed by a ministerial reading of "lessons." A chapter from the Old Testament, as prescribed for the day, would be read with a loud voice or sung "in a plain tune" by the priest "turning him so, as he may best be heard."

16. We have discussed and illustrated this issue in *Milton and the Hermeneutic Journey* (Baton Rouge, 1994), Introduction and *passim.*

17. See Articles 9–15 of the "Thirty-nine Articles of Religion."

The congregation in their turn responded to the first lesson with the fifth-century hymn "Te Deum laudamus," sung or intoned, or the apocryphal biblical canticle "O all ye workes of the Lord, blesse ye the Lorde."[18] The latter, always textually present whether or not often part of the doings, stood (and stands) as an anti-Gnostic, anti-Manichaean reminder that all created things were not merely neutral but were implicated in glorifying God (stars, winds, dews and frosts, light and darkness, whales, fowls of the air "magnifie him for ever").

After the Gloria, a "second lesson," a New Testament chapter, was read, followed by the canticle "Benedictus" (derived from Luke 1:68–79) or Psalm 10, then the Gloria. "Then shall be sayd the Crede, by the Minister and the people, standinge." This was (and is) the Apostle's Creed, with its acknowledgment of eternity and transcendence: "Maker of heaven and earth . . . life everlastinge"; of immanence and history: "Borne of the virgin Mary, suffred under Pontius Pilate"; of immanence both individual and corporate: "I beleve in the holy ghost. The holy Catholique Church. The communion of saincts."

The notes regarding ceremonies, in the front matter of the Prayer Book, stipulated that "If there bee a sermone . . . the Curate . . . may leave out the Letanye . . . the Crede, t[he] homely." The Litany was prescribed for Wednesday and Friday and was certainly used occasionally on Sundays. The "homely" would have been one or another from the first or second *Book of Homilies,* as endorsed by Article 35, providing insipid institutional boiler plate for country curates and the like who were deemed too unlettered or untrustworthy to compose their own sermons. A homily read from the book would be thematic: "Of Prayer" or "Of Alm-doing" or "Of Repentance," good advice to supplement the Good News. But the same notes on ceremonies stipulated it "seemely that Graduates, when they dooe preache, should use such hoodes as pertayneth to theyr severall degrees." The Protestant reformers wanted a learned ministry; the pulpit and the university lectern were not yet alienated worlds. The golden age of English preaching, Hugh Latimer to John Tillotson, was under way.

Essentially a sermon embodied a serious effort of the Anglican *dual* ministry of word and sacrament. The preacher tried to exemplify devout engage-

18. "Benedicite omnia opera"—apocryphal, as John E. Booty notes, with reference to *The Oxford Annotated Bible with Apocrypha* (New York, 1965); *The Book of Common Prayer, 1559* (Charlottesville, 1976), 392.

ment with a biblical text, often a verse or more from the first or second lesson. T. S. Eliot's lines in "Journey of the Magi" and elsewhere, virtually verbatim from Lancelot Andrewes' Nativity sermons, illustrated an important preacher imagining his way into a biblical scene as part of unfolding its timeless significance. The mode of proceeding broadly exemplified in a momentous generic way the profound debt or kinship of English Protestant devotion to Continental formal religious meditation, a matter invaluably described by Louis Martz. Of course, Donne, like others in the learned ministry, drew also on Bible commentaries, *ars praedicandi* back to Augustine (indeed to the Bible itself), concordances, and the Latin tradition of arts of grammar, logic, and rhetoric (*i.e.,* discourse).[19] Whatever the source, the preacher sought to bring the arts of rhetoric to the service of Christian understanding and reformation.

A homily might be theologically tendentious (*e.g.,* "Of Rebellion") and undistinguished or slurred and mumbled by a careless preacher, yet it could still deliver a serious message. A sermon was even trickier: It could be, and in Elizabeth's or James's view sermons often were, politically and theologically

19. See Louis L. Martz, *The Poetry of Meditation* (New Haven, 1954), revisionarily challenged by Barbara Kiefer Lewalski, *Protestant Poetics and the Seventeenth-Century Religious Lyric* (Princeton, 1979), thoughtfully reviewed by Martz, *Modern Philology,* LXXX (1982), 168–74 and revisited in his "The Poetry of Meditation: Searching the Memory," in *New Perspectives on the Seventeenth-Century Religious Lyric,* ed. John R. Roberts (Columbia, Mo., 1994), 188–200; and see Anthony Low, *Love's Architecture: Devotional Modes in Seventeenth-Century English Poetry* (New York, 1978). With regard to Renaissance commentarists and traditions of preaching and discourse more generally, see the standard edition, *The Sermons of John Donne,* ed. George R. Potter and Evelyn Simpson (10 vols.; Berkeley, 1953–62), esp. Vols. X and VIII, Appendix (referenced hereafter in the text by volume, sermon number, and, when appropriate, line numbers), but stronger and more thoughtfully sensitive exposition is available in the apparatus to Janel M. Mueller's edition of *Donne's Prebend Sermons* (Cambridge, Mass., 1970). For surveys long standard (but biassed), see William Fraser Mitchell, *English Pulpit Oratory, from Andrewes to Tillotson* (London, 1932) and Gerald Robert Owst, *Literature and Pulpit in Medieval England: A Neglected Chapter in the History of English Letters and of the English People* (Rev. ed.; Cambridge, Eng., 1961); more recent work bearing on the critical-discursive background includes James S. Baumlin, *John Donne and the Rhetorics of Renaissance Discourse* (Columbia, Mo., 1991), though his concern is Donne's poetry; so, too, is Thomas O. Sloane's *Donne, Milton, and the End of Humanist Rhetoric* (Berkeley, 1985)—Donne as skeptical controversialist, Milton as formalist expositor of truth (not description we would adopt for Donne's sermons or Milton's poetry). See also the almost positivistically methodological John S. Chamberlin, *Increase and Multiply: Arts-of-Discourse Procedure in the Preaching of Donne* (Chapel Hill, 1976).

dangerous. But essentially it represented a particularly rich moment in the service in which the preacher variously enlightened and represented the citizenry, with whom at other moments he would stand or kneel, in the slow dance of liturgical doing.

The sermon, contextually dialogic, was followed by elaborate interaction in closing prayers. The minister would say, "The Lorde be wyth you," and be answered, "And wyth thy spyryte" (from the Latin Mass, "dominis vobiscum" and "et cum spiritu tuo").[20] Upon the invitation "Let us praye," all would kneel and say or sing a threefold *kyrie:* "Lorde, have mercy upon us. Christ, have mercy upon us. Lorde, have mercy upon us." Then, still kneeling, "Minister, Clerkes, and people, shall say the Lordes prayer in Englishe, with a loude voyce."

The unison of the Lord's Prayer resolved into the prayer of (to use a Renaissance sermonic term) *application* of beliefs articulated in the creed. The prayers covered sentence by sentence the whole purpose of Morning Prayer; monarch, community, clergy, and people, with the emphasis on the last, were all included in alternating petition and response. The priest began with a general call upon the Lord:

Priest. O Lord, shewe thy mercy upon us.
Aunswere. And graunt us thy salvacion.
Priest. O Lorde, save the kynge.[21]
Aunswere. And mercyfully hear us, when we call upon thee.
Priest. Indue thy ministers with righteousnes.
Aunswere. And make thy chosen people joyeful.
Priest. O Lorde, save thy people.
Aunswere. And blesse thine inheritaunce.
Priest. Give peace in oure time, O Lorde.
Aunswere. Because there is none other that fyghteth for us, but onely thou, O God.
Priest. O God, make clean our heartes within us.
Aunswere. And take not thyne holy spyryte from us.

The prayers ended as they had begun, with a call for mercy by a priest and congregation who knew they were always in need of it and who deemed it was

20. Harrison and Sansom, *Worship in the Church of England,* 112.

21. "Save the kynge" became "save the Queen" in 1559, "the king" in 1604, "the President . . . and all in Civil Authority" in (a longer prayer in) the American Episcopal Prayer Book.

always available. The familiar figures of *battle* and *cleanliness* above are secondary: Each adverts to a special case of the omnipotent action of divine love, alludes perhaps to vicissitude on the journey.

A less Catholic Protestant service might end at that point. The Prayer Book, however, concluded with three collects, that is, prayers of strong biblical or patristic sanction, enunciated by the priest (standing) on behalf of all the still-kneeling congregation. The first varied from week to week, being taken from the calendar of "Introits": collects, Epistles, and Gospels to be used at communion services. The invariant second and third asked again for peace, safety, and righteousness, ideas of weight and familiarity in Renaissance English society.

> *The seconde Collecte for Peace.*
>
> O God, whiche art aucthor of peace, and lover of concorde, in knowledge of whome standeth our eternal lyfe, whose service is perfecte freedome; defend us, thy humble servants, in al assaults of our enemies, that we surely trusting in thy defence, may not feare the power of any adversaries: through the might of Jesu Christ our Lord. Amen.

> *The thyrde Collecte: for Grace.*
>
> O Lord, our heavenly father, almighty and everlasting God, which hast safely broughte us to the beginninge of this daye: defend us in the same wyth thy mightie power, and graunt that this day we fall into no synne, nether runne into any kind of daunger: but that all our doynges may be ordred by thy governaunce, to doe alwayes that is righteous in thy syght: through Jesus Christe our Lorde. Amen.

Monarch, minister, and people were here similarly, even if not identically, understood to be in needy dependence. The world of ambassadorial service and fallen journey, taken alone, was a Manichaean battleground of "adversaries," but it was also for and with God, who by definition could not fail. In the words of the Psalmist (every twenty-seventh day of the month), God "keepeth Israel" and "shall neither slumber nor sleep." He may manifest himself as more distant and mysterious than any earthly father and see (more infallibly than any earthly father) human falling or running from the path of return, yet he has "safely brought us to the beginninge of this daye." And he may manifest himself with profounder intimacy than any human father in Holy Communion, to which office we now turn.

◈

One anxious aim of the Protestant reformers was to bring, by design and "exhortation," each parishioner to take Holy Communion at least four times a year. What was the problem? Three attitudes, or spiritual conditions, seem to have been responsible for the lay reluctance to participate in the Eucharist: slack indifference, neurotic diffidence ("I cannot be worthy"), and the magical-spectatorial stance ("It is sufficient to watch the clergy do it"). What the reformers sought, and generally failed to obtain, was regular, profound engagement of the communicant, whether the Eucharist was deemed "real presence" or a memorial. Pastorally the same for every Protestant denomination, participation in communion was theologically more serious for a sacramental "real presence" church, where the doctrine held that the Eucharist was an occasion for grace. In these circumstances failure to take communion was a denial of the church's sacramental and ecclesiological doctrine and was adjudged the more serious for that reason.

Perhaps the first point to note about the Eucharist is that it was a humbling experience, universally humbling. No sovereign, duke, or prince of commerce had cause or leave, any more than the Pharisee, to stand aside and thank the Lord that he was not as other men are. All confessed their sinfulness of omission and commission (as at Morning Prayer) in a context proclaiming such sinfulness so onerous that "very God of very God" had to die to atone and redeem. Who could feel efficacious, or even adequate, in a service and a psychodrama dominated by such considerations? Moreover, while free will was explicitly and implicitly affirmed by the service of Holy Communion, any pretense to benign efficacy in human power was undermined by the overwhelming historical record ("we killed Christ"), and so was any pretension of human power to radical independence. The Pelagian triumphalism of alleging sin to be conquered was denied by the very fact of communion and by the "contrite heart" of the sinner who did "repente hym of hys syn" and turned to grace. Therefore, the services of 1559 and 1604 opened with the Lord's Prayer, among other things an acknowledgment of whose the kingdom and the power and the glory really are. They immediately continued with the Collect for Purity, a prayer that an omniscient and omnipotent God would "cleanse the thoughts of our hearts": *hearts,* not minds, making it an acknowledgment of taint in ideas, desires, and attitudes. The cleansing would be not a merely passive purity but a strenuous and permanent activity, so "that we may perfectly love thee, and worthily magnify thy holy name," a matter of orientation, calling, and progress on the journey.

Love was surely the second point about the service, second in thematic sequence to failure-transgression-need but not second in importance. From the greatest matter, of the divine death in love for humanity, to the lesser matter, of the individual's need for divine help to "perfectly love" divinity, love was repeatedly indicated as the remedy for abuses and failures of human power and as human power's only legitimate goal. Love and the need for grace to be able to love were reinforced when the Collect for Purity was followed by the priest reading "distinctly" each of the Ten Commandments and the kneeling people responding, "Lord have mercy upon us, and incline our hearts to keep this law." This, in turn, was followed by a collect for the particular Sunday of the liturgical year (or major feast) and a Collect for the Queen (or King), "that she (knowing whose minister she is) may above all things seek thy honor and glory." In a collect about power, love was the appropriate attitude, as the monarch sought "thy" not her or his honor and glory.

Following the opening collects, the Service of the Word moved to the central affirmation of faith and community, the readings from Scripture, the creed, the sermon, the offering of alms, and the exhortations to partake of the communion. The readings, one from an Epistle, the second from a Gospel, presented the "pure Word of God" to the congregation, giving a distinctly Protestant cast to the service and recalling Calvin's insistence that teaching was one of the four primary functions of the Christian community.[22] The creed from the Council of Nicaea (and from Constantinople in A.D. 381) followed the readings and was recited collectively by the whole congregation. Faith heard and faith affirmed became faith explained in the sermon or homily and faith practiced in the offering of alms, with all designed to transform the individuals in the congregation into a community of love.

These elements of hearing, affirmation, understanding, and practice were combined in the two exhortations to the community to participate in the sacrament of the Eucharist. Appearing in the 1559 Prayer Book, they were drastically abbreviated in 1662 and in subsequent revisions and seem almost absent

22. An example of teaching: There was a superficial contradiction between Job's "I shall see God in my flesh" in the opening sentences and Paul's "flesh and blood cannot inherit the kingdom of God" (1 Cor. 15:50). Donne preached companion sermons reconciling the texts (III, S3, S4), a characteristic Renaissance effort of unification.

from recent scholarly notice. But they manifested at arresting length the threefold rationale for communion identified above; and they reinforced the communion service's central concern with love, the potential communicants being "lovingly called and bidden of God himself." More particularly, the first, used "when the curate shall see the people negligent to come to the Holy Communion," exhibited warrant and precedent for John Donne's distinctive sermonic "beloveds": "Dearly beloved brethren . . . most dearly beloved in Christ, take ye good heed." Noncommunicants were said to "offend God . . . in refusing this holy banquet," the more so "if [they] stand by as gazers and lookers on them that do communicate, and be no partakers of the same [themselves] . . . a further contempt and unkindness unto God." Thus, with profound reprehension the objectifying gaze was condemned as theatrical spectatorship antipathetic to love, to involvement, and indeed (in a broad sense) to dialogue ("to say nay when ye be called").

The second exhortation prescribed a program of self-examination, confession, and reconciliation with those who had wronged one's self, by forgiving them, and with those whom one had wronged, by "restitution and satisfaction," with recourse at need to "discreet and learned minister" for "ghostly counsel, advice, and comfort" when one's conscience remained troubled. With regard to the pulpit and altar, or the place of ministerial consultation, out of sight could obviously be out of mind for any believer. It scarcely needs adding that persons with power, from James Stuart on down, could rationalize a range of conduct extending to countless enormities (so definable by a Jonson or other moralist) as consonant with the reign of love, with quasi-fatherly duty, or the like. But even such rationalizations (not to mention "turn[s] from . . . wickedness [to] live") acknowledged subordination of the self to the ideal of the reign of love. They differed fundamentally and permanently from fantasies of omnipotence and from unabashed worship at altars of power or profit.

The service would proceed (typically after a sermon, in London churches and chapels) with "one or more" of a score of offertory "sentences," bits of Scripture bearing on alms-giving. The first two, both from the Sermon on the Mount and not improbably the ones most frequently enunciated by the priest, call for mention:

> Let your light so shine before men, that they may see your good works, and glorify your Father which is in heaven
>
> (Matt. 5:16)

> Lay not up for yourselves treasure upon the earth where the rust and moth doth corrupt, and where thieves break through and steal. But lay up for yourselves treasures in heaven, where neither rust nor moth doth corrupt, and where thieves do not break through and steal.
>
> (Matt. 6:19–20)

The first epitomized the thesis of this chapter: the liturgy as the *only* true and lively theater, though as the quoted exhortation warned, even this theater could be degraded from productive participation to sterile, unloving spectatorship. The second was a particularly poignant variation on the essential need for the journey from fallen, decaying *here* to benignly enduring *there.*

After the offering, the priest would offer for all the prayer "for the whole state of Christ's Church militant here in earth." Not so anachronistically ecumenical as to include Jews and others, the prayer did in that era of religious wars among professed Christians petition that all Christians "may agree in the truth of thy holy Word, and live in unity and godly love." It followed with petitions for the spirit of *justice* to animate all in civil authority, for *grace* to animate to all "bishops, pastors, and curates," for *grace* to animate "all thy people," and for God "to comfort and succor all them which in this transitory life be in trouble, sorrow, need, sickness, or any other adversity."

Thus, the systole and diastole, of acknowledgment of fault and need, met by reassurances, continued. This interplay between *sacrificium* and *beneficium* intensified in the priestly invitation to communion, the "General Confession," and the priestly absolution. These three prayers completed the Service of the Word and provided a transition to the Service of the Sacrament. They collectively emphasized the faith as repentance and preparation, the two being indissoluably linked in the trope of journey. The invitation emphasized (1) the moment of *retorqueo,* (2) the complementary trope of ongoing journey, (3) the primacy of love over power in human affairs, and (4) the utter subordination of human power (or power-pretensions) to divine power, all expressed (5) conditionally, as an acknowledgment of free will, and (6) the complementary notion of calling: "You that [5] do truly and earnestly [1] repent you of your sins, and [3] be in love and charity with your neighbors, and [2] intend to lead a new life, [6] following the commandments of God, and walking from henceforth in his holy ways: [1, 2, 3, 6] Draw near, and take this holy Sacrament to your comfort; [3, 4, 6] make your humble confession to Almighty God before this congregation here gathered together in his holy name, [4] meekly kneeling upon your knees."

The central action-clause of the invitation ("Draw near, and take") defined, in context, at once a metonymic part and synecdochic model of the *itinerarium* toward God. First, however, the interior turning of repentance was made openly and corporately social, with a priest or his designee enunciating on behalf of all the general confession of sins "committed, by thought, word, and deed, against thy divine majesty" (the more concrete and social after 1662, when priest and people would speak it together). The form of the vocal prayer betokened in the very copiousness characteristic of oral society the dialogue (Mikhail Bakhtin would call it) of that older English society with the newer Latinate literacy ("thy wrath and indignation") and with the syntax of the Psalms ("have mercy . . . have mercy").

The priest responded by pronouncing absolution, a short prayer that a divine *general* promise, "forgiveness of sins to all them which . . . turn unto him," will in *particular* "deliver *you* . . . strengthen *you* . . . bring *you* to everlasting life" (our emphases). The priest continued with "comfortable words" of quotation, "Come unto me," which were brief praise, in dialogue with the congregation. The "comfortable words" marked the end of the Service of the Word, which concluded as it had started, with prayer and Scripture. As a collective unit, the Service of the Word had a generally rabbinical function, to teach by the various modes of hymns, prayers, readings, instruction, and practice the essentials of the faith. Exposition of the faith, both insistently and by several modes, was all that the Puritans wished, in conformity to the Calvinist position that God's chosen saints, those predestined for salvation, would respond to the pure Word of God, if only they had a chance to hear and read it, with conversion by grace and a proper assurance of faith. Thus, while many Puritans wished to replace the *Book of Common Prayer* with the Middleburg Liturgy or the Scottish service, they still found only detail to criticize in the Anglican Service of the Word. So far, disagreements between Anglicans and Calvinists were local or aesthetic or were problems of the sequence of elements of the service, and while these differences were often passionately expressed, they were still within the general realm of Protestant climate of opinion, liturgies, and sensibilities.

But all broad general ground and possibility of agreement at once evaporated when one came to the Service of the Sacrament. Calvinist denominations, Baptists, Congregationalists, the Pilgrims, Presbyterians, and other groups of Brethren did not regard communion as a sacramental occasion; that is, they saw it not as an outward and visible sign of inward and spiritual grace but rather as a memorial the efficacy of which depended on the ready hearts of those who received the elements. This "real absence" or (depending upon the congregation) "virtual presence" was resolutely receptionist and incompatible with the Prayer Book service, and all efforts by the Thirty-nine Articles to disguise this fact convinced no one. At this point in the liturgy, the established church and its Puritan critics had come to the end of the possibility of reconciliation.

Part of the problem of the Service of the Sacrament, beyond its real-presence theology (not precisely or clearly defined, in the Anglican manner), which not everyone would grasp, was the undeniable fact that the sacramental service sounded so Catholic. The service began with the Preface to the Canon of the Mass, in precisely the Roman manner. It consisted of the Sursum Corda and the Sanctus:

Lift up your hearts. We lift them up unto the Lord. Let us give thanks unto our Lord God. It is meet and right so to do.	Sursum Corda. Habemus ad Dominum. Gratias agamus Domine Deo nostro. Dignum et justum est.
It is very meet right and our bounden duty that we should at all times, and in all places, give thanks unto thee, O Lord, holy Father, almighty, everlasting God.	Vere dignum et justum est, aequum et salutare, nos tibi semper et ubique gratias agere: Domine, sancte Pater omnipotens aeterne Deus.

A glance at the Latin will show that the prayer was a translation into powerful and poetic English, but a translation nonetheless and one that preserved the function and meaning, as well as the words, of the Roman Catholic original. The Sanctus departed somewhat further from the Latin Low Mass but only in particular words, not in general tenor:

Holy, holy, holy, Lord God of hosts; heaven and earth are full of thy glory; glory be to thee, O Lord most high.	Sanctus, Sanctus Sanctus Dominus Deus Sabaoth. Pleni sunt coeli et terra gloria tua. Hosanna in excelsis.

Within the Prayer Book, the Preface to the Canon of the Mass was an integral part of the Canon rather than a separate introduction, and it differed in this respect sharply from the Latin Low Mass, where it was strictly a preparation. Since the Prayer Book communion service omitted the catalog of the saints, along with most of the prayers so prominent in the Low Mass, the Preface became the initial prayer of the sacramental occasion. It was followed by the Prayer of Humble Access. Here was acknowledgment of divine mercy, then the carefully nuanced petition:

> Grant us therefore . . . *so* to eat the flesh of thy dear Son Jesus Christ, and to drink his blood, *that* our sinful bodies may be *made clean* by his body, and our souls *washed* through his most precious blood.
>
> (our emphases)[23]

The Prayer of Humble Access led directly to the central portion of the communion service, the Prayer of Consecration, distribution of the elements, the Prayers of Oblation and the Thanksgiving. The Prayer of Consecration began with an acknowledgment:

> [Christ's] death upon the cross for our redemption; who made there (by his one oblation of himself once offered) a full, perfect, and sufficient sacrifice, oblation; and satisfaction for the sins of the whole world.

This was followed by the petition:

> Grant that we receiving these thy creatures of bread and wine, according to thy Son our Savior Jesus Christ's holy institution, in remembrance of his death and passion, may be partakers of his most blessed Body and Blood.

In the 1559 Prayer Book the distribution of the elements followed immediately after the Consecration. The distribution contained a long and theologically ambiguous formula:

> The body of our Lord Jesus Christ which was given for thee, preserve thy body and soul into everlasting life: and take and eat this, in remembrance that Christ died for thee, and feed on him in thy heart by faith, with Thanksgiving.

23. Significantly, the rubric printed at the end of the communion services includes the following paragraph among the directions to clergy: "And to take away the superstition, which any person hath or might have in the bread and wine, it shall suffice that the bread be such as is usual to be eaten at the table with other meats, but the best and purest wheat bread that conveniently may be gotten. And if any of the bread or wine remain, the curate shall have it to his own use."

This formula, like the similar one for the cup, was broad enough to include all standard Christian views of the eucharistic meal except the Roman Catholic doctrine of Tridentine transubstantiation. Justification by faith, an undefined real presence, a general receptionist view, accompanied by at most a virtual presence, all were encompassed by the carefully crafted formula of administration. It was an act of political generosity and calculation. The Catholic-minded communicant intent on real presence had no obligation to cavil at the word *remembrance* (the Savior had used it); the Zwinglian Calvinist abhorrent of popery at the altar could focus on his own reception of the creaturely bread and wine.[24] Each was nudged to recognize that it was love, not power, that must animate human memories; it was divine and human love, not ecclesiastic or alchemic power, that must transform creatures of bread and wine. Similarly, the immediately following priestly words to each communicant invite a sense of real presence: "The body . . . the blood." But they *admit* a Puritan construction: "Eat *this,* in *remembrance* that Christ died for thee, and feed on him in thy heart by faith. . . . drink *this* in *remembrance* . . . and be thankful" (our emphases). What could not legitimately be avoided was an acute sense of enormous participatory responsibility toward an "everlasting kingdom." That sense might be amplified, with enhanced contrastive regard to the kingdoms of this world, as both Donne and Milton were to witness.

After the administration of the sacrament came the Prayer of Oblation, when the communicants say:

> [We] offer and present unto thee, O Lord, ourselves, our souls and bodies, to be a reasonable, holy and lively sacrifice unto thee.

Again, in contrast to the usual Protestant view of communion, the Prayer Book service retained the Roman Catholic aspect of the Mass involving sacrifice: of the worshippers themselves to Christ, of Christ's sacrifice for the "whole world," and of the sacrifice of praise and thanksgiving by the community in remembrance of his "blessed passion, mightie ressurection and gloryous ascension." Again, the interplay of *sacrificium* and *beneficium,* resonant of the real presence, now appeared as a postcommunion commentary on the meal at "God's board."

The Canon of the Mass ended with three prayers. The first was of thanks-

24. Thompson, *Liturgies of the Western Church,* 151–55. See n. 5, above, for the Tridentine and other formulations of transubstantiation.

giving for those who had "duly received these holy mysteries," described here as "spiritual food." They were assured that "thereby" they were "very members incorporate in thy mystical body . . . and be also heirs through hope of thy everlasting Kingdom," a kind of ultimate dramatic denouement. The second was the Gloria, a prayer of praise, and the third was the petition that the "peace of God which passeth all understanding, keep your hearts and minds in the knowledge and love of God." This last blessing had particular poignancy when considered in connection with the pervasive Puritan anxiety over salvation or as petitionary rising action in contrast to the conventional "falling action" or "restoration of order" in secular drama.

Thus the service of communion, both word and sacrament, which began on a note of personal inadequacy and petition, ended with praise and assurance that God had dealt graciously with his people. The service was a moment for God "to assist us with [his] grace" in the longer, but not larger, trope of journey. Here was incarnate the theater of heaven, the ultimately unmasked masque, the insistent calling for the ambassadorship of witness and "all such good works as thou hast prepared for us to walk in."

While communion could be vitally the heart of Christian worship in the English seventeenth century (George Herbert to witness), the other great services marking stages of life should be assumed to have had by their intensity considerable impact on parishioners' habits in construing their world. The occasional service of "Public Baptism" signaled recruitment to that "blessed company of faithful people." The opening words, "Dearly beloved" (as at the beginning of the marriage service, echoed by Donne's vocative in sermons, "Beloved"), emphasized the "mystical body" as essentially an association of love. Godparents, speaking as ambassadors both for the child and for the faithful company, would in dialog with the priest *renounce* in order the devil's works, the vanities of the world, and, last, "the carnal desires of the flesh" and would *affirm* the historicity and majesty of God and the desire for baptism. The priest thereupon prayed for the child, affirmed the mercy of God, beseeched divine "regard" for the "supplications of thy congregation," would "take the child in his hands" to "dip it in the water" (but "discreetly and warily"), and "naming the child" pronounced the solemn formula "I baptize thee in the name of the Father, and of the Son, and of the Holy Ghost. Amen."

The tropic actions of ritual ambassadorship and of momentous washing and rebirth, at the very heart of the service, were reinforced by the opening prayer and Gospel reading and the concluding exhortation to godparents. The prayer cited "Noah and his family" and "the children of Israel . . . through the Red Sea" as typological acts of divine mercy "figuring thereby thy holy Baptism . . . into the ark of Christ's Church" and petitions that "these children . . . may so pass the waves of this troublesome world, that finally they may come to the land of everlasting life." That more or less corporate and civic image of journey was individualized and given intimacy by a following reading from Mark 10, featuring Christ's words "Suffer little children to come unto me." The exhortation in conclusion construed a future in terms of godly theater, calling, and journey: "It is your parts and duties to see that these infants be taught . . . be virtuously brought up . . . remembering always that baptism doth represent unto us our profession, which is to follow the example of our Savior . . . die from sin, and rise again unto righteousness . . . daily proceeding in all virtue."

The witnesses to baptisms would similarly be witnesses to regular services of confirmation and no doubt in the latter instance recalled their own. Confirmation was a service of reinforcement to the "mystical body which is the blessed company of all faithful people" in that the prerequisite to it was a period of dialogic instruction in articles of faith, the Ten Commandments, the Lord's Prayer, and a brief catechism about baptism and Christian life, further that the brief service was itself dialogic, and finally that its climactic action was (indeed still is) a moment of devout theater.

The officiant was not the parish priest but the bishop, sumptuously and symbolically vested as good shepherd. He would, the rubric stipulated, "lay his hand upon every child severally, saying":

> Defend, O Lord, this child with thy heavenly grace, that [he or she] may continue thine forever, and daily increase in thy Holy Spirit more and more, until [he or she] come unto thy everlasting kingdom. Amen.

Then the bishop offered a short prayer on behalf of the group of confirmands, speaking for the congregation and, by implication, for the whole body of the faithful. The prayer included the following resonant explication: "These children, upon whom (after the example of thy holy Apostles) we have laid our hands, to certify them (by this sign) of thy favor and gracious goodness toward them. Let thy fatherly hand, we beseech thee, ever be over them." There has been in recent years speculation and supposition about abusive parenting in Western Europe in the Renaissance and (even more poignantly) parental emotional numbing as a defense against the horrific child-mortality rate. No doubt. Still, as everyone has noticed, Shakespeare explored a spectrum of parent-child relationships, and Jonson's elegies on lost daughter and son betokened tenderness and pain rather than numbness. In any case, the moment of confirmation affirmed, with its intense verbal, visual, kinesthetic imagery, a fatherly touch, caring and perhaps sensed as tender.

There remain "The Form of Solemnization of Matrimony" and "The Order for the Burial of the Dead." The former resonated allegorical theater: "Holy matrimony . . . an honorable estate . . . signifying unto us the mystical union, that is betwixt Christ and his Church." The mystical union was declared to be signified by the devout, but no less physical for that, and indeed festive, union of man and woman. The officiating priest, not unlikely a married man himself, suggested the festive note and amplified the Christly implication in matrimony and his endorsement of it by recalling for all "the first miracle," the conversion of water into wine at the wedding "in Cana of Galilee."

The priest, in his substantial opening statement, reminded bridal pair and congregation alike of the three "causes for which matrimony was ordained." The first was *not* simply procreation of children, as it is sometimes misleadingly abbreviated; it was (as if the words were all joined by hyphens) "the procreation of children to be brought up in the fear and nurture of the Lord, and praise of God." A life in praise of God was thus a general *calling,* amenable to the joint and several particular callings of the faithful in the world. "Secondly," matrimony "was ordained for a remedy against sin, and to avoid fornication, that such persons as have not the gift of continency might marry, and keep themselves undefiled members of Christ's body." *Undefiled:* Not only was sex in marriage potentially, perhaps even essentially, sinless (notwithstanding the nod toward the patristic doctrine of continency), but the phrase "Christ's body" would remind the listeners of the allegory of mystical union, accordingly the more hospitable point (biblical and Augustinian) about good living as essentially right ordering and orientation of loves. Thirdly, matrimony was designed to foster "the mutual society, help, and comfort, that the one ought to have of the other." Literary critical discourse about the English Renaissance has often emphasized (like Juliet's murderously foolish father) the family as a little state, meaning a miniature power structure. The Prayer

Book here in the Latinate resonance of *society* and the liturgical resonance of *comfort* emphasized the husband-wife relationship as properly ("one ought") a pattern for states of love. But the enunciation of these three "causes for which matrimony was ordained" was expunged after 1662.

Even without those explicit statements, however, the "Solemnization" epitomized Prayer Book liturgy as sacred theater and ambassadorship. The priest, in a role analogous to God the Father in unfallen paradise and to Christ at Cana, blessed and commissioned the bridal couple to the great, lifelong role—a role much of which *they must themselves script*—of "signifying" and representing in their joint and fleshly lives the "mystical union." They were here called to that ambassadorship particularly with regard to any children of the union and within the community at large.

As the "Solemnization of Matrimony" put a fine point on the tropes of theater and ambassadorship, so, similarly, was "The Order for the Burial of the Dead" a particularly intense pointing of the tropes of journey and moment in contexts of true love and power and mere (and merely apparent) worldly power.[25] Physically and as it were theatrically, one journey ended. The rubric, so like a stage direction, read: "The priest meeting the corpse at the church stile, shall say or else the priests and clerks shall sing, and so go either unto the church, or toward the grave." The "stile" would be the lych-gate, or corpse gate, where pallbearers could pause (in rural parishes mayhap at an actual gate that could be closed against domestic animals). The grave could have been either within the church (in privileged cases) or in the adjacent churchyard (as for the humbly born folk elegized by Thomas Gray in mid-eighteenth century).

What was said or sung? A triad of lections: "I am the resurrection and the life" from John 11; "I know that my redeemer liveth" from Job 19; and "We brought nothing into this world. . . . blessed be the name of the Lord," a conjuncture of verses from 1 Timothy 6 and Job 1. The effect initially, maintained through the burial service, was to emphasize the loving power of resurrection, obviating any concession to the Roman Catholic doctrine of Purgatory.[26]

25. Marriage itself, thus, is tropic; for illuminating exposition of some of the riches in that, see Anthony Low, *The Reinvention of Love: Poetry, Politics, and Culture from Sidney to Milton* (Cambridge, Eng., 1993).

26. See n. 22 above for reference to a Donnean sermon on the Burial Office's text from Job (III, S3).

"Whiles the corpse is made ready to be laid into the earth," the priest would say or sing a passage from Job 14 ("cut down like a flower. . . . In the midst of life, we be in death"). Then, while earth was "cast upon the body," the priest pronounced the formula marking the worldly end of the bodily journey: this body "to the ground, earth to earth, ashes to ashes, dust to dust." But that formula turned forthwith to "sure and certain hope of resurrection" and to the combination of love and power in "Christ, who shall change our vile body that it may be like to his glorious body, according to the mighty working, whereby he is able to subdue all things to himself."

The primary focus on the end of the worldly body's journey concluded with a following verse from Revelation said or sung: "The dead which die in the Lord . . . rest from their labors" (Rev. 13:14). Abruptly, with a reading of 1 Corinthians 15:20–58, the focus shifted to divine love and power: "Christ is risen from the dead. . . . we shall all be changed, and that in a moment, in the twinkling of an eye by the last trump." This was the moment of all moments, the apocalyptic transformation to journeyless, embodied "incorruption" in eternity. Thus, there was no contradiction in the concluding verse "be ye steadfast and unmovable, always rich in the work of the Lord." The implicit frame was something like "rather than diverted, perverted, or seduced from the path," as confirmed by the immediately following Lord's Prayer, in which the priest would say, "And lead us not into temptation," and be answered by those present, "But deliver us from evil."

Finally, the service concluded with a short, anti-Purgatorial prayer of thanks for deliverance of the deceased "out of the miseries of this sinful world" and a truly remarkable collect. The collect was a theologically, psychologically, and *generically* instructive prayer. There was, of course, the conventional parallelism: "That when we shall depart this life, we may rest in him, as our hope is this our brother doth." More profoundly and in the manner of a masque, "We meekly beseech thee (O Father) to raise us from the death of sin unto the life of righteousness." We, the mourners, somewhat like dancers in a masque, have been redefined as more deeply participatory: We are also dead (like our lamented brother or sister); we could rise from our death in and of sin by amendment of *this* life; insofar as we did so, we validated to ourselves the resurrection that is "our hope" for her (or him).

The contemporary secular theater, in public wooden O or in private, had, even for its greatest defenders like Shakespeare and Jonson and Middleton, always a stigma of faintly or faithlessly representing a world actually available outside the playhouse (though the playhouse might be "as dirty as Smithfield, and as stinking, every whit"). The liturgy, by definition, gave the best possible representation of a world that, by definition, transcended the world outside the sanctuary. The liturgy, including the sermon, gave, by definition, the best instruction for the journey thither, the best commissioning for the calling of ambassadorship in that journey as a corporate responsibility, and the best propaedeutic for graced moments of *retorqueo,* ecstasy, or death.

4

Love, Power, Dust Royall, Gavelkinde

Beloved . . .

—Donne's favorite term of address
to his congregations

No man is a good Counsellor, for all his wisdome, for all his liberty of speech, except he love the person whom he counsels.

—Donne's sermon, Candlemas Day, February 2, 1622,
on Romans 13:7

As preacher to part of the legal establishment at Lincoln's Inn, to the *polis* as Dean of St. Paul's, to Kings James and Charles, and to court nobility at Whitehall and elsewhere, John Donne was *ipso facto* a political figure in his preaching, no matter what he said. But his politics may best be construed in terms of his theology and Prayer Book liturgy, the tropes of religious life, and the fact of dialogue.

In a society of active surveillance and censorship, particularly in the capital, Donne rendered unto Caesar the small change we should expect of anyone who wanted to continue his ministry in the Church of England and indeed avoid arrest with ears unclipped. He briefly praised King James as lawful and a peacemaker, praised him for wisdom and zeal in connection with foiling the Powder Plot, urged civil and ceremonial debts to him, and proposed regard for him as father to ecclesiastical appointments: measured praise, usually qualified in context.[1] In 1627 (probably), he preached to King Charles the conventional formula that "Kings are blessings, because they are Images of God," yet even at Whitehall, he hedged the formula with radical conditions and contingencies (VII, S14, 300ff.). Again, at Whitehall, he disclaimed it as "somewhat an Eccentrique notion . . . to speake of the Duties of subjects before the King," but he did so in a context noting that "Honour is . . . the noblest reward of the greatest Princes, yet the more have it, the lesse every one hath it" (with obvious application to Charles' royal father; VII, S16, 360–440). A moment later, he followed with biblically ballasted advice not to curse the king, though the biblical precedent from 2 Samuel ironically involved Shimei, whose curse King David deemed inspired by God and forgave. Donne further advised not defaming unnamed wives of "very religious Kings," even if they did have "some tincture . . . of errour . . . sucked in their infancy, from another Church" (VII, S16, 515–86). This was not, on inspection, sycophancy, though one must grant that by the end of the 1630s, even such discounted small change rendered unto Caesar would look and sound to many like unforgivably heavy money.

The received view, as articulated by ecclesiastical historians such as Horton Davies and by the editors of the standard California edition, Evelyn Simpson and George Potter, all with scholarly roots in the nineteenth century, has too often taken the small change to be the entire transaction. Recently scholars, notably David Norbrook, Paul Sellin, Jeanne Shami, and more ambiguously Debora Shuger, have convincingly modified the old view by their nuanced and discerning redefinitions of Donnean options and Donnean choices in particular preaching situations. From (mostly) court sermons, Shami has argued that Donne made deflating comparisons of the king to God or Christ; made *law* dependent on God (not on king) and made it the foundation of the state; and made the minister a figure of *honest discretion* called to interpret God to the state. We agree and would amplify her second and third points by noting that Donne meant natural or normative law, rather than positive (common, statutory, or jurisprudential) law as the foundation. And for him

1. *The Sermons of John Donne,* ed. George R. Potter and Evelyn M. Simpson (10 vols.; Berkeley, 1953–62). James was praised as a peace-maker, for example, at I, S3, 1305ff. (but compared there with Queen Elizabeth), at III, S2, 26, and repeatedly in IV, S7 (at royal command, but again with reference to Elizabeth); praised for foiling the Powder Plot at IV, S9, 869ff.; acknowledged to be focus for civil and ceremonial debts at IV, S12, 364ff. and to be father to ecclesiastical appointments, VI, S3, 312ff.

part of the king's duty was to reconcile positive to normative law, insofar as the fallen world would permit.

In making her argument, Shami generously acknowledged and subsumed the earlier point by Jonathan Goldberg that patriarchy subjects the king to God, reconstrued Annabel Patterson's construal of Donne's dependency, and (of course) dismissed John Carey's cartoon of a "thwarted, grasping, parasitic" apostate.[2] In general, we find that fine sifting through Donne's sermons for hints as to his politics on specific events will yield only the indecisive and secondary. It is Donne's continuing orientation *ad regnem caritatis,* not his tran-

2. Jeanne Shami, "Kings and Desperate Men: John Donne Preaches at Court," *John Donne Journal,* VI (1987), 9–23, and "Donne's Sermons and the Absolutist Politics of Quotation," in *John Donne's Religious Imagination: Essays in Honor of John Shawcross,* ed. Raymond-Jean Frontain and Frances M. Malpezzi (Conway, Ark., 1995), 380–412, which is an essential collection. Shami refutes current arguments (especially Shuger's) that Donne preached royalist-absolutist propaganda; with similar force and effect, Donne's position, as discernible primarily in prose and poetry certainly or probably of 1606 to 1615, is explored by Annabel M. Patterson, "*Quod oportet* versus *quod convenit:* John Donne, Kingsman?," 160–209, in her *Reading Between the Lines* (Madison, Wisc., 1993), subsuming some of her earlier writing. Horton Davies, *Like Angels from a Cloud: English Metaphysical Preachers, 1588–1645* (San Marino, 1986); David Norbrook, "The Monarchy of Wit and the Republic of Letters: Donne's Politics," in *Soliciting Interpretation: Literary Theory and Seventeenth-Century English Poetry,* ed. Elizabeth D. Harvey and Katharine Eisaman Maus (Chicago, 1990), 3–36; Paul R. Sellin, *So Doth, So Is Religion: John Donne and Diplomatic Contexts in the Reformed Netherlands, 1619–1620* (Columbia, Mo., 1988), and *John Donne and "Calvinist" Views of Grace* (Amsterdam, 1983); Debora Shuger, *Habits of Thought in the English Renaissance: Religion, Politics, and the Dominant Culture* (Berkeley, 1990); Jonathan Goldberg, *James I and the Politics of Literature* (Baltimore, 1983); John Carey, *John Donne: Life, Mind and Art* (London, 1981). See also John B. Gleason, "Dr. Donne in the Courts of Kings: A Glimpse from Marginalia," *Journal of English and Germanic Philology,* LXIX (1970), 599–612.

See M. L. Donnelly's well-situated study of the very long sermon on Proverbs 22:11 (March 24, 1617, I, S3) in relation to patronage in "Saving the King's Friend and Redeeming Appearances: Dr. Donne Constructs a Scriptural Model for Patronage," in *Patronage, Politics, and Literary Traditions in England, 1558–1658,* ed. Cedric C. Brown (Detroit, 1993), 79–92. We agree that Donne aggrandizes perception, reciprocity under God, and calling (see esp. 88–90), all, we would insist, for more inclusive devotional and tropic reasons having to do with love. For its fertile suggestiveness about the triangulation of court, secular or quasi-liturgical drama, and church, see Steven Mullaney, *The Place of the Stage: License, Play, and Power in Renaissance England* (Chicago, 1988), esp. the chapter on *Measure for Measure* (88–115), more particularly Angelo's "excruciating self-awareness" and the conclusion that James's power could not utterly contain or control the theater (113).

sient attitudes toward things here, that forms the key to Donne's real politics, and it is that which we have used as a guide in this examination of Donne's sermonic corpus. Explicit references to secular events, such as the Spanish Match and the war in Europe, and even references to kingship are brief compared to the extent, emphasis, and explicitness of his treatment of differences with Roman Catholicism and Separatist Protestantism. All this has sometimes been taken, perhaps abetted by Donne's own disclaimers, to indicate a political posture of acquiescent quietude. But it is more nearly adequate to say Donne's pastoral theology tended to look beyond vicissitude, especially beyond the transient manifestations of political power, toward natural, graced anticipations of Divine eternity and ultimate loving fulfillment in the *civitas Dei.*

Donne's sermons, like virtually all Anglican sermons, were framed by the liturgy of the Prayer Book, in contrast to the long tradition of free-standing sermons, often political, by Continental Catholic and Protestant and English Puritan figures from St. Dominic to Jan Hus to John and Charles Wesley. On Ascension Day, 1622, Donne preached a notable sermon at Lincoln's Inn on Deuteronomy 12:30: "Take heed to thy self, that thou be not snared by following them after they be destroyed from before thee." The sermon was preached in the intimacy of the Society of Lincoln's Inn to listeners personally friendly to Donne, preached in what were inferably even more cozily intimate surroundings than the present chapel.[3] He dwelled on the private individual's, or the household head's, relation to Roman Catholicism. But he observed paren-

3. For Donne's collegiality in the Society of Lincoln's Inn, see the introductions by Simpson and Potter to Vols. II (esp. with frontispiece of 1623 pulpit), III, and IV. The Society built a new and presumably finer chapel, in which Donne, by then Dean of St. Paul's, preached the dedicatory sermon (Ascension Day, 1623, IV, S15). With an eighteenth-century false ceiling removed and despite some late-Victorian embellishment and enlargement, that "new" chapel remains today a space of some intimacy, at least as compared to typical American city churches or university (as opposed to small college or particular denominational) chapels. He warned the Company of the Virginia Plantation to be preachers of the Gospel, rather than to have "emergent affaires . . . their Text . . . [or] humors of the hearers their Bible . . . but to knocke . . . to delight the eare, and not to search the House, to ransacke the conscience" (IV, S10, 424–30). See also John F. H. New, *Anglican and Puritan: The Basis of Their Opposition, 1558–1640* (Palo Alto, 1964).

thetically that the text's words "*following* . . . *not after them* . . . (if we were to reflect at all, which we always avoid, upon publick things) would afford a good note for the publick, for the Magistrate." Just a few sentences later, he added, "But that is not our sphear, the Publick, the State; but yet States consist of Families, and Families of private persons, and they are in our sphear, in our charge" (IV, S4, 272–75, 287–89). He concluded that line of argument, his explication of his chosen biblical text, and the entire sermon, with a complex exhortation: "To end all, embrace Fundamental, Dogmatical, evident Divinity." *Embrace:* an act more of love than of power. He also reminded his lawyer-auditors that they had just done that in reciting beliefs together in the Prayer Book creed and reciting needs and subordination together in the Lord's Prayer. He had directed their attention to the two tables of the Decalogue, conventionally emplaced on the walls of churches and chapels, as the familiar list of "things which we are to do":

> The first Table begins with that, *Thou shalt have no other gods but me.* God is a Monarch alone, not a Consul with a Colleague. And the second Table begins with Honor to Parents, that is to Magistrates, to lawful Authority. . . . *If it be possible,* saith the Apostle, *as much as in you lies, have peace with all men* [Rom. 12:18], with all kind of men. Obedience is the first Commandment of the second Table, *and* [our emphasis] that never destroys the first Table, of which the first Commandment is, Keep thy self, that is, those that belong to thee and thy house, intire and upright in the worship of the true God, not only not to admit Idols for gods, but not to admit Idolatry in the worship of the true God. (IV, S4, 448–62)[4]

As always, Donne had called upon his people to embrace the true *God.*

So alert and anti-idolatrous a conscience would reject idolatries of king or kingship or ecclesia or Royal Exchange or practical expertise (what we might call technology). Donne would and did. One may suppose mild collegial irony, edged by the known petulance of James I over criticism of the Spanish Match, when Donne said, "we always avoid . . . publick things." In any case, the privation was undone explicitly here and implicitly throughout the 160 surviving sermons by the theologically and psychologically interactive analogies of "States . . . Families . . . private persons." It is the familiar synecdoche

4. See J. Sears McGee, *The Godly Man in Stuart England: Anglicans, Puritans, and the Two Tables, 1620–1670* (New Haven, 1976).

of inner for outer, as well as small for large: "Cities are built of families, and so are Churches too" (IV, S9, 983, "Powder Day," November 5, 1622); "Every Christian is a state, a common wealth to himselfe, and in him, the *Scripture* is his *law,* and the conscience is his *Judge*" (IV, S8, 229–30, October 13, 1622, at St. Paul's).[5] That conventionally familiar structural and hermeneutic interrelationship, like microcosm to macrocosm, suggests much of what Donne as preacher said immediately or through analogy about political order and the state.

By analogy, then, and by "such words as stretch, in large characters, from one end of the chart to the other" (as in the "game of puzzles" adverted to by Edgar Allan Poe's Dupin), Donne construed a politics far more for the *civitas Dei* of love than merely for ephemeral power contests in the *civitas terrena.* And he did so largely with an Augustinian vocabulary current then and familiar today. Their extended significances, however, so powerfully developed by Donne, can still be overlooked. As Rebecca West remarked, men resist learning truths which are complex and tend to forget truths which are simple.[6]

In briefest brief: Donne's politics were God-oriented, heaven-oriented, eternity-oriented, and dialogic. They were centered on what he conceived as his God's loving call and his own and his auditors' charitable response to it, as against the rising current of civil, ecclesiastical, or technological shows and idolatries. His politics were centered on heaven-oriented journey, in rejection of world as narcissistic end (excessive love of self, sensation, power, and *praxis* here). His orientation toward heavenly eternity was implicit in the innumerable metaphors and metonymies of Christian journey and was synecdochically suggested by the *moment* of loving revelation or graced *retorqueo,* as opposed to the moment of apocalyptic loss or the endlessly disjunctive moments of tychastic time.[7] His politics were dialogic, as opposed to royal show and decree.

5. In that sermon, IV, S8, his third of three on John 1:8, Donne is strongly opposed to any idolatry of the state, a point affirmed to be characteristic by Gale H. Carrithers, Jr., *Donne at Sermons: A Christian Existential World* (Albany, 1972), 156. In heaven, "if thou look down and see kings fighting for Crownes, thou, canst look off as easily, as from boyes at stool-ball for points here: And from Kings triumphing after victories, as easily, as a Philosopher from a pageant of children here" (V, S2, 640–44). Here, admittedly, one cannot look off so easily.

6. Rebecca West, *The Meaning of Treason* (New York, 1945), Epilogue. Donne never forgot that his nation and church, albeit imperfect, were, as West understood, a hearth giving warmth.

7. Tychastic, as previously indicated, the temporal disconnection of mere chance, isolated events, or (coming to the same thing) *merely* mechanical chronometry. Mikhail Bakhtin de-

Finally, Donne, "our Augustine," as Izaak Walton called him, was no Manichaean; the City of God, present here and even now in the mysterious workings of grace, was the true end of humankind, and it was understood to surpass incalculably and outrank ontologically the *civitas terrena.* Even the *Jerusalem* of this world as a literal place or as a figure for London was seen as "a tumultuary place, a place of distraction" (IV, S8, 676).

Partial illustration of these elements of Donne's general politics emerges from a splendid sermon "Preached at St. Pauls upon Christmasse day, 1621." It was the first of three sermons he preached in that liturgical year on John 1:8: "He was not that light, but was sent to bear witnesse of that light." Donne had argued that the *reason* of man "must first be satisfied"—satisfied by the design of the world, which should be understood to argue not only a Designer but a Designer who "would still retain the *Administration* thereof in his owne hands" to "*sustaine* it still by his watchfull Providence" (III, S17, 363–72). The administrative and sustaining will implied for Donne a written and thereby permanent supralegal record. For him the Bible was obviously such a record and was so not by "Demonstration" but by such rhetorical, "Historicall . . . Grammaticall . . . Logical" evidence as properly to entail belief. It did not, must not *compel* belief but rather operate by dialogic, indeed hermeneutic, successive approximations and accumulations:

> *Knowledge* cannot save us, but we cannot be saved without [405] Knowledge; Faith is not on this side Knowledge, but beyond it; we must necessarily come to *Knowledge* first, though we must not stay at it, when we are come thither. For, a regenerate Christian, being now a *new Creature,* hath also *a new facultie of Reason;* and so believeth the Mysteries of Religion, out of another Reason, then as a [410] meere naturall Man, he believed naturall and morall things. He believeth them for their own sake, by *Faith,* though he take *Knowledge* of them before, by that common Reason, and by those humane Arguments, which worke upon other men, in naturall or morall things. Divers men may walke by

scribed it in the genre of romance; see *The Dialogic Imagination: Four Essays,* trans. Caryl Emerson and Michael Holquist (Austin, 1981). Some sense of it was inferably part of Donne's uneasiness with "the scurrilities of comedy and the drums and ejulations of tragedy" (III, S12, 578–79). For derivation of the term, and something of its use in twentieth-century cultural critiques, see Gale H. Carrithers, Jr., *Mumford, Tate, Eiseley: Watchers in the Night* (Baton Rouge, 1991), index entries for *time.* For a famous Donnean instance of bad moment, see the opening of his *Devotions.*

the Sea side, and the same beames of the Sunne giving light to them all, one gathereth by the benefit of that light pebles, or speckled shells, for curious vanitie, and another gathers precious Pearle, or medicinall Ambar, by the same light. So the common light of reason illumins us all, but one imployes this light upon the searching of impertinent vanities, another by a better use of the same light, finds out the Mysteries of Religion; and when he hath found them, loves them, not for the lights sake, but for the naturall and true worth of the thing it self. Some men by the benefit of this light of Reason, have found out things profitable and usefull to the whole world; As in particular, *Printing,* by which the learning of the whole world is communicable to one another, and our minds and our inventions, our wits and compositions may trade and have commerce together, and we may participate of one anothers understandings, as well as of our Clothes, and Wines, and Oyles, and other Merchandize: So by the benefit of this light of reason, they have found out *Artillery,* by which warres come to quicker ends then heretofore, and the great expence of bloud is avoyded: for the numbers of men slain now, since the invention of Artillery, are much lesse then before, when the sword was the executioner. Others, by the benefit of this light have searched and found the secret corners of gaine, and profit, wheresoever they lie. They have found wherein the weakenesse of another man consisteth, and made their profit of that, by circumventing him in a bargain: They have found his riotous, and wastefull inclination, and they have fed and fomented that disorder, and kept open that leake, to their advantage, and the others ruine. They have found where was the easiest, and most accessible way, to sollicite the Chastitie of a woman, whether *Discourse, Musicke,* or *Presents,* and according to that discovery, they have pursued *hers,* and *their* own eternall destruction. By the benefit of this light, men see through the darkest, and most impervious places, that are, that is, *Courts of Princes,* and the greatest *Officers* in Courts; and can submit themselves to second, and to advance the humours of men in great place, and so make their profit of the weaknesses which they have discovered in these great men. All the wayes, both of *Wisdome,* and of *Craft* lie open to this light, this light of naturall reason: But when they have gone all these wayes by the benefit of this light, they have got no further, then to have walked by a tempestuous Sea, and to have gathered pebles, and speckled cockle shells. Their light seems to be great out of the same reason, that a Torch in a misty night, seemeth greater then in a clear, because it hath kindled and inflamed much thicke and grosse Ayre round about it. So the light and wisedome of worldly men, seemeth great, because he hath kindled an admiration, or an applause in Aiery flatterers, not because it is so in deed.

This side, beyond, come to, stay at, come thither (405–407), *wayes* (448, 450): it is the biblical, Augustinian, Prayer Book trope of life as journey which pervaded Donne's sermons. Norbrook has recently enlarged upon that point, with reference to a later sermon, preached on the biblical text "Take heed what you hear." He wrote that as "soon as Donne has set up the figure of the *via media* he starts to deconstruct it: precisely because it is a way, a process, the middle is constantly changing its position."[8] What did not change for Donne is that wisdom associates most properly with the path of love, craft all-too-readily with aggressive unlove or with the merely narcissistic love of power. *Only* divine power-and-love (grace) does not deconstruct or deteriorate.

As Donne moved, in the passage above, from the concept and category of knowledge to the human faculty that conceives and articulates it, reason, especially natural or "common Reason" (412), the underlying metaphor and metonymy of journey expanded into allegories of "Sea side," natural illumination as punning "beames of the Sunne," and "medicinall Ambar" (417), this last resonant of spiritual sickness and *Christus medicus.*[9] The *"new facultie of Reason"* (408) should be loving reason, directed toward the gifts of divine love allegorized as nature and amber and also, in neighborly, good Samaritan fashion, toward "things profitable and usefulle to the whole world" (423–24). Donne here pioneered the argument (did one think it was Marshall McLuhan's discovery?) that printing was the most important example of such good works: "Communicable . . . commerce together . . . participate of one anothers understandings." The intensity of iteration and the associations of the

8. Norbrook, "The Monarchy of Wit," 23; his reference is to VII, S11, preached at St. Paul's on Christmas, 1626, on Luke 2:29–30 (*nunc dimittis*); but *cf.* Shami, "Kings and Desperate Men," 19, on the same sermon. For early soundings of the importance of journey, see Carrithers, *Donne at Sermons,* 21–22, 90–98, and Winfried Schleiner, *The Imagery of John Donne's Sermons* (Providence, 1970), 85–94.

9. For Christ as physician (with reference to Luke 4:23) or variations on medicine, illness, patient, and the like, see, for example: I, S2, 381, S3, 812, S9, 90, 268, 412–13; II, S12, 232–46; III, S5, 569, S7, 307–42, S8, 161, S17, 417, and *passim.* These sermonic employments of the complex trope need to be interrelated with the *Devotions* (1623) and the two *Anniversaries* (1612). For the non-Pelagian Donne, persons partly *choose* sin (unlike sickness) but can get well only by grace.

word *communicable* in a context of Prayer Book worship all suggested appreciation as profound as Milton's for printing as medium of sociable citizenship.[10]

Printing threatened not only the mores and stability of oral culture; it also threatened absolutism. It threatened absolutism by disseminating the possibility of investigating assertions that previously had to be accepted on faith (mapped boundaries, biblical texts, law, worship, political theories, and stories about "wonders"). All could now be brought into endless question and counterquestion through the persistence and expansiveness of printing. Moreover, a fugitive press could put out too many copies of a subversive pamphlet ever to be quite suppressed, as Elizabeth Eisenstein has so magnificently shown.[11] Of course, the congregation were using the printed Prayer Book as liturgical context of Donne's very sermon.

Artillery, in this excerpt, epitomized power as gadgetry. Trade and its negotiable instruments, Donne seemed to imply, comprised an equivalent power *abstraction.* Suddenly reader / hearers were moved toward the world of Jonsonian or Middletonian comedy: buyers aggressively diminished by corner or staple or monopoly pricing, unguarded heirs blown up by usury or commod-

10. Norbrook, "The Monarchy of Wit," 7, speaks of Donnean allegiance to "an international republic of letters, an ideal community," but does not at all develop what seems to us the framing importance of love, nor does he acknowledge Donne's Augustinian sense of the *civitas dei* as both immanent and transcendent. Rightly arguing that Donne conflated the Augustinian middle between fallen here and eternal there and the Aristotelian mean between vicious extremes here (as between cowardice and recklessness, "inordinate criticism and . . . candor") is Joshua Scodel, "John Donne and the Religious Politics of the Mean," in *John Donne's Religious Imagination,* ed. Frontain and Malpezzi, 45–80, esp. 65–69. See Daniel W. Doerksen, *Conforming to the Word: Herbert, Donne, and the English Church Before Laud* (Lewisburg, Pa., 1997); received while this book was in press, Doerksen's is a learned and helpful *taxonomy* of an English Channel middle-wayfaring between Rome and the "separated brethren" of Amsterdam (not Geneva), a church not emphatically predestinarian but otherwise preponderantly Calvinist, certainly so while the reign of James I (1603–25) overlapped the tenure of George Abbot as archbishop of Canterbury (1611–33). But "word centered"? The static, visual taxonomy of the metaphor occludes the dynamism of the Donnean poetic in prose and verse and the sacramentalizing preoccupation with love animating the sermons.

11. Elizabeth Eisenstein, *The Printing Press as an Agent of Change in Early Modern Europe* (2 vols.; Cambridge, Eng., 1979); or see her more lavishly illustrated, brief account: *The Printing Revolution in Early Modern Europe* (Cambridge, Eng., 1983). And see, of course, the foundational work of Walter Ong, much of it conveniently summarized in *Orality and Literacy: The Technologizing of the Word* (London, 1982).

ity swindles, chaste women beseiged by lovelessly delusive sallies and sorties. But Donne extended the scene whither Jonson (in drama apart from "Rome" or apart from masque) and Middleton had scarcely dared: to court. In this sermon on Christ as *light essential* and on the God-given light of natural understanding, he called *"Courts of Princes"* and their "greatest *Officers*" the "darkest, and most impervious places" (444–45). In an immediate context of chastity beguiled to "eternall destruction," he posited men who "submit themselves" to "advance the humours" of "great men," by, the implication seems unavoidable, the prostitute mechanics of strength plying weakness. If any had lost track of the parallel alternatives, he reminded them of ways "of *Wisdome*" (448), associated with loving reason or a transcendent orientation, and ways "of *Craft*" (449), mere leverage in the *civitas terrena.* As the remarkably weighty paragraph concluded, the whole court and its deceptions registered as a masque of blackness, antimasque to the *civitas Dei.*[12]

To be sure, Donne's terms were tactfully general: *courts, princes, officers.* But the next paragraph in this sermon was more about valid love than about power; it generalized about "worldly men" (498) as gatherers of "nothing but shels and pebles" (504), whatever their *wit, learning, industry, fortune,* or *favor.* No one likely to be in London at St. Paul's on Christmas Day in 1621 would have needed much prompting for particular application to the Court of James I and to James's scandalous sale of honors and preferments, disgraceful favoritism in connection with his series of infatuations, and the demoralization attending courtly whoring and pimping. Which was more subversive from the pulpit: eloquent argument calling in the secular arm to attack perceived heresy or other wrong-doing, or eloquent (and anti-Manichaean) argument that idolatries and shows of power are darkly, ontologically insubstantial, that they are the relatively ephemeral, relatively trivial annoyance merely of "thicke . . . grosse Ayre" [455]?[13]

After all, were not all biblically assured, here in the *civitas terrena,* that here

12. *Cf.* Jonson's *The Masque of Blacknesse* and *The Masque of Beauty,* which would altogether more likely have been received as the sort of too-welcome-to-the-Court compliment that we all call flattery. In fairness to Jonson, though, one might note that the Queen was more the object of compliment than James.

13. This instance is not atypical. In a paragraph on the knowledge and the love of God, he observed: "To know how near nothing, how meer nothing, all the glory of the world is, is a good, a great degree of learning" (IV, S3, 1226–28).

is no continuing city?[14] Were congregations not, whenever witnesses to baptism, enjoined by the *Book of Common Prayer* to side with the godparents to help the newly-baptized "forsake the devil and all his works, the vain pomp, and glory of the world" and (last) "the carnal desires of the flesh"? Was King James ever specifically named or indicated, unless to praise him for being a peacemaker? Kings were conventionally acknowledged and *called* to be God's agents, but everyone knew what could happen to agents or to calls.

Donne preached at Lincoln's Inn, probably in 1620, on Job 19:26: "And though, after my skin, wormes destroy this body, yet in my flesh shall I see God." A theologically orthodox occasion, certainly: After all, congregations vocally and regularly reaffirmed their belief in "the resurrection of the body, and the life of the world to come" as part of the Prayer Book credo. With more obvious political point, there was late in the sermon indulgence of royalty as spectacle (III, S3, 781–87), albeit ironically theatrical, we believe; and the flesh to be resurrected and transfigured was acknowledged to have aspersed and slandered "persons in authority" (796).

Yet there was no moment in the sermon more wittily pointed than one on the destruction of body and worldly things "as may justly remove us from any high valuation, or any great confidence in them" (532–33): "The knife, the marble, the skinne, the body are ground away, trod away, they are destroy'd, who knows the revolutions of dust? Dust upon the Kings high-way, and dust upon the Kings grave, are both, or neither Dust Royall, and may change places; who knows the revolution of dust?"(540–45). The highway could be the king's, and Donne exhibited conventional alacrity in rendering or acknowledging it unto Caesar, but any road, the whole *way* of the world here below, was pervasively understood as a way of process or flux or vicissitude.

On Candlemas Day (perhaps in 1622 / 23), in a place not identified, Donne preached on Romans 13:7: "Render therefore to all men their dues" (IV, S12). The remark we employ as epigraph occurred two-thirds of the way through that sermon, but it appropriately begins this chapter because the sermon was

14. Hebrews 13:14, cited at II, S14, 726–27, and of course read aloud in Morning Prayer approximately every six months. The insistence on airiness and ephemerality helps to gloss such passages as that where he averred of "the state of Princes," "all that is but ceremony; and I would be loath to put a *Master of ceremonies* . . . to include so various a thing as ceremony, in so constant a thing, as a Definition" (III, S3, 755–58), the passage adverted to below, in the text. When Henry Fielding's Parson Adams cites Hebrews 13:14, it is partly in favor of earthly countryside.

itself doubly framed by affirmations of the primacy of love. Donne opened with the conventional and almost lecturelike outline of topic-headings (debts to God: praise and prayer; to neighbors: superordinate and subordinate; to self: early and late). But he really began the engagement of the sermon with text and liturgy by negations: "Contentious men" discounted because "their food and delight, [is] disputation" (84–85) clearly represented the mischoice of kakocharist over Eucharist. The pulpit itself could be degraded and diverted from its calling, which was to enable the people's work of the liturgy in that valid theater, and could instead be "made the shop, and the theatre of praise upon present men, and God left out" (166–67). Later he spoke of ceremonial respect being due up the chain of order but all proper respect ending properly in God (477–87). This situated his climactic point about improper respect to superordinate neighbors: "To encourage him in his ill purposes . . . is too high a ceremony, and too transcendant a complement, to be damned for his sake, by concurring with my superior in his sins" (500–503). It was a point about conscience, as identified in Shami's analysis, and a point Donne confirmed with an even heavier term to end the whole sermon. He contrasted counseling from love with counsels of power: The satirist / calumniator "seeks to exercise his authority"; and others are guilty of "trusting too much in learning, for worldly gain," what we might call idols of the reference collection. Thereupon Donne echoed the caution of the Psalmist, "Except the Lord keep the city" (Ps. 127:2), and many would have responded mentally from remembrance of liturgic repetitions, "the watchman waketh but in vain" (514–671). Accordingly, he came to conclude for himself and the other individual "Romans" of his own day: "Thou shalt have rendered to all their dues, when thou hast given the King, Honour; the poore, almes; thy selfe, peace; and God thy soule" (737–39).

In a sermon on the call to love Christ, he spoke of Christ giving the individual soul "a capacity which it hath not, to comprehend the joyes and glory of Heaven." He continued:

> To save this body from the condemnation of everlasting corruption, where the wormes that we breed are our betters, because they have a life, where the dust of dead Kings is blowne into the street, and the dust of the street blowne into the River, and the muddy River tumbled into the Sea, and the Sea remaunded into all the veynes and channels of the earth; to save this body from everlasting dissolution, dispersion, dissipation, and to make it in a glorious Resurection,

> not onely a Temple of the holy Ghost, but a Companion of the holy Ghost in the kingdome of heaven, This *Christ* became this *Jesus.* (III, S14, 377–86)

The indiscriminateness of dust and the invidious discriminateness of lords and tenants were contrasted with the self as *Temple* and *Companion.* Or when the general way of the world was quite specifically the king's, the road must have two directions and may have strange turnings: "Have we not seen often, that the bed-chambers of Kings have back-doores into prisons" (III, S12, 191–92). Or again, when Christ's "pleasure is to execute a just judgement upon a Nation, upon a Church, upon a Man, in the infatuation of Princes, in the recidivation of the Clergy, in the consternation of particular consciences, *Quis stabit*?" (III, S15, 467–69).[15] Whether auditors thought of Somerset in the Tower or of any other prisons or of other infatuators / infatuatees of King James, the point had general force. Elsewhere, in general confirmation of the nature of love and politics, Donne would quote Romans 8:28: "All things work together for good, to them that *love* God" (III, S7, 398).

Moreover, the general implications were by no means exclusively passive or quietist. In that same sermon about "Wo unto the world because of offences," he quoted from Matthew's next verses and elaborated: "*If thy foot, thy hand, thine eye, scandalize thee* . . . Though hee bee the foot upon which thou standest, thy Master, thy Patron, thy Benefactor; Though hee be thy hand by which thou gettest thy living, thy meanes, the instrument of thy maintenance, or preferment; Though hee bee thine eye, the man from whom thou receivest all thy Light, and upon whose learning thou engagest thy Religion . . . *cut off, pull out, and cast away*" (II, S7, 320–25, 341–42, probably 1620, but perhaps earlier, at Lincoln's Inn). No bishop, no king could be immune to so decisive an individual conscience.[16]

15. Sermons 12, 14, and 15 in Vol. III were originally printed as 38, 40, and 41 in *LXXX Sermons* (1640), there ascribed by John Donne, Jr. (presumably) to "Trinity Sunday." Potter and Simpson seem right in ascribing them to a single Trinity *term* at Lincoln's Inn, not implausible in supposing it to be 1621. In IV, S1, 294–302, Donne spoke again of dust of wretch, prince, patrician, or plebian as indistinguishable. We acknowledge that *dust,* like almost any image, *can* work honorifically and not disparagingly. Ulysses S. Grant was praised as a dusty general, meaning one not afraid to get close to the action. But we can find little ambiguity in Donne's sermonic usage in his biblical and liturgical contexts.

16. For Shami, on conscience, see "Kings and Desperate Men," esp. pp. 15–17, and her earlier article "Donne's Protestant Casuistry: Cases of Conscience in the *Sermons,*" *Studies in Philology,* LXXX (1983), 53–66. For important recent general consideration, see Keith Thomas,

This may sound too radically Protestant, too little the establishmentarian Anglo-Catholic Donne of some redactions. But Donne was an inclusivist of the middle way and engaged, more in Lutheran senses than Calvinist, the Protestant tropes of calling and ambassadorship.[17] The trope of calling may for purposes of analytic explication be taxonomically separated from the trope of journey. For the pastoral Donne, however, in devout lived experience the two must coalesce and amalgamate. The Christian was understood to be called by the Triune God from birth (into sin) through the fallen world to redemption in eternal community; the call was a general commission, always ambassadorlike, to represent the true God in the welter of would-be gods of place or power and to return to the loving Creator, rather than stultifying in any besotted stasis. *Vae mihi si non,* says Donne repeatedly of his own particular calling to preach.[18]

To the Prince and Princess Palatine at Heidelberg in June of 1619, Donne, a ranking member of Viscount Doncaster's embassy, preached on salvation, preached on it as a calling to action: "As the Blessed Virgin speaks, *Thy soul shall magnify the Lord;* all thy natural faculties shall be employed upon an assent to the Gospel, thou shalt be able to prove it to thy self, and to prove it to others, to be the Gospel of Salvation."[19] He characteristically added, a bit

"Cases of Conscience in Seventeenth-Century England," in *Public Duty and Private Conscience in Seventeenth-Century England: Essays Presented to G. E. Aylmer,* ed. John Morrill, Paul Slack, and Daniel Woolf (New York, 1993), 29–53. See Meg Lota Brown, *John Donne and the Politics of Conscience in Early Modern England* (Leiden, 1995), for, especially, the considerable relevance of Protestant and Catholic discourse on casuistry to Donne's poetry, minor prose, and his sermon on Esther (V, S11).

17. Briefly, Calvin conceived a dual calling: special, to the ministry; and (relatively) general, to election. Luther espoused a *more* general calling, of each to find her or his way to embody in this world divine will and thereby to enhance divine glory; see *Luther's Works,* (45 vols.), Vol. LII, trans. and ed. Hans J. Hillebrand (Philadelphia, 1974), 123–24; Vol. XLIV, trans. and ed. James Atkinson (Philadelphia, 1966), 130, 269, 294–95; Vol. III, trans. and ed. Jaroslav Pelikan (St. Louis, 1961), 130. Donne's not-much-noticed "To Mr. *Tilman* after he had taken orders" asks, "What function is so noble as to bee / Embassadour to God and destinie?" (ll. 37–38). And see Daniel W. Doerksen, " 'Saint Pauls Puritan': John Donne's 'Puritan' Imagination in the Sermons," in *John Donne's Religious Imagination,* ed. Frontain and Malpezzi, and discussion in n. 23, below.

18. Donne condenses I Corinthians 9:16; the more private and internal aspect of this was addressed by Carrithers, *Donne at Sermons,* 117.

19. Sellin argues persuasively that Donne was integral, not merely adjunctive, to the embassy, especially in *So Doth, So Is Religion.*

later: "To be a lively faith, expressed in charity" (II, S12, 456–57, 491). Every English communicant would recognize the "Magnificat" from uncounted services of Evening Prayer and could recall something of the Prayer Book context: "He hath scattered the proud. . . . He hath put down the mighty . . . and exalted the humble and meek."

Returning in December, 1619, the more literal and particular embassy having failed, Donne preached at The Hague on the text "I will make you fishers of men." In 1630, he "digested" his "short notes" (he wrote) into two sermons, presumably for publication. He wrote in 1630, whether or not he had spoken in 1619, of the more general—the literal, political, and more than political—calling. He averred that contemporary ministers had not the *special* callings of apostles or prophets to "chide Kings openly" but rather the *regular* callings, "like Justices in their Sessions or Judges in their Circuits . . . due tryall by a course of Law" (II, S14, 564ff.).[20] Here, as in the citation before it, he evinced a marked variation of Calvinist doctrine: There is a universal calling to the priesthood of all believers, which is to magnify the Lord; and (he elaborated here) each person must find a special calling from God, like a sailing ship *in* the waterway of the world but *directed* by the *Hagia Pneuma* (680ff.).

Given the combination of Christian orthodoxy and Donnean wit, the former including journey, calling, and estimation of this world's attractions as "but *nothing* multiplied" or "but an *Occasional* world . . . but as it directs and conduces" to the joy of heaven (IV, S6, 300; III, S8, 56–63), one should not be surprised to find witty and subtle segues and permutations into variations on the commonplace that "all the world's a stage." After all, what was an omniscient God if not the arch-spectator, and what was his call if not to (the) true and self-fulfilling action? "Hath God made this World his theatre that man may represent God in his conversation; and wilt thou play no part?" (I, S3, 899–902, in 1617).[21] The Bible can accordingly become a kind of promptbook in the hands of the preacher: "Our text is an amphitheater in which all may sit, and see themselves acted" (VIII, S15, 75–77, in 1629 at Whitehall on James 2:12: "So speake, and so do, as they that shall be judged by the law of liberty").

20. On law, see especially Shami, "Kings and Desperate Men," 13–14; she would presumably agree with our sense of Donne's usual (though not *always* clear in him) distinction between the greater normative, or natural, law and the lesser positive law.

21. So Donne at I, S3, 899–902, translates "ut exhibeatur ludus deorum," substituting *God* for *gods,* and notes in the margin "Plato," a not-uncharacteristic instance of his almost Miltonicly imperial way with sources.

Sooner or later innumerable experiential variations introduced by these formulations got developed, and so, too, did innumerable others from like pronouncements. The imperfection of the player in her or his true part—imperfection caused by sloth or more explicit idolatry—may be anatomized as the self-divinizing tendency to script self or others into mere roles and scenarios, the trumpery and mummery of a fallen world.

Before King James, in Lent, 1621, Donne preached on 1 Timothy 3:16: "And without controversie, great is the mystery of godliness: God was manifest in the flesh, justified in the spirit, seen of angels, preached unto the gentiles, believed on in the world, received up into glory." He divided his sermon into major parts on "the mystery" and "the manifestation" and on each of those offered elaborated exposition and reflection for his auditors' immediate apprehension and later meditation. In a shrewdly developed subsection on "seen of angels," he extended angelic seeing from Christ to ourselves (by the authority of St. Paul and St. Jerome): "*We are made a spectacle to men and angels.* The word is there *theatrum,* and so *S. Hierom* reads it." The application included urging neither to "sollicite a woman's chastity nor calumniate an absent person in the Kings ear" nor to offend "those angels which see Christ Jesus now" by obliging them to "see the same Christ in thee crucified again in thy irreligious conversation" (III, S9, 430–51).

His long concluding section, on "received up into glory," looked both ways: toward the true and lively theater of the transcendent manifest here, toward true calling engaged here, toward *civitas Dei* reached and manifest here, and toward *civitas terrena* as meretricious mummery, going nowhere unless to inanity.[22] Having argued in the longer second part of the sermon that manifestations had established "meanes for believing in" Christ, he reminded all at Whitehall of the ontological distance, which was likewise hermeneutic and political distance: "This which we are fain to call *glory,* is an inexpressible thing, and an incommunicable: *Surely I will not give my glory unto another,* says God, in *Esay* [48:11]." This remark implicitly about the distance between divine being and human apprehension debouched into more about titles than any merely cautious preacher would have poured into the ears of a monarch so disesteemed for giving and selling many titles as James had been and had

22. *Cf.* IV, S6, 75–77 (1622, at Hanworth, to the Earls of Carlisle, Northumberland, and Buckingham, on Job 36:25): "Every error begins in *blindnesse,* and ignorance, but proceeds, and ends, in *absurdity,* in frivolousnesse."

done. The passage came to a summary view of the *fallen* terrene end of the axis and its shows: "Great titles have been taken, Ambition goes far; and great given, Flattery goes as far. . . . But not to 'your Glory' or 'our Glory'; *Glory be to God,*" *i.e.,* to the Trinity only. "As long as that scurff, that leprosie sticks to every thing in this world, *Vanitas Vanitatum, that all is vanity;* can any glory in any thing of this world, be other than vain-glory?" (III, S9, 598–99, 629–38).

Coronets and titles of the two realms were contrasted. On one heading were those that one had out of the "abundant Greatness and Goodness" of kings here, by which receivers "*are Consanguinei Regis,* the King's Cousins" (645–48). In contrast to the passive receptivity of status, Donne posited the active doing in response to the other kingdom's calling:

> The glory of Gods Saints in Heaven, is not so much to have a Crown, as to lay down that Crown at the Feet of the Lamb. The glory of good men here upon earth, is not so much to have Honour, and Favour, and Fortune, as to employ those Beams of Glory, to his glory that gave them. . . . glorifie him in that wherein you may see him, in that wherein he hath manifested himself in his glorious Gospel: employ your Beams of Glory, Honour, Favour, Fortune, in transmitting his Gospel in the same Glory to your Children, as you receiv'd it from your Fathers: for in this consists this Mystery of Godliness, which is, Faith with a pure Conscience: And in this lies your best Evidence, That you are already co-assumed with Christ Jesus into glory . . . that Kingdom . . . purchased for you, with the inestimable price of his incorruptible Blood. (652–69)

Officially, James *was* transmitting the Gospel as he had received it, neither remitting it to Rome nor hailing it into Geneva. So he could have felt praised without flattery by a definition of the good that corresponded to his supposed policy but that was offered as advice to follow. But could he have received complacently the implicit message to all the other auditors: 'Glorify God for all good fortune, including favors from the King. If in good men's judgments you deserve them, *that* is by the grace of God to you and through the royal giver; if you don't deserve them, you will come nearer so by glorifying God. If the King wishes to be glorified himself for the favors he gives, he is so much the less worthy of his own crown.'

On the first of July, 1627, Donne preached a commemorative sermon for his old friend, the recently deceased Magdalen Herbert, Lady Danvers. We infer that the church in suburban Chelsea would have been crowded with persons of political and economic importance; and the sermon, quite long, was published in duodecimo the same year. He took as his text 2 Peter 3:13: "Nevertheless, we, according to his promises, looke for new heavens, and new earth, wherein dwelleth righteousnesse" (VIII, 52). He divided less the text than the sermon into "Two Workes . . . That wee may walke together two miles, in this Sabbath daies journey; First, *to instruct the Living,* and then *To commemorate the Dead.*" The "mile" of instruction trebled in length and equaled in fervor the mile of commemoration.

Deep in that first mile, Donne ascribed to "*regenerate* man" a God-given, "endlesse, and Undeterminable desire of more, then this life can minister unto him" (454–55). *"Man,"* Donne averred, "is a *future Creature*" (459). Worldly honor could be *at best* only a gift and typological shadow of eternal heavenly honor. And so it was, in the stunning climactic syntactic gallop through three paragraphs on Righteousness, Justice, and Righteousness to the end of the instruction. We give them in part, eliding mainly remarks on righteousness, which took it as the more private and interiorly personal face of justice:

> Here, the *holy Ghost* proceeds not that way; by *improvement* of things, which wee *have,* [740] and *love* here; *riches,* or *beauty,* or *musicke,* or *honour,* or *feasts;* but by an everlasting possession of that, which wee hunger, and thirst, and pant after, here, and cannot compasse, that is *Justice,* or *Righteousnesse*. . . . [Justice] What would a worne and macerated *suter,* opprest by the bribery of the rich, or by the might of a potent Adversary, *give,* or *doe,* or *suffer,* that he might have *Justice?* . . . Here there is none that doe's right, none that executes *Justice;* or, not for *Justice* sake. Hee that doe's *Justice,* doe's it not at first. . . . *Justice* is no *Justice,* that is done for feare of an *Appeale,* or a *Commission.* There may bee found, that may doe *Justice* at first; At their first entrance into a place, to make good impressions, to establish good opinions, they may doe some *Acts* of *Justice;* But after, either an [760] *Uxoriousnesse* towards the wife, or a *Solicitude* for children, or a *facility* towards servants, or a *vastnesse* of expence, quenches, and overcom's the love of *Justice* in them; *Non habitat,* In most [justice] is not; but it *dwels* not in any . . . my comfort [is] that when I come thither, I shall have *Justice* at *God's* hands. . . .
>
> [Righteousnesse] *Justice dwels* there, and there *dwels Righteousnes;* Of which there is none in this world; None that growes in this world; none that is mine owne. . . . But in this new *state,* these *new Heavens,* and *new Earth, Justicia habitat,* This *Righteousnesse* shall dwell; I shall have an *innocence,* and a *constant in-*

> *nocence;* a present *impeccancy,* and an *impeccability* for the future. But, in this especially, is [790] *Righteousnes* said to *dwell* there, because this *Righteousnesse,* is the very *Son of God,* the *Sonne* of *Righteousnesse* himselfe. . . . these *new Heavens,* and *new Earth* shall bee his *standing house,* where hee shall *dwell,* and wee with him; as himselfe hath said [Matt. 13:43]. . . . *God* shall impart to us all, a mysterious *Gavelkinde,* a mysterious *Equality* of *fulnesse* of *Glory,* to us *all.*

Gavelkinde was the Kentish alternative to primogeniture: roughly, "equal inheritance." Of course Donne was no church-court-and-chancery burning Leveller *avant la lettre.* But the implications of his liturgic and sermonic orientation toward gavelkinde reward reflection. Most of that which would magnify status in any secular perspective is nugatory. But love, and within its nature justice, is always to be construed in heavenly perspectives, where in valid manifestations it will always look majestic, where in invalid or misoriented manifestations it will evaporate as gross air (though that might be temporarily consequential). Elsewhere, he identified "Heires of heaven, which is not a Gavel-kinde, every son, every man alike; but it is a universall primogeniture, every man full" (V, S2, 629–30).

Such samples, excerpted from the sermons, are representative. His preaching manifested a sort of parable or allegory of the biblical, Augustinian, liturgical Christian journey of rightly ordered loves. He proceeded with a zealous alertness that tried to avoid the dejection of spirit or uncharitable disputatiousness he associated with Separatism and to avoid the power-mongering tendentiousness he associated with spiritual complacency, Pelagianism, and Rome. He gathered or was liturgically confronted by biblical texts that his meditations could develop as "arguments" expansible into scenarios for God- and heaven-oriented action rather than action idolatrous of inferior powers or shows and eternity-minded and dialogic rather than entropically or disjunctively temporal or narcissistic. Such a preacher of the "True and lively word" may be thought of as Protestant in zeal of conscience, as Catholic in his sense of alternatives as unlively, existentially attenuated, but as tempered by his calling to speak from love.[23] He would need to be a "preacher, crying according

23. Shami finds honest *discretion* in the sermons, and so do we. But she takes that as antipathetic to Puritan or suchlike *zeal.* There are certainly Donnean animadversions against stirrers-up of strife, but our *general* sense of his passionate distinction between the City of God here and hereafter, as opposed to near or mere nothings, and of the testimony on his elocutionary style (in the elegies to him by acquaintances) places us closer to Norbrook's position that Donne

to Gods ordinance, shaking the soule, troubling the conscience, and pinching the bowels, by denouncing Gods Judgements, these beare witnesse of the light when other wise men would sleep it out" (IV, S8, 45–47). The King's court and political world adjacent to the pulpit—those necessary but problematic expediencies of a fallen world—need likewise take lights from light's source in the godly city, he believed, else they would sink to emitting light squibs, mere shows in the somnolent dark.[24]

For all the quasi-diagrammatic "branches" into which Donne regularly divided the biblical texts he chose for his sermons, for all the occasionally forced or far-fetched quality to his *applications* of a biblical term, there was a stoutly

"preferred evangelical 'zeal' to the decency that was so much a feature of High Church rhetoric" ("The Monarchy of Wit," 23). The issue is "zeale to the assistance of others" (V, S14, 970)—zeal of love rather than bad zeal of reprehension; or for nonzeal, think of the high, dry, wry rhetoric of Andrewes. See the helpful Doerksen, "'Saint Pauls Puritan,'" 350–65. We agree Donne did not hate Puritans, but we are not persuaded his was a "word-centered piety"; it could not be, in the context of the liturgy, though it could have (as the dual ministry proposed but more complexly) a dual center. Doerksen equates "church doctrine" with "spiritual well being," jointly opposed to "outward forms of worship," but for Donne, the crucial polarity was between theatricalized (literally hypocritical) worship and inner worship accordant with essential doctrine and expressive in outward forms.

24. We deliberately echo "light squibs, no constant rayes," from "A Nocturnall upon St. Lucies Day," and "light squibs of mirth," from "A Litanie," to acknowledge the issue of continuity of Donne's thought from late poetry to later prose, an interesting issue, marginal here. Catherine Gimelli Martin has argued "Donne's lyrics enlarge the private sphere," implicitly criticizing the mystificatory "divine right ideology of the Stuart court" ("Pygmalion's Progress in the Garden of Love, or Wit's Work Is Never Donne," in *The Wit of Seventeenth-Century Poetry,* ed. Claude Summers and Ted-Larry Pebworth [Columbia, Mo., 1995], 78–100, esp. 99). The good case for continuity, with complex change especially in connection with Anne More Donne's death but no *radical* break between "Jack Donne" and "Dr. Donne," has been made with emphases political, ecclesiastical (and transcendent), and erotic: see, respectively, Patterson, *Reading Between the Lines;* Claude J. Summers, "The Bride of the Apocalypse and the Quest for True Religion: Donne, Herbert, and Spenser," in *"Bright Shootes of Everlastingnesse": The Seventeenth-Century Religious Lyric,* ed. Claude Summers and Ted-Larry Pebworth (Columbia, Mo., 1987), 72–94; and, too recent for full consideration here, M. Thomas Hester, ed., *John Donne's "desire of more": The Subject of Anne More Donne in His Poetry* (Newark, Del., 1996). See esp. there Kate Gartner Frost, "'Preparing towards her': Contexts of *A Nocturnall upon S. Lucies Day,*" 149–71; Theresa M. Di Pasquale, "Ambivalent Mourning in 'Since she

orthodox and coherent theology, particularly if sought in general, thematic terms. God and the joys of heaven were devoutly extolled in encomiastic preference to favors of this world, in admonitory reprimand to idolatries of the devil, the world, or the flesh. Divine times and devout articulations of time were enjoined against secular degradations of time: blessed eternity, moment decisive with regard to that, and the Christian year's precession of needful opportunities in a seductive fallen world. Correspondingly, divinely sanctioned communions of call and witness were privileged over secular conversations, not to mention profane communication.[25]

The richness of implication in Donne's sense of his society, and its history unfolding so ambiguously around him, emerged to a considerable degree in his construal of that society in the tropes of journey, theater, calling, and moment and the action of dialogue.[26] The tropic moment in particular and time in general have been especially scanted in previous attention to the sermons, and consideration of those issues first will enrich subsequent consideration of journey, theater, and calling on following pages.

A definition of Donnean time by partial contrast: Milton seemed to have been engaged by the problem of how to conceive a God who must by definition be superior to human time. Most notably in *Paradise Lost* and *Paradise Regain'd,* the solution was love. Human love at its best was metaphor and me-

---

whome I lovd,' " 183–95; Achsah Guibbory, "Fear of 'loving more': Death and the Loss of Sacramental Love," 204–207; Maurine Sabine, "No Marriage in Heaven: John Donne, Anne Donne, and the Kingdom Come," 228–55.

25. Time, even Time, was from his earliest preaching construed as yielding to divine power-and-love, as Donne meditated the difference from fallen process, as with the penitent thief "suddenly a Convertite . . . Confessor . . . Martyr . . . Doctor" (I, S6, 73–76), and likewise four *suddenlies* with regard to Paul's conversion (I, S6, 73–76, 109–11). See, collaterally, Anthony Low, "John Donne: 'The Holy Ghost Is Amorous in His Metaphors,' " in *New Perspectives on the Seventeenth-Century Religious Lyric,* ed. John R. Roberts (Columbia, Mo., 1994), 201–21; we agree on Donne's frequent (with him and others) construal of sacred love with reference to secular and in both "timeless moments of . . . intimate mutuality . . . never passivity, still less . . . admitted inferiority" (203, 210–11); but we're uneasy with the sweeping claim of "failure of love in Donne's divine poems" (221), since what Low calls the marriage-trope may fail, but other tropes do not, still less in those prose poems, the sermons.

26. This is not to slight but rather to supplement and in some instances modify the essential work on political, doctrinal, and personal statement and implication in the sermons—work that has tended recently to occlude tropics. See n. 1 above. Potter and Simpson made only desultory references to imagery and metaphor in the introductions to the ten volumes of their edition of *The Sermons.*

tonymy of the peace and joy of heavenly eternity; the antilovers in the place of antilove, lost amid endless mazes of argument over fate, free will, and foreknowledge and ever-burning sulfur unconsumed, were too self-absorbed to have a *telos.* Donne was no less concerned with love than Milton but seemingly less anxious to anatomize the problem of eternity. He more readily dismissed extreme Puritan anguishing over fate / free will / foreknowledge as impertinent, in modern terms "intellectually arrogant" and "neurotic." His visions of heaven emphasized *community* rather than eternity, as in a sermon at Hanworth to the Earls of Carlisle, Northumberland, and Buckingham where he spoke of "the *communion of Saints,* the fellowship of the faithfull," with children, martyrs, prophets, evangelists, matrons, virgins, "*Princes,* and *Subjects* crowned all with one crowne" (IV, S6, 492–509). What evidently engaged Donne was the perceptible variability of time as metaphor and metonymy of divine power immeasurably transcending the merely theatrical power of any royal *fiat* or commercial gadgetry.

All Donne said in sermons about sacred or profane time was framed by the defining actions and terms of the liturgy. The parishioner might come into the church, as the sermons routinely suggest, as a secular-minded individual observer or even as a self-styled devil of a fellow. But in a moment the opening sentence defined the situation differently, and in the General Confession the parishioner acknowledged herself or himself as *social* and as a *sinner.* Thereupon, the priest in a (temporarily and contingently) decisive moment pronounced absolution, including the phrase that the sinner "turn from his wickedness and live" (Morning Prayer) or "turn unto him" (Holy Communion). That movement of reorientation, of Augustinian *retorqueo,* by its potentially enormous consequentiality measured the power of the grace that enabled it. "*Revertere,* turn to God, and thou shalt not dy the death, not the second death . . . though . . . thou must turn into the grave" (III, S3, 427–30), as the absolution was expressed in a Donne sermon. The sermons, by their placement in the liturgy, spoke at least implicitly to the trope of salvific moment.

Similarly, in a Christmas sermon at St. Paul's, he quoted from the Latin version of St. Luke's account of the Crucifixion: "Hodie mecum eris in paradiso." He translated it, however, with expansive emphasis on divine power, which is able to collapse the very *categories* of time, change, and space: "This day, this minute thou shalt be, now thou art with me in Paradise" (IV, S11, 526–28). Earlier in that same sermon, on Colossians 1:19–20, he reflected on "all fulnesse" of the Father dwelling in the Son. That would include, with special regard to the Son and the Church, "the Spirit in those beames, in those functions, in those operations, as conduce to government, that is, Wisedome, and Counsell, and Power." Thus, he concludes "that this is Christ's fulnesse, that he is in a continuall administration of his Church . . . [so] *have all we received* . . . power by his grace, to derive grace upon the Congregation" (225–31). Donne, long the shrewd political observer, well knew that wisdom might fail, counsel miscounsel, and power in the fallen world might tend to other than the gifts of grace. But, he understood as Milton came to understand, power in a fallen world must remain the essence of government. Nonetheless, if love could not be institutionalized, at least wisdom and counsel could commend reorientation of highest loves to highest objects and define profane power by contrast with sacred power.

Theologically, time is always proportional to its implication in the fallenness of humanity and to the benign magnitude of an act's consequences. Donne understood this relationship between time and action on both human and divine levels. In an Easter sermon on resurrection, Donne said, "For all God's works are intire, and done in him at once, and perfect as soon as begun," but "Here, Grace works not that Resurrection upon thy soul, in an absolute instant." He continued: "In thy first, thy spirituall Resurrection from sin, make haste. The last is to be done *In raptu,* in a rapture. Let this rapture in the first Resurrection be, to teare thy self from that company and conversation that leads thee into tentation." Accordingly, he advises: "Let the opening of thine eyes be, to look upon God in every object, to represent to thy self the beauty of his holinesse, and the honour of his service in every action. And in this rapture, and in this twinkling of an eye, will thy Resurrection soon . . . though not instantly be accomplished" (IV, S2, 498–99, 474–95). Theoretically, everyone in England could have enjoyed such a resurrection, though no joint or several consummation could be effectively commanded, still less institutionalized. But in hearing or reading the Donnean unfolding of such turning to life and conceiving how life might be if such were general among their neighbors, citizens would have understood a reproachful distance between that resultant City of God and the London at hand.

Donne varied the theme in a sermon preached on Easter Monday, 1622, the day after the sermon cited just above, if Simpson and Potter's all-too-confident assumption is correct.[27] He addressed 2 Corinthians 4:6 and, in one division of that text, how God "hath shined in our hearts":

27. Evelyn Simpson, it seems, was primarily responsible for the argument that "As the Dean of St. Paul's was required by statute to preach on Easter Day, and we have dated sermons for all

> And we consider also the dispatch, how soon he made light, with a word. . . . So if we consider the dispatch of Christ Jesus in all his Miracles, there went but a *Tolle, Take up thy bed and walk,* to the lame man; but an *Ephphatha, Be opened,* to the deaf man; but a *Quid vides, What seest thou?* to the blind man. If we consider his dispatch upon the thief on the cross, how soon he brought him from reviling, to glorifying; and if any in this Auditory feel that dispatch of the Holy Ghost, in his heart; that whereas he came hither but to see, he hath heard; or if he came to hear the man, he hath heard God in the man, and . . . must confess that as *God commanded light out of darkness, so he hath shin'd in his heart: So,* that is, by the same means, by his Word; and so that is with the same speed and dispatch. (IV, S3, 999–1014)

Again, as *passim,* "dispatch" was a conclusive attestation of power so profound it could transform life from errancy or stasis to heavenward mobility, imperception to perception, rancor or indifference to love, in the instant of a word. Donne's God, like Milton's, was conceived to unite power and love perfectly, in poignant contrast to all fallen worldly agencies, with their tendencies toward ineffectual love or unloving power. The transformations cataloged in this excerpt represented loving calls and something like loving responses to grace, for those who "hath heard . . . hath heard God in the man."

Donne's sermonic ideas about divine time of power and love and their emplacement in the Prayer Book's Christian year (essentially a cycle of ever-renewed opportunity for loving response to call) reinforced his consistent anti-Manichaeanism and anti-Pelagianism. (These were arguably the recognized heresies that most concerned him because of their perennial, metamorphic vitality). But what were the alternatives to divine time? What was life in the Age of Iron, from which the sinner may turn or arise and live? Clearly no one in Donne's century had the option of thinking in terms of geological time or the lesser scope of biological-evolutionary time.[28] For Donne, even

---

the other Easters of Donne's tenure of the Deanery, it [IV, S2] obviously must belong here" (IV, Prefatory Note, and p. 29). But the statute could not ensure that his health or circumstances allowed him to preach or that he would preserve (or even write out) any sermon he may have preached. The absence of date, when other St. Paul's Easter sermons were dated, suggests to us an earlier Easter at Lincoln's Inn, though conceivably elsewhere. The speed of grace in the penitent thief was on his mind both earlier and later; and did he really preach his longest extant sermon the day after this very long Easter sermon?

28. See Ricardo Quinones, *The Renaissance Discovery of Time* (Cambridge, Mass., 1972), and trenchant review by Marvin Mudrick, "The Asp and the Entrails," *Hudson Review,* XXVI

botanical-seasonal time, whether of annual harvest or the several seasons until vines would have tender grapes or fig trees would bear, seems to have been infrequently present to his consciousness. The liturgical year, a vocabulary of postures of the fallen soul focused toward eternity, was Donne's preferred measure of *chronos,* where there was no present, merely past and future. The essence and realization of time as *kairos* was for Donne social interaction. It might be within the self, a "dialogue of one." It would ideally be ambassadorial to the earthly city in service to the heavenly city. At a marriage sermon (for Margaret Washington, in 1621), he spoke of Christ marrying the receptive / responsive soul, and averred: "This is his abundant and his present fecundity, that working now, by me in you, in one instant he hath children in me and grand children by me" (III, S11, 402–404).

The liturgy, as we have argued, was for Renaissance Anglicans the by-definition-valid scenario for redeeming time in the fallen world. In the sermon to the Virginia Company cited above, Donne defined the call to ambassadorial witness partly in the light of the ultimate call when "time shall be no more," the call to judgment, after the abrupt leveling by death: "The *Angell* that shall call us out of that dust, will not stand to survay, who lyes naked, who in a Coffin, who in Wood, who in Lead, who in a fine, who in a courser Sheet; In that one day of the Resurrection, there is not a forenoone for Lords to rise first, and an afternoone for meaner persons to rise after" (IV, S10, 435–39).[29] The wood, lead, and linen, or "filthy dowlas" of which Falstaff complained, were the props and acts of meretricious scenarios, tendentious temporizings.[30] For Donne, time in the literal theater or figurative *theatrum mundi* was ridiculous not because it squeezed events of years into two hours' traffic of the stage but on the contrary because it *attenuated* time-as-life.

In contrast, the suddenness, to human perception, of divine actions was a function of intensification. Extended human scenarios would seem com-

(1973), 219–24. We attend more to Donne's vocabulary of love and power than did Quinones. See, for provocative variation, Loren Eiseley on Bacon, in *The Man Who Saw Through Time* (New York, 1973).

29. The citation from Apocalypse 10:6, "time shall be no more," concludes the section on *nunc* in the magnificent "Sermon of Valediction" (II, S11). Both sermons are *inter alia* calls to redeem the time, amid vicissitude signalized by leave takings into danger. See also I, S5, 326–40 and VIII, S10.

30. *Cf.* at Whitehall (but with King James absent), "the miserable equality" in dust of "so unequall persons" as king, slave, bishop, heretic, counsellor, fool (IV, S13, 361–67).

pressed into points because of divine time more abundantly concentrating life. Life between the "fulnesse" of God and the *nihil* that *peccatum* was understood to be (in Scholastic doctrine) would necessarily be somewhat attenuated even at its fallen secular best. For just one example, a sermon on 1 Peter 1:17 invoked the temporal comparison in "Contemplation of that judgement," the final one by God as Judge: "There shall be Information, Examination, Publication, Hearing, Judgement, and Execution in a minute" (III, S13, 592–94).[31]

Donne honored the law, among whose students and practitioners he had himself as student and as chaplain spent relatively happy years. And he insisted on the judicial function of the individual conscience, even as he endorsed the concentration of executive power (and perhaps most legislative initiative) in a king. He understood, though, that in a fallen world some attenuation, some parceling out of power into powers—legislative, executive, judicial—might be prudent, and so, too, the attenuation or parceling out of powers into procedures. It was not, or was scarcely, for Donne a matter of what we have come tendentiously to call either "checks and balances" or "gridlock." It was rather a matter of providing maximum occasion, as if "space," for saving turnings back from wickedness toward life, a way of redeeming time, for the days were (as if spatially) evil.

Time as life was for Donne, as for Milton, essentially *not* a metaphoric double of space (a usual confusion of latter-day discourses in English, abetted by print). Only thought and behavior degradative of love could so reify time. "Nine times the Space that measures Day and Night," we recall, describes the *falling* angels. "Doe not think that your *Sundayes zeale* once a weeke, can burn out all your extortions, and oppressions, and usury, and butchery, and simony, and chambering and wantonesse practised from Monday to Saturday" (IV, S4, 901–904, at St. Paul's). Sin may be conceptually and theologically nothing, but it is existentially and consequentially something: unloving instrumentations that crowded a rejected way of life somewhat as stage-props in a sordid scenario (solid but not "real life"), commercial and military instrumentalisms, love reduced to lustful athletics, and zeal itself a kind of autoclave-of-convenience. Similarly, in a sermon preached and printed by

31. Recall that the loving, sexual, quasi-atemporal transport of the "dialogue of one" in "The Extasie" would look to a dull observer like nothing much "all the day." How much of the irony about *peccatum nihil* was Donne's, not merely ours, was shown by his petition in "A Litanie": "As sin is nothing, let it nowhere be."

command of King James, when he glossed why neither Reuben and his company nor Dan and his (Judg. 5:16, 17), joined with the Israelites against Sisera, he interpreted Reuben's failure as political pride: "Ambition of precedencie . . . greatness of heart." Simple. But "why did Dan remain in his ships?" A "confidence in their owne strength, a sacrifice to their owne Nets, an attributing of their securitie to their owne wisdome or power . . . retard[ed] the cause of God" (IV, S7, 430–33). Thus, Donne construed the somewhat cryptic biblical account as indicative of power scenarios he could see embraced near at hand. That of Dan developed far beyond the biblical hint into a scenario with props of technology. Ships and nets and expertise were embraced in a species of idolatry, while reality passed them by in amazing fashion (the "stars in their courses fought against Sisera," and Jael nailed his head to her tent floor).

While Donne infrequently but consistently disparaged stage comedies as "not . . . unlawfull . . . but . . . prophane diversions" and while he scarcely noticed tragedy, the comparison with the Christian moralist Ben Jonson is suggestive.[32] Jonson, in message and medium, in argument, folio, and stage productions, was taking theater more seriously than Donne. He regarded the stage as a better representative of the truth and as more vigorously redemptive than Donne would allow. Yet we see a certain reinforcing complementarity: For Donne, waxing instrumentalisms and technologies appeared as the ephemeral props of a perennial meretricious theatricalism. Jonson's resent-

32. The words quoted are from V, S16, 120–25. Elsewhere, Donne characterized comedies as "unseasonable comforts" (III, S8, 468–70), associated with merely seeing the company (IV, S6, 490–92, spectatorship "even to Church") or "lighter affections" (V, S14, 972–74), as "miserable comforters" (VIII, S10, 330–32, S13, 490–92), as that which would merely "weare out . . . the afternoon" (IX, S18, 387–88) or (ironically) "passe my time" (X, S1, 541–44). The fault is not in our genres but in our selves: "The book of *Job* is a representation of God, in a Tragique-Comedy, lamentable beginnings, comfortably ended" (IX, S5, 38–39). The world can be made a tragic stage: Any son or daughter of the King of Heaven who is indifferent to society "prepares for a Tragedy . . . in the Amphitheater, the double Theater, this world and the next too" (IX, S13, 482–83). The Renaissance stage tragedy of blood can suggest divine order, though with limited forcefulness (VIII, S14, 748–51). Of course, secular drama is liable both onstage and in the perceiver's attitude to decay to mere titillation: the already-cited "obscenities and scurrilities of a Comedy, or the drums and ejulations of a Tragedy" (III, S12, 578–79). These were the later expressions, this was the philosophically coherent (albeit with some ambivalence) view of the Donne who had, when young, been "not dissolute but very neat; a great visitor of Ladies, a great frequenter of Playes" (Sir Richard Baker, *A Chronicle of the Kings of England* [London, 1643], 156).

ment of eclipse by Inigo Jones and of masque flummery is well known. More important, his *Alchemist, The Devil Is an Ass,* and *The Staple of News* powerfully dramatized meretricious assorted idols of the laboratory, engineering site, or factoid factory. For Donne, however distracting (*e.g.,* from sadness) stage time may be, it will, absent grace, be time and representation unredeemed. For Jonson, the increasingly hectic quality of stage time was part of the beneficently cautionary message for the reflective viewer. Donne had his own version of raging comic acceleration, what Claudius in a tragic context called "the hectic in my blood." It was disarticulated event time, of *tuchē,* latterly identified as something like a mental virus of the modern world, tychastic time.[33] At St. Paul's on Midsummer Day, 1622, Donne reflected on the miracle of God having created each person from nothing and on how God might well have stopped short (at toad or heathen or Papist) of placing the human listener / reader there and then in a peaceful land and reformed church. But the response could be to act as if all this from nothing were "done . . . for nothing":

> Thou passest thorough this world, like a *flash,* like a *lightning,* whose beginning or end no body knowes, like an *Ignis fatuus* in the aire, which does not onely not give light for any use, but not so much as portend or signifie any thing; and thou passest out of the world, as thy hand passes out of a basin of water, which may bee somewhat the fouler for thy washing it, but retaines no other impression of thy having been there; and so does the world for thy life in it. (IV, S5, 135–42)

This was the reverse of benign moment as generative of profounder, more abundant life: chronological time as meaningless moments disconnected from one another by their emptiness of charitable love. Donne liked the formulation so well that he repeated it verbatim but with expansions for emphasis at Whitehall early in 1628 (VIII, S7, 70–118).[34]

33. By, for notable examples, Loren Eiseley, historian of science; Allen Tate, classically educated critic and poet; and Lewis Mumford, urbanist-historian. See n. 7, above; see, too, Bakhtin on time in the romance in "Forms of Time and of the Chronotope in the Novel" in *The Dialogic Imagination,* esp. 94.

34. Similarly, with glances at the prototypical bad moment of unlife (and Donne's nearest feint toward Manichaeanism): of *relapse* into a former sin, "it is born an *Adam,* in full strength the first minute; born a Giant, born a Devil, and possesses us in an instant" (I, S3, 403–405); of "ill senses" of images, "an ill serpent, that did devour us all at once" (IV, S3, 506–508). The

As we have urged before, the theologically, liturgically, existentially critical trope of moment worked in a dialectic of complementarity with the tropes of theater, journey, and calling, which foregrounded *continuing* temporality as action in space, even narrative. The sermon itself is in swiftest reading no thing of a moment. Insofar as it was in delivery an argumentative exposition, it proceeded linearly through *parts,* even *branches* or *rooms.*[35] Insofar as it was an appeal to the affections of the communicant's will, including the appeal by enactment of the quickening of the preacher's own devotion, it was semidramatic.[36] The preacher's argumentative and affective action was, of course, confined to the small circuit of the pulpit. But the pulpit was an elegantly crafted site of exposition on the mighty acts of God held in mind by altar with crucifix, the tablets of the law, and the baptismal font. The pulpit was auditorily commanding in the space of the people's *work,* the *leitourgos.*

Milton's unfallen Adam and Eve did the people's work, in both a morning hymn and an evening—both expressions manifestly as heartfelt and elegant as their verse is blank, expressions that were intimated (albeit not shown) to be always a new song. But here and now, Donne implicitly said, the fall and human freedom in conjunction have endowed divine omniscience with a quality of spectatorship.[37] The world was a stage in that sense and all persons necessarily players, but in their freedom they may be players for well or ill. To the Virginia Company, in exhortation to "act over the *Acts* of the *Apostles,*" he

carnival license may long have been regarded by Donne as another sort of bad moment; he paid to decline the Mastership of the Revels at Lincoln's Inn in 1594 (R. C. Bald, *John Donne: A Life* [New York, 1970], 56–57).

35. See, for example, the three *scenes,* "three objects, three subjects" in the sermon for the marriage of Margaret Washington, May 30, 1621, on Hosea 2:19: "And I will marry thee unto me for ever."

36. And was received as somewhat dramatic. See, for example, the testimonies to Donne's delivery in the commendatory poems furnished posthumously for his *Poems* (1633). *Cf.* Jonson's Epigram No. 75: The Puritan "*Lippe,* at *Pauls,* ranne from his text away, / T'inveigh 'gainst playes: What did he then but play?"

37. See Peter King, "The Reasons for the Abolition of the Book of Common Prayer in 1645," *Journal of Ecclesiastical History,* XXI (1970), 327–39. He judges that *abolitionist* Scots and London Presbyterians overcame a *reform*-minded Puritan majority, on grounds of anticommunal, particularist individualism and notions of "lethargy" rather than liturgy as the antithesis of extemporaneity, but they "turned an unpopular work into a popular one."

affirmed, "Beloved, you are *Actors* upon the same Stage" (IV, S10, 5–6). Conversely, "Not solitude, but company is the scene of pride" (II, S14, 294), the compulsive scripting of a self-centered world through idolatry of self-regarding would-be-gods. More inclusively, not to embrace the true and lively play of ambassadorship was to be implicated in both acting and scripting manifold sordid feignings: "Where there is not the fear of God in great persons, other men dare not proceed clearly with them, but with disguises and Modifications . . . where there is not this fear of God, there is no directness." (I, S6, 447–52).[38]

Fortunately, hopeful occasions were powerfully at hand because the church afforded them liturgically, and the church was everyone's place of weekly resort to a degree that Court, Temple, Exchange, or other scenes of "great persons" were not. The church supplied and structured those moments that could serve as beginnings for good actions: the "new man" to "put on a new-production, and generation of effects out of other causes" (III, S16, 47–49) or the guests of a marriage service and sermon wherein those witnesses, like a cast at a rehearsal, could hear the preacher "shift the scene thrice" to delineate marriages in Paradise, in the Church, and finally in heaven, where an ultimate denouement would abrogate all disguises and false selves before an audience of the true (III, S11, on Hosea 2:19).[39] Lenten observances "celebrate by a poor and weak imitation, the fasting of our Savior"—poor and weak but not reprehensible for that (I, S6, 52–53). In the moment of Holy Communion, taken in its liturgical context, "all that that body suffered, is offered again . . . and the Father is intreated" and "in the absolution of the Minister there is a concur-

38. At one point he quotes from Augustine's Sermon 19 of *De Verbis Apostoli*: "*Quale certamen! Theatrum mundus, spectator Deus*" (III, S10, 205–206). Neither there at Whitehall nor in III, S3, 56–57 at Lincoln's Inn did a parenthesis about theatricality seem to need explanation or excuse. Something like the movement toward love we identify in Donne's sermons is identified in Augustine's *Confessions* and *On Christian Doctrine* by Geoffrey Galt Harpham, *The Ascetic Imperative in Culture and Criticism* (Chicago, 1987); relevant to Donne is the concluding (and metatheatrical) point that all reader-interpreters "are ascetics" in the sense of finally subjecting "subjectivity to the extra subjective" (134).

39. See Richard A. Batey, "Sepphoris: An Urban Portrait of Jesus," *Biblical Archaeology Review,* XVIII, No. 3 (May / June, 1992), 50–62, and (behind it) his *Jesus and the Forgotten City* (Grand Rapids, 1991). Sepphoris, with its open-air theater, was within sight of Nazareth. See, further, "disguises . . . pretenses of *publique good,* with which men of power and authority apparel their oppressions of the poore" (III, S17, 561–65). And see n. 47, below, for connections with issues of relative distance or mediation.

rence of medecines of all qualities; purgative in confession, and restorative in absolution; corasive in the preaching of Judgements, and cordial in the balm of the sacrament" (II, S12, 222–23, 243–46). The Church by ministry of sacrament and word could direct and prompt the middle of any action: "*We are made a spectacle to men and angels* [1 Cor. 4:9]. The word is there *theatrum*. . . . therefore let us be careful to play those parts well, which even the *Angels* desire to see well acted" (III, S9, 429–33).[40]

The liturgy and sermon together also embraced the trope of theater, which afforded a medium for the preacher to caution himself as well as his parishioners. "Nay, how often is the Pulpit it selfe, made the shop, and the theatre of praise upon present men, and God left out?" (IV, S12, 166–67). "Shop" and "theatre" betokened differing disorders of love: the less selfish and the more selfish misattribution of love. Often enough, twentieth-century readers fastidiously disdain Renaissance flattery; too seldom has notice been taken of such stern recognition.

Thoughtful hearers or readers of the words quoted above would understand them to reinforce the unobtrusive tropism of a passage a little earlier: "A recognition . . . a second, a ruminated, a reflected knowledge: Beasts doe remember, but they doe not remember that they remember; they doe not reflect upon it, which is that that constitutes memory" (114–16, Candlemas Day, on Rom. 13:7: "Render therefore to all men their dues"). Human memory implied and entailed reflection: the mind as theater with self as spectator, a potentially graced and regenerate configuration. Correlatively, glossing cryptic mental activity as theater could externalize it in communal discourse, likewise a redemptive activity. So Donne said with more emphatic explicitness in a sermon at St. Paul's at Easter Evening Prayer, 1623, when he explained at the end of his preliminary division of Acts 2:36 that speaker / auditor participation in the sermon would be analogous to enactment of a masque: "And when we have paced, and passed through all these steps, we shall in some measure have solemnized this day of the Resurrection of Christ; and in some measure have made it the day of our Redemption too" (IV, S14, 47–50).

"In some measure": The measure depended, not of course on Whitehall, Lambeth Palace, or any institutionalized power, but on love. In its absence or

40. All such language of putting on (new man, armor of light, Christ) alludes to Romans 13:12–14. Resurrection (leading bodily to Judgment) was, of course, "the last scean of this last act of man" (IV, S2, 23).

misorientation, entrance to church could be, equally with attendance at secular "Comedies . . . Masques," a scene of inspection, in polar contrast to scene of entrance to heaven as grateful love (IV, S6, 490–509). The course or scenario of seriously misoriented loves may be unpredictably punctuated with ironic denouements: "He can sink down the Stage and the Player, the bed of wantonness, and the wanton actor, into the jaws of the earth, into the mouth of hell: he can surprise thee, even in the act of sin" (I, S2, 318–21, at Whitehall, on Ecclesiastes 8:11).

Opposite the numberless sordid feignings when there was "not the fear of God in great persons" was the ramifying typological drama of love of God and neighbor, "that is, faith and works" (II, S12, 207–208):

> Heare in those words, the Word. . . . that whole Sermon is not the word of God. But yet all the Sermon is the Ordinance of God. . . . Take delight in God's ordinance, in mans preaching, and thou wilt finde Gods Word in that. . . . if ye will heare the same Jesus . . . The holy Ghost shall fall upon you . . . accompany you home . . . make your domestique peace there, *a type* of your union with God in heaven; and make your eating and drinking there, *a type* of the abundance, and fulnesse of heaven; and make every dayes rising to you there, *a type* of your joyfull Resurrection to heaven; and every nights rest, *a type* of your eternall Sabbath; and your very dreames, prayers, and meditations, and sacrifices to Almighty God. (V, S1, 762–98; our emphases)

Theater and theatricality as properly humane (*i.e.,* created good) self-consciousness, as rehearsal or reconfirmation of true self, and as acting faithfully one's true ambassadorial calling not only redeemed the trope but also redeemed theater itself as a possible location of the hope of salvific journey. Debased theatricality—life as irreality (mummery), life as powerlessness (scripted by others), life as falsity (in response), life as power (unloving scripter / director)—might accord with journey as misdirection either perverse or seduced. Of course; that went without saying, though Puritans said it tediously and often. That mattered little theologically because Donne was as anti-Manichaean as the Martin Luther whose familiar hymn alluded to "our ancient foe" and proclaimed, "lo! his doom is sure." But it mattered socially, because Donne saw his world threatened with increasing disintegration, at home and abroad, into discord, division, and war.

Finally, for Donne, the trope of journey gave welcome coherence and substantiality to features of life as day-to-day flux (and even to the salvific round of the liturgical year) that the trope of theater slighted. On the one hand, the notion of lifelong journey back to God (or at least to judgment) affirmed a coherence subsuming all missteps, detours, and theatrical ludes and interludes. On the other hand, as any traveler knew, the notion of journey also implied unscripted vicissitude and casualty: shipwreck and "exit pursued by a bear."[41] It was the perception of destination or its lack, of purpose or its lack, that governed the different views of journey.

Journey tended also to emphasize a self and to emphasize it as an oriented and bodily self. So journey as trope tended to reinforce calling to ambassadorship as trope and to supplement (as an alternative) the bounded self often implicit in the trope of theater (bounded by scripted role, by sanctioned costume, or by conventional disguises) as well as the temporal limitations implied in the trope of moment. While it may be vital (as our poets agreed) for the self to be *centered,* love and power alike testified to the unsatisfactory quality of the image of *bounded* self and pointed toward the more spacious tropes of journey and ambassadorship.[42]

Journey as metonymy, metaphor, or synecdoche aptly repairs, supplements, or contests theatrics in other ways. Donne contested any tendency to idolatries of scene or scenario, as when he said and wrote, "Here we are but *Viatores*. . . . thou canst not build thy hopes here. . . . bury not thy selfe, thy labours, thy affections upon this world" (III, S13, 499–502). It supplements

41. For misscripting or misdirection of the self to or into comedies and tragedies (in playhouse or at large), see, for example, III, S12, 56–79, and I, S3, 899–901; see also Bakhtin, *The Dialogic Imagination,* esp. 99–126.

42. For an excellent critique of the bad metaphor of a bounded self, see Jennifer Nedalsky, "Law, Boundaries, and the Bounded Self," *Representations,* No. 30 (Spring, 1990), 162–89. See also Jonathan Crewe, "The Theatre of the Idols: Marlowe, Rankins, and Theatrical Images," *Theatre Journal,* XXXVI (1984), 321–44. For Rankins, "*all* theatrical phenomena" are monstrous and culturally threatening; for Crewe (albeit unthreatened), the "substance of the self . . . dissolves in the Elizabethan theatrical world of magnified appearances." Dissolved into or bounded by theatrical images comes to much the same thing. Crewe, like Rankins and subsequent Puritans, has the Bad News right but not the Good News that Donne, Jonson, Marvell, and Milton believed in; for Shakespeare, more than for Milton, theater could be either deceptive or instrumental in identifying "What our seemers be." See also, for its richly extensive treatment, Jonas Barish, *The Antitheatrical Prejudice* (Berkeley, 1981), and Timothy Murray, *Theatrical Legitimation: Allegories of Genius in Seventeenth Century England and France* (New York, 1987). For overt alignments of journey with calling, see, for example, the high (as if ridgeline) middle way and thoroughfare at III, S11, 383–85, and the thicket at III, S17, 323–30.

and repairs the tendency of theatrics to exaggerate the literal surface of costume and the figurative surface of the publicly audible and observable by always implying the solidity, kinesthetics, and partial hiddenness of *body.* Donne referred to this tendency early in his ministry, to the strayings of the vagabond heart, or heart in perpetual motion but potentially ballasted by love of purity (I, S2, 421ff., S3, 787ff.). Somewhat later, he quoted approvingly Deuteronomy 30:17–18: "If the heart turn away . . . you shall surely perish" (III, S4, 584).

The trope of journey, moreover, critically qualified the trope of moment. A few lines after professing us *Viatores,* he characteristically specified his meaning: "Here thou art no more then a *sojourner;* but yet remember withall that thou art so much, thou art a *sojourner.* This life is not a Parenthesis . . . that belongs not to the sense . . . that might be left out, as well as put in. More depends upon this life then so: upon every moment of this life, depends millions of yeares in the next, and I shall be glorified eternally, or eternally lost, for my good or ill use of God's grace offered to me in this house" (III, S13, 510–17). This glossed somewhat more generally and abstractly some remarks made in more particular, secondarily metaphorical terms in earlier sermons: In our "course of Sanctification . . . we must be thrifty all our life" and not rely on a potentially bankrupting death-bed splurge of charity (I, S1, 191ff.); we must follow a course of diet, not "physick" (I, S3, 479ff.); "we must not coast and cross the nearest way," not take temporal shortcuts but abide God's seasons. Although the journey may be a very long haul, each moment was understood as vital though usually limited, some moments crucial, all in opposition to that tychastic time "that might be left out as well as put in." Donne in the pulpit stood with the creator of Sansjoy *et al.,* the creator of the unfortunate traveler Jack Wilton, the creator of Macbeth "deep in blood," the creator of serpent gourmandizers of Dead Sea apples. Donne's parenthetical time was mere event-time, tychastic time, toward which lived experience degenerated insofar as it was not articulated by the syntax of *caritas* and freedom, by the liturgic scenario of reparative journeying. Time connected with eternity or not, and every moment was vital or not, insofar as it afforded a choice taken for or against love.

Donne was so given to construing lived experience in terms of journey that other metaphors, even when entailed by his chosen text, could give way to it. In a sermon on Proverbs 25:16 about eating only a sufficiency of honey, an obsessive-compulsive "appetite" for office and tithes suddenly modulated into "a winding staire," a ladder "set a slope"; for "though our meanes be direct in their owne nature, yet wee put them upon crooked wayes" (III, S10, 335–46). Apt for imaging occasional or compulsive deviousness, the trope could in his hands likewise image alternative attitudes from the grimly over-controlling to the feckless. As above, there was a hint of alternative scenarios: "Be not apt to thinke . . . the way to heaven a sullen *melancholy;* Heaven, and the way to it, is a *Communion of Saints,* is a holy cheerfulnesse. Get thou thither . . . but be not too hasty to think, *that no body* gets thither, except he go thy way in all opinions, and all actions. . . . Since God has brought us into a fair prospect, let us have *no retrospect* back; In Canaan, let us not look towards Aegypt, nor towards *Sodom,* being got to the Mountain" (III, S4, 275–79, 668–70).[43] So the journey was understood to be neither a quasi-military close-order drill nor a fortuitous errancy. Indeed, its dependency on the love of God (as grace) and the love of individual and communal selves for God (as constancy in faith), both conjunctions of the world and the transcendent, implicated the trope in paradox: "To follow [Christ] to the end . . . to beare afflictions . . . to bring our crosses to the Crosse of Christ . . . is a royall progresse, not a pilgrimage" (II, S14, 459–62). "Pilgrimage" here may be understood as what the secular world sees. Love as constancy in faith would give it (in Hamlet's words) "that within which passeth show."[44]

Beyond Eden, beyond Babel, the Church itself must be on the move, both morally and historically. In one place, he characterized it as something of a mobile Travelers' Aid: "Our Church hath gone a middle, and a moderate way" in appointing for Trinity Sunday an Old Testament lesson that "is an awaken-

43. See also III, S15, esp. 28–32, 187–88, 592–604: journey as divagation and *retorqueo* with regard to both persons and instruments and the self as "embarking" or passively undergoing "negligent passage" as a "fragmentary and incoherent" man who "embraces no Calling." Donne, who more than once embarked, did not use the word *embraces* without abundant sense of body and of care.

44. It was within the range of Donne's imagination and temper (but far less usual) to take the smoothing, regularizing, as-if-from-seven-miles-aloft view, as when he characterized our adoption in Christ and "our resurrection determine[d] in him" as the first and "last point of our Circle" (IV, S2, 175–81). See Walter R. Davis, "Meditation, Typology, and the Structure of Donne's Sermons," in *The Eagle and the Dove: Reassessing John Donne,* ed. Claude J. Summers and Ted-Larry Pebworth (Columbia, Mo., 1986), 166–88; meditation and typology are indeed resources of structuration as of distantiation and intimacy, potentially interactive. Davis' climactic instance of the Easter, 1628, sermon on 1 Corinthians 13:12 (VIII, S9) is particularly apposite in our view because of its terminus *explicitly* in love.

ing of that former knowledge which we had of the Trinity" (III, S5, 348–53). Tychastic time and teleological time were valid distinctions in the social as well as the individual spheres as Milton made clear in the last two books of *Paradise Lost.*

Journey could foster recognition of other forms of mediation, for example, of "natural reason," which might warn, like Balaam's ass, of misdirection (III, S17, 968–78). Or, more complexly, by the model of the Wise Men, who "by a Star . . . found the Son," we could come by "the beames of comfort in this life . . . to the body of the Sun, by the Rivers, to the Ocean" (III, S12, 516–31).[45] Again, mediation was subordinate to goal, which essentially gave character to the journey and to the individual's understanding of time.

Any designedly paradigmatic selection like this risks muting the edgy ambivalence of Donne's range as he advised himself and his city in response to what he saw as an ambiguously seductive century. The very modeling urged in the excerpt above (and elsewhere in his sermons) could emphasize the radical otherness of transcendence: "Were it not an impertinent thing for him that went to lye in France, to study Dutch? So if wee pretend to make the joyes of heaven our residence, it is madness to study the joys of the world" (III, S16, 289–90). Or the journey abruptly could become reflexive and unmollified by any communal first person plurals: Christ "hath been in a pilgrimage towards thee long . . . and how far is he got into thee yet?" (I, S9, 259–61).[46]

Finally, we conclude abruptly in regard to Donne's tireless engagement with the trope of journey, whether upward-bound, return-bound, reflexive, surprising or errant, with the mode of recognition: "He came to save; And whom? Sinners. Those, who the more they acknowledg themselves to be so, the nearer they are to this salvation" (I, S9, 47–49). Donne understood in theological terms that presence (short of heaven) also embodied absence and that presence depended on relationships of care and recognition of the need for grace rather than on visibility.[47] One corollary was that any "royal Pres-

45. See also III, S11, 383–85.

46. Citations could be multiplied illustrating his edgy sense of exacting demands and distracting misdirections through his modern "Israel" or "Jerusalem," so suggestive of Babel. The way is narrow and the gate strait (IV, S2, 402–406); afflictions need be borne in love of Christ, not with "the stupidity of a Stoique" or the "pertinacy of a Heretique" (I, S7, 105–10).

47. This can be confirmed by considering passages where he spoke of nearness. See, for some particularly useful examples: preacher's nearness to worshipper in III, S5, 297; the analogous nearness of divinity in III, S2, 523, S10, 73, S12, 401, S17, 316, and IV, S5, 538, S6, 131; wor-

ence" or "Presence chamber" was quite ironically so designated unless the king were truly and hence subordinately acting as agent of God *and* subjects were honoring the king only for that.

In the sermon at Whitehall in 1618 cited above, Donne repeated the point about recognition with a metadialogic meaning: "The end of preaching, [is] to make men capable of salvation by acknowledging themselves to be sinners" (489–90); it is essentially an outer and general dialogue aimed at an inner and individual one. Any hearer or reader of Donnean dialogue is urged to a sense of the *contingency* of that dialogue. We are "not in the School, but in the Pulpit," "not upon a Lecture, but a Sermon," he remarked in two of his earlier sermons (I, S4, 429–30; II, S15, 352).[48] The distinction, for him, was between

shipper in the liturgy as thereby nearer to the "Communion of Saints" in IV, S2, 788. Conversely, for hypocrisy as *distance,* see IV, S2, 842–60. Separatists might, of course, deny that any script repeated by a second person could in the fallen world be free of hypocrisy, might deny that "Common Prayer" could be the people's Godly work. For the valuable political construal of seeking "nearness," see Shami, "Donne's Sermons and the Absolutist Politics of Quotation," esp. 391, which cites the first example above.

Before canvassing other and secondary responses to the issue, it should be noted that *hypocrisy* from Greek classical and biblical times has referred to, or at least been associated with, stage playing and ambiguously so. More exactly, the root (*krino / krina / kritas,* to judge / judgment / a judge) is not negative in classical Greek. The derived forms *hupocrisis,* a reply or answer, a part played, or the declamation of a poem or formal speech, and *hupokritas,* one who answers or expounds or acts a part on stage, give, secondarily for both words, the sinister meaning of (respectively) "feigning" and "dissembler." In New Testament Greek, the sinister meaning prevailed in the usages of Matthew, Mark, and Luke and in the words attributed to Jesus. But the literally theatrical element has been obscured by the translation, which, in the Authorized Version as in others, has sometimes simply been transliterated (as with Jesus speaking of the Pharisees at Matthew 22 and 23), or translated as "feign," as of the spies who would feign to be just (Luke 20:20). Similarly, but in a further half-turn, the privative *anhupokritos* has been translated "unfeigned," as in "unfeigned love" (1 Pet. 1:22) and as in "faith unfeigned" (1 Tim. 1:5). As archaeological scholarship has reinforced our sense of the urban and commercial elements in the biblical landscape, of Nazareth itself seemingly adjunctive to a city, it is proper to recognize the trope of theater in biblical uses of words from the verb *hupokrinomai.*

48. We would urge caution in attaching any other than arithmetical significance to the mere "earliness" or "lateness" (in Donne's preaching career) of a given sermon. The claims of the liturgy (always), of the greater or lesser learning or the greater or lesser intimacy of the auditory (slightly), and of political urgencies (very occasionally) all impinge more discernibly on

mere conveyance of information, or linear explanation, and encouraging devotion. Moreover, "the School" adverts to Rome and Tridentine theology as well as to an academic setting, and "a Lecture" presumably discounts the practice, typically Puritan, of what we have called "free-standing" sermons. Puritans even endowed them, called them lectures or lectureships, and expected and got hortatory argument standing clear of liturgy, though perchance tied to a liturgical time such as Easter or a secular anniversary such as "Powder Day," November 5. The Paul's Cross sermons, including Donne's (IV, S7; VII, S17; IX, S4; and " 'Spital Cross," IV, S3) probably best represent the Church of England's traffic in that mode.[49]

Thus for him the sermon stood between taxonomic theological monologue and monologically coercive harangue. The sermon was dialogic in two senses, encouraging the hearer / reader to take a "responsive attitude" toward the sermon and to take an active step toward salvation. Walter Ong long ago scotched the bad analogy of speaking / hearing to radio sending / receiving, and Mikhail Bakhtin, that magnificent enhancer of intellectual images we rudimentarily already had, has elaborated: "The fact is that when the listener perceives and understands the meaning of speech, he simultaneously takes an active, responsive attitude toward it. . . . Any understanding of live speech, a live utterance, is inherently responsive, although the degree of this activity varies extremely."[50] The question here is far less how responsive Donne's actual listeners were in surveyable historical fact (even if it were surveyable) than how far the responses of the implied, the invited readers / hearers of the text, of which Donne himself was one, went in terms of the rhetorically im-

---

the sermons than any supposed curve of development. Donne began preaching as an ecclesiologically and rhetorically learned man and died lamentably few years later; no quasi-Beethovenian periodization is appropriate for that sixteen-year period. We note the general agreement, on this point, of Paul Stanwood, "Donne's Earliest Sermons and the Penitential Tradition," in *John Donne's Religious Imagination,* ed. Frontain and Malpezzi, 366–79; on the political consistency, Shami notes advice both principled and acceptable to both James I and Charles I ("Donne's Sermons and the Absolutist Politics of Quotation," 404).

49. See Millar MacLure, *The Paul's Cross Sermons, 1534–1642* (Toronto, 1958).

50. Walter J. Ong, "Voice as Summons to Belief," in *Literature and Belief,* ed. Meyer Abrams (New York, 1957); Mikhail Bakhtin, "The Problem of Speech Genres," in *Speech Genres and Other Late Essays,* trans. Vern W. McGee (Austin, 1986), 68, and *The Dialogic Imagination,* esp. 249, 259ff. For interactive taxonomies of time / typology and soul / meditation, see Davis, "Meditation, Typology, and the Structure of John Donne's Sermons," 166–88.

plicit journey toward salvation. Bakhtin put it concisely: "Any speaker is himself a respondent to a greater or lesser degree. He is not, after all, the first speaker, the one who disturbs the eternal silence of the universe."[51] The Donne situated in the liturgy was always responding to a universe in the beginning of which was the Word.

For Donne, the responsiveness of himself or of anyone else in the priesthood of all believers, of any member of the body of faithful people with Christ as head, would be responsiveness of degree so critical as to become dispositive in kind. In a very important sermon on Acts 10:22 at the dedication of the new chapel at Lincoln's Inn, he referred to the Holy Ghost as respondent (earlier in Acts 10) to St. Peter. Donne's reflections featured the hope of divinely and abruptly decisive moment:

> When the holy Ghost takes a man into his schoole, he deales not with him, as a Painter . . . but he deales as a Printer, that in one straine delivers a whole story. We see that in this example of St. *Peter,* St. *Peter* had conceived a doubt, whether it were lawfull for him to preach the Gospel to any of the Gentiles, because they were not within the Covenant. . . . This very scruple was the voyce and question of God in him: to come to a doubt, and to a debatement in any religious duty, is the voyce of God in our conscience: Would you know the truth? Doubt, and then you will inquire: And *facile solutionem accepit anima, quae prius dubitavit,* sayes St. *Chrysostome.* As no man resolves of any thing wisely, firmely, safely, of which he never doubted, so neither doth God withdraw a resolution from any man, that doubts with an humble purpose to settle his owne faith, and not with a wrangling purpose to shake another mans. . . . *Peter* thus prepared by the Holy Ghost, was to prepare others for the Holy Ghost. (V, S1, 95–128)

We pass by the theological point of Peter's scruple being defined as Ghostly questioning (an enormous special case of prevenient grace, in that it extended to "*our* conscience"). The more culturally pertinent point began with the extension to *any religious duty.* Where would "religious duty" begin or end? To say that a duty was purely secular would be to make a religious determination that would perforce make the secular duty analogous to the ecclesiastic category of *adiaphora,* that is, 'things indifferent' to salvation because not intrinsic

51. Bakhtin, "The Problem of Speech Genres," 69.

to the faith and to obedience embodying the love of the believer for God. So Donne extended "religious duty" to "any thing," making all duty, social and personal, subject to debate in religious terms. Or rather, the only absolutism acknowledged was the claim of God. Claims of church, king, or *polis* must be construed in subordination to it.

And what of *adiaphora*? We suppose he would have included in that category the merest conventions and practices of everyday life, like reading left to right, hat with brim up or down . . . perhaps child's play. But though Donne spoke in various roles in the sermons, and sometimes proposed therein something like scenarios for his auditors' adoption, we understand him as doing so less in the dramatistic sense than as a statesman in the City of God. His sense of contingency and his noncoerciveness were the dialogue of love, as the great alternative to secular power.[52]

"Beloved," said Donne again and again in dialogic address to his auditories at Lincoln's Inn and St. Paul's, thereby decisively altering discourse for the better. Who does not always already know that? Yet Latimer, Andrewes, and Tillotson did not talk that way. It was as a dialogic statesman of the City of God that Donne respectfully quoted and expansively amended St. John Chrysostom. It was as loving subordinate to God that he trusted to serene *settling* (not annihilation) of doubts for those similarly humble in spirit and disdained the uncharity of wrangling. Peter was defined with the Holy Ghost as prerequisite to dialogue "to prepare others" for dialogue with the Holy Ghost. Likewise Donne in the pulpit of chapel or cathedral and in the implicit pulpit of quarto or folio page.[53]

As if out of the pulpit and brother at the elbow of reader or pew-occupant,

52. Thus we resolve in disagreement with Anna Nardo's "John Donne at Play in Between" in her *The Ludic Self* (Albany, 1990), though her consideration of the sermons as devout and serious play is a necessary part of our "debatement."

53. "Wrangling" was for Donne, as for Hooker, dispute with charity absent, as "The more disputing the less believing" (III, S10, 549, and context). Donne acknowledged the lesser forcefulness of "things written" in comparison to things spoken, in a cover letter to the Countess of Montgomerie, along with his sermon on Matthew 21:44. But, he insists, "The Spirit of God that . . . is present in his tongue or hand, meets himself again . . . in the eise and eares and hearts of the hearers and readers: and that Spirit, which is ever the same to an equall devotion [*i.e.,* love of God], makes a writing and a speaking equall meanes to edification" (II, p. 179). Jane Tylus, *Writing and Vulnerability in the Late Renaissance* (Palo Alto, 1993), argues resistance as the implied and inevitable other of power; perhaps, but in her neo-Foucauldian terms there

Donne always insisted the human option was one dialogue or else another: "We may pore upon *books,* stare upon *preachers,* yet if we reflect nothing, nothing upon our *conversation,* we shall still remain under the increpation and malediction of St. *Paul*" (IV, S8, 82–85). Refusal of response and action on the one hand could only mean being talked to and talked *about* (a reductive status) on the other. Reflective dialogue with the preacher would be variously internalization, exteriorization, and model (metonymy, metaphor, synecdoche) of dialogue with the self. The self must perennially "proceed" with the self in attempting "competent witness" to conscience, as in the "*Civill warre*" of "flesh . . . against the Spirit" (IV, S5, 198, 224; IV, S7, 531).

For Donne, dialogue with the self and dialogue of the self with God in spirit, Scripture, or liturgy were less bounded and distinct actions than matters of hermeneutic recirculation. He asked, "What did you mean by it, when, even now, you said with me, in the *Lords prayer, thy kingdome come*?" And he reflected that we surely must not have been presuming on the Day of Judgment, but rather intending "the blessed state . . . in the Kingdome of God in this life; Peace in the State, peace in the Church, peace in our Conscience," considering that "In this, wee answer the motions of his blessed Spirit here" (III, S3, 434–36, 494–97). Accordingly, too, he concluded that Job's and Paul's "texts [on bodily resurrection] answer one another, so your resurrections may answer one another too" (III, S4, 693–94, with references to III, S3), in a "resurrection of grace" in answer to the preacher. Beyond that, "God is often said to *heare* and *answer* in the Scriptures, when they to whom he speaks, have said nothing" (IV, S2, 780).

Thus, the ideal of dialogue was understood as divinely instituted and indeed enscripted in the Book of Creatures, where it remained available for human embrace and enactment. In an early Whitehall sermon, an immense paragraph on divine saying was centered on "a Dialogue in the making of man" and, there and in a gigantic following paragraph, on the dialogic "shadow, a representation of our second Creation, our Regeneration in Christ, and of the saving knowledge of God" (I, S8, 160–65). That modeling in turn was to be the quintessential work, not of the king (however much de-

---

would be no way out, since truly new knowledges or vocabularies would be unintelligible, whereas in her example of *The Winter's Tale,* as in ours of the sermons (and some Jonson), love is the Klein-bottle topology of outside and inside being continuous.

fender of the faith and father of the realm) but rather a work of the preacher and dialogue: "If, then, we have begot you in Christ, by our preaching, you also beget by your holy life and conversation. . . . you have preached over our Sermons again, as fruitfully as we our selves" (III, S16, 548–51). *If:* characteristically contingent, incipiently interrogative. As liturgy was the supremely legitimate theater, so the liturgical interaction of the preacher and listener or reader in challenge and response and identification and differentiation was, never necessarily, the supremely generative dialogue.[54]

But what of the commanding, title-creating voice of the king? Did not the king speak? Of course, and ideally his speech would be animated by the Spirit of God. In any case, however, his speech would be accepted responsively, ideally parsed by that same Spirit in the listener. Did money talk? Yes, Donne might have said, but such instruments, like jesting Pilate, damnably stayed not for an answer.

"We," the hearers and readers, must also respond. Neither intentional nor affective fallacy is involved in so saying. One who *has* heard or read has been too multifariously engaged not to respond, albeit in some unpredictable mixture of acquiescence, denial, or resistance. Some Puritanical hearers demurred, one of Donne's elegists indicated. The original hearer actually and subsequent reader implicitly had liturgically confessed faith and sin and been absolved of the latter in the strength of the former by (the Prayer Book insisted) the grace of God. Accordingly, that addressee, that "beloved," must as quasi-theatrical actor / spectator / director decide whose journey and where, decide significant moment or not, accept or not accept calling as ambassadorship. More particularly, believers, Puritans, and secularists had to contend with the implications of such questions as "[Shall we] change all our disputation into thanksgiving, and all our *utrums,* and *quares,* and *quandos* of the school, to the *Benedictus* and *Alelujahs* and *Osanna's* of the Church?" (I, S9, 126–29). Or, again, was there still "Here, in the militant Church upon earth . . . a reconciliation to be made; not only toward one another, in the band of charity, but in our selves?" (IV, S11, 646–48). Would we all, to what degree do we all, say as the preacher said (in the voice of the Apocalyptic John) to the wedding guests at St. Clement Danes, whom he hoped to meet again in

54. See also Shami, on the aggrandizement of preacherly conscience with respect to the king, "Kings and Desperate Men," esp. 14–15. Donne famously engaged the patristic exegetical tradition, sometimes like a chief of staff (as in III, S18, 221–22, 335–73, and *passim*), sometimes with diffidence (as at IV, S2, 57–78).

Heaven, "I shall see the Sunne black as sackcloth of hair . . . the Starres fall as a Figge-tree casts her untimely Figges . . . I shall see a divorce between Princes and their Prerogatives" (III, S11, 495–98). It was a wedding sermon, ending in apocalyptic vision and concluding prayer for the present moment. Princes were acknowledged to be souls as properly brides of Christ as were other souls. Their other prerogatives, however, were judged superfluous to the *saeculum* of love.

5

"O Rare Ben Jonson"

We begin with the Westminster Abbey epitaph that has become a commonplace but still retains its truth. For it is the rarity of Ben Jonson that we shall consider—rarity in the sense of Jonson's fierce and undeviating devotion to virtue on earth and the Christian journey to Paradise. Furthermore, Jonson was that rarest sort of moralist, one who was neither a Puritan or Jansenist nor a joyless curmudgeon who saw only malice and distemper everywhere. We also understand Jonson to have described both the *civitas terrena* and the *civitas Dei* in his poetry and plays, as moral instruction in classical virtue and Christian journey and as a witty depiction of urban and courtly life as Londoners then knew it. Like Donne, Jonson was intensely a London poet and additionally a London playwright, one of many writing and publishing for a metropolis of letters, including the court as well as the city, in an environment of substantial freedom of thought, for all the censorship, combined with even more substantial opportunities for profit, place, preferment, and patronage.[1] And, finally, we concur with massive contemporary opinion that Jonson possessed that rarest thing of all, that which Kent had seen in the face of Lear, authority.

In his "ripest . . . studies," his *Epigrammes,* published in 1616, Jonson included this couplet:

1. Barbara Everett, "Donne: A London Poet," *Proceedings of the British Academy,* LVIII (1972), 245–73; David Norbrook, "The Monarchy of Wit and the Republic of Letters: Donne's Politics," in *Soliciting Interpretation: Literary Theory and Seventeenth-Century English Poetry,* ed. Elizabeth D. Harvey and Katharine Eisaman Maus (Chicago, 1990), 3–36.

He that feares death, or mournes it, in the just
Shewes of the resurrection little trust.
(XXXIV)[2]

The assertion that human life centered on the "blessed Passion, mightie ressurreccyon and gloryous ascencion," as the communion service of *The Book of Common Prayer* phrased it, might seem out of place in a book of poems devoted ostensibly to praise and blame within the secular temporal realm. So, too, might our contention for the centrality to that collection of that center, since there were certainly epigrams in wide variety upon human vice, folly, virtue, or early death. The poems in praise of Sir John Roe, a close friend who died in Jonson's arms, celebrated civic virtue, which Jonson valued and wished both to anatomize and to increase.[3] But even here, where civic virtue, a humanist and Stoic good, was eulogized, the scent of death and the expectation of salvation followed:

Glad-mention'd *Roe:* thou art but gone before,
Whither the world must follow. And I, now,
Breathe to expect my when, and make my how.
(XXXIII, 2–4)

The "better ornaments, my teares and verse" (XXVII, 2) were directed not only to praise of human virtue, here given knightly form (scutcheons), but

2. We are using William B. Hunter, Jr., ed., *The Complete Poetry of Ben Jonson* (Garden City, N.Y., 1963). We have ignored the printer's convention of capitalizing the second letter of each poem's initial word. We have consulted the long-standard but increasingly contested *Ben Jonson,* ed. C. H. Herford and Percy and Evelyn Simpson (11 vols.; Oxford, 1925–52). We have quoted from *Ben Jonson, Five Plays,* ed. G. A. Wilkes (Oxford, 1988); *Catiline,* ed. W. F. Bolton and Jane F. Gardner (Lincoln, 1973); *Sejanus,* ed. W. F. Bolton (London, 1966); *The Staple of News,* ed. Devra Rowland Kifer (Lincoln, 1975).

3. See, for example, *Epigrammes,* XXVII, XXXII, XXXIII. See Katharine Eisaman Maus, *Ben Jonson and the Roman Frame of Mind* (Princeton, 1984), for the definitive treatment of this element of Jonson's horizon (which we judge secondary to his Christianity). For a particular element of Jonsonian classicism well shown to open out to more, see Robert C. Evans, "Wit and the Power of Jonson's *Epigrammes,*" in *The Wit of Seventeenth-Century Poetry,* ed. Claude Summers and Ted-Larry Pebworth (Columbia, Mo., 1995), 101–18. Horace's *ingenium,* from 'to beget,' Jonson translated "wit," by which he understood a life-giving power of both conceiving and judging; in a *moment,* we would add. See also n. 13 below. W. David Kay points out, shrewdly, that classicism was a valuable card to play in the rivalry for patronage in *Ben Jonson: A Literary Life* (New York, 1995), 41–42.

more importantly to heaven, where Roe's virtues had presumably directed him. The thought of heaven, however, was not confined just to Roe. The first of the three epigrams on him ended with a direction outward to those who still lived—a direction concerning their own just expectations:

> If any pious life ere lifted man
> To heaven; his hath: O happy state! Wherein
> Wee, sad for him, may glorie, and not sinne.
> (XXVII, 6–8)

What applied to virtue also applied to folly and vice, though not always as explicitly. Sir Voluptuous Beast, who earned a pair of epigrams, certainly fell short of civic virtue, or even private decency, as he instructed his "faire, and innocent wife" in the sensual techniques he had relished elsewhere. Even after the phase of debauching his "chast wife,"

> He' adulters still: his thoughts lye with a whore.
> (XXVI, 2)

Admittedly such epigrammatic sentiment, sternly moralistic and impeccably orthodox, was far from idiosyncratic with Ben Jonson. (We are reminded of the young groom in Jules Romain's *Men of Good Will* who was told by his father that his wife deserved respect and was not an appropriate object for the husband's sexual enthusiasm.)[4] Sir Voluptuous Beast, having corrupted himself, was further and obviously damned by corrupting the one person whom he had sworn, before God, to love and honor. This betrayal was explicitly cosmic in scale and consequence, hence the knight's full fall from a human, personal name to mere categorical label within a subhuman genus.

The same moral judgment appeared in the epigram to Banck the Usurer. Here a physical infirmity, gout, reflected a moral one, lending at excessive interest. If Banck's legs would not carry him well, his money would, and the destination of this journey of predatory profit was "to be at hell" (XXXI, 4). Similarly, the twin couplets addressed to Sir Cod reflected on the physical and spiritual odor of unsanctity. Sir Cod, the ill-favored wooer of women of a certain age and property, had used perfume to disguise his physical reek as well as his spiritual depravity. But the expense of aromatics was a vain thing, Jonson declared, unless Sir Cod could "weare them within," in his soul (XIX, XX). Or again, in the couplet "On Baudes, and Usurers" (LVII), prostitution and

4. Jules Romains, *Les Hommes de bonne volonté* (27 vols.; Paris, 1932–46).

money-lending were combined in profit and disease, with damnation the implied ultimate judgment, an ironic riddling equation of *ends* as money and *final* journey's ends, and *fruits* as enjoyments and those results by which "ye shall know them."

A similar pairing occurred in epigram XCVIII, "On Gut." Gut, an energetic and dedicated sinner, ate all day and whored all night, a kind of prodigy. Gut could "double his delight," while becoming a "thorough-fare of vice," as the wayfarer became the fairway. There was a further elaboration of Gut's virtuoso performance in sin:

> Thus, in his belly, can he change a sin
> Lust it comes out, that gluttony went in.
> (CXVIII, 5–6)

The final couplet was clever, and compared to Juvenal the touch was light, but its humor was grimly reductive of conventional poetic transformations, whether thought of as Ovidian or alchemical. Jonson wrote of Gut familiarly and identified him as depersonalized by his besetting sins, which had completely overborne all other aspects of his personality. The internal journey that was Gut's misplaced and misoriented love had carried him into degraded metonymic identity, far from the image and likeness of God (albeit with original sin), in which Jonson would assume every city neighbor to have been created (*cf.* Spenser's Gelousy). Such was the rationale for all the depersonalized metonymic or generic or vague identities, Groyne, Spies, Lady Would-bee, Some-Thing: they were more than fallen; they were seduced or self-perverted and were actively, transgressively departing from the Source of all identity. In contrast, the folk celebrated in many of the longer epigrams were understood to *fare well* (like the departed Elizabeth, L. H.) toward the Creator of male and female in the divine image, hence to manifest much more individualized human identity, as initially betokened by their proper names in titles.

Jonson was, of course, not engaged in sermonic explications of biblical texts, as was Donne, but the very embeddedness of the tropes suggests how he had internalized them. His "first daughter" and "first son," epigrammatically elegized, have in her case "parted," in his case been —shall we say *called*?— "exacted," both "hence," she to "virgin-traine," he "scap'd worlds, and fleshes rage." The grieving father *here* can only wish that his son *fare* well and vow that *hence* forth in time and symbolic space he will keep his loves in good (as if Augustinian) order (*Epig.*, XXII and XLV).

More overtly, journey helps organize the "Epitaph on Elizabeth, L. H."

(*Epig.*, CXXIV) and the scenario of "To the World: A Farewell [to the world *stage*] for a Gentle-woman, Vertuous and Noble" (IV in the fifteen-poem *The Forrest,* which immediately follows *Epigrammes*). In the first, the journeying "thou" is invited to pause and reflect, a "stay" to consider a lady who gave "harbour" to virtue presumably storm-tossed in a fallen world, the better to "Farewell."

The latter, a stage-exit speech, is even reflexively theatrical in that the departing lady herself characterizes the "world" as a "shrunke up, and old" vice-like figure that proffers "baits," false goods or props to distract others on their journey. But the lady will neither bate nor "rome" (*cf.* the "labyrinth of love" in *Love's Triumph to Callipolis*): she will, rather, make the true journey to something like grace, a journey within the bosom. It is a journey from and within that fallen state of "age, misfortune, sicknesse, griefe," which perfuses an experimental landscape very like that "state . . . full of shame and scorne / . . . and unto labour borne" that the poet acknowledges in his own voice in "To Heaven" (*Forrest,* XV, concluding the group).

That much noticed Ignatian meditation in "To Heaven"—four lines of proposal (as double question), sixteen lines of analysis, and six lines of colloquy of mixed feelings—epitomizes Jonsonian dependence on the tropes. The poem enacts the always critical moment of choice occurring whenever a thought of God comes to mind. The poet attests to self-enactment, the true theater of liturgy, not the meretricious theater of *show* or *pretend.* In such enactment he would be seen by God and by sympathetic reader / observers as pilgrim-journeyer, "unto labour" (as by maternal labor) "borne," "laden with sinnes," "exil'd from thee," but "rap'd now," "destin'd unto judgement" and *called* to (in the poem's very last words) "love of thee."

In contrast, the "Ode: To Himselfe" (25 in *Under-wood,* the ninety-one-poem miscellany following *The Forrest*) is apparently more secular than "To Heaven" or "A Farewell for a Gentle-woman" but like the latter is theatrical. With Jonson, the classicist and celebrant of Lucius Cary and Henry Morison, the ode is generically to be understood as—or at least as if—a vocal performance on stage. Yet animating the classical allusions to Aonian springs, Thespia, and Clarius is a psychic movement less a *psychomachia* than a Christianized turn, counter-turn, and stand. That movement rejects the "where" of mortally sinful *sloth,* canvasses (as noted) the region of classical understanding (part of the map of any respectable poet's mind), and notes a crypto-Christian aspect of it: words (and the Word?) desecrated "by chattring Pies" dropping birdlime. The poet calls himself to "quicken," to seek a higher region than Fortuna's, calls himself to no secular-Petrarchan page-boy service to a strumpet-stage but rather to a prophetic minstrelsy in "Japhet's line," something (notwithstanding the conventional and transparent code of "Jove") veritably liturgic. Japhet (Prometheus, as Herford and Simpson note) stole fire from pagan gods. For all Jonson's difference from Donne and Milton, the poem invites comparison with the former's treatment of the London stages in his sermons and the latter's notorious strictures on classicism voiced by the Son in *Paradise Regain'd* (which we have discussed in *Milton and the Hermeneutic Journey*).[5]

In further token of Jonson's vitality in varying the tropes, not least that of calling, note the false "embassies" of Captain Hungry's "pompous lies" (*Epig.*, CVII) and "worthy scorne" in "On the Famous Voyage" for wayward souls on "some in-land passage / of sixe times to, and fro, without embassage" (34–35). That longest of the epigrams was the last. The form was avowedly mock-epic:

> No more let *Greece* her bolder fables tell
> Of *Hercules,* or *Theseus* going to *hell.*
> (CXXXIII, 1–2)

But the Famous Voyage was and is both humorously and seriously more than that. It was, like the "Epode" in *The Forrest,* an extended comment on sin, on the voyage one might choose to take since "Man may securely sinne, but safely never" ("Epode," 116). In the "Famous Voyage," this central concern was festooned in classical learning, theatricalized as a neo-Juvenalian or neo-Perseun scenario, with the allusions, mythic and heroic, serving both to support and to skew the epic form. The classical, however, was soon left behind. The four rivers of Hades were outdone in stink and refuse by the Fleet Ditch, and the two adventurous knaves were both "laden with plague-sores" and "Lash'd by their consciences." Biology befouled formed the setting for even fouler souls.

This judgment on London was not, of course, restricted to Jonson or even very new. One may recall Wyatt's "Mine Own John Poyns," Spenser's Colin Clouts, and the bitter denunciation of the capital by Nashe in *Christ's Tears.*

5. Gale H. Carrithers, Jr., and James D. Hardy, Jr., *Milton and the Hermeneutic Journey* (Baton Rouge, 1994).

Jonson's poem, though, goes beyond the conventional comparison of the idyllic countryside of pastoral and Arcadian poetry with the dismal and automatic corruption of court and capital. Here the poet declared that the city befouled pure nature herself, using it as an emblem to stigmatize the grime of worldly urban souls.

The voyage, traversing polluted London, was declared more dangerous than rowing across the Channel, and its hazards were increased by the poet's neglecting to call upon supernatural protection, a "golden bough, / Or magick sacrifice" (48–49), a resonant and ironic comment since the magic that protected classical pagan heroes was a mortal sin to Christians. With only Hercules to hold the poetic torch, the two adventurers began rowing at Bridewell Dock, stirring the sewage at the river bank. "Car-men" passed, driving privy wagons to dump their cargo in the river, described in phantasmagoric terms as "Centaures," Gorgons, and Harpies. Privy sludge was compounded by waste mercury compounds poured into the river from the buildings above. These chemical poisons, fed to gulls by quacks, were joined by the "Fleet-lane Furies, and hot cookes" (143), who added to the rain of filth the dregs of their macabre trade of selling boiled, stewed, and minced dog and cat to those foolish enough to buy:

> The sinkes ran grease, and haire of meazled hogs,
> The heads, houghs, entrailes, and the hides of dogs:
> For, to say truth, what scullion is so nastie,
> To put the skins, and offall in a pastie?
>
> (145–48)

Many a scullion along the river, as Jonson well knew. On past walls plastered with excrement, the intrepid voyagers rowed until they reached Holborn, itself described in terms of the three judges of hell. Everyone could be supposed to cheer such a voyage, and, accordingly,

> In memorie of which most liquid deed,
> The citie since hath rais'd a Pyramide.
>
> (193–94)

This jaundiced physical description of the London streamfront, generally accurate until the twentieth century, was not the chief message of this lengthy-beyond-the-usual epigram. The real "stinke" and the real "sinke" of London were moral failures metaphorized into the familiar disgusting physical aspect of the city. From its position as the last of the 133 *Epigrammes,* the "Famous Voyage" stood both as summary in terms of cityscape of the spectacular examples of Original and Extratemporal Sin earlier described and as a contrast to the human virtue and divine grace that were the subjects of many of the epigrams and that presumably warrant the weirdly jaunty tone. The voyage thus betokened a journey of dis-grace through a universe of "stinkes" and wretchedness, should one be so foolish as to want to undertake it. Sir Gut and Court Worme and Sir Cod had done so. Let others beware.

In "To Penshurst," the second poem collected in *The Forrest,* Jonson took moral instruction from epigram to description and from London to the countryside of Kent. "To Penshurst" has been expansively analyzed, lately by Don Wayne. While we agree with much of Wayne's analysis, it is more theoretical (synchronicity and diachronicity in history), technical, and physical (nature and culture, estate and architectural description) than it is theological, and it is within this last category that we find Jonson's conception of the great, good place.[6]

The varieties of goodness found at Penshurst were the central concern of the poem, as similar concerns animated the succeeding poem "To Sir Robert Wroth." As Marvell would later do in "On Appleton House," Jonson identified the good in a small and cooperative community. The good house was "not . . . built to envious show, / Of touch, or marble" (1–2), was not, in de-

6. Don E. Wayne, *Penshurst: The Semiotics of Place and the Poetics of History* (Madison, Wisc., 1984). But see Richard Harp, "Jonson's 'To Penshurst': The Country House as Church," *John Donne Journal,* VII (1988), 73–89, for a view that is generally sceptical of Wayne's thesis. Harp concentrates on the house and estate as church and sees a "country estate that was also a spiritual house composed of living stones" (87). Although perhaps he goes a metaphor too far, we are in general agreement. Jonson's poems on the Sidneys are not the only way of evaluating the moral and political condition of that family; in "Jonson's House of Wisdom," *Ben Jonson Journal,* I (1994), 1–13, Harp invaluably details Jonson's theology, especially of his Roman Catholic years (1598–1610) as articulating a mode of dwelling for contemplation in "To Penshurst." We agree and would only add that the dwelling, the poetizing, and (upon completion) the reading are enacted calling, which is to say a personally conceived, semiprivate liturgy (*cf.* Donne's "A Litanie"). There is also Arthur Collins, *Letters and Memorials of State* (2 vols.; New York, 1973), a photographic copy of the 1746 London edition. Much of this eighteenth-century collection was centered on the papers of Sir Henry, Sir Philip, and Sir Robert Sidney. See the judicious exposition by Malcolm Kelsall, *The Great Good Place: The Country House and English Literature* (New York, 1993), esp. Chaps. 1 and 2. Still useful is William A. McClung, *The Country House in English Poetry* (Berkeley, 1977).

fining contrast, one of "Those proud, ambitious heaps, and nothing else" (101). Penshurst was not a work of overweening assertion of power but, instead, a shelter for family and community where "Thy Lord dwells" (102).

Moreover, the place itself, though architecturally and socially attractive, was primarily an occasion for moral and natural good. Jonson dealt first with nature, in the second section of the poem (9–44). Here the poet described nature in terms of bounteousness, fecundity, beauty, and variety, as if thinking of Paradise, where in Christian orthodoxy the natural order manifested the moral order, which had pre-existed any material creation. Penshurst thus had:

> thy orchard fruit, thy garden flowers,
>   Fresh as the ayre, and new as are the houres.
> The earely cherry, with the later plum,
>   Fig, grape, and quince, each in his time doth come:
> The blushing apricot, and woolly peach
>   Hang on thy walls, that every child may reach.
>
> (39–44)

This description of fruit and flower was complemented by praise of pond and river, wild and domestic fauna, woods and fields, walks and hills. All combined to present a picture of ordered nature in what George Orwell was later to call the "sleekest landscape in the world."

As the house led the poet-celebrator to nature, within the poem, so nature invited attention to the moral worthiness of the inhabitants whose lives were emblematized by Penshurst. The last two sections of the poem, from line forty-five to the end, dealt with the community found in this place of architectural and natural favor. The lord and lady received the open and freely offered gifts of the manor's farmers:

> Some bring a capon, some a rurall cake,
>   Some nuts, some apples; some that thinke they make
> The better cheeses, bring 'hem. . . .
>
> (51–53)

All of these go to "more then expresse their love" (57). The lord and lady expended these gifts, and much more, in the "liberall boord" of "hospitalitie" to all who came, from the poet (sometime bricklayer) to King James. This was a household where the gods of the hearth were honored and where the "good lady . . . reap'd / The just reward of her high huswifery" (84–85). Here was praised the ancient noble virtues of largesse and hospitality, in which substance was invested not in capital formation, an urban and mercantilist value that Jonson did not support, but rather in the rural virtues of sharing between classes and of the responsibility of the great for the small that tied society together. The Sidneys looked backward to the always-idealized-but-not-totally-imaginary virtues of the past when social grace and generosity outranked mere wealth. The virtues, even if more aspired or pretended to than practiced, were identified, praised, and enjoined by the lections in every parish church. Thus, the estate without signified the moral estate appropriately, perhaps even habitually, within the inhabitants of the manor. This point was repeated and strongly re-emphasized in the last section of the poem:

> These, *Penshurst,* are thy praise, and yet not all.
> Thy lady's noble, fruitfull, chaste withall.
> His children thy great lord may call his owne:
> A fortune, in this age, but rarely knowne.
> (89–92)

Certainly, such a circumstance was rarely known within the ambit of the Famous Voyage, where all was deceit, disease, or filth. But within a household where all were "taught to pray," such noble chastity and trust could be deemed to survive and flourish, if anywhere.

Implicit in this poem, as in "To Sir Robert Wroth," which immediately followed "Penshurst" in *The Forrest* (and hence in the 1616 Folio), was the difference between country and city, used in part, and in part only, as a metaphor for the difference between good and evil. The physical difference between the two, described in terms of "jewells, stuffes, the paines, the wit / Thus wasted" ("To Sir Robert Wroth," 11–12) was compared:

> at home, in thy securer rest,
> Live, with un-bought provision blest;
> Free from proud porches, or their guilded roofes,
> 'Mongst loughing heards, and solide hoofes.
> (13–16)

And the difference was certainly great enough. But the London poet (who did not *relocate* to the country) saw the moral difference as even greater. It was the difference between the falsity of the *theatrum mundi* and the goodness of ambassadorship, between ambassadorship and the "stinke" of sin. It was the difference in journeys between the Famous Voyage and the life of Sir Robert Wroth, a Sidney in-law, in which journey Wroth was instructed to "live long innocent," thinking "life, a thing but lent." Thus, in the last line, with "life, a thing but lent," the implicit difference between virtue and vice was again made clear. Jonson was thinking in terms of the Creed: "Et vitam venturi saeculi." That was the direction of the real journey, in which the virtues of this life were not only Stoic ends but also Christian means.

These themes of the Christian tropes of ambassadorship, journey, and the falsity of the world's theater were made pellucidly clear in "To the World: A Farewell for a Gentle-woman, Vertuous and Noble," adverted to above and the third poem in the Penshurst-Wroth triptych, if placement means anything. "To the World" was, from the first line, uncompromisingly clear:

> False world, good-night: since thou has brought
> That houre upon my morne of age,
> Hence-forth I quit thee from my thought,
> My part is ended on thy stage.
> Doe not once hope, that thou canst tempt
> A spirit so resolv'd to tread
> Upon thy throate, and live exempt
> From all the nets that thou canst spread.
>
> (1–8)

But if the world could be held *in contemptu* (as theater deceitful *in toto* or stage of betrayals in particular), it could not be expunged from reality. Humanity must accept it, as trial or as goal, as end or as journey, as ambiguous theater or not, for "what we'are borne for, we must beare" (53), however understood or undertaken the journey. Jonson understood it as an interior progress of *conversio,* marked by outward virtue, life figured as a continuing sacrament:

> But make my strengths, such as they are
> Here in my bosome, and at home.
>
> (67–68)

The melding in integrity of virtues (the true strengths), "bosome," and home was one chief Jonsonian counter to the power pretensions of worldly theatricalism: a kind of private liturgy.

The external element of the sacramental life may be seen in the "Epode," the eleventh poem in *The Forrest.* Here the emphasis was on virtue and vice, with the opening of the poem anticipatory of Milton's understanding of Adam and Eve living without past or sin in paradise:

> Not to know vice at all, and keepe true state
> Is vertue, and not *Fate:*
> Next, to that vertue, is to know vice well
> And her blacke spight expell.
>
> (1–4)

The first was not possible—if not in Eden, certainly not now in the world—and the second could only be achieved through grace. "Wakefull reason," particularly insofar as it ordered "affections," was an imperfect guard against sin, but it was the "securest policie we have," though, of course, mere "policie" could not by itself attain to grace. The affection and passions must "strike reason blinde" anyway, and true love, that is *agape,* could deteriorate into "blinde Desire." Still, it was the true and chaste love that really mattered, that could identify and make inviting the right path. Jonson closed this philosophical, largely Neoplatonic, meditation with the already cited sharp reminder about the world of sin:

> Man may securely sinne, but safely never.
>
> (116)

Remembrance of the inward and spiritual grace may be seen in epigram XLV, "On my First Sonne." One is here again brought back into the reality of death, but of death seen by those who were

> also heirs through hope of thy everlasting kingdom, by the merits of the most precious death and passion of thy dear Son.
>
> (Communion Thanksgiving, *Book of Common Prayer*)

Ben Jonson bid a painful farewell to his eldest son Benjamin and did so within the Christian context of redemption and salvation:

> For why
> Will man lament the state he should envie?
> To have so soone scap'd worlds, and fleshes rage,
>
> (5–7)

His regret was for himself, for having loved his son too much, which was to say imperfectly, but not for his son's destination "out of the miseries of this sinful world" (Burial Service, *Book of Common Prayer*). The grace that could make of life a salvific journey would not, Jonson made clear, desert humanity "at the hour of our death," though neither would our fallen tendency toward disordered loves. Epigram XXXIV, cited at the beginning of this section, is relevant here. Jonson was a God-centered poet who construed his world by "blessed passion, mightie ressurreccyon and gloryous ascension," even as he felt his own and others' disgrace, frailty, and fall.

In addition to the orthodox world of redemption, which posited divine willingness to forgive along with human freedom, we judge that Jonson's poetry presented an ample metonymic survey through that moral world, more externally and descriptively through the city in *Epigrammes* and more internally through the diversely sacred and secular wood of the psyche in *The Forrest* and *Under-wood.* In the *Epigrammes* Jonson examined both sin and virtue in the social context of London. The poetry of the *Epigrammes* emphasized the consequences of human free will and moral choice, the individual subject of the epigram being subsumed in the defining act or attitude that outwardly exemplified the interior life of grace or dis-grace. The cityscape depicted not primarily the act or turmoil of personal moral change but rather the status of more or less achieved individuality interspersed with more or less degraded stereotypicality.[7] The prevailing theme was the poet surveying, canvassing, indicting, praising, above all stabilizing in quasi-emblematic identification with relation to charity and power. What Jonson found was certainly conventional enough within the realm of moral theology, though here expressed with great descriptive vigor. Gut, Sir Voluptuous Beast, Banck, Cod, Chev'rill the Lawyer (XXXVII, LIV), the English Mounsieur (LXXXVIII), and the Poet-Ape (LVI) were all guilty of one of the seven deadly sins, while Fine Lady

7. See Susan Wells, *The Dialectics of Representation* (Baltimore, 1985), esp. Chap. 3, "Typicality and Indeterminacy in Jacobean City Comedy," for a brilliant exposition of these notions as adumbrating a dialectic vital to Renaissance drama (and certain later texts), with Jonson evidently privileging the typical. We generally agree but demur with regard to the uniquely named, in essence the beloved. For a fine exposition in similar terms of Jonson's elegy on his son, cited above, see H. W. Matalene, "Patriarchal Fatherhood in Ben Jonson's Epigram 45," in *Traditions and Innovations: Essays on British Literature of the Middle Ages and the Renaissance,* ed. David G. Allen and Robert A. White (Newark, Del., 1990), 102–12: "Not a nurturing middle-class daddy in mourning, but a covetous patriarch in repentance" (110).

Would-Bee (LXII) was described as a murderer, and the Some-Thing, That Walkes Some-Where (XI) as having so far died to charity and society as to be utterly nameless. In being dead to charity, Some-Thing was de-specied. Viewed within the context of ambient attention, with the reader a sort of *flâneur* of disgrace, the Famous Voyage emerged as an epitome of the *Epigrammes,* a book of vice condensed into an epigrammatic series, narrative as raucous gallery of *tableaux vivant.* Redemption was far away, and forgiveness was a human (though not divine) improbability.

But the *flâneur* encountered as much virtue in the city as vice, indeed, encountered more. There was William Camden (XIV) and John Donne (XXIII), standing rebukes to Chev'rill or the Poet-Ape, and Sir John Roe, the opposite of Gut, Beast, Banck, or Cod. Margaret Ratcliffe's epitaph concluded: "For wit, feature, and true passion / Earth, thou hast not such another" (XL, 15–17). She was a paradigm of general good, as was the Earle of Salisburie (XLIII). So was King James (of course), though praise here carried pregnant advice: "Looke not upon thy dangers, but our feares" (LI, 10). Sir Henrie Cary (LXVI) was a model of military courage and steadfastness in the face of disaster. In these, as in the Countess of Rutland and the Countess of Bedford or Sir John Radcliffe, virtue and nobility made them ambassadors of goodness to all. More, they stood in opposition to the city of the Famous Voyage. The cityscape of Jonson was a universe of free will and thus of all categories of human experience. But such opposition, balanced or even tilted toward ill in this local place or that brief time *sub specie aeternitatis,* could not for so Christian a poet as Jonson be Manichaean. The rich personhood of the graced attested to that.

The Forrest and *Under-wood* depicted a different scape, an atlas and survey of the psyche, of interiority, reflection, retirement, and meditation. The themes of grace and disgrace, of love and power, were the same in *The Forrest* and the later large collection *Under-wood* as they had been in the *Epigrammes,* but they appeared in a different light. Meditation dominated description as the medium for illustrating the virtues and their absence. Meditative poetry was also acutely Platonic, participating fully in Scholastic realism, reflecting always on what was real and what was shadow. As Louis Martz put it in *The Poem of the Mind,* meditative poetry dealt with the "interior life, where the mind, acutely aware of an outer world of drifting, unstable forms, finds within itself the power to create coherence and significance." Martz himself referred to Wallace Stevens to sharpen the definition of meditative poetry, a gift from modern secularism to help characterize such concern with the Incarnation and Resurrection as marked Jonson's meditation on virtue and its forms:

> The poem of the mind in the act of finding
> What will suffice. . . .

This was Stevens' description of the process of meditation. The end of meditation Stevens identified in a neighboring work in the same collection, *Parts of a World:*

> the mind
> . . . declares
> "This image, this love, I compose myself
> Of these. In these, I come forth outwardly." [8]

The invocation of love certainly accorded with Jonson, and we descry an especially Jonsonian version of the general meditative practice that stretched back to Bernard of Clairvaux, a Jonsonian rearticulation of older continental norms. The Jonsonian meditative mode as represented in his poetry was *receptionist* in its dynamic, civic in substance and composition, oriented to the end of love, that philadelphic love to be realized as the illumination of the reader.[9]

8. Louis L. Martz, *The Poem of the Mind: Essays on Poetry English and American* (New York, 1966), ix; Wallace Stevens, "Of Modern Poetry" and "Poem with Rhythms," in *The Collected Poems of Wallace Stevens* (New York, 1955), 239, 246.

9. Receptionism, in both narrow eucharistic meaning and broader cultural setting, had a theological resonance, consistent, in cultural terms, with the religious base to English Renaissance "habits of thought." For the Eucharist understood in terms of receptionism and / or memorialism, and specifically rejecting transubstantiation, see John Wycliffe, *On the Eucharist,* ed. and trans. Ford Lewis Battles, in *Advocates of Reform,* ed. Matthew Spinka (Philadelphia, 1953), 61–88, Vol. XIV of *The Library of Christian Classics,* ed. John Baillie, John McNeill, and Henry Van Dusen, 26 vols. On the question of indulgence, which extended the granting of grace to an analogy of the sacrament of confession, penance, and absolution, see B. J. Kidd, ed., *Documents Illustrative of the Continental Reformation* (Oxford, 1911), 1–12, where one finds the papal bull *Unigenitus Dei Filius* of Clement VI (1343), which is regarded as the foundation of indulgences; the papal bull *Salvator noster* of Sixtus V (1476), the earliest indulgence for the dead; the bull *Liquet omnibus Christianae* of Julius II (1510), which was the origin of Luther's protest; as well as various *Formula absolutionis* of 1513–17. These extensions of grace-giving to what many in the sixteenth and seventeenth centuries deemed the all-too-human level of the church were of course one of the causes of the Protestant insurrection against the Roman Catholic hierarchy.

We apply this description to the poetry as a whole, because it was the whole that invited the reader to an illuminated sense of the true city.

As the inwardness and meditative quality of Jonson's poetry increased from *Epigrammes* to *The Forrest* and *Under-wood,* the pace slowed, the variety of poetic subjects diminished, and the attention given to each expanded. Jonson returned to people again and again, expanding and altering his plane of vision in accord with recognized meditative practice. The poetry became more explicitly devotional, an examination of love gained and lost, rightly bestowed and ill-directed, but the poems still beginning, as meditations must, with a specific person or event, still ending, as meditations ought, in illumination.[10]

The shift from the exterior to the interior was facilitated by an extended consideration of the Sidney family, who were prominent subjects in both *Epigrammes* and *The Forrest.* In epigram LXXIX, Jonson praised the Countesse of Rutland, daughter of Sir Philip Sidney, comparing her to her father's book. Two epigrams, CIII and CV, extolled the beauty, wit, and virtue of Lady Mary Wroth, the daughter of Sir Robert Sidney. Jonson ended the first of these with the compliment:

> My praise is plaine, and where so ere profest,
> Becomes none more than you, who need it least.
> (CIII, 13–14)

This was expanded in epigram CV, with mythological comparisons added and an even more lavish compliment at the end:

> So are you *Natures Index,* and restore
> I' your selfe, all treasure lost of th'age before.
> (19–20)

In her own person Her Ladyship (dedicatee of *The Alchemist*) restored . . . should we say the lost age of gold? or more politically and pointedly the last age of Elizabeth? Jonson was too prudent to answer. This theme was carried further in epigram CXIV, as Jonson praised Philippa Sidney, also a daughter of Sir Robert, as "miracle" of "so much beautie met with vertue." In *The Forrest,* the Sidneys reappeared in a now-familiar role. "To Penshurst" (II), as argued above, depicted Sir Robert Sidney as lord of a great good place where virtue nurtured both humanity and nature and love overcame even physical

10. See "Collect on Illumination," in *The Book of Common Prayer* (1559).

distance (as it partly does in the mind). In "To Sir Robert Wroth" (III), a poem that guardedly repeated the theme of "Penshurst," the subject was praised for having wisdom and strength of character to love the country and avoid city show and vice. Again, the Countess of Rutland was addressed, this time directly in a classical "Epistle" (XII), which extended the praise of virtue and wit only mentioned earlier. Finally an "Ode" (XIV) to Sir William Sidney, son of Sir Robert and the Countess's cousin, emphasized the now-familiar themes of family and virtue, here more in exhortation than in confident report.

These eight poems, to which must be added "An Epigram. To the Honour'd ———, Countesse of ———," from *Under-wood* (52) and "A Sonnet, to the Noble Lady, the Lady Mary Wroth" (30), made of the Sidneys both an occasion for the consideration of love and a starting point for further exploration. We note that this further meditative exploration began with a denial of what was manifestly true with the short poem "Why I Write Not of Love" (I). "Notness," negation, denial resonated in *The Forrest,* as Catherine Bates has pointed out, but that very "notness" and denial were false.[11] Jonson was writing essentially about love—love of place, of family, of nature, of tradition, of virtue, and of eros itself ("To Celia," V, VI, IX); these were the subjects of the fifteen poems in *The Forrest* and were themes continued in *Under-wood.* Here the *flâneur* would find: the fruits of love cut off in "To Elizabeth, Countesse of Rutland" (*Forrest,* XII); love remembered, continued, and cherished in refinement in "A Farewell for a Gentle-woman, Vertuous and Noble" (*Forrest,* IV); love rightly directed in the trinity of "To the Holy Trinitie," "A Hymne to God the Father," and "A Hymne on the Nativitie of My Saviour" (*Under-wood,* 1, 2, and 3).The *flâneur* would find a lengthy and ruefully antic-

11. Catherine Bates, "Much Ado About Nothing: The Contents of Jonson's *Forrest,*" *Essays in Criticism,* XLII (1992), 24–35, a witty article in which we have found a good deal to like. See also Alastair Fowler, "The Silva Tradition in Jonson's *The Forrest,*" in *Poetic Traditions of the English Renaissance,* ed. Maynard Mack and George de F. Lord (New Haven, 1982), 85–101; Fowler notes a movement (journey, we would say) from the secular world in orientation toward heaven. We would add that in the final *Forrest* poem, "To Heaven," "my state, both full of shame and scorne . . . And destin'd unto judgement after all" is too often taken as exclusively confessional on Jonson's part. He took it to be the general human estate. This is not to deny Sara van den Berg's point in *The Action of Ben Jonson's Poetry* (Newark, Del., 1987) about Jonson inscribing and privileging relationships. See also Gary Waller, *The Sidney Family Romance: Mary Wroth, William Herbert, and the Early Modern Construction of Gender* (Detroit, 1993), esp. Chap. 7, "Sidney Cousins in the Theater, Court, and Country."

Petrarchan examination of earthly love in "A Celebration of Charis in Ten Lyrick Peeces" (*Under-wood,* 4); would find love not quite lost and not fully enjoyed as a bittersweet elegy in "An Elegie" (*Under-wood,* 21, 42, 43); would find love sequentially semidramatized, first as urgent "sport," then as bittersweet retrospect, in what *The Forrest* presents as a series of poems (V, VI, IX) "To Celia"; or would find love as beauty radiated in "An Elegie" (*Under-wood,* 24) and beauty disfigured in "An Epigram, To the Small Poxe" (*Under-wood,* 36). The interior stroll was not less varied than the patrol through the city.

For Jonson as for Anaximander, however, behind the facade of variety there was unity, the "Boundless" for the Greek philosopher, the allness of God for the English poet.[12] If one would obey the injunction of the opening epigram and "understand" Jonson's poetry, we propose a return to the epigrams "Of Life and Death" (LXXX) and "Of Death" (XXXIV). In both, Jonson dealt with the two themes that underlay the whole of his poetry: virtue and the "sure and certain hope" of the resurrection.

> The ports of death are sinnes; of life, good deeds:
>
> . . . .
>
> For good man but see death, the wicked tast it.
>
> (LXXX, 1, 8)

But the core of the message was contained in the couplet with which we started:

> He that feares death, or mournes it, in the just,
> Shewes of the resurrection little trust.
>
> (XXXIV)

Many Christians say such things. We think Jonson believed them.

H. L. Mencken once defined a Puritan as someone who had "the haunting fear that someone, somewhere, may be happy."[13] For the seventeenth century,

12. Charles H. Kahn, *Anaximander and the Origins of Greek Cosmology* (New York, 1960), deals with this issue; see Chap. 1, n. 15, above.

13. H. L. Mencken, "Sententiae," excerpted in Alastair Cooke, ed., *The Vintage Mencken* (New York, 1955), 233.

as for the twentieth, this was not in every instance inaccurate. The contemporary portrait of the Puritan, coming in part from Jonson's plays, of a person who manifested a fragile inner assurance of grace by an outward sniffish disapproval of all that constituted the world, was too often repeated to have been entirely imaginary. But Jonson, who had a lively moral sense and who in "To the Holy Trinitie" called for "Helpe, helpe to lift / My selfe up to thee" (4–5), could not bring himself to the relentless censoriousness of the dedicated Puritan. Jonson drank (a lot) and ate (substantially) and entertained (heartily), nourished ambition, strove to climb socially on the none-too-reliable ladder of talent, hung around the court and its smarmy but dangerous politicians, laughed, and wrote comedy. Until the last difficult years of poverty and lost favor, and of defeat by fire in his library and by illnesses in his body, he maintained a cheerful and optimistic disposition. A happy moralist, a cheerful man of deep religious conviction and consciousness, Jonson was an author who ridiculed and condemned actions and perverse courses of life but did not damn sinners, a poet who loved many persons while loving God. So deeply is dour and antisocial Puritanism engrained in our cultural sensibility that such a combination as described above seems contradictory and repugnant to good sense. But it was not, and the difficulty in recognizing a man of great faith who loved God and enjoyed human society yet fretted at waxing misadventures of power is a lapse of historical imagination on the part of a modern and secular age, not a failure of Jonsonian poetic or psychology.

In an important article on Jonson's comedies, "Ben Jonson and the Publicke Riot," Peggy Knapp has contended that "Ben Jonson saw his world quite clearly, but he liked almost nothing in what he saw."[14] We can agree completely with only the first clause. In the first place, Jonson's disapprobation focused primarily on individual and personal sins, with society itself mostly an afterthought or a setting. Jonson was a serious Christian who lived long before Jean-Jacques Rousseau convinced the Enlightenment West to move the loca-

14. Peggy Knapp, "Ben Jonson and the Publicke Riot: Ben Jonson's Comedies," in *Staging the Renaissance: Reinterpretation of Elizabethan and Jacobean Drama,* ed. David Scott Kastan and Peter Stallybrass (New York, 1991), 164. A recent, more general essay is John Creaser, "Enigmatic Ben Jonson," in *English Comedy,* ed. Michael Cordner, Peter Holland, and John Kerrigan (Cambridge, Eng., 1994), 100–17: an enigmatic but not ungenerous, nonrelativistic, and finally exhilarating Jonson we believe in. See also C. A. Patrides, "A Poet Nearly Anonymous," in *Figures in a Renaissance Context,* ed. Claude J. Summers and Ted-Larry Pebworth (Ann Arbor, 1989), 73–87.

tion of sin from the individual to secular society in general. Jonson believed humankind were born not good and virtuous but rather with a massive propensity to evil (Original Sin). If society led to corruption, and the city certainly contributed to that end, this was basically because social temptations were working on already fallen individuals. *Aversio* was an individual turn or tangent away from God within the single soul, not a description of social ills, however horrific these might have become. And the fault and cause of social ills could be found in the cumulative effects of individual sin, of numerous persons choosing power over love, of abusing the obligations of charity in the squalid pursuit of transient private aggrandizement.

Moreover, though Jonson criticized, he also praised, more often in poetry than in theater, more often in masque than either, but he found acts and qualities and persons to praise in all genres. There was, in *The Devil Is an Ass,* a virtuous wife who combined decency with good sense and a repentant conspirator who came to admire both.[15] In the masques there was (to be sure) ritual approval of king and monarchy but no reason to suppose that praise of the royal *officium* was anything but genuine. Having lived through 1603, Jonson knew the importance of the monarchy to England and had serious grounds for hoping the best with regard to James Stuart. And the poetry was primarily a genre of praise, with moral instruction and social improvement coming more extensively from good extolled than from evil condemned.

Finally, when Jonson did condemn, he usually did so with an eye to improvement. Rare Ben was no Juvenal, writing to annihilate; taking his lead from God, he did not desire the death of a sinner. What Jonson did not like could be fixed through the moment of *retorqueo* demanded by the Augustinian journey, so that the sinner would incline toward God, explicitly proclaimed in "fecisti nobis ad te."[16] Conversion was always possible, perhaps

15. St. Augustine, *Confessions,* Bks. II–VII, on the varieties of sin; see also Gamini Salgado, *Four Jacobean City Comedies* (London, 1985), 189–309, for a convenient text of *The Devil Is an Ass.*

16. St. Augustine, *Confessions,* Bk. 1; see also *On the Grace of Christ* (*De gratia Christi*) (418); *On Original Sin* (*De peccato originali*) (418); *On Nature and Grace* (*De natura et gratia*) (418), trans. Peter Holmes, in *A Select Library of the Nicene and Post-Nicene Fathers of the Christian Church,* ed. Philip Schaff (14 vols.; New York, 1886–90) V, 116–51, 214–55. See also an earlier work of Augustine, not occasioned by the Pelagian controversy, *On Christian Doctrine (De doctrina Christiana),* Bks. 1–3, 397, Bk. 4, 426, trans. J. F. Shaw, in *Nicene and Post-Nicene Fathers,* ed. Schaff, II, 513–97; see particularly Bk. I, Chaps. 13–19, 38, which emphasize love rather than

even imminent, for grace was always abounding, always pursuing the sinner through conscience, admonition, and good example. We cannot assert that Jonson, like Donne at sermons, thought that speculation about human power to resist grace was impertinent; Jonson at poems and plays was not so explicit. But Jonson clearly believed in the abundance and power of grace, in the wonders it could work, in the human need of gracious assistance, and in the ultimate good for humanity through the divine plan. The "blessed passion, mightie ressurreccyon and gloryous ascension" were sign enough of that for Ben Jonson.

Not imperturbable, he would cry out when gored and might follow hurt with anger and imprecation, as in *Under-wood,* 51, "Epigram on the Court Pucell" (who was elsewhere praised), or *Under-wood,* 25, his "Ode to Himself," with its self-consoling and rededicatory promise to "sing high and aloofe / Safe from the wolves black jaw, and dull Asses hoofe." Perhaps Jonson is a kind of Rorschach: This last generation of criticism has seen a morose Jonson, "full of rage and scorn," which has been no doubt a shrewder portrait than the previous generation's cartoon of him as a dry and prosy classicist. (He was a classicist all right, as Katharine Eisaman Maus and others have shown, but rarely dry or prosy.) We note that his self-description as "full of rage and scorn" must be understood as penitence for what he would have seen as sinful falls into uncharity. We see him as generally full of cheer, however satiric in particular. He noted in the partly satiric "An Epistle to a Friend, to Perswade Him to the Warres" (*Under-wood,* 17) that "Who falls for love of God, shall rise a Starre" (196). And we most identify him with how consistently he rebounded to "cheerefull worke" (his term in "An Epigram. To the Honour'd Countesse," *Under-wood,* 52). The commander of the verse in "A Fit of Rime Against Rime" and "An Execration upon Vulcan" surely exhibits something close to urbane command of himself. Even late in life, his physical condition woeful, he could assert, "no Palsi's in thy braine," a chin-up line, albeit indirect discourse. Exaggeration is what we see, where Hunter saw "utter subserviency" in "An Elegie" (*Under-wood,* 40). Rather than self-abasement, apparently after some drunken impropriety of speech, it is the familiar chagrined hyperbole of mannerly reparation, complete with theatrics:

punishment, an important distinction of emphasis, though not of underlying systematic theology. For an outstanding recent interpretation of Augustine on sin and shame, see Elaine Pagels, *Adam, Eve, and the Serpent* (New York, 1988), esp. Chaps. 5 and 6.

"Regenerate now . . . the child / Of [her] compassion . . . / I the penitents here emulate" (39–40, 86). The final line of his "Grace Before Kinge James" seems emblematic of his usual buoyancy: "And God bless mee and God blesse Raphe." So we reiterate our identification of Jonson the cheerful and optimistic and good-tempered moralist who believed in the power of grace over sin, who believed that the result of evil was a later and greater good, who believed in God's ultimate redemption of humanity.

Jonson's moral vision, which combined personal optimism and a comic voice with strong condemnation of sin, was the result of an Anglo-Catholic imagination. On the reality of Original Sin both Catholics and Protestants agreed; it had, after all, been a fundamental part of Christian moral theology at least since Augustine.[17] But from that common doctrine arose profound differences of interpretation, emphasis, and pastoral psychology. These differences revolved less around sin, usually described in terms of defective human will, misdirected human love, or inappropriate use of human reason and imagination, and more around virtue. The Catholic view of virtue was comparative rather than absolute. Absolute virtue was reserved, of course, for Christ, not the commonality, but merely because human beings could not act in an absolutely virtuous manner did not therefore imply that there was absolutely "no health in" them. That phrase in the Prayer Book General Confession was alleviated by the contextual sense that there *is* blessedly designed, vigorous, free-willful, and redeemable *life* in those confessing. There were sharp moral differences within human conduct. Evil eschewed, whether out of pride or fear or principle, was different from and preferable to evil embraced. While it was morally more creditable not to steal because it was wrong (see Exodus 20:15) than not to steal because someone was watching, it was, for any reason, better not to steal than to have stolen. The three possibilities aforementioned were three different moral conditions. Arising from the Scholastic division of an act into intention and action, the Catholic view was that the moral condition of humanity, while tending to the bad, was basically variable. Virtue was not the absolute rejection of temptation and the avoidance of

17. St. Augustine, *Confessions,* Bks. I–VI: the progression of sin from childhood by false doctrine and will weakened by the Fall. St. Thomas Aquinas, *Summa Theologiae,* ed. Thomas Gilbey, O. P., *et al.* (60 vols.; London 1964–65), *Prima Pars, Ia,* q. 48, a. 5, r. (VIII, 124–27); *Prima Secundae, Ia IIae,* q. 18, a. 8, r. (XVIII, 32–35); (*Ia IIae*), q. 20, a. 3, s.c., r. (XVIII, 90–95). We have generally found the "Dicendum quod" to be particularly useful. For the best modern meditation on this issue as Augustinian and general, see Paul Ricoeur, n. 19, below.

sin (see Luke 4:1–12), which was humanly impossible, but rather doing the best one could to avoid evil action and to act from good motives, which was difficult but sometimes attainable.[18] While people could not in this life attain the good (short of miracle or sainthood, certainly), they could always do better. Sin could be reduced. Decency could be expanded. It was the function of the Christian so to do. (The heretical extreme of this view was, of course, Pelagianism: 'no need for grace; up by one's spiritual boot-straps to salvation.' We see no sign of that in Jonson.)[19]

18. Aquinas, *Summa Theologiae, Ia IIae,* q. 55 ("utrum virtus convenientur definiatur"), a. 4.6, x.c., r. (XXII, 10–17); *Ia IIae,* q. 71 ("de vitriis et peccatis secundum se"), a. 6, r. (XXVI, 20–25); see also Anton Pegis, ed., *Saint Thomas Aquinas, Summa Contra Gentiles* (4 vols.; South Bend, 1975), Bk. IV, art. 50–52; and see St. Thomas Aquinas, *Omnia Opera* (Rome, 1982), XXIII, *De malo,* q. 4 ("de peccato originali"), in particular, a. 1, r. (pp. 103–28). See James Weisheipl, *Friar Thomas d'Aquino* (Garden City, N.Y., 1974), for an excellent bibliography of the saint's works and editions.

19. The Pelagians were declared heretics many times, particularly at the Council of Carthage (417) and the Council of Orange (July 3, 529), which specifically accepted Augustine's theology and, indeed, Augustine's own words. See Philip Labey and Gabriel Cossarti, *Sacrosancta Concilia* (17 vols.; Paris, 1671–72), II, 1533–36, "Concilium Carthaginese contra Pelaginos"; IV, 1666–78, "Concilium Arausicanum II de Gratia et Libero Arbitrio." See, in particular, Capitula IV, which condemned the heart of the Pelagian doctrine: "Si quis, ut a peccato purgemur, voluntatem [will] nostram Deum expectare contendit, non autem ut etiam purgari velimus, per sancti spiritus infusionem et operationen in nos fieri confitetur." All who believed this were condemned. This was confirmed by the Council of Trent in session V, June 17, 1546. See also Labey and Cossarti, *Sacrasancta Concilia,* XIV, 748–55, esp. 748 for "Decretum de peccato originali." A more convenient source for conciliar action on Pelagianism and original sin is C.-J. Hefele and Dom H. Leclercq, *Histoire des conciles d'aprés les documents originaux* (11 vols.; Paris, 1907–52), II, Pt. 1, 190–96, for Carthage, II, Pt. 2, 1085–110, for Orange, X, Pt. 1, 33–64, for Trent I, session V (see 42–43 for text of Decretum). Recently published is Norman P. Tanner, S. J., *Decrees of the Ecumenical Councils* (2 vols.; Washington, D.C., 1990), II, 665–67, for Trent. See also, of course, Aquinas, *De malo,* q. 4, a. 1, r., and Augustine, *De peccato originali,* esp. No. 14, pp. 241–42, for a succinct statement of how Pelagian doctrine differed from Augustine's theology; see the essential text, Augustine's *De libero arbitrio, e.g.,* in John S. Burleigh, ed. *Augustine: Earlier Writings* (Philadelphia, 1953), 102–218, esp. Bk. I; see also William J. Collinge and John A. Mourant, *Saint Augustine: Four Anti-Pelagian Writings* (Washington, D.C., 1990), Vol. LXXXVI of the *Fathers of the Church,* 221 vols. (The writings are: *On Nature and Grace, On the Proceedings of Pelagius, On the Predestination of the Saints, On the Gift of Perseverance*). For richly provocative reflection on Augustine Agonistes (so to speak), see Paul Ricoeur, "'Original Sin': A Study in Meaning," and "The Hermeneutics of Symbols and Philosophical Reflection," in his *The Conflict of Interpretations: Essays in Hermeneutics,* ed. Don Ihde (Evanston, 1974), 269–334; we are generally indebted to this brilliant work of contextualizing.

This notion of virtue consisting partly of one's best effort was an element of the general doctrine of salvation through faith and works. Luther had, at the very dawn of Protestantism, denied the use of works in the salvific journey, arguing that Original Sin had rendered unworthy any human *sacrificium* offered to God.[20] In *De servo arbitrio,* written in 1526 to oppose Erasmus' earlier treatise in defense of free will, Luther argued that humanity, because of the Fall and Original Sin, had freedom only to sin. He took the position Augustine had enunciated in the assaults on the Pelagians, "non posse non peccare," and extended it.

> When it has been proved that salvation is beyond our own powers and devices and depends on the work of God alone does it not follow that when God is not present and at work in us everything we do is evil and we necessarily do what is of no avail for salvation? For if it is not we, but only God, who works salvation in us, thus before he works we can do nothing of saving significance, whether we wish or not.[21]

Luther tied Original Sin, with its denial of a human soteriological capacity, to a fundamental lack of human freedom, which denied humanity the ability to do good (sinless) works and which made salvation entirely a matter for God, both in outcome and in daily human activity. This Bad News, which occluded the trope of salvific journey, was a general position that much of Reformation Protestantism would embrace, in spite of denominational differences. John Calvin agreed with that general position but was more rigorous in his adherence to the logical consequences thereof. Beginning with the absolute sovereignty of God and the total depravity of humanity, with their corollary that humanity was utterly different from God in every way and lacked some aspects of free will, Calvin argued that humanity was subject to predestination either to salvation or damnation.[22] No human action could be good be-

---

Accordingly, the clients of Jonson's alchemist are moved by no "heroic passion, but an ordinary madness"; John S. Mebane, "Renaissance Magic and the Return of the Golden Age: Utopianism and Religious Enthusiasm in *The Alchemist,*" *Renaissance Drama,* X (1979), 117–39.

20. On the liturgical result of the rejection of *sacrificium* in favor of *beneficium,* see Luther's "Formula Missae" and particularly the "Deutsche Messe" in Bard Thompson, *Liturgies of the Western Church* (Cleveland, 1961), 95–137.

21. Martin Luther, *De servo arbitrio,* ed. Philip Watson, in *Luther's Works,* ed. Jaroslav Pelikan and Helmut Lehmann (55 vols.; Philadelphia, 1958–86), XXXIII, 64.

22. John Calvin, *Institutes of the Christian Religion,* Bk. II, Chaps. 2, 3, 5; Bk. III, Chap. 21,

cause every human action was obviously and conclusively evil in motivation and probably in execution as well.[23] The rigorist view that virtue was congruent with perfection meant that every sinful act—and that was every act and thought—drew one further from God and must by itself merit the punishments for disobedience so thoroughly outlined in Deuteronomy 28:15–68. The journey was rationalized and etherialized as if to a Ramistically diagrammatic dichotomy. Only God could intervene within this rigorously binary logical system, and, indeed, he had:

> For whom he did foreknow, he also did predestinate to be conformed to the image of his Son, that he might be the firstborn among many brethren.
> Moreover, whom he did predestinate, them he also called: and whom he called, them he also justified: and whom he justified, them he also glorified.
> (Rom. 9:29–30, Authorized Version)

But this intervention was not in favor of all mankind, even all of those who were believing Christians. Calvin believed that God had predestined some to be saved (the elect) and some, certainly many and probably most, to be lost (the reprobates).[24] Everyone was "foreknown," and God's sovereignty was ab-

---

trans. Ford Lewis Battles (Philadelphia, 1954), Vol. XX, 241–309, 316–40, Vol. XXII, 920–32, of *The Library of Christian Classics,* ed. Baillie, McNeill, and Van Dusen, 26 vols. See also the Canons of the Synod of Dort, held from November 13, 1618, to May 28, 1619. The 154 sessions produced a strict predestinarian doctrine, firmly faithful to Calvin and equally firmly rejecting the contemporary theology of Jakob Arminius (d. 1609) that allowed the cooperation of the human will in salvation, thus moving toward the Catholic position of justification by faith and works and clearly compromising predestination. The synod produced canons that defined the basic five points of Calvinism: total depravity of mankind, unconditional election, limited atonement for the elect only, irresistible grace, and the perseverance of the saints (T. U. L.I. P.). A convenient and excellent book on Calvinism is John T. McNeill, *The History and Character of Calvinism* (London, 1954), 265, on Dort. See also Horton Davies, *The Worship of the English Puritans* (London, 1948), and Charles Davis Cremeans, *The Reception of Calvinist Thought in England* (Urbana, 1949), two standard older books. See also Calvin, *Institutes,* Bk. III, Chap. 21, ¶ 5: "For all are not created in equal condition; rather eternal life is foreordained for some, eternal damnation for others. Therefore, as any man has been created to one or the other of these ends, we speak of him as predestined to life or death" (XXI, 926).

23. Calvin, *Institutes,* Bk. II, Chap. 1, in XX, 241–55, and Bk. III, Chap. 21, in XXI, 920–32.

24. *Ibid.,* Bk. III, Chap. 21; Bk. II, Chap. 3, ¶ 13–14. See Bk. III, Chap. 21, ¶ 7: "For experience shows that of the great multitude many fall away and disappear, so that only a slight portion remaine" (XXI, 930).

solute in an absolute sense. Nothing human could affect this divine arrangement, which was perfect, unchanging, and just.

This powerfully reductive argument at once threw Puritans, conformist or separatist, of whatever formal church, into one of two groups, the saved or the damned. But into which group? How was one to know the answer to life's most important question? All, of course, were "geven into . . . perversnesse" and, therefore, could know "nothing certain about their own salvation." Among even those people who seemed saved were reprobates, on whom Calvin gave this judgment:

> Only those predestined to salvation receive the light of faith . . . yet experience shows that the reprobate are sometimes affected by almost the same feeling as the elect, so that even in their own judgement they do not in any way differ from the elect . . . because the Lord, to render them more convicted and inexcusable, steals into their minds to the extent that his goodness may be tasted without the spirit of adoption.[25]

This was designed by God to make the reprobate feel the horror of hell even more keenly by allowing a taste of salvation. It also, of course, made everyone psychologically into a hypocrite and then a reprobate.

No true Puritan could object to such treatment for reprobation, but, again, what were the signs to tell that one was saved? Calvin could come up with no answer other than a stout and invincible personal conviction of election. An apparently virtuous life was of no soteriological force since there was actually no virtue and since salvation came only from predestined grace. The sacraments were not occasions for grace since they were of human invention and all the grace needed for salvation was foreordained through predestination. Calvin wrote: "There is a far different feeling of full assurance that in Scriptures is always attributed to faith. It is this which puts beyond doubt God's goodness. . . . For this reason the apostle derives confidence from faith. . . . This is so true, that the word 'faith' is very often used for confidence."[26] Confidence alone was both the buttress against doubt and the sole earthly sign of election. In the nature of Calvinism, however, nothing that a person could do or think could be used to support this confidence, so far had human will and apprehension fallen. Additionally, everything must, psychologically and

25. *Ibid.,* Bk. III, Chap. 2, ¶ 11, in Vol. XX, 555.
26. *Ibid.,* Bk. III, Chap. 2, ¶ 15, in Vol. XX, 561.

theologically, undermine confidence, even to despair, since everything a person did or thought was tainted with sin.

How could the needed sublime confidence of election be *maintained* among the vicissitudes of a fallen world? Even the stoutest conscience always must be cognizant of sin and doubt. Imagine the obsessiveness, the compulsivity, finally the despair that this utterly constant need for assurance and reassurance would powerfully tend to evoke in the pious, who always saw utter damnation lurking behind every small daily activity, who saw doubt, by reason of pride, reside in the very condition of confidence. How often must condemnation of sin in others have been a confession of reprobation in oneself? For who could claim in all honesty all the time that they did not fall short of the glory of God? Who was not, in his heart, a hypocrite? How could such crypto-Manichaean hypostatizing of sin and vice not position such a believer as an adversary to God, mocked by absurdly incommunicable Good News? Surely these considerations added to the pervasiveness and ambivalence of the trope of theater in Renaissance habits of thought.

The essentially pathological pastoral theology of rigorist Protestantism has received extended discussion from several sources, though not in terms of darkly ironic inner theatricality. One historical exemplum was the tortured life of Nehemiah Wallington, a London turner who despaired of salvation so often and so fiercely because of sin and doubt that he thought the devil must take him, and he several times tried suicide. The theology of suffering meted out as Godly admonition to quicken the soul of the elect was in Wallington's psyche frequently confused with the foretaste of hell assigned to reprobates, and he was never able to acquire the necessary confidence in being elected.[27]

27. See the crucially important book by Paul R. Seaver, *Wallington's World: A Puritan Artisan in Seventeenth-Century London* (Stanford, 1985), and, equally important, John Stachniewski, *The Persecutory Imagination: English Puritanism and the Literature of Religious Despair* (Oxford, 1991). Stachniewski makes the vital point that the pathology of the Puritan imagination has often been softened or overlooked by modern historians and critics who had difficulty believing that any faith could have been so dark and despairing. But despair and the assurance of damnation were at the core of Calvinist psychology in the years from 1570 to 1640, and they must not be overlooked in assessing Jonson's (and Marvell's and Milton's) view of Calvinism. Here the historian has, of course, produced a shapely narrative of times the *exact* shape of which, and persons the *exact* exemplarity and number of whom, cannot be known, vividly though the narrative plays in the theater of each reader's mind. There are several books on Calvinism and Puritanism in England that we have found useful as historical context for the phenomenon of the English Puritan imagination and practice: Lucy Hutchinson, *Memoirs of the Life of Colonel Hutchinson,* ed. James Sutherland (Oxford, 1973), which was particularly useful;

A second and earlier case searchingly analyzed was Martin Luther himself, in the celebrated *Young Man Luther* of Erik Erikson. A sympathetic psychoanalytic approach characterized Erikson's description, drawn from the *Tischreden,* of Luther's *anfechtung,* his conviction that God's anger was turned against him and he could never be justified. But Luther drew from his dark night of the soul the message that faith followed doubt and that faith, the gift of grace, justified.[28] The Letter to the Romans came to his rescue (3:26–28). This was soft stuff, though; strict Calvinism had a much harder psychological edge.

Ironically—and the history of religion is nothing if not ironic—one of the fundamental reasons for the initial success of Protestantism, particularly in the towns, was the moral paranoia that afflicted many Catholics in the late fifteenth century. Driven by the feeling that they were devoured by sin, many literate and urban Catholics on the continent took to performing a wide variety of "good works." They listened to sermons (a constant practice likewise of Nehemiah Wallington), they went on pilgrimages, they purchased indulgences, they purchased books like *The Mirror of a Christian Way,* an influential manual of devotion by Dietrich Coelde, an Augustinian friar, which went through twenty-nine editions between 1480 and 1520.[29] Like other devotion-

---

Owen C. Watkins, *The Puritan Experience: Studies in Spiritual Autobiography* (New York, 1972); and Paul S. Seaver, *The Puritan Lectureships: The Politics of Religious Dissent, 1560–1662* (Stanford, 1970). For the important international aspect of Puritanism, see Keith L. Sprunger, *The Learned Doctor William Ames: Dutch Backgrounds of English and American Puritanism* (Urbana, 1972). On the movement toward Separatism, see Timothy George, *John Robinson and the English Separatist Tradition* (Macon, Ga., 1982). On the general Elizabethan background of moderates, as opposed to separatists, see Peter Lake, *Moderate Puritans and the Elizabethan Church* (Cambridge, Eng., 1982).

Allied with Lake and focused on the following years of James I and Archbishops Bancroft and Abbot is Daniel W. Doerksen, *Conforming to the Word: Herbert, Donne, and the English Church Before Laud* (Lewisburg, Pa., 1997); in various doctrinal senses (see Chaps. 1–3, 6–7), the median of the middle way may have been a moderate and conforming Calvinism friendly to Dort (and to Hippo and Wittenburg), unfriendly to Rome and Amsterdam. But he takes Donne's love as a tone or tactic of his doctrine; we take it as intrinsic to the heart of his doctrine, and his sacramentalism of sermon, calling, and liturgy implicated in it. One (fortunately) didn't have to cherish Andrewes or Laud to cherish sacramentalism.

28. Luther's psychology has proved fascinating in the modern West. See Erik Erikson, *Young Man Luther* (New York, 1958); for a standard biography of Luther, see Roland H. Bainton, *Here I Stand: A Life of Martin Luther* (New York, 1950).

29. See the important book by Steven E. Ozment, *The Reformation in the Cities: The Appeal of Protestantism to Sixteenth and Seventeenth Century Germany and Switzerland* (New Haven,

als, from Thomas à Kempis to Francis de Sales, Coelde advocated a lay version of the life of the convent. Article seven recommended the following prayer upon rising:

> O dear God, how I waste my precious time! How tired and slow I am! How I must burn for my sloth! During the night all spiritual souls have sung God's praise and I have overslept! There has been great joy in heaven and I have given it no thought. There has been great lamentation in purgatory, and I have not prayed. Many have died during the night, yet God has spared me.[30]

Wallington also overslept and had the same sense of spiritual failure and impending damnation and present reprobation. Coelde included seven things one might (must!) do to be assured that one was a friend of God. These included the Calvinist practices of attendence at sermons, constant prayer for forgiveness, and a continuous searching of one's conscience. These described the Calvinist interior life, tormented by terrifying anxiety concerning salvation. But Coelde was addressing Catholics who could partake of sacraments and good works. The Calvinist could do nothing but suffer. Or die. Despair-driven suicide was common enough that there were constant reminders and several books and pamphlets warning against it.[31] With the trope of journey so largely discounted, the trope of moment did not always suffice. Enough felt themselves reprobates and ignored the warnings so that attempted suicides and utter despair became one of the major problems of Calvinist pastoral care, comparable only to sin and the role of the elect in a sinful world.

1975), 24–32. See also Gerald Strauss, ed., *Pre-Reformation Germany* (New York, 1972), particularly the article by Bernd Moeller, "Religious Life in Germany on the Eve of the Reformation," 13–42, and Hermann Heinipel, "Characteristics of the Late Middle Ages in Germany," 43–72. Although German cities present an interesting point of contrast, our interest is primarily with English cities. While the demographics of English towns during the Reformation are somewhat tangential to our main focus on literature and religion, urban studies do provide significant context. For English towns, see Roger Finlay, *Population and Metropolis: The Demography of London, 1580–1650* (Cambridge, Eng., 1981); David Levine, *Family Formation in an Age of Nascent Capitalism* (New York, 1977); and Peter Clark and Paul Slack, eds., *Crisis and Order in English Towns, 1500–1700* (London, 1972). A long-valued illuminator of the Protestant lower bourgeoisie of London is George Unwin, *The Guilds and Companies of London* (4th ed.; New York, 1963).

30. Ozment, *The Reformation in the Cities,* 30–32.

31. Stachniewski, *The Persecutory Imagination,* Chap. 1, "English Puritanism and the Social Reality of Religious Despair," esp. 46–52; James D. Boulger, *The Calvinist Temper in English Poetry* (The Hague, 1980), 35–46; Seaver, *Wallington's World,* 21–24, 199–203.

Ben Jonson could find abundant reason in his culture to feel "full of rage and scorn," to use his own phrase, which William Kerrigan in a prominent essay has taken as characterizing the Jonsonian stance.[32] The poetic cries from such moments have, like Cordelia's tears, great power as reality tests, and we join the throng in honoring them and additionally would assert, from such considerations as those above, as well as their poetic expressivity, that Jonson himself took his turns to satire or complaint very seriously indeed. But we insist they were *occasional,* less fundamental to Jonsonian ontology (or, if you prefer, psychology) than his Christian hope and his range of love. Cordelia's tears, while important and implicated in her love, were less fundamental than her love. The analogy is limited but not casual. So, too, Jonson's poems of rage and scorn were special cases of his hopeful, nonrigorist, and presumably imperfect love, rather than the other way around.

Indeed, Jonson understood the Calvinist psychic experience only as an outside observer, not as a participant in the desperate feeling of helpless reprobation. He described the free-floating angst of Puritans as social priggishness and pecksniffery, not as *anfechtung* and potential suicide. Jonson's Puritans were essentially cartoon characters whose function was to disapprove, not deeply tragic persons whose entire life was given over to the "perverseness" of unrelenting scrupulosity, of a constant search, always successful, for the slightest sign of rising doubt or flagging confidence in salvation. Ananias and Pastor Tribulation Wholesome, the two Puritan and separatist characters in *The Alchemist,* fit into this exterior view of the saints as social pests and hypocrites. The surface of Puritanism could be fair game for fun. He satirized the turgid and politically correct speech of the Brethren, Christ-tide for Christmas (III, ii, 43), or the "visible mark of the beast in his forehead" (III, i, 8) or the saints' pretended forbearance in the face of disapproval:

> These chastisements are common to the saints,
> And such rebukes we of the separation
> Must bear with willing shoulders, as the trials
> Sent forth to tempt our frailties.
>
> (III, i, 1–4)

The language of self-justifying self-pity needed then and needs now glossing no more than do the Puritan names—names designed to beg a religious question.

32. William Kerrigan, "Ben Jonson Full of Rage and Scorn," *Studies in the Literary Imagination,* VI (1973), rpr. in *Ben Jonson,* ed. Harold Bloom (New York, 1987), 111–28.

But these were off-hand hits. Jonson reserved his main fire for what he conceived as the fundamental faults of the Puritans, their greed for money, their slippery moral standards and sharp practice, and their self-righteous hypocrisy in defending and justifying their conduct. Thus, in Act III of *The Alchemist:*

Tribulation: Good brother, we must bend unto all means,
That may give furtherance to the holy cause.
Ananias: Which his cannot: the sanctified cause
Should have a sanctified course.
Tribulation: Not always necessary.
The children of perdition are oft-times,
Made instruments even of the greatest works.

(III, i, 11–16)

What actor would not savor that "Not *always*"! The unsanctified course here involved buying the philosopher's stone, and thus supporting the damnable practice of magic, stealing from orphans, and counterfeiting money, hanging offenses every one. Coining money was now to be called "casting"; the synod had deliberated and redesignation made everything proper. Appropriating the orphans' mite was prudent investment; the iron and pewter would be greatly increased in value after the philosopher's stone turned it into gold. The philosopher's stone would only aid the "sanctified cause" of the saints and, by the way, align God's function of turning all evil into ultimate good with the Puritans. Everything, in the words of William S. Gilbert's cynical Pish-Tush, would be "right as right could be." Not to Jonson. This was serious satire, meant to point out serious sin and a threat to the peace of the Commonwealth.

Nevertheless, we continue to argue that Jonson was a cheerful moralist. It is not merely that he omitted the genuine horror attendant on Puritan spirituality; Jonson also gave his two Puritans a good end in *The Alchemist.* Although Ananias was depicted as a zealot (and thus a fool), and Tribulation as a darker sort of trickster, they did not suffer the implicitly fatal sentence of Volpone or Mosca, neither of whom could be called Puritans. At play's end, Ananias and Tribulation Wholesome faced frustration in recovering the orphans' goods, at a loss only of time and anticipated profit and perhaps *amour propre.* Beyond this, the two Puritans talked about crime but committed none. They were nuisances, but they were not arch-criminals.

What was true in *The Alchemist* was repeated in the later *Bartholomew Fair*, produced in 1614. Here again were Puritans with zany names (Win-the-Fight and Zeal-of-the-Land Busy) and characteristic hostility to joy and fun. He ridiculed again their propensity to turn every speech into a sermon. Zeal-of-the-Land Busy, for example, sermonizes on roast pig:

> [It] may be eaten, and in the Fair. I take it, in a booth, the tents of the wicked. The place is not much, not very much; we may be religious in midst of the profane, so it be eaten with a reformed mouth, with sobriety, and humbleness, not gorged in with gluttony or greediness; there's the fear . . . it were not well, it were not fit, it were abominable, and not good.
>
> (I, v, 70–79)

Such persons Jonson again freely called hypocrites, but he did not depict them as thieves or cut-purses, and he laughed at their exterior affectations, not at the profound depression and stark terror in their interior lives. Fallen like all humanity, they were perhaps exasperating but more pitiful than vile. Their hypocrisy and greed and self-righteousness were transparent and dismissible. Of course, it was still early. By 1639, to those of Jonson's or Donne's persuasion, the saints would seem far more threatening.

Beyond Jonson's charity toward Puritans was his equal consideration for Dol Common in *The Alchemist.* Dol was certainly a common woman and probably a wicked one as well; certainly she was engaged in two outlawed professions, prostitution and bunco. Her own references to the cart and whip indicated an awareness of both social disapproval and personal danger. But Jonson made it impossible to dislike her, something that could not be said of his Puritans. She was sensible and intelligent, trying to compose the endemic quarrel between her two rascally co-conspirators in the venture tripartite, an effort always both needed and doomed by male greed and bad faith. She played her roles with ingenuity and good humor, in spite of the constant threat of betrayal from both Face and Subtle, who were scheming to marry Dame Pliant. Of all the active characters in *The Alchemist,* Dol was by far the most honest, striving to keep faith, however bad the cause, while everyone else was a user of people, a cynical profiteer, and a liar. One may be tempted to ask what a relatively nice girl like Dol was doing in a place like Face's den.

Whether or not Jonson intended it (as he well may have), the analogy with the dynamic in *The Taming of the Shrew* is suggestive. In the Shakespearean comedy, a socially disapproved woman achieved love and amiability while her socially approved sister Bianca achieved the status of shrew apparent. In *The Alchemist* the socially disapproved "suster" earned our recognition of essential decency (something akin to charity), while "suster" Pliant gave a hint of spirit. Can one doubt that expressed impatience with the "Spaniard's" slowness will find repair from hende Jeremy? We cannot prove but we suspect: Jonson was deliberately surpassing in ironic subtlety his rival and superior playwright's conclusion (itself subtle enough to be misconstrued by undergraduates even now). We are more confident that a poet and dramatist so skilled in ironic distance must leaven his moral criticism with humor and affection.

All comedy is city comedy. So we believe, though we will *argue* only that Renaissance stage comedy in English is, all of it, city comedy.[33] While rural inhabitants had chivarees, routs, jokes, gossip, mimicry, pratfalls, and village fairs to "spend a merrier hour," only the city could body forth and reciprocally be represented by a genre as organized, as extended over time, as artificially constructed and institutionally implicated as comedy. Only the city could elaborate on the stock situations, characters, and plots used by the Renaissance, that is to say, Plautine comedy. The basic requirements of Plautine / Renaissance comedy: literacy, a money economy, a substantial variety of caste and contiguous class, juxtaposition of sophistication and social ignorance, freedom for social climbing and rampant ambition in general, an asymmetry that assigned greater natural endowments to the socially weaker but not powerless characters, a plot that led to *limited* transformation and / or humbling, and a marriage or reconciliation at the end in celebration of love, understand-

33. On the notion of a specifically Renaissance city comedy, see Brian Gibbons, *Jacobean City Comedy* (London, 1980). See, at large, Jonathan Haynes, *The Social Relations of Jonson's Theater* (Cambridge, Eng., 1992). For several "micropolitical" contexts, especially of patronage, see Robert C. Evans, *Ben Jonson and the Contexts of His Time* (Lewisburg, Pa., 1994); he also shows Jonson's notions of wit "very much involved in questions of . . . power" (questions we see as adjudicated by love) in "Wit and the Power of Jonson's *Epigrammes*," in *The Wit of Seventeenth-Century Poetry,* ed. Summers and Pebworth, 101–18. More particularly at this point, see Jonathan Haynes, "Representing the Underworld: *The Alchemist,*" *Studies in Philology,* LXXXVI (1989), 18–41, narrowly but informatively focused on cony-catching, criminality, and "nascent capitalism."

ing, and forgiveness to indicate that there could be right order in this world, though limited in scope and time. All this could be understood as a psychic description of the city, and it certainly did not exist in any such configuration in the countryside. Indeed, comedies that had a rural locale generally revolved around the doings and misdoings of the dislocated urban folk, only temporarily in Belmont or Arden or Caliban's island (or adventitiously in Windsor, Heartbreak House, or Horseback Hall). We remember that Mr. Deeds went to town, Mr. Smith went to Washington, and Petrucchio and the would-be Duke of Drown'd-Lands also headed for the city, like Aaron Slick.

Literacy might seem a doubtful or peripheral requirement for comedy, but it played three necessary roles within the plot. At the simplest and most obvious level, characters sent notes, read and signed contracts, or, like Portia and Isabella, went to law. Beyond that, Renaissance comedic plots and situations often assumed varying degrees of literacy in the characters. The venture tripartite in *The Alchemist,* albeit oral, made no sense in an oral setting; they could not have hatched a scheme based on medieval and Renaissance natural philosophy had they or their gulls not been literate and in a context of literacy. Finally, comedy required at least an appreciation of the social power given by literacy, even if—perhaps especially if—the individual member of the audience could not read. Literacy added to the sense of social recognition that was essential to comedy.[34]

Further, comedy required a money economy, which during the Renaissance functioned most completely in town. The complicated and sophisticated bunco schemes to cheat the unwary, which formed so central a part of Jonson's comedy, were not believable in an economy of barter and farthings. Nor were they worth the trouble; the projectors in *The Staple of News* were not going to gain an ignoble living by selling penny items to old countrywomen. Alchemical secrets were not part of the village barter market, jumbled with leeks and goose grease. We also note the thriving urban market in rank, preferment, and wives, all involving money and all staples of comedy. This aspect

34. Gale H. Carrithers, Jr., "City Comedy's Sardonic Hierarchy of Literacy," *SEL,* XXIX (1989), 337–55. For Jonson as himself consummate textualist, see Richard Dutton, *Ben Jonson: To the First Folio* (Cambridge, Eng., 1983), and his *Ben Jonson: Authority: Criticism* (London, 1996), esp. 40–53, 140–62; the nine essays in *Ben Jonson's 1616 Folio,* ed. Jennifer Brady and W. H. Herendeen (Newark, Del., 1991); and (opening into issues of real self-change versus mere theatrical role-playing) Raphael Falco, *Conceived Presences: Literary Genealogy in Renaissance England* (Amherst, 1994), Chap. 3.

has particular resonance for Renaissance comedy, in view of the work by Max Weber on urban religion (Calvinism), literacy, money, and the social attitudes this mix might be expected to include.[35]

Beyond this, comedy required a wide variety of class and caste along with the genuine possibility of rapid social mobility in the time span, say, of five acts or a few days. The village could provide nothing like this. Birth and land, the stable and traditional requirements of position or its lack in the countryside, restricted mobility to the time span of generations (fit for novels). Moreover, rural social rigidity was compounded by wide distinctions among the few social classes. Variety in trade or calling was limited on the land. The asymmetricality of Renaissance comedy was thwarted by stolid rural social endurance. Only in a city did the rich variation of social power, class, money, literacy, talent, physical attractiveness, intelligence or cunning, perceived or real, have both scope and propinquity for full comic development. Only in town did the frog turn into the prince or the servant become the master. In the village the servant might outwit the master, and frequently did, but this was class guerilla warfare, not mobility, for the servant could never thereby become the master. It was not for nothing that Dick Whittington came to London, for only there could he make his fortune and meet Geoffrey Chaucer. All was possible in the city; at least Petrucchio thought so, and the gaudy and enticing menu of urban possibility to transcend external limits gave comedy its compelling interest. A tart could impersonate a foreign duchess and, for an act, get away with it. The oft-noted disparity in comedy between appearance and reality, the almost omnipresent (and successful) use of mask and disguise in comedy, the moment of unveiling and discovery, the anxiety over tricks that might be discovered, the juggling of hope and failure, all this was urban. In town, the asymmetry of talent and formal position was clever, the bunco schemes were daring, the bumbling elderly would-be lovers were funny, the disguised swain or maid, charming. In the village, where everyone and everything was known and settled, such schemes were madness, unequal loves were impudence and presumption, and tricks were mean-spirited villainy. If the lord's daughter eloped with the coachman, they ran away to town, where they might cease being criminals and become interesting.

35. Max Weber, *The Protestant Ethic and the Spirit of Capitalism* (Los Angeles, 1996). On Jonson and news, see Paul R. Sellin, "The Politics of Ben Jonson's 'Newes from the New World Discover'd in the Moone,'" *Viator,* XVII (1986), 321–37.

Comedy thus afforded scope for the outrageous, for social climbers, and for the crazily ambitious. The German social proverb that the city air made one free was true not only in law but also in existential reality. No one climbed quickly in the country, and most did not climb at all. The declining gentry, such an issue for a generation of historians after 1945, were always considered to be declining (or not) over generations, not days or even years. In the city, however, the lucky could move up through the contiguous social classes to the very edge of caste, the hereditary aristocracy, where title but not birth could be bought. Such determined and impudent social climbing was often held in contempt, as by the Belle Époque French countess who remarked that in her day one did not arrive. But in comedy one almost did, if only to be embarrassingly denied at the threshold of acceptance, yet often still above one's lower-class origins. Ultimate failure crowned substantial, though partial, success. The rampant ambition of the hyperkinetic projectors in Jonson's comedies fared the same way. The scam described in the play was not completely successful, but the idea was a good one and the schemers might, to quote Mickey Mantle, "get them next time." The city freed people to try to change their lives, by fair means or foul, by "luck or pluck," and, after one failure, often permitted another effort. The artistic acceleration of the pace of such activities by a Jonson or a Middleton yielded a sort of dizzy delirium that was an important generic component of comedy, as Rogier Caillois has theorized and innumerable cinematic chases have shown.[36]

Still more, comedy often juxtaposed the (sometimes only seemingly) sophisticated urban bunco-steerer with the green rural rube. The author could string together a series of jokes, from costume to accent to inappropriate replies and gestures, that mocked the countryman's lack of comprehension of the latest urban modes. As the rural butt-of-all-jokes stood confused by the endless and often implausible kaleidoscope of urban change and complexity, the audience, smug from being *dans le vent,* could see plot advanced and character delineated. Social embarrassment or potential embarrassment were part of the Renaissance stock in trade, and their resolution was an element of the plot, as with the mixed-up lovers of *A Midsummer Night's Dream* or the pageant-makers and -viewers in *Love's Labors Lost.*

Beyond this, we judge that Renaissance comedy rested upon a foundation

36. Rogier Caillois, *Jeux et Sports* (Davis, Calif., 1967), 5–16, 150–80. His four elements are *agon* (contest of skill), *alea* (chance), *mimesis* (mimicry), and *ilinx* (delirium or vertigo).

of asymmetry of social status and power, inside information, intelligence, beauty, ambition, capacity, virtue, and nobility or baseness among the characters. Social nobility of rank ought to be congruent with natural nobility of character. Gods should be more moderate than men, Euripides argued in *The Bacchae,* and, in the same way, the mighty should be wiser and more forbearing than the meek. But they were not, and a great deal of medieval and Renaissance social commentary, including the entire "Mirror of Princes" genre, was devoted to how this glaring social defect might be remedied. It could not be repaired, though, not by good example or good precept, not in any way, for a fallen world was, in part, defined by the oppression and hypocrisy of such asymmetry. Comedy touched this exposed and vulnerable social nerve, showing the audience (viewers and readers) the hideous results of asymmetry: marriage loveless, fraud rewarded, hypocrisy triumphant, justice denied, "insolence of office," good order confounded in ways both large and small. In comedy asymmetry was itself adjusted, a temporal and therefore temporary (and comic) analogy to death that had lost its sting. In comedy good order triumphed over social power put to vicious use; the tables were turned in the fifth act, and the schemes of the (comparatively) virtuous succeeded (for a time). The abyss had been avoided. The audience smiled, though reassurance that things would work out well was tempered by the knowledge that they almost had not and did not always. Comedy made asymmetry both starkly visible and socially bearable.

In comedy, therefore, this inequality, this asymmetry, was the mainspring of the plot. With Plautus, the clever and attractive characters were concentrated at the bottom of the social scale, with the virgin and the slave outwitting the *miles gloriosus* or the *senex amans.* It was the same in Niccolo Machiavelli's *Mandragola.* With Jonson, the asymmetry tended to run to virtue and vice rather than to stupidity and intelligence, the latter of which was not uncommonly linked to vice, thus making right order both more humanly ambiguous and also moral (*caritas*) rather than intellectual or a function of erotic love. But the mechanism was the same: The vicious with apparent advantage were undone, those who were unserious or even silly frequently escaped more or less intact, and those with even modest capacity to do good were rewarded. With Jonson, though, the rewards of marriage were frequently murky at best, and the plotters often escaped hanging. Ben had lived in London too long to be even theatrically convinced that the good moral order would clearly triumph. Thus, with Jonson, the humbling of the proud or malicious was not the occasion for beginning a new life. Jonson saw situations reversed, not people and not society in general. Indeed, for Jonson, the undoing of wrong-doing had about it almost the character of an accident. With a little more luck the plotters would have gotten away with it. In the short run anything was possible, and the divine beneficence certain in the long run might involve a very long run indeed. Didn't he increasingly suspect as much? Certainly, he was no millenarian.

The moral statement made by Renaissance theatrical comedy, whether made through marriage or through other reconciliation, was often ambiguous, if not genuinely cynical. Of the three newlywed couples in *The Taming of the Shrew,* only Kate and Petrucchio, at play's conclusion, seem to have achieved love and harmony. Although Theseus claimed he was wedding Hippolyta by love, not force, most adults would question that thin though romantic and well-meant imposture. The reconciliation in the *Midsummer Night's Dream* within the commonwealth and between fairy time and human time was also tentative and ambiguous.[37] We see in this hauntingly beautiful play more hope for good than firm conviction that right order will be established.

Shakespeare's comedy was more optimistic than Jonson's. The latter's rarely even hinted that good order was coming, that there would be reconciliation among characters and within the commonwealth. The best Jonson could find was that the would-be Duke of Drown'd-Lands was going to keep his marriage, would listen more to a virtuous and sensible wife, and would not have to be told that he was the greatest fool in Christendom not currently ruling a country. Jonson always remembered that the world was fallen and that, while individuals might be saved, the commonwealth could not be. The attempt to build a city on a hill, a constant ambition of the Puritans both at home and in New England, was, for Jonson, akin to the attempt to build the Tower of Babel. Its failure was inevitable; its attempt, impudent; its very concept, disgraceful and antisocial. For Jonson, the city as a character was a context of fallenness, *though not of reprobation.* The city was classically comedic, a setting of nuances and shadows where the inclination toward goodness coexisted with the slide to perdition, usually in the same character. The issue was always im-

37. See Carrithers and Hardy, *Milton and the Hermeneutic Journey,* 108. For the most strenuous explication of Jonson's unique adaptation of the pastoral tradition and its general civic (as opposed to merely topical) implications, see Joseph Loewenstein, *Responsive Readings: Versions of Echo in Pastoral, Epic, and the Jonsonian Masque* (New Haven, 1984).

mediately in doubt, though eschatologically never in doubt; so in some characters and on some level, the play turned toward reconciliation, a reminder in comedy of the tropes and of the ultimate destination of all humanity. The *civitas terrena* was, after all, a glass darkly reflecting the *civitas Dei.* As a genre comedy never forgot that.

Within this theoretical framework, we turn to several of Jonson's comedies with all of their dark edges, their ambiguities, their sense that virtue triumphed as much by good luck as by the overreaching of vice and folly. The six comedies we here notice all centered on specific social / moral disorders: projectors (today called developers) of expensive, large, fraudulent, and antisocial schemes of "improvement" and "progress"; disordered households; the worship of gold; elaborate confidence schemes; the prevalence of public vulgarity and rout; the elaboration of canting; the general construal of virtue as fit only for (some) women, the stupid, or the gulled. These are all bad things, and comedy is required to set them right; "Of that there is no shadow of doubt," as Gilbert's Grand Inquisitor in *The Gondoliers* sang. For Jonson there was doubt, at least as to the efficacy of comedy. We would not forget the darkness, the ambiguities. In *Volpone,* the vulture, the raven, and the crow were as morally culpable as the fox or the fly, yet the former lived, albeit in diminished circumstances.

Begin with the quintessential man of the theatrical trope, Jeremy / Face / Lungs: a quintuple fraud—to his partners in gulling whom he hustled over the back fence with no loot and the watch in pursuit; to the gulls themselves; to his master Lovewit, whose house he turned into a den of confidence tricksters and whom he certainly will crown with horns; to his new mistress whom he has hustled into a dubious marriage; and, finally, to himself, becoming a "no-face" who scarcely has a self to know, having become mere opportunism and appetite. If theater was the trope of dissimulation, from *carpe diem* to the technological power fix, then Jeremy *et al.* was the end result of such a life.

The masking implicit in theatricality can be seen as well in *Volpone,* in the antimasque in Act I, scene ii, with the charade of Volpone playing the mountebank and, in imaginary form, with the chimeras of grandiose scheme and gnostic knowledge that the self-deluded Sir Politic Would-be so desperately wished to believe.[38] The antimasque was a crazed parody of transformation, from Apollo to Calvinism, that "will drop you forth a libel, or a sanctified lie, / Betwixt every spoonful of a nativity-pie"(*Volpone,* I, ii, 45–46). Whether

38. Jonas A. Barish, "The Double Plot in *Volpone,*" *Modern Philology,* LI (1953), 83–92.

this sequence of transformation was advance or decline may be left to individual judgment, but the series was at an end. Androgyno the hermaphrodite was changing no more, being delighted with his / her present state. Such stability was not sexual but fatuous: "Your Fool wherewith I am so taken" (I, ii, 50). As Mosca sang to close the entertainment:

> Fools, they are the only nation
> Worth men's envy or admiration;
> Free from care or sorrow-taking,
>
> . . . .
>
> He's the grace of every feast
> And, sometimes, the chiefest guest.
> (I, ii, 66–68, 76–77)

The praise of fools, sharp enough in echoes of the literature of folly and in contemporary application, gained theatrical resonance from its association with Volpone's three creatures, the dwarf, the eunuch, and the hermaphrodite. All were monsters and added to the trope of *theatrum mundi* the additional weight of unnaturalness, of carrying dissimulation beyond the merely human masking, whether social or criminal. If not Volpone's biological offspring (can we know?), they are in allegorical masque-terms the proper issue of his spirit, his likeliest family.

In *Bartholomew Fair,* masking and pretense were a considerable subplot, involving the pompous Justice Overdo, working always "in Justice' name, and the King's and for the Commonwealth!" in his lugubrious search for "enormities." Imitating his betters in the "Mirror for Magistrates" genre or the duke in *Measure for Measure,* Adam Overdo wished to do justice, not to be fooled on the bench by the "unintelligible perjuries" (in Mencken's phrase) of the rabble brought before him. While touring the fair in disguise, Overdo failed to detect the real crime, was praised by a madman in between assorted thrashings and a sojourn in the stocks, and lost his ward to a marriage he did not choose. No matter. After the puppet play within the play, a familiar Renaissance device for showing both the truth and the theater of theater, all was straightened out.[39] Crime was forgiven, stupidity overlooked, defensible marriages arranged, and, in a gust of generosity and forgiveness, Justice Overdo forgot enormities and invited all to dinner:

39. The puppet play is in Jonson's *Bartholomew Fair,* V, iv, and V, v. Interrupted continuously by comments from the audience, it acts as a mirror for the rest of the play.

> I will have none fear to go
> along, for my intents are *ad*
> *correctionem non ad destructionem;*
> *ad aedificandum, non ad diruendum.*
> (V, vi, 110–12)

Only Zeal-of-the-Land Busy did Jonson leave unregenerate. Zeal's last speeches were not *ad regnem caritatis* but toward denunciation, this time of the theater. It was not a proper calling, Zeal said, but instead "a beam, a very beam, not a beam of the sun, nor a beam of the moon, nor a beam of balance, neither a house-beam nor a weaver's beam, but a beam in the eye, in the eye of the Brethren; a very great beam, an exceeding great beam; such as are your stage-players, rhymers" (V, v, 5–9). It was going to take more than a good supper to reconcile Zeal-of-the-Land to reconciliation. It may be taken as Jonson's comment on self-righteousness.

In *Bartholomew Fair,* the trope of theatricality took yet another form, not of masking and disguise or of truth discovered and right order established and true nobility rewarded, but of stretching the genre of comedy to include a variety of dramatic and symbolic styles and forms. Jonson here wrote a loose string of vignettes connected by the background of the fair, similar in many ways to the Elizabethan tilts or the earlier mystery plays depicting the cosmic *Commedia.*[40] The Coventry or Wakefield cycles on their pageant wagons or the tilts with their royal pavilion, the tents, and the crowd of jousters were comparable in form to *Bartholomew Fair* with its line of canvas booths. Nonetheless, behind the wagons rose the church and its service of salvation; behind the tilt stood the quasi-divine authority of the queen; but behind the canvas booths lay the mixed terrestrial, but potentially Godly city. We recall from the "Famous Voyage" what authority and character the city possessed. A playgoer did not have to be a Puritan to understand the city as a place of sin and deception (whatever local and temporary evidences of grace it might present). But the comparison was not all to the disadvantage of the stage or of the city. As he did from the Church and the Monarch, Jonson sought justice from theatricality. The fair *was* the occasion for improving the social order. The trickster's scheme served to reward all according to need, though not always according to desire. Ragged as it was dramatically, *Bartholomew Fair* gave a hint

40. Roy Strong, *The Cult of Elizabeth: Elizabethan Portraiture and Pageantry* (Berkeley, 1986), Chaps. 4 and 5; see also Peter Happe, ed., *English Mystery Plays* (London, 1975).

of the betterment of the Commonwealth in a secular exercise in pageantry. As the wretched puppet playlet was to the classical story behind it and to serious London theater framing it, so was the theatricalized canvas fair to the city of wood and stone wherein love, justice, learning, and beauty had some intermittent purchase, and it to the never-fully-imaginable community of the City of God.

In contrast to *Bartholomew Fair, Epicoene* was a tightly constructed Plautine comedy, built in the great classical tradition. Here were all the right characters, such as the Plautine *senex* or Panteleone from the commedia dell'arte, with the added Jonsonian touch of a false Columbine. *Epicoene* abounded with fools. The knights, Sir Jack Daw and Sir Amorous La Foole, held obviously purchased rank, which could not cover their personal defects as cowards, liars, and cads. Lawyers and parsons, as a class, did not escape ridicule; the learned debate on divorce, half in Latin, between the barber Cutbeard, disguised as a canon lawyer, and Otter, impersonating a cleric, had sufficient verisimilitude to require an advance retraction of satirical intent. The snobbish ladies of the college were perhaps no better, though the playwright did not use them so badly. The presumptive heir, Sir Dauphine Eugenie, was possessed of true nobility, at least on the testimony of the fools and snobs, though he gained control of his inheritance through a low and abominable trick, which the audience applauds. As Plautine comedy demanded, (comparatively) good social order triumphed, asymmetry was overcome, fools looked foolish, and, at the end, all was (partly) forgiven. The ending of *Epicoene* also contained a genuine surprise, giving an additional comic twist to all that had gone before. Epicoene, the supposedly silent woman who had become a common scold upon marriage, was unmasked as a boy, which was instantly recognized by those two giants in canon law, Cutbeard and Otter, as a "justum impedimentum in primo gradu." In *Epicoene,* the disguise was not merely incidental as in *Volpone* or *The Alchemist* or *Bartholomew Fair;* it went here to the very core of identity. The entire play was brought together by the unmasking of the silent woman turned scold now turned boy. All of the previous tricks were shown to have been in the nature of puppet theater and now made sense as part of a coherent whole engineered by the master puppeteer Sir Dauphine. Was it true that in comedy there was truth? Or was so managerial a figure as Sir Dauphine not alarming?

In a manner more alarming, potentially terrifying, Jonson hinted that it might be truthful, in *The Devil Is an Ass,* written about projects and projectors in 1616. *The Devil Is an Ass* began with a metaphorical and comic exemplum of the greatest project of them all, the corruption of humanity by Satan. But Satan's emissary, a minor devil named Pug, soon discovered that things were worse up here than they were down there, a deeply serious suggestion in the early seventeenth century, even when posed in a comic context. Pug asks:

> Can any fiend
> Boast of a better Vice than here by nature
> And Art they're owners of?
>
> (II, i, 187–89)

A good question, though not a new one. Jonson was not the first moralist to suggest that there is "no hell / To a lady of fashion" (V, ii, 14–15). Poor Pug was always "out-gone," being merely "an Everydevil, taken beyond his depth in depravity by the self-serving plots of all the human beings around him."[41] All of the evil imaginable was already on tap.

Corruption is always promising material for comedy, and Jonson constructed an appropriate plot around it, the conning of Squire Fitzdottrel, who was so greedy, so naïve, so perfect a combination of sin and stupidity that he was a gull to the manner born. This individual mark stood as the reflection in miniature of the whole satanic project of the corruption of humanity, which was the framing megaplot of the play. Pug and Satan were Merecraft *et al.* writ large, though only in the sense of enduring. As the metaphysical project ended, Satan whisked poor Pug back to hell to the accompaniment of violent abuse. Pug was nothing but "dull, damn'd defects" who had less evil in "a finger and a thumb" than the cut-purse whose body he had borrowed.

The human project involved a group of complex and related schemes hatched by Merecraft to gull Fitzdottrel to invest in draining the Norfolk fens, thus becoming the Duke of Drown'd-Lands and to enroll Mistress Fitzdottrel in a fake school of etiquette to learn how to be a duchess. In the early Stuart years of projects and arrivistes, this was a plausible imposture, but it was well beyond the power of Merecraft and his gang of grifters. Here was

41. Robert N. Watson, *Ben Jonson's Parodic Strategy: Literary Imperialism in the Comedies* (Cambridge, Mass., 1987), 173; Chap. 7 deals with *The Devil Is an Ass.* The term *Everydevil* comes from C. G. Thayer, *Ben Jonson: Studies in the Plays* (Norman, Okla., 1963), 162. W. David Kay argues Jonson there "narrows his satire's focus": yes, insofar as its target is the Earl of Argyle and Sir Robert Carr; no, insofar as it is the religion of *projects,* of technological-economic power (*Ben Jonson,* 152).

Jonson's wry realism; some of the credit virtue gets ought to go to incompetence. Some, but not all. The hard rock on which the fanciful improvisation of Merecraft foundered was the one he least expected because he could never see it: love. Rescued from participation in the ruin of the squire by his love for his wife, Wittipol, the confidence trickster manqué, conveyed control of the squire's lands and destiny to the honest and capable Eustace Manly. Again, we notice Jonson's irony. While goodness in the form of love defeated human fraud, evil in the form of human ability to outsin Pug defeated the satanic scheme. Again, the improbable occurred; asymmetry was overcome, and a simulacrum of good order was established. But it was unconvincing. The trope of theater, with its innumerable variety of seemings, disguises, masks, recognitions, and surprises, was attenuated here. For the believing audience of 1616, the devil was not an ass, and a human soul that dealt in witchcraft, as Fitzdottrel did in the last act, was preternaturally fortunate to escape with merely being an ass.[42]

The most modern of Jonson's comedies was *The Staple of News,* produced in 1625, a play from what Dryden called his "dotage." In *Staple,* the truth was presented, not as what actually happened, not as what was reported to have happened, not even as what was understood to have been reported to have happened (now called spin), but *only* as what was *sold* about the understanding of the report of the event. Anything unsold or unsalable (without a sponsor) ceased to have the name of "news" but became instead a form of technological waste. Information treated as a product created a triple mirror of theatricality, as event was thrice refracted through reportage, spin, and sale before becoming reality. Only through the parable of the projectors and their new business / scam / public service could so extended a metaphor of the *theatrum mundi* be launched. In this case, Marshall McLuhan was right: The medium was the heart of the message.

Jonson's acute social vision went beyond a new and startling definition of news; it also included an appreciation of the sources of news. Some news came from the maid Joan Hearsay or other sources "of doubtful credit: as barber's news / And tailor's news, porters' and watermans' news" (I, v, 9–10). Of doubtful credit? This is precisely the news we all believe, even though it is di-

42. Keith Thomas, *Religion and the Decline of Magic: Studies in Popular Beliefs in Sixteenth- and Seventeenth-Century England* (London, 1971), esp. Chaps. 15 and 17 on the religious and social implications of witchcraft.

minished and devalued by the name of gossip. Today, gossip is supposed to be sharply separated from news. Secrecy is part of the separation; gossip has retained its original secret character whereas orthodox news is disseminated everywhere. Hence the popularity of the "inside story," or "exclusive." Accuracy is another supposed differentiation; news is thought (or imagined) to be true. Source is a third alleged distinction, with gossip coming from biased neighbors, whereas news is purveyed by affluent professionals. Breadth also divides the two, with gossip treating of the relatively private only whereas news involves public affairs (and persons). During Jonson's time, however, none of these purported distinctions existed, either in fact or in cultural psychology. Baroque government and society were still intensely personal. The rise and fall of Somerset in the estimation of James I was both news and gossip, as was the later career of the Duke of Buckingham. The "faceless bureaucrat" had not yet replaced real persons. The health of the state, and not infrequently its life as well, really depended on the intellect and character of monarchs and ministers and their vulnerability to flattery.[43] The irony in *The Staple of News* came not from confusing news with gossip and travel and "wonders" in a single potpourri; it arose from confusion over which news was valuable, who was more likely to provide a bit of truth, and who was most likely to be gulled.

There was more in *Staple,* however, than the words of news; there was also the news of the Word. Jonson had profound mistrust for "projects" or public power without moral purpose or legitimacy, as we have previously argued when discussing the masques. Here Jonson echoed Augustine, who, in the *Confessions,* gave far more attention to sins of false doctrine, false teaching,

43. On the reliability of news and its personal nature, see the generally available English translation by Edward Seymour Forster, *The Turkish Letters of Ogier Ghieslin de Busbecq* (London, 1927). Although the first English translation was not until 1694, there were several printed editions in the sixteenth and seventeenth centuries. For a contemporary example of news management that produced news less accurate than Busbecq's, though probably more reliable than the staple office, see Jonathan Schell, *The Time of Illusion* (New York, 1975), about the Nixon White House. Finally, in discussing news and flattery, one must consider the foremost Renaissance authority on things political: see Niccolo Machiavelli, *The Prince,* ed. and trans. James B. Atkinson (Indianapolis, 1976), Chap. 23, on flattery, and Chap. 21, on prestige. See also, of course, the recent and superb study on Machiavelli: Sebastian de Grazia, *Machiavelli in Hell* (New York, 1989), Chaps. 8–12, esp. Chap. 10. Machiavelli, in his political thought, did not forget that humanity was fallen; thus, republican civic humanist that he clearly was, he was also profoundly pessimistic.

and false report than he did to the myriad sins of the flesh.[44] There was, of course, news other than the Good News, indeed, so much that the Good News was hard to hear. But the fallen din should neither be increased nor applauded (still less, falsified), for any such misordering detracted from the good of the community.

Jonson's comedy participated in the dominant tropes beyond theater, which here displayed itself in dramatic representation. He also exploited the trope of moment, usually in antic form, from the moment of recognition and unmasking, through a Plautine acceleration of pace portraying a kaleidoscope of moments as manic-disjunctive secular busyness, to a parody of the salvific moment. As with theater, moment was softened in Jonson's comedy (and, we would suggest, all comedy) so that the characters on stage escaped the direst consequences of their crucial action and were let off with a warning or a wedding.

The moment of unmasking and recognition in *Epicoene* fit such a pattern. Sir Dauphine removed Epicoene's wig, revealing the *soi-disant* and *ci-devant* silent woman as "a boy, a gentleman's son that [he] ha[d] brought up this half year" (V, 4). This single stroke of recognition resolved every plot and subplot, even those we (the readers and audience) had not previously been aware existed. Everyone was gulled by the master of events, Sir Dauphine. Morose suffered a lot, Truewit and Clerimont only a bit, Otter and Cutbeard all in fun, Daw and La Foole with more malice, the ladies collegiate with less animus. And, at the end, all was revealed. All? Do we not now see "through a glass darkly" and only then "face to face"? Plautine comedy finesses moment as it does the *theatrum mundi,* making revelation an occasion for levity and turning Dantesque fraud into social masks.

Moment also appeared as a series of events, as in the "progress" toward goals and / or the philosopher's stone in *The Alchemist.* Here the moment was, like modern "recovery," divided into twelve steps, these being the stages of alchemical transformation leading to projection, when success in the form of gold was to be achieved.[45] But cohobation, inceration, or maceration never

44. See Augustine, *Confessions,* Bks. 3–7.

45. See Michael Jamieson, ed., *Three Comedies: Ben Jonson* (London, 1966), 179–84, for a brief "Note on Alchemy." This excellent epitome of the alchemical knowledge needed to understand the play also refers the reader to C. G. Jung, *Psychology and Alchemy* (London, 1953), an examination of alchemy as part of the Renaissance "habits of thought." Now, more at large, see Stanton J. Linden, *Darke Hierogliphicks: Alchemy in English Literature from Chaucer to the*

quite arrived, and projection remained always in the middle distance. In the play, of course, the apparatus and the scheme literally exploded to the ironic cry of "God and all the saints be good to us" (IV, vi, 55–56). Every instance of human moment, from carefully designed fraud to accidental and unanticipated truth, was engaged in the description of alchemy.

The Alchemist and *Bartholomew Fair* also depicted moment as skewed by the accelerated pace demanded by situation comedy. Not only did characters enter and depart suddenly, but subplots were multiplied as the play progressed. By the last act both the subplots and the various characters were competing for attention and resolution. A neat and clever resolution in *Epicoene* was the exception; elsewhere the trope of moment deteriorated to the mundane level of human busyness, of hustle and hassle not quite mindless or purposeless, that was instantly recognizable by its urban audience (then and now) and was genuinely funny (and pathetic). Such a parody of moment, though, a comforting gumbo of confusion, mistake, misunderstanding, opportune outcome, and "come-uppance," depicted just the local face of tropic truth. Jonson did not forget, though some in his audience might have, the serious interrelationships of city, comedy, and theatrical stage-setting:

> For here we have no continuing city, but we seek one to come.
> (Heb. 13:14, Authorized Version)

All statecraft, when not farcical, is potentially tragic. Whether Jonson would have generalized thus or not, certainly tragedy of state was for him far more bleak than the image depicted by Sir Joshua Reynolds in his soulful portrait of *Mrs. Sarah Siddons as the Tragic Muse.* In two Senecan tragedies on Roman themes, one from the republic and one from the empire, *Sejanus: His Fall,* produced in 1603, and *Catiline,* in 1611, Jonson dwelt on the tragic general implications of the inevitable corruption of the fallen state. Indeed, the essential and indispensable element of classical and Renaissance tragedy was its public aspect. There was very little tragedy, until the Enlightenment, that did not deal with the state, either in the person of the ruler or in the implications of ambition, pride, and conspiracy around the king. The folly of Lear was com-

Restoration (Lexington, Ky., 1996); Jonson's *Alchemist* and *Mercury Vindicated* are considered in Chap. 7, the latter as championing "nature" over the "art" of Bacon and the New Science; yes, but Jonson was as concerned with grace as nature.

pounded by the vice of his daughters and their husbands. The arrogance of Caesar fell easy victim to the self-righteousness of Brutus and the malignant plotting of Cassius. From Agamemnon and Clytemnestra, Electra and Orestes on, the state had always worn a tragic, theatrical aspect, and politics had been the occasion for themes of destruction, despair, and death. The geographic scope of the state might be reduced to Faustus' study (if augmented by the Kingdom of Darkness) or Malta or Cyprus. But even domestic tragedy, from Thomas Heywood to George Lillo to Fyodor Dostoyevsky to Theodore Dreiser and Arthur Miller, has depended heavily on some surrogate for the state as power-complex, on construals as if of the City of God, or on permutations of the family as principality or of economic order as more or less ironized *imperium* (City of Mammon).[46]

The constant tragic role of the state had some variation in style and intensity. In *Antigone,* the polis, in the persons of Creon and the Chorus, was a tragic actor / commentator in view of the audience. In *King Lear* the tragic pall of the kingdom covered the actors and the action and, by implication, all of the people as well. In *Sejanus* control of the empire was the prize to be won, and political greed sharpened the instinct to evil. In the Scottish play, Macbeth and his Lady had their heads turned by the golden glitter of royal power, but in reality they turned from peace, prosperity, and honor to death, dissimulation, barrenness, fear, and damnation. Could the tragic import of the state be made clearer than that? Yes. In *Antony and Cleopatra.* By one modern editor called the "sunniest" of Shakespeare's tragedies, it was arguably the most poignant and resonant. A parade of death occupied the last act of this "sunny" work, but never mind that. Death was familiar enough in daily life, and people aspired to a good end (to *Holy Dying,* in Jeremy Taylor's midcentury title). In *Antony,* it was the time and place of the drama that had a special meaning to a culture that knew Roman history more intimately than its own national past. *Antony* represented precisely that historical moment when the Roman Empire, the best and most just realm in history, was created. But how good and just was Rome? It is enough to say that the Renaissance had recovered Tacitus. Caligula, Nero, Domitian, Sejanus all suggested that even the best was hideously flawed. Antony's "fortunes" had corrupted honest men,

46. Even a casual comparison of the *Agamemnon* with *The London Merchant; or, The History of George Barnwell* (1751), by George Lillo, will reveal a difference in magnitude that is genuinely breathtaking.

and Octavius was portrayed as a frigid statist android. And Rome had the mandate of heaven, though in limited form, as Augustine had pointed out.[47] No modern (Renaissance) kingdom or commonwealth could easily compare itself to mighty Rome (though a couple of Caroline masques tried) without risking evocation of distance and difference rather than closeness and similarity. If Roman politics were murderously flawed, what might be said of Renaissance statecraft? Machiavelli's *The Prince* and *The Reason of State* of Giovanni Botero may come to readers' minds today as they manifestly did to Renaissance minds.[48]

Yet the suggestive power of *Antony* was ambiguous. Augustus did establish relative peace and justice, and the Roman Empire did survive for several centuries. Nostalgia for Rome, so poignant and powerful during the Renaissance, of course embraced the recognition of Roman success. Perhaps, as Thomas Aquinas implied it might be, politics was partially redemptive, partially journey, even if mostly theater, a medium for regenerate ambassadorship as well as chicanery.

The essential participation of the state, forms of polity extending from Renaissance city-state to Christian kingdom and universal empire, conformed to the Aristotelian description of tragedy as being serious in subject and having a certain magnitude. Only the *res publica* possessed the requisite magnitude and seriousness. Everything and everyone else might exhibit *hamartia* (in the sense of defect or circumstance, a virtue or good fortune in other contexts), that is to say, the ironic imperfection in people and their doings, providing the occasion for disaster. A private citizen unconnected to the state might, as in *Cavaleria Rusticana,* a product of nineteenth-century *verismo,* suffer a hideous fate, but while the pain was real, the magnitude was insufficient.[49] Recall the description of Denmark by the usefully commonplace Rosencrantz:

47. St. Augustine, *The City of God,* trans. M. Dods (New York, 1950), Bk. IV, Chap. 33, 140. Achsah Guibbory emphasizes the Stoic sense (and with it Jonson's sense) of cyclicism in history: "England . . . like Rome, involved in the process of cyclical decline" (108–109, 130 n. 7). We see in Jonson a Christian orthodoxy so Augustinian and teleological that power peaks are meretricious. But see her exceedingly valuable study *The Map of Time: Seventeenth-Century English Literature and Ideas of Pattern in History* (Urbana, 1986), esp. Chap. 4.

48. See P. J. Waley and D. P. Waley, eds. and trans., *Giovanni Botero: The Reason of State* (London, 1956).

49. Aristotle, *Poetics,* Chap. 6; *Cavaleria Rusticana,* Metropolitan Opera libretto, Milanov performance, April 10, 1953.

The cess of majesty
Dies not alone, but like a gulf doth draw
What's near it with it; or it is a massy wheel
Fixed on the summit of the highest mound,
To whose huge spokes ten thousand lesser things
Are mortised and adjoined, which when it falls,
Each small annexment, petty consequence,
Attends the boist'rous ruin. Never alone
Did the king sigh, but with a general groan.
(*Hamlet,* III, iii, 15–23)

It was the "boist'rous ruin" and "general groan" that mattered. Again, recall the authority recognized by Kent in Lear.

History, for ancients the prose form of epic though below it on the scale of generic seriousness, added the weight of politics to Aristotle's observation concerning drama. History dealt with the state in general, institutionally, politically, but also morally, whereas epic dealt with the state in the allegory of an individual, morally more emphatic. Tacitus, Caesar, Livy, Polybius all ratified what the *Aeneid* had taught: the catastrophic results of failure of character, of failure to do one's duty. "Character is destiny" (*daimon*), Heraclitus had observed, and all of Roman history and epic combined to proclaim that this was the truest thing the Romans knew.[50]

The Divine Comedy of Christianity added salvation and mystery to Stoic duty. This went beyond the role Rome had played in universal history as described by Augustine in *The City of God.* In the letter of Pope Gelasius I to the emperor Anastasius in 494, the pope declared: "There are two, august emperor by which this world is ruled, the sacred authority [*auctoritas*] of the priesthood and the royal power [*potestas*]."[51] This view was repeated in the *Novellae* of the *Corpus Juris Civilis* of 535: "The greatest gifts given by God to men from his heavenly clemency are priesthood and empire [*sacerdotium et imperium*]."[52] The secular state thus sacralized by being both a gift from God

50. Heraclitus, frag. 121, in Milton C. Nahm, ed., *Selections from Early Greek Philosophy* (New York, 1947), 95.

51. Augustine, *The City of God,* esp. Bks. IV and XV; Pope Gelasius I, "Epistola VIII ad Anastasium imperatorem" in Migne, ed., *Patrologia Latina,* LIX, col. 42: "Duo quippe sunt, imperator Auguste, quibus principaliter mundus hic regitur: auctoritas sacra [alt. sacrato] pontificum, et regalis potestas."

52. T. Mommsen *et al.,* eds., *Corpus Iuris Civilis* (3 vols.; Berlin, 1954), III *(Novellae),* 35, *N,* 6 pr.: "Maxima quidem in hominibus sunt dona dei a superna colata clemertia sacerdotium

and responsible to God came to have a role in the salvation of its citizens. From city, that most essentially comic of human inventions, to empire, that most essentially tragic, the state became also a help to heaven, without ever losing its tragic implications. At its best, working from bad means to good end, a common enough direction among Christians, the secular state utilized defective human justice, with all its huge and constant failures, to assist the believer on the road to God. To those uncomfortable with irony, and most of humanity—certainly nonliterate humanity—has always been so, the tragic was swallowed up in the salvific, and the state was often seen as the secular arm called in to enforce the true faith and the pure word of God. The tragic aspect of the state remained, however, though reassuringly (for the faithful) converted into good, and tragic drama continued to assert the doubtful outcome of the public sphere.

Jonson, in his two tragedies, avoided this quandary formally and dealt

---

et imperium."; see also T. Mommsen, P. Krueger, and Alan Watson, eds. and trans., *The Digest of Justinian* (4 vols.; Philadelphia, 1985), I, xlvi–xlix (December 15, 530): "Deo auctore nostrum nubernater imperium, quod nobis a caelesti maiestate traditum est."; see also Thomas Collett Sandars, ed. and trans., *The Institutes of Justinian* (Chicago, 1876), 2.1.7–9, pp. 160–61, "Nullius antem sunt res sacrae et religiosae et sanctae; quod enim divini iuris est, id nullius in bonis est." This restated an old principle from Gaius (*Institutiones,* ii, 4) that religious things were the property not of a single person but of the entire commonwealth and thus under the jurisdiction of the emperor. In the East this reinforced the divine character of kingship as coming directly from God and being responsible in an unmediated manner to God. On the Christian sacralization of the secular state, see the opening sentence of Zeno's *Henotican* (482), an ultimately heterodox document, in P. R. Coleman-Norton, *Roman State and Christian Church* (3 vols.; London, 1966), III, 925 ("Considering the source and the constitution and the power and the invincible shield of our Empire as the only right and true faith"), or the Letter of Anastasius I convoking the Heraclean Council (514), *ibid.,* III, 955 ("Divine matters must be set above all affairs and indeed we are confident that when Almighty God is propitious the State should be both preserved and improved"). See also the edict of Justinian I on Theopaschism (533), in the *Codex* of the *Corpus Iuris Civilis, C* 1.1.6, or the letters of Pope John II and Justinian I on Theopaschism (533–34) *C* 1.1.8. In every case the state had, directly from God, the divine mission of ensuring the correct behavior and doctrine on the part of the subjects, thus helping lead them to salvation. The opposite of the hierarchical royal commonwealth inherited by the Renaissance from Christian doctrine and Roman Law was seen in the anonymous Huguenot pamphlet *Vindiciae Contra Tyrannos* (1579). The pamphlet posited a series of covenants between the king, God, the people, and the magistrates—covenants that bound the commonwealth to the true faith and the monarch to right action with regard to that true faith. Such a conventual doctrine lay at the roots of the view of English Puritans, and of course Milton, as in "The Tenure of Kings and Magistrates."

with pagan Rome. But if the ironies of Christian salvation being aided by a fallen though ultimately good yet still tragic state were avoided by a pagan setting, the choice of Rome brought its own baggage. Although pagan and in spite of the contempt expressed by Augustine in *The City of God,* Rome yet glittered for the Renaissance. The Renaissance anticipated Edward Gibbon's judgment that the Roman Empire was a model for polity, desirable to emulate and impossible to equal. Machiavelli, after all, had written his *Discourses* on the Roman history of Livy; especially there one could find the universal historical truth about the city and the state.[53] During the Renaissance, commentary on Rome was always understood to imply something about the present and about what the state might become.[54]

In both *Sejanus* and *Catiline,* the tragedy did not come from the fall of the title characters, both of whom were notorious for the cynical corruption they had brought to statecraft. Indeed, if one considers only the fate of these antiheroes, the plays might be regarded as comedy: The better cause triumphed (if only in *Catiline*), and vile plotters were dashed to defeat and obloquy. Moreover, conspiracy thwarted invariably caused rejoicing among contemporaries who had learned only six years before *Catiline* of the Gunpowder Plot, who believed in the ubiquity of conspiracy and the cunning of loathsome conspirators to an even greater extent than Americans after 1963. But these were not comedies, because they dealt with the state. The tragic tone went be-

53. Leslie J. Walker, ed. and trans., *The Discourses of Niccolo Machiavelli* (2 vols.; New Haven, 1950). See especially Discourse I, 2 (on the kinds of commonwealths and the nature of Rome), I, 39 (on recurring events, even to different peoples), I, 42 (on the ease of corrupting the people), I, 49 (on the difficulty of maintaining liberty), I, 55 (on the impossibility of setting up a principality where equality prevails), II, 1 (on empire, virtue, and fortune), III, 6 and 7 (on conspiracies and revolutions). But this was not the only paradigm of universal history. See Augustine, *The City of God,* esp. Bks. 4, 15, and 17. In a subsection on "Virtue, Constancy, and the Past," Guibbory speaks of "virtue (which [Jonson] equates with reason)" yet of "a kind of individual moral progress . . . [which] contrasts with the cyclical pattern of history" (*Map of Time,* 116–19). We judge Jonson *associated* virtue with reason but *equated* virtue with grace. And grace, as we earlier argued, was deemed to work individually *even* in the ministrations of the church.

54. See, as the obvious examples, Shakespeare's Roman plays, as well as those on Roman subjects by Jonson. See W. David Kay, *Ben Jonson,* for the immediate but intermittent topicality ("not . . . rigid allegory") of *Sejanus* (63–77) and in *Catiline* the proportioning, at once blunt and faint, of Robert Cecil, Lord Salisbury, and his exposure of the Powder Plot, to Cicero (120–25).

yond the generic; the tragedy in Jonson's Roman plays came from the realization that even great Rome itself was not immune to such threats, to criminal efforts to seize power, or to the wormwood work of hypocrites, flatterers, and official murderers, to what St. Paul and Augustine had called the mystery of iniquity. "If gold rust, then what shall iron do?" in the words of Chaucer's Parson.

In both of the Roman plays, the tone and emphasis were institutional, not personal. In *Sejanus,* for example, love was linked to death and politics; the passion of Sejanus and Livia was not for each other but for power. The institutional tone was enhanced by the long set of speeches on the nature of power and the qualities of rule— speeches that were speckled with political know-how:

> The way to rise, is to obey, and please.
> He that will thrive in state, he must neglect
> The trodden paths, that truth and right respect;
> And prove new, wilder ways; for virtue, there,
> Is not that narrow thing, she is elsewhere.
> Men's fortune there is virtue; reason, their will:
> Their licence, law; and their observance, skill.
> Occasion, is their foil; conscience, their stain;
> Profit, their lustre; and what else is, vain.
>
> (III, ii, 735–43)

The advice here, unlike that in Machiavelli's ironic *Prince,* was meant to be taken literally, especially since preceded by Macro's observation:

> A prince's power makes all his actions virtue.
>
> (III, ii, 717)

This was reason of state served raw without garnish, as was the personal and individual lesson to be drawn from such a view of the moral quality of public power:

> All best turns
> With doubtful princes, turn deep injuries
> In estimation.
>
> (III, i, 302–304)

This cynicism concerning the state and its princes and ministers quite overwhelmed the pious Silius, who argued:

> Men are deceived, who think there can be thrall
> Beneath a virtuous prince. Wished liberty
> Ne're lovelier looks, than under such a crown.
>
> (I, i, 407–409)

Such a crown was what Tiberius fondly thought or pretended that he wore when he said he would "not endure the flatteries" (I, i, 375). Jonson thus compressed his entire tragedy into Tiberius' opening line, describing both Caesar's recognition of the evil of flattery and his having succumbed to the very danger he professed himself to be on guard against.

Catiline, also about "plots and conspiracies to subvert the fundamental laws of the Kingdom and to introduce Arbitrarie and Tyrannicall government by the most pernicious Councils," was a play in which the hideous and perverse personal characters of the conspirators were added to the general stain of treasonous actions.[55] Political subversion would expectably include murder, hence the dispatch of Drusus occasioned no surprise, but in *Catiline* the monstrous conspirators drank blood of a butchered slave mixed with wine. To contemporaries so shocking a reference to the Eucharist was far more telling than the expected hypocrisy of Catiline denouncing the rich who have taken over Rome (I, 374–420), while at the same time plotting to gain wealth (I, 429–484). Sacrilege sealed the viewers' and readers' opinions. Catiline and his cohorts were dis-graceful on a scale that presumably reminded the English of the legendary enormities of the Jesuits or the even more horrifying rites of the worshippers of Satan. In *Catiline,* conspiracy was associated with damnation.

Taken together, though they differed in the vehicle for presenting the theme of conspiracy, both of Jonson's Roman tragedies eschewed a focus on

55. An example of "Tyrannicall government by the most pernicious Councils" was "The Association Oath" of 1641, a common practice in seventeenth-century England, where Parliament purposed an oath and every male citizen was invited to subscribe. See W. E. Tate, *The Parish Chest: A Study of the Records of Parochial Administration in England* (Cambridge, Eng., 1946), 71–72, and J. Charles Cox, *Parish Registers of England* (London, 1910). But see Philip J. Ayres, "The Nature of Jonson's Roman History," in *Renaissance Historicism: Selections from "English Literary Renaissance,"* ed. Arthur F. Kinney and Dan S. Collins (Amherst, 1987), 207–22; we agree that Jonson was more the philosophical poet than the chronicle historian but focus on the tropes as means and the order of his loves as motive.

the individual characters and renovated the medieval mirror of princes. Jonson's tragedies were quite different from the *Polycraticus* of John of Salisbury or the *Traité de Police* of Claude de Seyssel or James Harrington's *The Commonwealth of Oceana,* but the differences were not too radical to be instructive. *Sejanus* and *Catiline* were dramatic rather than expository in form, but they performed the same public function: giving good moral and social advice to princes. The plays lauded virtue, though they were realistic enough to recognize that virtue was rare in high places, and they showed rather than explained the disastrous results of flattery, unbounded ambition, rancor, rage, lack of moderation, and ordinary evil when it obtained on the magnified stage of statecraft. We suggest that the *speculum* genre went beyond the narrow limits of earnest and often unimaginative exposition, plodding sermon, and theological polemic to include works of tact, delicacy, and indirection: the sustained irony of Machiavelli's *The Prince,* the ambiguous drama of Jonson's Roman plays, the epic defamiliarization of Spenser's *Faerie Queene,* and satiric lyric such as Wyatt's "Mine Own John Poyns," as well as the more conventional epistle (Petrarch's Letter to Francesca da Carrara) or fable (*Utopia*).[56] In an age when the personal character of the prince subsumed the roles of bureaucracy, press, and important elements of law, no one doubted that if the prince were vicious, the people would perish.

Finally, we note a major difference between Jonson's Roman plays and those of Shakespeare. *Sejanus* and *Catiline* were (comparatively) didactic, clear, and emphatic. No one could doubt their message of clear restoration of the right commonwealth or their basic position of total support for legitimate authority. The one great ambiguity was the degree of *application* of Rome to London. Contemporary and continuing arguments about topicality in the plays and masques witnesses to this. Shakespeare's several Roman plays were far from simple, as we have already urged in the case of *Antony and Cleopatra.* In *Julius Caesar* even the encomium for Brutus was qualified, the claim that he alone, not just among the conspirators but among the rest of the characters as well, had acted "only in a general honest thought / And common good to all" (V, v, 71–72). The pronouncement came from Antony, a man not without (as the phrase goes) his own agenda; and we have seen Brutus' self-theatricalizing (as with the news of his wife's death).

56. The Letter of Francesco Petrarca to Francesco da Carrara (1373) is edited and translated in Benjamin Kohl, Ronald Witt, and Elizabeth Welles, *The Earthly Republic: Italian Humanists on Government and Society* (Philadelphia, 1978), 25–78.

But it would be unthinkable even to propose such an opinion of either *Sejanus* or *Catiline.* These tragedies did not include praise for conspirators. In Jonson, the ambiguity, indirection, and unanswered questions of Shakespeare became such didactic directness that we suspect a kind of nervous edginess in the lesser playwright. Jonson suspected that the right moral / political order could not be maintained, that the center could not hold against the religion of power. His older contemporaries had been overly optimistic in agreeing with Sir John Davies that now was "this, our golden age." It had only been at best a golden moment, now past, notwithstanding the poignant claim of *The Golden Age Restored,* in the eponymous masque from January 6, 1616, in the wake of the Overbury murder trial.

Jonson's moral lessons, observations and concerns, hopes and fears, though in certain respects obvious and direct, were not cynical or fashionable, not taken because they were demanded by monarchs of courtiers. In this respect, Jonsonian tragedy hardly differed from his comedy or poetry; all were informed by a constant consciousness of the Christian journey and the call to Pauline ambassadorship amid a fallen world of fragile social order. This was never a common habit of thought among the manic place-seekers and time-servers at court, however widespread among soberer parishioners. It reinforces our belief in Jonson's epitaph. Rarely has so much truth been got for eighteen pence.

6

Marvell and Milton: Moment and Era

Indisputably the line of Milton's achievement was majestic, long, and heavy: the mostly short but rich and problematic earlier poetry, the polemical prose of middle years, the inexhaustible epics and closet-tragedy. As against this, the Marvellian line, from teasing and distanced early poems to polemical poems and reportorial prose, seems altogether slighter, even intermittent. And the two poets have not regularly been considered in tandem, not in the terms we propose.[1] We see the two as suggestively comparable in their poetic response to crisis, to the tropes, and to the *Book of Common Prayer.* Additionally, we see

1. An early exception was Christopher Hill, "Milton and Marvell," in *Approaches to Marvell: The York Tercentenary Essays,* ed. C. A. Patrides (London, 1978), 1–30. More discerning in reading the texts of both friends in their political settings has been Annabel M. Patterson, first, on Marvell's "Cromwell Poems" and "Fairfax Poems," in *Marvel and the Civic Crown* (Princeton, 1978), 26–30, 59–110, second, on "The Good Old Cause" as ideologeme for both men after the Restoration, in Chap. 7 of *Reading Between the Lines* (Madison, Wisc., 1993); we agree with most of her points, though we emphasize the poetic critique of the emergent cultural movement larger and less familiar than abusive new Presbyters, old Bishop, or King. Still valuable is Judith Scherer Hertz, "Milton and Marvell: The Poet as Fit Reader," *Modern Language Quarterly,* XXXIX (1978), 239–63. See Warren L. Chernaik, *The Poet's Time: Politics and Religion in the Work of Andrew Marvell* (Cambridge, Eng., 1983), indispensable for its sensitive particular readings and for its analysis of the generic and discursive rationale of Marvell's whole writing career, with frequent reference to Milton's and seen as diverging after "the mid-1650's" into literature of activist engagement as Milton (after 1660) "withdrew" into the more contemplative world of epic; we construe the division as somewhat less sharp, because the theological distinction between realms of nature and grace (theoretically sharp enough for both men) was mediated by tropes of power (fallen worldly or otherwise) and love (gracious or otherwise).

a *framing* comparability, a hermeneutic journey, often explicitly combined with commitment to the trope of life as journey.[2] Beginnings are understood partly in terms of ends; steps or parts, by wholes; times, by eternity; and all of these both prospectively and retrospectively, by a dynamic, successive approximation that must be open-ended because human nature does not permit godlike absoluteness and closure.

If comparable in their poetic enactments of the hermeneutic journey, however, Milton and Marvell differed in their understanding of the trope of moment. For Marvell, the decisive, salvific, turning (*retorqueo*) moment never came and ceased to be sought, or was at most occluded and subsumed in the metonymic contiguities of pious dutifulness. There is more than a hint of the modern sense of existential alienation from all that is important, only partially relieved by Marvell's devotion to becoming, the trope of journey. For Milton, in contrast, the salvific moment was always *at hand.* There was little ambiguous about God's call, though there was plenty of ambiguity in the human response. Humanity thus lived, as it were, in a constant moment of crisis of choice. Milton wrote again and again of the illuminating and defining critical moments within the always-understood and -present trope of salvific journey. The moment, for Milton, was always the same, the fateful choice, always made and remade by all, between love and power. For Milton, the moment and its calling to love were always present; for Marvell, they were dissipated among efficient and material causes and human ambiguities occasionally gauged with reference to a God who increasingly was *merely* transcendent.

This Marvellian ambivalence or indifference concerning moment can be seen in the poems that celebrated the particular public journey England was taking under Oliver Cromwell. In 1650 Andrew Marvell wrote "An Horatian Ode upon Cromwell's Return from Ireland," a consciously classical poem about the new world that had suddenly emerged in the year after the execution of the king and the bludgeoning of the Irish. In the "Horatian Ode" Marvell caught the violence and terror and strangeness of the sudden new world cut adrift from the immemorial dock of king, church, and nobility and caught in the freshet of an unknown government, a new church, an army that could be compared only to Roman legions, an iron commander, an unimag-

2. See our *Milton and the Hermeneutic Journey* (Baton Rouge, 1994). We hope for the present chapter to have an independence proper to this book of which it is a part, but we are anxious to minimize repetition.

inable destination. Contemplating Cromwell's works, the poet knew well enough what he was seeing. This was the *stupor mundi,* and he had remade the polity. Marvell's most confident analogy to describe such a thing was a force of nature:

> And, like the three-fork'd Lightning, first
> Breaking the Clouds where it was nurst,
> Did thorough his own Side
> His fiery way divide.
> . . . .
> 'Tis Madness to resist or blame
> The force of angry Heavens flame;
> . . . .
> And to all States not free
> Shall *Clymacterick* be.
>
> (13–16, 25–26, 103–104)[3]

This did not exhaust the language of violence, natural and human, or the ambiguity of whether "Heavens flame" was a transcendent ministry or merely sublunary. Cromwell himself was "reserved and austere," appropriately Olympian characteristics for the magisterial destroyer and creator, the Scripter of Kings:

> Thence the *Royal Actor* born
> The *Tragick Scaffold* might adorn,
> While round the armed Bands
> Did clap their bloody hands.
>
> (53–56)

But this was only the start. Would Cromwell cast himself as "A *Caesar*" to conquer France or be a new Hannibal to Italy, or would he next take "*Caledonian* Deer"? All were possible, of course, but one single thing was certain:

> The Wars and Fortunes Son
> March indefatigably on.
>
> (113–14)

3. In our examination of the poetry of Marvell, we used the edition of George deF. Lord, *Andrew Marvell: Complete Poetry* (New York, 1968). We have consulted H. M. Margoliouth, ed., *The Poems and Letters of Andrew Marvell* (2nd ed.; Oxford, 1952).

While it was clear to Marvell that Cromwell was a force of nature, what exactly was the nature of that force? Within the "Horatian Ode," the trope of defining moment for England and for the man himself was obvious. In the month between the return from Ireland in May and the beginning of the campaign in Scotland in July, Lord Thomas Fairfax had resigned as commander of the Puritan / Parliamentary armies to be succeeded by the all-conquering Cromwell. The man who was "fit for highest trust" now held all real power in Britain.[4] Parliament, with its large Presbyterian contingent began its slide into irrelevance and dissolution. The war would continue, as the ode again noted in its somber conclusion:

> The same *Arts* that did *gain*
> A *Pow'r,* must it *maintain.*
> (119–20)

The moment served, like Revelation itself, both to illuminate and to hide, to bring into sharp focus and to make ambiguous and indistinct, a flash of lightning punctuating a storm. No alternative to power (love?) seemed recognizable, scarcely even different acts *of* power. Most indistinct of all was the question of good and evil. Lavishly described, Cromwell was barely judged. His fitness to rule was affirmed—indeed, it could hardly be denied—but the good he might bring went discreetly unmentioned. Would the future Lord Protector bring England closer to God's kingdom, unite or divide the *civitas terrena?* Readers were invited to wonder.

Of course, the general future is always clearest within the trope of journey. And so it was for young Marvell, not yet thirty. He began the poem on an unmistakably personal note:

4. On the period in 1650 when Fairfax resigned and Cromwell assumed command, see Samuel Rawson Gardiner, *History of the Commonwealth and Protectorate, 1649–1660* (3 vols.; London, 1897–1901), I, Chaps. XI, XII, and XIV, which include Cromwell's success in Scotland. For Fairfax's resignation on June 26, 1650, see 291; for Cromwell's appointment to succeed to command, 292. See also, of course, Edward Hyde, Earl of Clarendon, *The History of the Rebellion and Civil Wars in England Begun in the Year 1641,* ed. W. Dunn Macray (6 vols.; Oxford, 1992), V, 144–50. All of this took place against the backdrop of the king's execution in January, 1649, and the emergence of socially radical movements. On the execution of the king, see Gardiner, *History of the Great Civil War, 1642–1649* (3 vols.; London, 1888–91), III, 599–601. Gardiner quoted Marvell's lines on Charles' death ("He nothing common did" to "Down, as upon a bed"), and historians have quoted the same lines ever since. The execution "was staged, largely by Charles" as the last of the Caroline masques, Patterson rightly noted (*Marvell and the Civic Crown,* 22).

The forward Youth that would appear
Must now forsake his *Muses* dear,
  Nor in the Shadows sing
  His Numbers languishing.
'Tis time to leave the Books in dust,
And oyl th' unused Armours rust.
(1–6)

The poet himself was not that "forward youth"; instead he was going into precisely the sort of retirement and communion with the muses that the "forward youth" must now leave behind. Before the year was out, Andrew Marvell would be ensconced at Lord Fairfax's country house in Yorkshire, Nun Appleton, as tutor to the former commander's twelve-year-old daughter, Maria. Cromwell's glory seemed to mean the poet's obscurity.

The "Horatian Ode" introduces our consideration of Andrew Marvell because it illustrates, by being on the margin of, the major features of Marvell's poetry: a pervasive sense of distance, a nostalgic longing for security and social stability, a love of botanical nature and countryside, a reflective and classical disposition, an ever-so-slightly ambivalent love of general order. Like Vita Sackville-West, we have put aside Marvell's political and polemical prose, his letters to his Hull constituents, his public tracts, and the thankless task of ascertaining his political inclinations from his poetry.[5] Rather, we have focused

5. See Vita Sackville-West, *Andrew Marvell* (London, 1929), 21. For a recent reargument, with comment on the extensive previous scholarship, see Christopher Wortham, "Marvell's Cromwell Poems: An Accidental Triptych," in *The Political Identity of Andrew Marvell,* ed. Conal Condren and A. D. Cousins (Aldershot, Eng., 1990), 16–52. Wortham emphasizes Hobbes and, accordingly, power. Blair Worden elaborates illuminatingly on immediate political contexts in "The Politics of Marvell's 'Horatian Ode,'" *Historical Journal,* XXVII (1984), 525–47, and in "Andrew Marvell, Oliver Cromwell, and the 'Horatian Ode,'" in *Politics of Discourse: The Literature and History of Seventeenth-Century England,* ed. Kevin Sharpe and Stephen Zwicker (Berkeley, 1987), 147–80; Adriana McCrea is especially helpful in identifying a current of neo-Stoic thought in "Reason's Muse: Andrew Marvell, R. Fletcher, and the Politics of Poetry in the Engagement Debate," *Albion,* XXIII (1991), 655–80; David Norbrook finds Horace out-troped, and contingent hopefulness at the end, in "Marvell's 'Horatian Ode' and the Politics of Genre," in *Literature and the English Civil War,* ed. Thomas Healy and Jonathan Sawday (Cambridge, Eng., 1990), 147–69; C. A. Patrides adduces Shakespeare's Julius Caesar

on the somewhat conflicted younger Marvell, who spoke (like William Butler Yeats) to some of the deepest conflicts of modern man and did so in the language of love and power so often articulated in the poetry of Renaissance self-awareness.

"Upon Appleton House, To my Lord Fairfax," that longest and most oblique of Marvell's poems, surely is the place to linger for reflection. The first ten stanzas surveyed the house, and the tetrameter couplets of each stanza built a modest shapeliness. This "sober Frame" contrasted, the reader on this house tour was instructed, with work of "Forrain" architect. A generation earlier Ben Jonson had defined Penshurst's sobriety partly by contrast with the cultural and moral extravagance of "proud ambitious heaps" in the domestic neighborhood. Marvell, alike yet different, defined Nun Appleton by partial contrast with *alien* despoilers of nature ("unto Caves the Quarries . . . Forrests to Pastures").

By the end of stanza iv, the culture of the ample house was construed as an outward and visible sign of its proprietor's human nature, an emblem of his and the best of his age's humility, "Like Nature, orderly and near." Readers may understand "That more sober Age and Mind," in stanza iv, as a surviving *civitas Dei* in the *civitas terrena,* and it was implicit in the contrast between builders of such as Nun Appleton and those who think "by Breadth the World t'unite / Though the first Builders fail'd in Height." Microcosmic delusions of grandeur were part and parcel of a macrocosmic neo-Babel and of the trope of fallen theater. (And what else was the royal actor's tragic scaffold?)

The following six stanzas, v–x, began with a political and not altogether secular supposition of canonization: "In *Pilgrimage,* / These sacred Places to adore, / By *Vere* and *Fairfax* trod before." It sacralized civic virtue as Donne had sacralized amatory virtue in "The Canonization," published in 1633. Similarly, and with an urbanity akin to that in "The Canonization," Marvell in stanzas vi and vii commented on the main hall's dome, the square grown "spherical." The allusion (beyond the direct reference) we believe was double, to Donne's lovers' souls in compass-figure and to St. Peter's in Rome, which

---

and theatricalism in the superb "Andrew Marvell: Engagements with Reality," in *Figures in a Renaissance Context,* ed. Claude J. Summers and Ted-Larry Pebworth (Ann Arbor, 1989), 273–94. Thomas M. Greene further emphasizes a legitimate quasi-liturgical theatricality of poetically achieved outer and inner poise between "cool perception and crude violence" in "The Balance of Power in Marvell's 'Horatian Ode,'" *ELH,* LX (1993), 379–96. See the generically kindred argument about Herrick and apprehensive royalist metamasque, Chap. 2, n. 66, above.

Marvell had seen and which he described as a kind of false "holy mathematics," lacking due proportion and thus truth. St. Peter's and Catholicism were here presented by this moderate Puritan poet as the false metaphysical geometry, as projectors only of the *civitas terrena,* which can only

> vainly strive t'immure
> The *Circle* in the *Quadrature.*[6]
> (vi, 45–46)

True community, vainly sought in the immense magnificence of St. Peter's, could be found at Nun Appleton, as the opening lines of stanza ix indicated, glossing the two previous stanzas in terms of "open Door" and "Daily new *Furniture of Friends*" (ix, 66, 68).

Thus, in the first eight stanzas Marvell, in his celebration of decorum and appropriateness, where "ev'ry Thing does answer Use," understood Appleton House as place essentially configured by love, philadelphic primarily, but love rising to God as well. The poem was consequently, in part, a meditation "upon" Appleton House in those terms and, accordingly, "to" Lord Fairfax as a communal and loving verse letter.

The house as *"Inn"* (ix, 71)—on the road to heaven, of course, in the omnipresent trope of journey—was defined partly as representative of the various relationships between nature and art:

6. Our interpretation differs from much received scholarship. See, notably, Rosalie Colie, *"My Ecchoing Song": Andrew Marvell's Poetry of Criticism* (Princeton, 1970); Isabel G. MacCaffrey, "The Scope of Imagination in 'Upon Appleton House,'" in *Tercentenary Essays in Honor of Andrew Marvell,* ed. Kenneth Friedenreich (Hamden, Conn., 1977), 224–44; Warren Chernaik, *The Poet's Time,* esp. 28; George de Forest Lord, *Classical Presences in Seventeenth-Century English Poetry* (New Haven, 1987), esp. 97; Douglas D. C. Chambers, "'To the Abyss': Gothic as a Metaphor for the Argument About Art and Nature in 'Upon Appleton House,'" in *On the Celebrated and Neglected Poems of Andrew Marvell,* ed. Claude J. Summers and Ted-Larry Pebworth (Columbia, Mo, 1992), 139–53. Barbara L. Estrin, *Laura: Uncovering Gender and Genre in Wyatt, Donne, and Marvell* (Durham, N. C., 1994), 278–303, on "Appleton House," sees the nuns as power-mongers (287–88), the fishing tackle as "masturbatory playthings" (298–99), but the final going in the house a defeatist "going into history" and the "cannibalizing instincts of family, sexuality, and power" (303), as opposed to lingering in a liquefaction of gender and other boundaries, where we see a victory of social love over narcissisms of solitude or power; and see Thomas Healy, "'Dark all without it knits': Vision and Authority in Marvell's *Upon Appleton House*" in *Literature and the English Civil War,* ed. Thomas and Sawday, 170–88; Leah S. Marcus reads less ironically than we do, in *The Politics of Mirth: Jonson, Herrick, Milton, Marvell, and the Defense of Old Holiday Pastimes* (Chicago, 1986), 215–22.

But Nature here hath been so free
As if she said leave this to me.
Art would more neatly have defac'd
What she had laid so sweetly waste.

(x, 75–78)

Art *defaced,* while Nature may lay waste, but *sweetly;* such was Marvell's ambivalence. But concurrently, while "slow Eyes . . . survey" the setting of art-enhanced nature and naturalized art, voice "opportunely may relate" the temporal survey.

That survey, in stanzas xi–xxxvi, began, as every attentive reader will have recognized, with eighteen stanzas focused on the seduction of the Fairfacian ancestor Isabel Thwaites by the *"Suttle Nunns,"* who would have had her (and her wealth) enveloped in their order and dwell in that building, now a "Neighbour-Ruine," from which Nun Appleton was "brought forth" as a veritable virgin birth. Less obvious was the implicit obverse of sacred history: Instead of a fall from timeless Eden into history in a climactic moment of mischoice, here was represented a deceptive scenario of seduction by carefully scripted appeals to vanity, power, spiritual pride as quasi-mythic, is-it-or-isn't-it-erotic fantasy, in which Isabel would be godlike:

"Each Night among us to your side
Appoint a fresh and Virgin Bride;
. . . .
Where you may lye as chaste in Bed,
As Pearls together billeted.
All Night embracing Arm in Arm,
Like Chrystal pure with Cotton warm."

(xxiv, 185–86, 189–92)

But Isabel Thwaites in a time of myth (with multiple soul-brides), who "Was in one instant dispossest" (272), was as signal an example of such transfigurative moments as may occur in the postlapsarian world. Indeed, Thwaites was delivered from myth into generative and putatively regenerative history, as represented by the Fairfax genealogy; similarly, from the Priory where "vice infects the very Wall" (216) came a *"Cloyster"* with "blest Bed" maritally fruitful of heroes ("no *Religious House* till now," 280) and ultimately Nun Appleton. The better journey had been taken and had become more sequence than moment.

The preliminary survey of place and time occasioned a more complex meditation (xxxvi–xlvi) on the first generation from Fairfax and Thwaites and on the *now* of the present Lord Fairfax, both in the estate gardens and in the garden of England at large. The earlier Fairfax laid out these "more gentle" (338) garden forts "in Sport" (285), from which sites the poet's sightlines ("Beams") now ambiguously threatened, played, or gazed (xlvi). Commentary has helpfully pointed out the affinity of this description with the temper of the mock-epic battle of the Priory earlier, the references to and gestures toward *play* (always a serious matter, though not always solemn), and the poet's reiterated affinity for nature and for georgic. But the tone was not always playful, and play was still peripheral; it is the mode of transformation we would emphasize.[7]

Transformation was not confined to Isabel Thwaites. It embraced nature, the gardens, young Maria Fairfax, and, at a general rather than local level, all of England. One notes floral petals scripted as "Silken Ensigns" (294), flowers "as at *Parade,* / Under their *Colours*" (309–10), gunpowder flasks filled with scent (296), and the like, with blooming Maria Fairfax as commanding flower, conventionally sweet of breath and fair of cheek. "No Ear can tell" the synesthetic floral musketry, but it "Ecchoes to the Eye and smell" (307–308).[8] This passage glossed local culture as nature, which was in turn construed to be consonant with macrocosmic nature, where "the vigilant *Patroul* / Of Stars"

7. On georgic, see Anthony Low, *The Georgic Revolution* (Princeton, 1985), Michael C. J. Putnam, *Virgil's Poem of the Earth: Studies in the "Georgics"* (Princeton, 1979), and his *The Georgics of Virgil: A Critical Survey* (Cambridge, Eng., 1969). On play, see Rogier Caillois, *Jeux et Sports* (Davis, Calif., 1967); Anna Nardo, *The Ludic Self* (Albany, 1990), esp. Chap. 6; and Frank Warnke, "Play and Metamorphosis in Marvell's Poetry," *SEL,* V (1965), 23–30. See the suggestive contrastive point by Joseph Loewenstein about Milton's *Mask* and subsequent "hard pastoral," in his *Responsive Readings: Versions of Echo in Pastoral, Epic, and the Jonsonian Masque* (New Haven, 1984), 146.

8. Louis L. Martz noted most of the data of theatricalism in the passage but interpreted it as "all only a harmless pastoral scene," in *The Wit of Love* (South Bend, 1969), 182–84; Martz cites the fine treatment of "masque-like qualities" by Ann E. Berthoff, *The Resolved Soul: A Study of Marvell's Major Poems* (Princeton, 1970), 163–93; later, he would suggestively emphasize competing temporalities and "a basic insecurity" in masques and masks (compared to liturgy, we would say) in "The Masks of Mannerism in Herrick and Marvell," in *Approaches to Marvell,* ed. Patrides, and, slightly revised, in *From Renaissance to Baroque: Essays on Literature and Art* (Columbia, Mo., 1991), 149–73. Is Marvell's not-exactly-oafish speaker deliberately made to sound like Bottom on his dream ("Eye hath not heard") and / or the Pauline text behind it?

walked nightly "round about the *Pole*" (313–14). This was, to be sure, a postlapsarian vision of nature: The "Bee as sentinel" in one or another flower "runs you through" (318, 320), if roused. Nature outside of Paradise remained perfect in its way while human naming and understanding of that nature were gravely impaired. Thus, it was a human impression or redisposition, not an inherent quality, that made nature seem arrayed in *"Bastions"* and "invisible *Artilery*" aimed at "proud" Cawood Castle (361–63).

But that sword, like powder-flasks, musketry, and the "watry if not flaming Sword" guarding the garden-isle of England, was masquelike and benign compared to the new order of degradation:

> War all this doth overgrow:
> We Ord'nance Plant and Powder sow.
>
> (xliii, 343–44)

The dark possibilities of the "Horatian Ode" now seemed to have been realized in a polity of permanent war. To the implicit question "Can we English do at large the reparative thing the Fairfax line has here done in small?"—to that question no answer could yet be given; human time could only be understood, as Augustine pointed out in Book XI of the *Confessions,* by looking, hermeneutically, *both* backward and forward. But Marvell was not hopeful, even about Fairfax himself:

> [He] had it pleased him and *God,*
> Might once have made our Gardens spring
> Fresh as his own and flourishing.
> But he preferr'd to the *Cinque Ports*
> These five imaginary Forts.
>
> (xliv, 346–50)

Fairfax could save or regenerate England not politically / militarily, if redemption is even conceivable in that mode, but only domestically. He will, as Marvell's poetic voice scripts him, stand as a model, for the edification of those who have eyes to see and ears to hear, of regenerative farming of the self and disposition of estate and family. The farming ("*Ambition* weed, but *Conscience* till," 354) and disposition of the estate in the stanzas immediately following (xlvii–lx) pointed provocatively in several directions, all of them at odds with the trope of moment.

One view is an ultimately critical stance toward Stuart court masque with its conventional purpose of aestheticizing politics into virtue and redemption but with its actuality, too often, of reducing politics to fatuity. "No Scene that turns with Engines strange / Does oftner than these Meadows change" (xlix, 385–86) is a reference to machinery as of the Stuart masques staged by Inigo Jones. Marvell also implied a contrast between the honest change of scene in nature and the showiness, even fraud, of mechanical theatricality. Engines were not yet things to be automatically praised. And the allusions to staginess and theatricality went beyond the comparison to stage engine and meadows. Among other examples, note the Mower's ambiguous "Traverse seemeth wrought / A Camp of Battail. . . . Women . . . with [pitch] forks . . . Do represent the Pillaging" (419–20, 423–24). Here the same comparison was proposed; the honest rural toil of gathering daily bread contrasted with the elaborate mythic unreality of strife in masque. A rural masque was suggested in the immediately following lines: "Victors play, / Dancing the Triumphs of the Hay. . . . Females . . . *Fairy Circles* tread. . . . at their Dances End they kiss" (425–26, 429–31). The description of the rural masque, simple, honest, and without fraud, continued a dozen lines later with: "This *Scene* again withdrawing brings / A new and empty Face of things . . . Clothes for *Lilly* strecht to stain . . . a Table rase and pure . . . this naked equal Flat / Which Levellers take Pattern at . . . the painted World" (441–42, 444–46, 449–50, 455). The rural masque here gave way to religious politics, the radical Levellers whom Cromwell opposed, and the poet moved from staginess to note subversion of both polity and the correct view of God's true and lively Word.[9]

These interpretations by the poet / observer certainly read like descriptions of, virtually stage directions for, a masque. But written masque tended to be, in itself alone, thin and unconvincing and artificial, a mere pastiche of mythological scenes that had courtly wit and classical learning but none of the mortal (and immemorial) reality of the rural drama of bringing in the sheaves. Such masque had availed Charles nothing and was demonstrably inefficacious against the malice, violence, and attendant disorder of the revolutionary world, even when amalgamated with the convention of dream vision, and Marvell made the failure reveal itself.

This next section of the poem (xlvii–lx) began with a radical defamiliarization akin to both dream and occasional masque settings:

9. On Levelers, see Christopher Hill, "Milton and Marvell," 20–25.

> And now to the Abbyss I pass
> Of that unfathomable Grass,
> Where Men like Grasshoppers appear,
> But Grasshoppers are Gyants there;
>
> . . . .
>
> And from the Precipices tall
> Of the green spires, to us do call.
>
> (369–72, 375–76)

The inversion of perspective continued with transformation of the very native element: "Men . . . Dive . . . As, under Water" (xlviii, 377, 379) and show they've reached bottom by bringing up not mud, as mariners' leaden sinkers do, but rather flowers. As a quasi-epic descent to the underworld, this one is more disorienting than revelatory.

Like the survey of flowers in "Lycidas," this dalliance, though no false surmise, gave way quickly to increasingly unsettling masquelike or dreamlike displacements: mowers as *"Israelites"* through a *green* sea (pursued by Pharaoh, as Royalists by Parliamentarians or Parliamentarians by Royalists?), grass, and rails ("for Quails") *massacred* (394–408). The radical aestheticizing pulled toward farce, reassuringly: The croaking death-trumpet note of "Orphan [rail] Parents" was the "*Sourdine* in their Throat" (413–16). This punned on the musical instrument, with young rails as young pikkards in this quasi-aquatic scene; it contrasted with the monstrous world of drowned Lycidas but not antithetically. The playful wit was both aesthetic and anaesthetic and came at a cost of both divine moment and personal momentousness in the world.

Yet again, the defamiliarizing inversion fostered unsettling generalization: "Lowness is unsafe as Hight / And Chance o'retakes what scapeth spight" (411–12), an appraisal from the vegetable point of view, according to which mowers were conquerors and women with hayforks, pillagers. The very haycocks resulting from their labors showed like rocks in a calm sea or poignantly like pyramids or Roman "Hills for Soldiers Obsequies" (lv, 433–40).

Or like a masque platform rotating, "This *Scene* again withdrawing brings / A new and empty Face of things" (441–42). This "Table rase," this "naked equal Flat" (partially in the sense of stage flat), the "*Levellers* take Pattern at" (446, 449–50). An egregious mistaking of a kind of nothing for something or, indeed, all? Marvell characteristically did not say so. Rather, he observed the villagers loosing their cattle to crop the stubble left by the mowers. The diction, however, was more suggestive than that:

> The Villagers in common chase
> Their Cattle, which it closer rase;
> And what below the Scythe increast
> Is pincht yet nearer by the Beast.
> Such, in the painted World, appear'd
> *Davenant* with th' Universal Heard.
>
> (lvii, 451–56)

"Pincht," not, say, "cropped"; and does the reference of "Beast" to "Cattle" stop antiseptically short of "Villagers"? H. M. Margoliouth, for all the readers since who have read Marvell but not Davenant, glossed the reference to the "painted World" in *Gondibert.* But the poet did not write "in Davenant's painted world, appears th' universal herd," as Margoliouth's gloss might suggest. In what "painted World" appeared Davenant, *with* what "Universal Heard"? It was court masque and Caroline polity in which Davenant was implicated.

While we are seemingly invited by the poet to judge court and polity, the poet further occluded himself by violent efforts of aestheticizing: cattle to field as freckles to face (landscape as selfscape), scene magnified (supposedly) like fleas under a microscope, cattle in field as if through spyglass reversed, like "*Constellations* . . . above" (464). But the increasingly drastic efforts at aestheticizing proved inconclusive, if not feckless, literally overwhelmed by the opened sluice-gates making the quasi-sea a literal one. This real water was implicitly a symbolic Second Flood, which "try's t' invite" Fairfax, as the political situation did (469–70). Or so the tactful poet may have invited us to infer. What we see was an emblem of revolution: "Fishes do the Stables scale. . . . *Salmons* trespassing . . . Pikes are taken in the Pound" (478–80).

With aestheticizing overwhelmed, the poet fled to "Sanctuary in the Wood" (lxi, 482), a flight that sixteen stanzas later eventuated in a self-aggrandizing pseudo-Christly quasi-Crucifixion. That the speaker's own (or seeming) religion of the forest was repeatedly metaphorized as *ecclesia* we take to be just the point. The poet, whether among Presbyterian "Elders" (518) or as Catholic "Prelate of the Grove," with *"Cope,"* amid *"Corinthian Porticoes"* and "Quires" (vocal or architectural; 591–92, 508, 511), modeled the very Fall from which Isabel Thwaites was rescued earlier in the poem. "I *easie Philosopher*"—too easy philosopher, clearly—"shall fly" as a god (561, 566), name things as had Adam, number leaves (like the sparrow's fall), weave "Prophecies . . . Mosaick" ('mosaic' and 'of Moses'; all this in lxxii–lxxiii *if* "not mistook"), take his rest as vainly as ever nun promised Thwaites, and fancy himself superior to the outer world and himself the gratifyingly crucified Christ within his own church. The degree to which Marvell was a forest lover is not the most useful question. Rather: Could any church be immune to the prevailing fallenness of humanity and the consequent corruption of society? Could any pillar of the temple of such a church or such a self, untested, be presumed free of corrupting worm (510 and lxx)? No seventeenth-century reader could properly say yes. Nor was the Elizabethan settlement of the established church forgotten. The briars that would, for his own good, nail him within the metaphorically botanized church were literally 'of the court,' *courteous.*

This ironic apotheosis modulated into four stanzas (lxxviii–lxxxi) of pastoral retreat into the quasi-regenerate world-after-the-Flood, configured by Lord Fairfax. Before him the "Trees . . . divide," as had earlier the grass, both trees and grass like, still earlier, the Red Sea for fleeing Israelites.

But worldly pastoral removal, piscatory or otherwise, could not resolve the poetic crisis here, anymore than in "Lycidas." *"Young Maria"* appeared, the reminder of the poet's tutorship and of daily responsibilities in history like those of Thwaites. Such reminders warranted the poet's description of his would-be fugitive self as "trifling youth" with "Pleasure slight . . . Toyes" (652, 654). Here again one may recall Milton; this time it is his *Mask,* the single example that was strong enough to survive the desuetude of that genre. Maria Fairfax stood akin to the Lady in the *Mask:* an heiress of family and position, beleaguered in a fallen world, though not so sore beset as the Lady who could not move, and each lady a hope for a bright, fruitful, and moral future. These were serious matters, a constant concern for the family as well as for the child, and a situation and circumstance in which Stoic virtue and steadfastness must be supported by grace. Utter seriousness underlay "trifling youth." In such a world, fecklessness would not do.

What would do? For Milton's speaker, at the last verge and moment, at Michael's Mount, it was Michael's angelic report of Lycidas triumphantly resurrected in heaven.[10] For Marvell's less elegiac or momentous, more encomiastic and secular poet, a more local and quotidian *modus* must suffice. As Michael's vision recommitted and reoriented the "swain," calling him in fidelity to "fresh woods and pastures new," Maria's self-presentation organized the whole landscape (*cf.* Wallace Stevens' jar in Tennessee) and made the pastoralizing "Youth" (652) an other to the "Man" (654), apostrophizing him. At this determinedly mundane verge, as sun set, Maria, like the Halcyon, reconciled day and night. Her virtuous qualities, "Pure, Sweet, Streight, and Fair" (695), validly aestheticized, literalized, and stabilized the hitherto dreamily metamorphic, disorganized, threatening, and metaphoric nature: "*Nature* is wholly *vitrifi'd.*"[11]

Although more secular in focus than the resolving vision in "Lycidas," this was theologically akin to it. Maria was an Augustinian figure who, "to higher Beauties rais'd, / Disdains to be for lesser prais'd" (705–706). A *"sprig of Misleto"* to be cut by "The *Priest*" from the *"Fairfacian Oak"* (of lineage and emblematic estate) for marriage (739, 742, 740), she was already for the poet something of a baptized version of the golden bough, cut from the sacred grove of Nemi. Her genetic separation for marriage, however, fatefully could ratify historic and cultural stability by "a *Fairfax* for our *Thwaites*" (748), and she, as sprig of Fairfacian oak, enabled our baptized *pius* Aeneas not to visit the dead but rather like Milton's swain to rejoin the living.

The great world (geographical *lebenswelt*) may yet be a "dark Hemisphere"

10. We are persuaded by William Madsen, "The Voice of Michael in 'Lycidas,'" *SEL,* III (1963), 1–7.

11. On Maria and the pastoral, see Harold Toliver, *Pastoral: Forms and Attitudes* (Berkeley, 1971), 146–49, for a brief discussion of "Upon Appleton House." But compare the less generically mediated, more ethically thematized emphasis on Maria as legitimate student contrasting with Fairfax as false contemplative: Patterson, *Marvell and the Civic Crown,* 101–109. Maria is antipoetic for Lynn Enterline, "The Mirror and the Snake: The Case of Marvell's Unfortunate Lover," *Critical Quarterly,* XXIX (1987), 107. But for a truly antipoetic, even disgraceful, epiphany, *cf.* Satan, touched by angelic spear, in *Paradise Lost,* V, or the disclosure of artillery, in *Paradise Lost,* VI. John Rogers, in "The Great Work of Time: Marvell's Pastoral Historiography," in *On the Celebrated and Neglected Poems,* ed. Summers and Pebworth, 207–32, shows that the "scriptural fall from grace" is used "to represent" the "recent national crisis of the civil wars" (211); yes, and both scriptural fall and civil fall-into-war, with priests and stagecraft, ambulation, temporalities, represented the more general cultural crisis; both represented and enacted, all the attention to theatrics has implied, and Frank J. Warnke insists ("The Meadow-sequence in 'Upon Appleton House,' in *Approaches to Marvell,* ed. Patrides, esp. 244–48).

of bizarre figures, "rational *Amphibii*" who have "shod theyr Heads in their *Canoos.*"[12] But "Let's in," with Maria into the smaller world (hardly cramped!) of Nun Appleton, where one may expect to find good learning and good society marked by reverent order and, in due time, regeneration. Thus Marvell, in the several metaphors of family, ancestry, building, garden, nature in general, and horrific dream vision of chaos, wrote for the values of community, of mutual caring and support, of social redemption through love and grace. He followed his own poetic invitation the rest of his life. Program, for Marvell, would avert apocalypse. Or, perhaps, the Second Coming could at least find us looking busy at our callings.

This considerable poem, we believe, thematically resembles Milton's *Mask* and "Lycidas," while a more obvious direction of comparison lies in the equally considerable kinship to Jonson's "To Penshurst." Penshurst, as apotheosized by Jonson, was a beacon of love and community, radiating love and good order to the world and inviting visitors into the community as full participants therein: Penshurst was emblem and exemplum and also a real place inhabited by real and good people. The good was not just theoretical, a pious hope entertained by the devout and the naïve. What had been achieved at Penshurst was within human grasp, including that of the king, himself specifically mentioned as a glad guest. As a good community, Penshurst was neither perfect nor static; its role instead was to influence the larger world outside the community with its *bienfaisance.* The poem would likewise instruct: The *now* at its end refers to the *reader's* newly informed understanding.

"Upon Appleton House" had an almost completely different ethos. In direction it looked inward upon itself, with the estate being a refuge—a beleaguered and perhaps doomed refuge—against the terrible storms of civil war and social disintegration. The Fairfax estate was an island of civility and community in a world run to ruin. Although, like Penshurst, the community around and within such a good place had much to teach the world beyond, that world was too far sunk in violence and disruption to be likely to observe, listen, and learn. The inhabitants of the good community could only huddle behind the metaphorical battlement of hedges and the real battlements of vir-

12. We take them to be (whether intentionally or not) cultural cousins to Jonson's idolatrous alchemists, their heads in their "limbecks." Variously subtle opposition to idolatry is one manifestation of Marvell's religion, which "trembles on the brink of non-existence," as Patrides put it. "Yet it is vital to his poetry . . . not of the supernatural order [but] the pendant world" ("Andrew Marvell: Engagements with Reality," 291).

tue and hope for the best. Marvell was not optimistic. As the frightening dream visions showed, the community of virtue was already hard pressed.[13] The poem's intimation of social redemption through love and grace seemed muted and ineffective in a world of "angry heaven's flame" and "War's and Fortune's Son."

Osip Mandelstam, who knew the way the wind blew as well as anyone, once began to write an ode to Joseph Stalin, but he could not bear to complete such dreadful lies, so he suffered the fate of all honest men in a Marxist regime. Andrew Marvell felt differently about power, at least about Cromwell in power. From an enigmatic position in 1650 on Cromwell's goodness, though not his greatness, Marvell moved to a positive assessment in "The First Anniversary of the Government Under His Highness The Lord Protector" in 1655.

He began with his usual theme, the incomparable vigor of Cromwell. In the "Horatian Ode," Cromwell had been a force of nature; in the "First Anniversary" he still was. While ordinary

> . . . man, declining always, disappears
> In the weak Circles of increasing Years;
> . . . .
> *Cromwell* alone with greater Vigour runs,
> (Sun-like) the Stages of succeeding Suns:
> And still the Day which he doth next restore,
> Is the just Wonder of the Day before.
> (3–4, 7–10)

The nature of the force, ambiguous in 1650, now was clear: It was the sun, a motif, ironically, later to be chosen by Cromwell's polar opposite, Louis XIV. But the sun non-king also possessed a second entitlement to power, and that was his proper success. Power was as power did, for the occasional political poet, and Cromwell

13. On the role of velocity and movement generally in these two poems, see Barbara Kiefer Lewalski, *Donne's Anniversaries and the Poetry of Praise: The Creation of a Symbolic Mode* (Princeton, 1973), 355–70 (Maria in terms of Elizabeth Drury). It will be seen that we differ somewhat from Lewalski's emphasis on movement in favor of a concentration on direction.

cuts his way still nearer to the Skyes,
Learning a Musique in the Region clear,
To tune this lower to that higher Sphere.
(45–47)

This theme of harmony across the Chain of Being was expanded in the next sixty-five lines of the "First Anniversary":

Such was that wondrous Order and Consent,
When *Cromwell* tun'd the ruling Instrument.
(67–68)

Some readers will inevitably take this as egregiously equivalent to praise for making the trains run on time. It is admittedly analogous—Maestro of the Concert—to Scripter / Producer of the Play. This harmony reached beyond the human, however, and embraced the Second Coming. "The path where holy Oracles do lead" was the preparation, the anteroom of the "great Designes kept for the latter Dayes" (108–10). There was, in the England of the early 1650s, a sense that the end of time (linear, not eternal) was at hand, and this was compounded by the view that some human action was the sole remaining requirement for the Second Coming described in Revelation.[14] Marvell's "First Anniversary" reflected both of these interconnected ideas. "Angelic Cromwell," who clearly portended the end of days through his enmity to religious falsehood and heresy (the "Roman den impure"), was the ruler meant:

High Grace should meet in one with highest Pow'r,
And then a seasonable People still
Should bend to his, as he to Heavens will,
What we might hope, what wonderfull Effect
From such a wish'd Conjuncture might reflect.
(132–36)

But just as human rule endowed with grace must predictably advance the divine fulfillment, so human folly must obscure the workings of Providence. And Marvell was not altogether optimistic. The latest day rendered the divine scheme impenetrable:

14. See B. S. Capp, *The Fifth Monarchy Men: A Study in Seventeenth-Century English Millenarianism* (Totowa, N.J., 1972), esp. Chap. 8, for religious and intellectual attitudes toward apocalypse.

But a thick Cloud about that Morning lyes,
And intercepts the Beams of Mortall eyes.
(141–42)

The refusal of humanity to see the true religion, to understand rightly the "pure Word of God," was beyond even the power of Cromwell to correct, though "to be *Cromwell* was a greater thing" than to be a king. The "great captain" could do only so much, and his power was the human power of ambassadorship.

Still, that power, exercised in Cromwell's case with love for both people and God, was redolent of the divine. The initially ambiguous image of Cromwell as the sun (Apollonian?) had, by the middle of the poem, been replaced by the Lord Protector being a figure from biblical prophecy. The force of nature was actually an instrument of God, something essentially miraculous and long awaited. "At the seventh time" Cromwell was called into public being as divine service. The doctrine of calling, familiar to and beloved by Protestants (Lutherans as well as Calvinists), placed the sacred at the heart of the mundane and gave even the smallest actor, like the falling sparrow, an eternal meaning as a part of God's place and will.[15] The sacralization of the world, seen in "Upon Appleton House" and elsewhere, was a general theme for Marvell. Nor was the doctrine of calling incompatible with a predestinarian Calvinism as defined by the Synod of Dort in 1619. Nor did sacralization of the mundane world violate the Protestant psychology and pastoral theology implicit in the doctrine of redemption through suffering or justification through grace that inspired works.[16] Here one had all of it: sacralization of the world's work, calling, predestination, God's wonder-working grace, humanity's requirement to respond to grace by undertaking God's manifest command:

What since he did, an higher Force him push'd
Still from behind, and it before him rush'd,

15. For a political-secular reading, see Wortham, "Marvell's Cromwell Poems" (n. 5, above); for a valuable semiotic (but too secular) reading, see Michael McKeon, "Andrew Marvell and the Problem of Mediation," in *Andrew Marvell: Modern Critical Views,* ed. Harold Bloom (New York, 1989), 205–26.

16. On the matter of grace and justification, see John Calvin, *Institutes of the Christian Religion,* trans. Ford Lewis Battles (Philadelphia, 1954), Bk. II, Chap. 6, in Vol. XXII, and Bk. III, Chaps. 1, 2, 3, 11, 21, 18, in Vol. XXIII of *The Library of Christian Classics,* ed. John Baillie, John McNeill, and Henry Van Dusen, 26 vols. On suffering (including reprobation), see Bk. III, Chaps. 8, 24, in Vol. XXIII.

Though undiscern'd among the tumult blind,
Who think those high Decrees by Man design'd.
'Twas Heav'n would not that his Pow'r should cease.
(239–43)

The "First Anniversary" continued by reinforcing by means of contrast the theme of sacralization of Cromwell and his works through grace. The first to earn the poet's scorn and wrath were the Fifth Monarchy men, a millenarian group steeped in biblical prophecy and hostile to Cromwell. For Marvell, they were numbered among those who were the

Accursed Locusts, whom your King does spit
Out of the Center of th' unbottom'd Pit;
Wand'rers, Adult'rers, Lyers, *Munser's* rest,
Sorcerers, Atheists, Jesuites, Possest;
You who the Scriptures and the Laws deface
(311–15)

They had misread the prophecy, and though they shared with Marvell and Cromwell the general view of the sacredness of the mundane, the Fifth Monarchy men, like the Catholics and those who practiced magic and witchcraft, stood against right religion and thus might delay the Second Coming.

That the "great captain" could do anything to advance (or impede) the Second Coming, however, was a theological position at some variance to Christian orthodoxy. Was God in any way dependent on the actions of humanity? Certainly the view that Christ could return only if mere people properly prepared the way was endemic within millenarian sects and radical prophetic Protestant groups. Within the context of seventeenth-century religion, this could only be described as a particular variety of Pelagianism, the doctrine that humanity's ultimate fate was in its own hands (or each person's), making God and grace irrelevant. In more modern, post-Enlightenment terms, human activity to compel God might be described as an assertion of human power over divine love, typically as techno-fix.

Where did Marvell himself stand? As always, that most hooded and careful of poets had it both ways. A deep social / religious longing for peace, appearing in masqued Arcadian form in Nun Appleton, appeared here again with Cromwell as divine instrument bringing stability to the polity. But if "an higher Force him push'd," Cromwell was only the implied preparer of God's way. The "wonderful effect" his rule might produce was a question, not a conclusion. The "thick cloud" of Fifth Monarchy men who defaced "the Scriptures and the Laws" was called "Accursed Locusts." Their effect, if any, on the Second Coming must be inferred by the reader. Perhaps Marvell hid behind his poetry's ambiguity and metaphoricity. Perhaps he dared say no more. Perhaps he flirted occasionally with Pelagianism. All we can say with assurance is that Marvell here used the language and ideas of millenarian Pelagians, not that he was one.

The final section of the poem dealt with the futile hostility of foreign princes to Cromwell and England. The English navy was lauded, and foreign princes were lampooned, but, as always, the focus was on Cromwell. Again, Cromwell was compared to the sun, bringing the opening conceit back and giving a unity of praise to the poem. Again, Cromwell was depicted as greater than a king, though he seems everywhere to be one. Again, this time as "the *Angell* of our Commonweal" (401), Cromwell appeared as the foundation on which the polity rested.[17] The man was both the personification of the regime and its perceived link to heaven, as Marvell so clearly represented, thus making the Protectorate the ironic ideal of divine-right absolutism.

The difference in tone between the "First Anniversary" and the "Horatian Ode," separated by five years, is unmistakable. In the first poem the facts were stated, but the question of their good import was left hanging; in the second the facts were largely ignored but the Godliness and goodness of the regime were affirmed on every level. But the "First Anniversary" went far beyond merely answering the question posed in the "Horatian Ode." The second poem was also a treatise in political theology, far closer in argument and conclusion to Bishop Jacques-Bénigne Bossuet's *Politique tirée* than to either the secular tone or power nexus found in Thomas Hobbes' *Leviathan.*[18] There was a cruel irony in this resemblance to divine-right absolutism. Presumably Marvell meant Davidic Kingship, a metaphor long associated with European royalty but now more familiar to Protestants with their biblical emphasis. But the Protestant and Catholic styles of kingship were not very different, in spite

17. M. L. Donnelly helpfully supports our reading in emphasizing vigorous angelic agency (John 5:4, the pool of Bethesda) in his provocative "Marvell, Cromwell, and the Problem of Representation," in *On the Celebrated and Neglected Poems,* ed. Summers and Pebworth, 154–68, esp. 166.

18. *Oeuvres complètes de Bossuet, Évêque de Meaux* (12 vols.; Paris, 1845–46), Vol. V, *Politique tirée des propres paroles de l'Écriture Sainte,* 134–309; see esp. Bks. VIII–X.

of Marvell's use of Cromwell as the Protestant champion and conveying "*Angell* of our Commonweal" who was doing God's work and might be hastening the Second Coming. It all could have been written (and was) about Louis XIV, from the emblem of the sun to the mandate of heaven to the divine disapproval of those opposing the king to the sense that the history of the monarchy was, in some real way, part of divine history.

Only the emphasis on the last days marked a specifically Protestant poem, and here Marvell seemed to be ambiguous. He affirmed Cromwell's divine role while denouncing the expectations of the Fifth Monarchy men, as noticed above. This sharp dichotomy, though, meant Cromwell alone filled the trope of ambassador on a truly cosmic scale—the one and necessary ambassador through whom the will of God would be made manifest. All ordinary ministerial journeys were subsumed in his great and more-than-royal pilgrimage (an idea shared with divine-right absolutism). The "First Anniversary" was thus a Neoplatonic poem of illumination and explanation, showing the hidden unity of God's grace behind the diversity and vicissitudes of the ordinary and the mundane. It was a seven-part reflection on the *gnosis* that affirmed the gracious connection between modern politics and biblical prophecy. This was poetic compliment of "stupendious force."

Marvell's final work on Cromwell, "A Poem upon the Death of His late Highnesse the Lord Protector," came three years later, in the winter of 1658. This elegiac work began with the conceit that Cromwell, his work done and with the Kingdom of God still firmly elsewhere, could now, by Heaven, be allowed to die and that his death was mysteriously tied to the death of his daughter, Eliza, a month earlier. The link between the two Cromwells, both slowly declining during that victorious summer of 1658, which saw the defeat of the Spanish at the Battle of the Dunes and the occupation of Dunkirque, was not casual but rather divinely coincidental:

> Doubling that knott which Destiny had ty'd;
> While they by sense, not knowing, comprehend
> How on each other both theyr Fates depend.
>
> (44–46)

But Cromwell was connected to more than his daughter. He was still a force of nature, an image carried from both previous poems, and nature itself paid homage to a death of such public importance. A great storm struck England the day before Cromwell's death and Marvell invoked the convention of nature's fury (or unusual natural occurrence) as a portent of disasters on the death of princes. This idea went beyond the realm of hackneyed poetic conceit to the level of a general social superstition, believed by virtually everyone. The general social currency of nature (personified or not) as a predicter of and commentator on human affairs, inherited from the ancients, was widespread enough that Pierre Bayle would utilize it in his *Pensées divers sur le comète,* published in 1682, where he launched his sustained attack on miracles and the supernatural. In 1691 Balthasar Bekker, in *The Enchanted World,* a study of folk superstition, found nature to lie at the heart of many of the beliefs about portents and prophecies.[19] But Marvell was using a figure that his audience unquestioningly accepted and that invoked a connection between humanity, God, and nature that had general approval. Building on that general connection between humanity, nature, and God, Marvell joined the storm, Eliza's death, and the death of Cromwell into a single stroke of fate:

> Nature it seem'd with him would Nature vye;
> He with *Eliza,* it with him would dye.
>
> (133–34)

19. For the points on Bayle and Bekker, see Paul Hazard, *The European Mind, 1680–1715,* trans. J. Lewis May (New York, 1963), 99–115, 155–79. This immensely important book, originally published in Paris in 1935, defined the beginnings of the Enlightenment, as well as clarifying its intellectual parameters. For Marvell in this general historical context, see Annabel M. Patterson, "Miscellaneous Marvell?," in *The Political Identity of Andrew Marvell,* ed. Condren and Cousins, 188–212; she reads the *Miscellaneous Poems* of 1681 as thoughtfully prearranged by Marvell or a sympathizer to show ideological movement "from innocuous and catholic devotion to worldliness, and from there through private versions of puritanism to the more unstable model of Fairfaxian [*sic*] politics in retreat, until they arrived at active republicanism" in the Cromwell poems (208). Christopher Hill, extravagant on the "Ode," is useful in delineating a Harringtonian (even if oversecularized) Marvell in 1659 and after; see his *The Experience of Defeat: Milton and Some Contemporaries* (London, 1984), 191, 243–51. Blair Worden marshals an abundance of ephemeral contemporary texts in a helpful article broader than its previously cited title suggests: "Andrew Marvell, Oliver Cromwell, and the 'Horatian Ode,'" 147–180; Worden conceives as do we that "alone of the Cavalier poets of the 1640s, Marvell looks the future in the face" (178), but he gauges that stare to be more complacently Machiavellian and Hobbesian than do we. Finally, we do not disagree with Lewalski in "Marvell as Religious Poet," in *Approaches to Marvell,* ed. Patrides, 251–79; she construes six of the poems as variations on the "dilemma" of life simultaneously in the order of nature and in the order of grace (see esp. 252–53), while we emphasize Marvell's concern with love and power as considerations in both and the tropes as the modes of intercommunication.

The poet then turned from nature and Eliza to Cromwell the victorious, whose triumphs transcended death:

> He first put Armes into *Religion's* hand,
> And tim'rous *Conscience* unto *Courage* mann'd.
> (179–80)

Perhaps a discreet reference to the Civil Wars and, if so, the only one; it also could refer with equal justice to the wars against the Scots and the Irish and the endless conflict with Spain and Catholicism. At least, only the victories since 1647 were mentioned: Preston, Dunbar, Worcester, Ireland, Jamaica, and the Dunes. All of this caused him to be classed with King Arthur among the English worthies; perhaps this was a reference to the imperial iconology of Charles I in the Banqueting House ceiling and in his masques (but not without "deniability," as we've learned to say).

Cromwell's glory, however, went beyond victory. He was also *"Heavens Favourite,"* for "To none / Have such high honours from above been showne" (157–58). He manifested perfection in character as he had manifested prowess in war. Marvell mentioned his valor, religion, friendship, and prudence but was most struck by the Lord Protector's clemency, his friendship, his "Tendernesse extended unto all" (204). The most redoubtable warrior had the heart most ready to forgive.

Finally, Marvell ended the poem of praise for Cromwell and sorrow for the English, now left unprotected by his death, with a short anticipation of Richard Cromwell. About the same age as Marvell himself and politically untried, Richard was both a puzzle and a danger. No one knew what to expect. Marvell chose to suggest mildness, as "Calme Peace succeeds a War" (321), a shrewd estimate. In the event, Richard ruled for only six months, resigning the office of Lord Protector in April, 1659. He had been unable to hold the center together, which meant the army. Marvell had written of Richard:

> Tempt not his Clemency to try his pow'r
> He threats no Deluge, yet foretells a Showre.
> (323–24)

In the modern world, economists and pollsters prophesy, warn, and explain; in the Renaissance it was the poets who did. The latter-day diviners appear to pride themselves on a more soberly factual style than that of poetry, but we see little increase in accuracy.

The three Cromwell poems, often treated together to divine something of Marvell's political identity, have little in common except their subject, but that was a very great deal. Different in occasion, style, mood, form, function, and genre, the three Cromwell poems together formed a small essay in the theology of politics. They examined the relationship between human affairs and the divine plan and the place Cromwell had in that view of politics. It was not Cromwell's abilities or achievements or even character that really interested Marvell but rather the use heaven was making of them. That Cromwell was called by God was obvious and self-evident (needing metaphorical mentioning but no explanation); the real question was the nature of that call. Was it within the realm of the theology of suffering? Was Cromwell a cross to bear, a sickness in the polity, an occasion for tribulation and lamentation, a rod of punishment to the wicked and those lost in error, a Godly reminder of grace to those "called according to his purpose"? Or was the call to Cromwell within the realm of the theology of redemption? Was the Lord Protector the instrument called to purify the church, gather the saints, reward the faithful, cleanse the polity, fulfill the prophecies, and bring on the Second Coming so ardently desired by "the blessed company of all faithful people"? Suffering or redemption, those were the possibilities that Marvell really considered. In an era when the unusual, in society as well as in nature, was a sign of Providence, Cromwell meant accordingly a visible link to God that must be correctly interpreted.

For Marvell, that interpretation was an open question in 1650, hence the tone of ambivalence and impersonal distance and dispassionate analysis in the "Horatian Ode." But it moved steadily away from suffering and toward redemption. In the "First Anniversary" Marvell both praised Cromwell's creation of a harmonious polity, using the simile of Amphion's building Thebes, and denounced the Lord Protector's enemies as those who fought "high grace . . . in one with highest power" and thus championed suffering in the place of redemption. Here the tone was one of hope and anticipation clouded by the recognition that "seasonable people" were lacking both at home (the Fifth Monarchy men) and abroad (Rome and monarchs). Could the prophecies really be fulfilled in such circumstances? Cromwell's death in 1658 and "A Poem upon the Death" answered such questions about the new Jerusalem but also confirmed the choice of redemption over suffering. Like the prophets, never mentioned because in a theologically literate society they were already present in mind, Cromwell pointed out the right way. Such a service was a pearl of great price; in such a service, joy outweighed grief, and the grave lost its victory. In "A Poem upon the Death," the victory is always Cromwell's, and mere death cannot efface it. It was Marvell's final judgment on the central drama of his times.

The Cromwellian moment, and in poetic compression the multiple triumphs come to that, was thus finally subsumed to journey. Marvell was quintessentially a poet of journey but in a somewhat new, print-cultural way. From the history of the Fairfax house and family to the public life of Cromwell to love itself in "To his Coy Mistress," the journey is conceived less in kinesthetic or orientational or even logistical terms than in print-cultural, abstractive-spatial terms of *time line.* Certainly Marvell's best poem, "To his Coy Mistress" (undatable, so far), participated in the standard genre of *carpe diem,* but it differed from most such in being more about the conflicting *paces* of entropic time and of love's progression than about love and power. The opening of the poem was an invocation to time and journey:

> Had we but World enough, and Time,
> This coyness Lady were no crime.
> We would sit down, and think which way
> To walk, and pass our long Loves Day.
>
> (1–4)

These lines, so well known they don't need quoting and so poignant they can't be omitted, led directly into a commentary on sharing, romance, and consent rather than conquest. In the catalog of the delights that endless time could bring, followed by the reality of "Times winged Charriot hurrying near," moment was metamorphosed into journey. But, it was supposed possible to "tear our Pleasures with rough strife, / Thorough the Iron gates of Life."[20] Marvell concluded:

> Thus, though we cannot make our Sun
> Stand still, yet we will make him run.
>
> (43–46)

20. Dale B. J. Randall has argued persuasively for the manuscript reading "grates," in "Once More to the G(r)ates: An Old Crux and a New Reading of 'To His Coy Mistress,'" in *On the Celebrated and Neglected Poems,* ed. Summers and Pebworth, 47–69.

the journey was both literal and existential, as time raced or slowed, all for the sake of love. We again are reminded of the night at once so busy, so long, so still in *A Midsummer Night's Dream.* Thus behind the glitter of "instant Fires" lies the even more enticing hope of love as journey of a lifetime, in which there certainly is world enough and time. And not of a lifetime only; in the seventeenth century the English believed in the resurrection of the body and the "life of the world to come."

This element of variable extendedness through time, frequently appearing in the *aigre-doux* elegiac mode of regret for love lost or love not taken ("The unfortunate Lover," "Daphnis and Chloe"), formed the central theme of Marvell's particular version of the trope of journey. The poet was always conscious of the wide range of possibilities and variations that must accompany every step of the journey actually made. It is always possible for things to have gone differently, in love, at home in the family, in politics, and Marvell was acutely aware that the journey was not simply a path, a *via,* but rather (in Newtonian style, an infinite series of points) a long series of decisions, any one of which could have been decided differently. A great Arminian, Marvell was the poet of the ambiguity of life, of the journey as multeity and alterity, of reassessment and regret, of being lost as well as being found. Not for him the ossifying certainties of the religious fanatic. In brief, Marvell never lost sight of the reality of things going wrong, of the poor choice being made with the best of motives, of the loveless and power-driven shadow journey lying always at the ear, eye, and foot of even the most determined pilgrim. Marvell was the poet of the fragile contingency of the journey of love.

This preoccupation with the trope of journey and his peculiar view of that trope made Marvell at once the most conventional of poets and the subtlest critic of the conventions. In commenting on the trope of journey, he was explaining the most fundamental element of Renaissance self-awareness, a convention familiar to all, indeed a commonplace, whether in poetry, visual art, liturgy, or the pastoral theology of suffering or redemption. Who, among the literate, was unfamiliar with love poetry, with the *carpe diem* motif, with nature or political poetry, generic modes and themes that so persuasively lent themselves to meditations on journey? Marvell was the poet of the familiar and thus the comfortable. But not exactly. Within the familiar horizons of genre, theme, and trope, Marvell offered doubts, not assurance; the hint of ambiguity and the unknowable always contained within the most ordinary idea or circumstance; the shadow of the other hiding within ourselves.

This can, of course, be described in terms of the Freudian uncanny, but the *unheimlich* is for modernity and present-minded scholars. For Marvell the metaphor was religious, the outcome of Original Sin, which had deranged memory, clouded the clear eye of right reason, and fatally damaged the will. It was sin that lay behind folly, that made the journey, theoretically so clear, actually so difficult to discern and understand. Marvell never tried to hide from the doubt and ambiguity inherent in a Christian, specifically a Protestant, view of life and polity. The Christian journey might be easy to describe but only in general, never day by day, act by act, choice by choice. Moreover, Marvell's poetry is famously suggestive and elusive in part because his mind, we infer, ran divergently to construals of his world and its tropology that were at once concrete in representation and unusually abstract in "argument." The Cromwell poems are as if programmed by concern with the ontology of power in a fallen world, the love poems, by concern with the ontology of love in that world (beyond character or interaction of lovers). Compared to the Prayer Book, to Donne, to Jonson, to Milton, there is with Marvell an element of greater abstraction in his rearticulations of all four tropes. Journey is relatively etherealized toward contingency, moment toward disjunctive event-time or chronometry, theater toward fanciful and rarified hypothesis, calling toward continuation. It seems he was indeed, albeit ambivalently, disposed toward "Annihilating all that's made / To a green Thought in a green Shade."

To conceive one such divergent tendency in Marvell's mind and its action with the cultural tropes is to understand something more of positions Marvell took in his underrated poem "On Mr. Milton's *Paradise Lost,*" written for the 1674 edition. Marvell could not but be uneasy with prophecy as always a *new* song, could not but be resistant to Samson as an image for Milton (notwithstanding Samson's popularity with Puritans), and could not but be disdainful of efforts (whether by Dryden, Davenant, or anyone else) "To change in Scenes, and show it in a Play" (22). These points were further developed, with others less central to our purpose, by Joseph Wittreich in what remains the most searching meditation we have seen on this poem.[21] Secular theater can reach at best only ephemeral play, will tend toward frivolity, absent the sacramental seriousness of liturgic theater. Samson had been shown by Milton (in the 1673 volume, with *Paradise Regain'd*) to be guilty by association with de-

21. Joseph A. Wittreich, Jr., "Perplexing the Explanation: Marvell's 'On Mr. Milton's *Paradise Lost,*'" in *Approaches to Marvell,* ed. Patrides, 280–305.

based theater and false liturgy. Theater will not be prophetic, and if time is linear and chronometrically sequential, song may have novelty but not sacramental newness.

Line 51 suggests this and more: "I, too, transported by the *Mode* offend." Marvell meant the mode of rhyming couplets, and Wittreich generously defends these particular couplets as "a scaled-down image of Milton's blank-verse paragraphs."[22] But notice how ironically secular a journey is suggested by *transported*! Felons in prison ships and drabs in carts must come to mind. Calling (*vates, poietes*) has been ironically secularized to being in fashion, to *"Mode."* Moment, as the "tinkling" couplet "Bells" signal, was not, as for Donne, a signal that "I am part of the main" or, as for Marvell's fellow-parishioners, a passage to eternity but only a passage in or out of fashion. Naturally, then, which is to say culturally for Marvell, personal industry, faithful and dutiful and annotated by verse, in linear or at most state-calendrical time, would be the recipe.

Marvell was the poet of journey, ambiguous but at least conceptually salvific, but Milton brought to that trope a livelier sense of the soteriological possibilities of the numberless moments (potentially) contained within that journey. The journey is then ambiguous only within the purely secular paradigm of vicissitude, in the sense that events can be ultimately meaningless, weltering within the realm of Platonic *tuchē,* chance. Such a world is devoid of Providence, which alone can transform *tuchē* into *telos,* can endow vicissitude with the name and character of journey. Providence and the consequent journey of grace do not, of course, eliminate crisis, though they do transform its meaning. Crisis elevated from the random does not by that account become less of a distinct and defining moment; indeed, the trope of moment is enabled by the action of Providence. In a providential universe, accordingly, crisis loses some of its terror and gains meaning within the totality of the order of Being, becoming, so to say, transfigured from the merely eventful to the consequential as well as the illuminative.

Crisis, as the moment of potentially moral decision, was the point of confluence where all of the tropes could come together, all providing illumina-

22. *Ibid.,* 287.

tion for a single event. It is one thing to know that crisis has tropic meaning for all, but it is another to feel and experience the death of a parent, the imminence of danger, the recognition of fault, or the loss of place. *Turning* at such occasions of crisis and decision was a psychological and theological inevitability, and this gave the tropes both their urgency and cultural generality. Crisis forced the individual and the culture at large to engage all the tropes, making the moment as-if-theatrically emblematic of journey and of ambassadorship and dispositive (one may hope) of the human theater of power. Institutionally, of course, viewing life as a whole within the tropic paradigms might occur within the liturgy or as the result of hearing a sermon. But the poets also spoke of crisis and decision in the ongoing and infinitely various cultural dialogue of trope.

Such a sense of crisis, as existing within the trope of providential and salvific moment, informed Milton's poetic corpus. From "On the Morning of Christ's Nativity" of 1629 or "An Epitaph on the Marchioness of Winchester" of 1631 or *A Mask* of 1634 or some of the later sonnets of the years 1647–1652 to the great works of his last years, Milton was not only a poet of meditation and exile and love but also a poet of crisis.[23] The crisis for Milton consisted of the Augustinian choice between a proper love of the greater good, God, and an improper love of things, situations, other persons, self before God. Crisis could equally be expressed as the fallen inclination to choose the *theatrum mundi,* inherently false and expressed in part as a hardy perennial Babel, visible in technology and edifice, implicit in law, ambition, politics, money, and the social rationalizations these have produced.[24] Or the crisis could be expressed in the calling to ambassadorship benign or Satanic. But always, the Miltonic vision of crisis was the moment of choice between love and power, and what recent generations have called the love of power was for him only

23. We refer especially to Louis L. Martz, *The Paradise Within* (New Haven, 1961), and *Poet of Exile: A Study of Milton's Poetry* (New Haven, 1980), secondarily to our own *Milton and the Hermeneutic Journey,* which argues that Milton was fundamentally a poet of love.

24. On this see Gale H. Carrithers, Jr., *Mumford, Tate, Eiseley: Watchers in the Night* (Baton Rouge, 1991), esp. Chaps. 1 and 2. By close analysis of the Pandemonic consult in *Paradise Lost,* Bk. II, Diana Treviño Benét shows that "*Paradise Lost* defines politics as the fallen method of conducting the business of the sinful world. . . . Milton deflates and in some respects indicts seventeenth-century politics and politicians" ("Hell, Satan, and the New Politician," in *Literary Milton: Text, Pretext, Context,* ed. Diana Treviño Benét and Michael Lieb [Pittsburgh, Pa., 1994], 91–113, esp. 113).

narcissistic, hence Nimrod's juxtaposition with Babel and the kinship of both to the Hellish councillors.

Milton, more than any other mind in England after Donne, realized the limitations as well as the implications of the tension between love and power. Love was individual and could never be institutionalized. Love might have general implications, even a general occasion or invitation, but never a general *cause* and hardly (short of God) a general form. Thus, for the Commonwealth, there remained no alternative to power. The *res publica,* as George Washington once remarked, was power. If the building of Babel could not be sanctified, that "black bituminous gurge" from the "mouth of Hell" to "build / Citie and Towr, whose top may reach to Heav'n" (*Paradise Lost,* XII, 41–44), neither could it be omitted or ignored. Milton understood that for the terminally lost, power was the earthly substitute for love, and for the Commonwealth, which was partial venue of the journey but not the going on the journey, power was its essence.[25]

For Milton, indeed for all Christians, the continuing personal crisis of choice extended well beyond the actual choice made. Mere virtue in the Stoic mode was not enough; that had been achieved by the virtuous pagans in Dante's Limbo (*Inferno,* canto IV). Moreover, virtue as sufficient unto itself

25. Wittreich, "Perplexing the Explanation," 280–305, esp. 290–301, but the whole essay should be consulted for its persuasive anatomization of the whole poem as Marvell's assertion of himself and as defense of both poets against evil days, evil tongues, "Town Boys," and the like. See, in juxtaposition, Michael Lieb, *Milton and the Culture of Violence* (Ithaca, 1994). We disagree that *Samson Agonistes* exults violence (237) or that Harapha is reducible to Salmasius (244 ff.) or that at the end "Manoa is right" (303). But insofar as a "sparagmatic sensibility" was in Milton or Marvell or was arising in a world beset by violence (263), it accords with our argument for a rising but suspect (to both) secular religion of power. In agreement, and with reference to processions and many lesser texts, see Laura Lunger Knoppers, *Historicizing Milton: Spectacle, Power, and Poetry in Restoration England* (Athens, Ga., 1994), esp. 117–22 (Milton and Marvell both ambivalent about Cromwell) and 165 (Milton challenging the royalist mode with "counter-spectacle, a kind of iconoclastic art," like beheading). See also Margarita Stocker, in *Apocalyptic Marvell: The Second Coming in Seventeenth-Century Poetry* (Athens, Ohio, 1986), esp. for its fine discussions of Marvell's quasi-spectacular "Last Instructions to a Painter," of its kinship in procedure to 901 lines of *Paradise Lost,* X, that became (in 1674) *Paradise Lost,* XI, and of its need at the end for "Christ the King, but he was nowhere to be found" (143–44, 186). Marvell could recognize moments of crisis, could hypothecate quasi-tropic moments (esp. in gardens), but increasingly could only *dwell* in a linear time of successive power temporizing, awaiting dulcification by the noncoercive power of love. See S. K. Heninger, "Marvell's 'Geometrick yeer': A Topos for Occasional Poetry," in *Approaches to Marvell,* ed. Patrides 87–107 (focused on the Hastings elegy, but with large implications).

without faith in Christ as the bearer of faith, hope, and salvation was, as Paul indicated in Romans 3:20–28, foul and rancid heresy. Not only had all "sinned, and come short of the glory of God," but humanity was "Being justified truly by his grace through the redemption that is in Christ Jesus" (Rom. 3:24). Therefore, human choice must be not only virtuous (to the limited extent possible in a fallen world) but also God-centered and faithful. This extended the sense of crisis beyond action to motivation, where there always lurked the likelihood of pride and constancy, where there always lurked the likelihood of failure.[26] For Milton, crisis involved faith as well as choice, with faith higher in the Chain of Being.

We have already discussed the road opened in Calvinism from anxiety to despair by obsession with pride (and consequent doubt of election) as opposed to emphasis on love and grace.[27] This was a road Milton avoided by his constant emphasis on love encompassing judgment and on mercy encompassing justice and by his view that sin was what one did, not what one merely recognized in thought as a possibility of doing or a symptom of doubtful election (*Paradise Lost,* V, 117–19). While Milton moved far from strict and orthodox Calvinism (as seen in the Synod of Dort) toward a Catholic view of Christian pastoral theology (virtue as sincere effort and prayerful contrition), this theological shift, we conclude, underscored his intense commitment to a God-centered base for human choice and judgment. For Milton, even while he eschewed predestination in favor of human freedom, the existential human crisis could only be understood across the levels of the Great Chain of Being as centered in love or its absence or debasement.[28]

26. Anthony Low has persuasively argued that finally Milton was really georgic and *Paradise Regain'd,* a heroic georgic poem, that "moment by moment labor" (Marvell's stance, in our view) rather than single battle is of the essence (*The Georgic Revolution,* 322–52, esp. 327).

27. Calvin, *Institutes,* Bk. III, Chap. 2, 11–16; John Stachniewski, *The Persecutory Imagination: English Puritanism and the Literature of Religious Despair* (Oxford, 1991), Chap. 1; J. Sears McGee, *The Godly Man in Stuart England: Anglicans, Puritans, and the Two Tables, 1620–1670* (New Haven, 1976), Chaps. 1 and 2; on Pelagianism, see our Chap. 5, n. 21, for a citation of Augustine and the Church's condemnation of that pastoral theology. For arresting argument with regard to a *literary* consequence, see Raphael Falco, *Conceived Presences: Literary Genealogy in Renaissance England* (Amherst, 1994), and his chapter "Repudiated Trees: Genealogy and Election in John Milton," 166–206, esp. 186 ff., where Sir Philip Sidney, Prince Henry, and Edward King are seen as a lineage of stricken promise repudiated in favor of election (subordinated in favor of grace, we would say).

28. See Joan S. Bennett, *Reviving Liberty: Radical Christian Humanism in Milton's Great Poems* (Cambridge, Mass., 1989). For a focus less on the concept of freedom and more on

Throughout Milton's more than forty-five-year career as a poet, this theme of love-based and God-centered crisis remained constant, not only through the years but also in the various aspects of life and death he examined. The poem "An Epitaph on the Marchioness of Winchester" focused sharply on communal loss and the salvific meaning of death. The young Marchioness was dead of childbirth, with the child dead as well. Here Milton struggled with a loss that was unexpected, profoundly poignant if not indeed tragic, and not an occasion for understanding or celebration. The poet, as he had with Hobson, concentrated less on the recently deceased than on a public effort to find meaning and, with that, some solace in a death that seemed to defy both.[29] The late Marchioness was now in heaven; of that there could be no doubt:

> Through pangs fled to felicity,
> . . . .
> No Marchioness, but now a Queen.
> (68–74)

But this was compliment, and while the compliment was Christian rather than courtly, "Queen" was still assertion, not explanation or understanding, and perhaps thin solace as well. The community would have to make do with compliment and would have to accept the implicit message that no explanation was possible. Revelation hid as well as revealed God's will. For Renais-

---

method, see the similarly analytic and indispensable book by Dayton Haskin, *Milton's Burden of Interpretation* (Philadelphia, 1994); by "conference of places," the parable of the talents, and the divorce tracts and other references different from ours in *Milton and the Hermeneutic Journey,* Haskin's less tropic exposition and analysis arrives at many similar interpretations and the same end: a Milton insisting on the hermeneutic situation, interpretation indeed a "constituent feature of paradise itself" (xvii). So, too, John P. Rumrich, in *Milton Unbound: Controversy and Reinterpretation* (Cambridge, Eng., 1996), esp. Chap. 6, argues mostly from Milton's and others' exposition (where we argue more from tropes) for a Milton no "carping didact" (XII) but a poet of an on-going hermeneutics" (24, and *passim*) for whom chaos:God::Eve:Adam. For the most thoughtful and extended exposition yet known to us of Milton's iconoclasm as a hermeneutic of transcendence, see Lana Cable, *Carnal Rhetoric: Milton's Iconoclasm and the Poetics of Desire* (Durham, N. C., 1995).

29. The Hobson poems, in their context in *Poems,* 1645, form a contrast not thematically so antithetical as their antiphony of jaunty wit might suggest. The generations of students who made a "Hobson's choice" are a community not to be quite replenished by students to be served by whatever successors follow Hobson-the-legend.

sance Christians, existential crisis, of whatever description and variety, was also in part a mystery.

The mystery in the Marchioness of Winchester poem was on a human scale, small enough to be clearly described, though too large to be truly understood. In the early poem "On the Morning of Christ's Nativity," the mystery was too large even to be taxonomically, as-if-Aristotelianly, described, and Milton accordingly employed mythic and Neoplatonic metaphor and metonymy. Here was the crisis of macrohistory, the time when the old covenant (albeit obscurely) gave way decisively to the new, and the poet gave this full measure. Pagan gods and goddesses along with their priests were described as receding into historical memory and theological absurdity:

> The Oracles are dumm,
> No voice or hideous humm
> Runs through the arched roof in words deceiving.
> (173–75)

Such a catalog, including Roman *lars* and *flamens,* the Greek oracle of Apollo, and twelve assorted Philistine, Phoenician, and Egyptian "deities" (xxii–xxv) gave an almost epic quality to the lyric; in this case the greatness of the subject aggrandized even the largest mode—hymn and ode—that lyric (conventionally lesser than epic) could afford.[30] The catalog of paganism was only the earthly aspect of the coming of the Savior. The heavenly and eternal meaning of this central point in universal history was described in two metaphors, celestial light and the music of the spheres, and the subsequent, as if mysteriously consequent virtue of concord / reconciliation:

> That glorious Form, that Light unsufferable,
> And that far-beaming blaze of Majesty,
> (8–9)

were coupled with

> such musick sweet
> Their hearts and ears did greet,
> As never was by mortall singer strook,

30. Barbara Everett, *Poets in Their Time: Essays on English Poetry from Donne to Larkin* (Boston, 1986), Chap. 3. As with all else in this book, Everett's comments on Milton's epic catalogs are witty, serious, and powerfully argued. See also Richard Helgerson, *Forms of Nationhood:*

Divinely-warbled voice
Answering the stringed noise,

(93–97)

bringing at long last

Yea, Truth and Justice then
Will down return to men,
   Orb'd in a Rain-bow; and like glories wearing
Mercy will sit between.

(141–44)

Neoplatonic imagery and evocation of concord were certainly conventional modes of describing the first Christmas, and Milton gave the familiar its due.

But coming before framing light, "musick sweet," and concord, was another theme, time, which articulated the moment of intersection between human time (*praeterito* and *futura: chronos*) and the divine eternity (*praesens: kairos*) that was the true meaning of the Nativity:

This is the Month, and this the happy morn
Wherin the Son of Heav'ns eternal King,
Of wedded Maid, and Virgin Mother born,
Our great redemption from above did bring;

(1–4)

Having begun with the idea that time, while not stopped, was changed by eternity entering in, Milton recapitulated that theme of crisis of history in his catalog of usefully-remembered-only-to-be-forgotten false simulacra of the true God. The nature of time, in a shift from *chronos* to *kairos,* was reality symbolically expressed by the metaphors of light and music and the almost kinesthetic notion of concord.

The source of moment as crisis was revisited by Milton in a far different setting, this time domestic and developmental, in *A Mask.* Here, general questions of virtue, steadfastness, temperance, and the proper relationship to God and community were personalized on the small stage of and by young people, the children of the Earl of Bridgewater. The Earl had just become the Lord President of Wales, and his daughter and two sons were coming to join him:

The Elizabethan Writing of England (Chicago, 1992), 59–62 ("A Miltonic Revision"), with its argument that Milton, in contrast to Daniel and Spenser, felt a (we would say) *calling* to be *eikonoklastes.*

but thir way
Lies through the perplext paths of this drear wood,
The nodding horror of whose shady brows
Threats the forlorn and wandring passinger.
(36–40)

Nature thus emblematically assumed the role of the world, which was morally far more "perplext" and "drear" than any wood and far more difficult to navigate yet impossible to avoid. Perhaps "the crown that vertue gives" (9) could repulse the "rank vapours of this sin-worn mould" (17). But mere "vertue" was not enough, strong though it might be, as the Lady's immobility showed.[31] It was not merely Comus' "words of glozing courtesie / Baited with reasons not unplausible" (161–62) that must be parsed and rejected for their meaning both here and hereafter; there must also be a reliance upon grace. Calling (famously) on faith, hope, and chastity, the Lady did what she could; her acceptance of Comus' promise of guidance was less dangerous than the Elder Brother's bland Pelagian assurance that chastity was "compleat steel," proof against "savage feirce, bandite, or mountaneer" (426).[32] This had never been the case before, and it would have been hard for Milton and his audience to believe it now. Nor were the brothers' swords of much use in this crisis of moral choice. Grace, in the mythic classical dress favored by masque, appeared as Sabrina and released the Lady to be led with brothers (also in jeopardy) to safety "while Heav'n lends us grace" (938).

In *A Mask,* Milton turned the genre upon its courtly head.[33] Usually cele-

31. The virtuous Lady's immobility may be seen as a frozen moment, her for-the-nonce-decisive mobility, a tropic moment by the grace of Sabrina. The trope of moment survives in later liturgical and evangelical contexts ("decision for Christ"), but much more pervasively, it appears in secular, spatialized usage: *point in time, choice point, decision-tree analysis,* and the like. Journey is omnipresent colloquially in countless locutions, "farther down the road" and the like, but typically with no transcendent *telos* considered. Theater flourishes, both in sinister contexts of mask or role and in innocent contexts in which speaker or auditors are variously styled as players in an athletic contest (but mundane, ordinarily).

32. For a contemporary view of the Renaissance understanding of Comus himself, see the Garland reprint of the 1578 French translation by Blaise de Vigenére of the *Icones* of Philostratus: Philostratus, *Les Images,* ed. Stephen Orgel (1611; rpr. New York, 1976), 9–17, "Comus est un Demon: d' où procède aux homines mortels le rive, gaudir ou baller" (10). See also Douglas Brooks-Davies, *The Mercurian Monarch: Magical Politics from Spenser to Pope* (Manchester, Eng., 1983), Chap. III. We do not agree on the primary role of magic in *A Mask.*

33. But see the masque of complaint, *Salmacida Spolia* of Davenant and Jones, in Stephen Orgel and Roy Strong, *Inigo Jones: The Theatre of the Stuart Court* (2 vols.; London, 1973), II,

bratory of statecraft, sophistication, and power, the masque here extolled familial simplicity, innocence, and love. Usually designed to reassure with a publicly useful delusion, that the king was wise and that God favored the royal "policie," here the masque illustrated the moral education of the young, with no assurances that all would turn out properly. While a sort of safety would be gained by arriving at the family home, there was no certainty that the safety could there endure. *A Mask* was ambiguous about the possibility of a good moral or social result. Thus, as social scale was inverted, a sober ambiguity replaced absurd assertions of certainty, and personal and familial virtue was preferred to courtly sophistication.

Milton also wrote about the continuing moral choice between love and power on the general communal level. Between 1647 and 1652 he wrote four "war sonnets" dealing with the issues and personalities of the years when the war against the king devolved into the war among the victors. Here the crisis had moved from the personal / familial to the middle ground of community. Much less than the divine turning of Incarnation, the community was still (ideally) the gathering of saints that would be the house of the Lord (Ps. 122:1). Milton found himself in defense of freedom, persuasion, and latitude in matters of liturgy and doctrine, perceiving as essential to the moral health

728–85; see also on *A Mask,* C. L. Barber, "*A Mask presented at Ludlow Castle:* The Masque as a Masque," in *The Lyric and Dramatic Milton,* ed. J. H. Summers (New York, 1965), 35–63; Thomas O. Calhoun, "On John Milton's *A Mask at Ludlow,*" *Milton Studies,* VI (1974), 165–79; Angus Fletcher, *The Transcendental Masque: An Essay on Milton's "Comus"* (Ithaca, 1971); John Demaray, *Milton and the Masque Tradition: The Early Poems, "Arcades," and "Comus"* (Cambridge, Mass., 1968). On the local background see Leah S. Marcus, "Justice for Margery Evans: A 'Local' Reading of *Comus,*" in *Milton and the Idea of Women,* ed. Julia Walker (Urbana, 1988), 66–85. An excellent short piece of criticism on *A Mask* may be found in Stephen Orgel, *The Jonsonian Masque* (Cambridge, Mass., 1967), esp. 55, 102–103, 151–53. We discuss the *Mask* and its Miltonic context at greater length in *Milton and the Hermeneutic Journey,* Chap. 6. More generally, David Loewenstein comments on Milton's disdainful critique in *Eikonoklastes* of self-seeking theatricalizing (as in *Eikon Basilikon*) in *Milton and the Drama of History: Historical Vision, Iconoclasm, and the Literary Imagination* (Cambridge, Eng., 1990), 57–58 and *passim.* Thomas Corns notes Milton's linkage with masque in *English Political Literature, 1640–1660* (Oxford, 1992), 209; there he also argues, under what we take to be inappropriate cultural materialist constraint, for the indeterminacy of Milton's ideology (111–26).

of the Commonwealth precisely those social representations of love that so many were fighting to repress. The poet did not conceal his outrage:

> From them whose sin ye envi'd, not abhorr'd,
> Dare ye for this adjure the civill sword
> To force our Consciences that Christ set free,
> And ride us with a classic Hierarchy
> . . . .
> New Presbyter is but old Preist writt large.
> ("On the Forcers of Conscience," 4–7, 20)

If the power move by Presbyterians was a clear and present danger, it was not the only one. War itself, even in a good cause, threatened love. In Sonnet 15, Sir Thomas Fairfax, the commander of the Parliamentary army, was praised for victory. But mere victory was not enough, precisely as mere power never was:

> For what can Warrs but endless warr still breed,
> Till Truth, and Right from Violence be freed,
> And Public Faith cleard from the shamefull brand
> Of Public Fraud.
> (10–13)

Milton returned to the themes of both previous sonnets in Sonnet 16 on Cromwell, "our chief of men." Here the war had not banished public fraud but revived it in the form of a proposal for the state to support and thus control the clergy. From Archbishop Laud to the Calvinists, the faces had sped by but the communal crisis had not changed: The *imperium* of power was to be substituted for the *auctoritas* of love.

An extended comment on love and power, largely in terms of the tropes of theater and ambassadorship, came in the "dramatic poem which is call'd tragedy," *Samson Agonistes.* Here again, the scale was middling, mindful of the intimacy of the personal and familial, mindful of divinity, but focused below the cosmic. *Samson,* however, involved more ambiguity than did the war sonnets. The chorus claimed that moral choice was clear:

> Just are the ways of God,
> And justifiable to Men;
> Unless there be who think not God at all.
> (293–95)

This dictum, the second line of which could be believed only by faith in general, was followed by an assertion of voluntarism:

> As if they would confine th' interminable,
> And tie him to his own prescript,
> Who made our Laws to bind us, not himself,
> And hath full right t' exempt
> Whom so it pleases him by choice.
>
> (307–11)

It did not please God, apparently, to exempt Samson, and the chorus, like Job's friends, were quick to point out Samson's sin, in this case, marrying outside the tribe. The chorus justified "the wayes of God to men" only by simplifying them so as to make of God a mere powerful man, thus making the chorus the fool it condemned (even while readers would remember New Testament injunctions against judging another person a fool).

What was clear to Samson was the need to repent, which involved, by definition, acceptance of fault and of responsibility:

> Nothing of all these evils hath befall'n me
> But justly; I my self have brought them on,
> Sole Author I, sole cause.
>
> (374–76)

Repulsing efforts by Manoa to substitute excuse and regression (and neglect of calling) for contrition, scornful of Dalila's plea for her own version of self-indulgence, Samson moved to the next step in the sacrament of Confession, a resolve to lead a new life and accept penance. What sounded to others like self-pity and breast-beating were, instead, Samson's *retorqueo* from theatricality ("like a petty god . . . admir'd of all," 529–30) to salvific moment and renewed journey. Samson's declaration was the central moment of the poem:

> Yet despair not of his final pardon
> Whose ear is ever open; and his eye
> Gracious to re-admit the suppliant.
>
> (1171–73)

One may recall a similar moment in Job: "For I know that my redeemer liveth" (19:25). Another occurs in *Paradise Lost,* when Adam and Eve

> both confess'd
> Humbly thir faults, and pardon beg'd, with tears
> Watering the ground, and with thir sighs the Air
> Frequenting, sent from hearts contrite, in sign
> Of sorrow unfeign'd, and humiliation meek.
>
> (X, 1100–04)

In all cases the penitents turned from world and self, transforming their moment of crisis into a judgment for love.

Paradise Lost ended with the human dimension of God's divine history. The "wandring steps and slow" implied continuing crisis combining both error in journey and hesitation in calling / ambassadorship. The final triptych depicted, of course, this human dimension within the general context of perpetuity but stopped short of describing general redemption within history. The promised redemption had already been briefly considered with "On the Morning of Christ's Nativity," and Milton returned to the center of history in *Paradise Regain'd.* The lines of choice were clearly drawn:

> His weakness shall o'recome Satanic strength
> And all the world.
>
> (I, 161–62)

Love expressed as weakness (in human terms) and as submission to God's will, conceived by Milton as perfect love combined with perfect power, would repair what an earlier crisis of tropic theater and moment had lost through Adam's reliance on self and human power and thus would "earn Salvation for the Sons of men" (I, 167). Only perfection, denied to fallen humanity, could *earn* what impiety had lost, repudiating the Satanic notion that gratitude to God was a "debt immense . . . / So burthensome still paying, still to ow" (*Paradise Lost,* IV, 52–53). Hence gift replaced debt.

The importance of love as the motive and the end of human choice and the nature of human crisis was emphasized also by the "glozing lies" of Satan. The "Arch Fiend now undisguised" asserted to the Son:

> though I have lost
> . . . .
> To be belov'd of God, I have not lost
> To love.
>
> (*Paradise Regain'd,* I, 377–80)

This temptation of (humanly) plausible assertion and argument the Savior easily repulsed, exposing Satan as "depos'd, / Ejected, emptied," who was "never more in Hell then when in Heav'n" (I, 414, 420). While the Son's rebuke had always been true, now it took on even more weight, as the turning of history back toward God:

> When his purpose is
> Among them to declare his Providence
> To thee not known.
>
> (I, 444–46)

At this point of redemptive history the magnitude of the stage suddenly expanded from local to cosmic, and Satan's dissimulation, though quantitatively the same, had become incalculably more important. Here again the trope of *theatrum mundi* clarified the paradox of the temptation. While Satan's glozing lies were powerfully menacing to humanity, they were exposed by the Son, who saw their seemings and their fraud. Yet the temptations of power and theater were portrayed by Milton as real:

> To which my Spirit aspir'd, victorious deeds
> Flam'd in my heart, heroic acts, one while
> To rescue *Israel* from the *Roman* yoke,
> Then to subdue and quell o'er all the earth
> Brute violence and proud Tyrannick power.
>
> (I, 215–19)

The validity of the Son's desert musings, demanded by Christian orthodoxy concerning the dual personae of Christ, paradoxically increased the threat of Satan's theatricality (since a man could not reject it outright), while raising the quality of the Son's (human) rejection to the level of human perfection. The Son did what Adam had not: He embraced grace and love to see him through a crisis rightly, thus avoiding acts and performances in the mere theater of power. Only, of course, this was *the* crisis, involving all, not just one, and declaring the general journey.

But a crisis can be more than a single moment, once surmounted and soon ended. It is the endless series of choices and moments that make up the calling and the journey, or alternatively the theater of the world, and the remainder of *Paradise Regain'd:*

How to begin, how to accomplish best
His end of being on Earth, and mission high.
(II, 113–14)

These are the questions of humanity, asked perfectly by the Son, whose gaze was defined as fixed upon his called and salvific journey and his heart, as fixed upon God in loving praise. It was this, Milton insisted, in which the Son's double perfection resided: the grace of the moments, all of them salvific, and the totality of the calling to ambassadorship, in the calm and persistent rejection of the hypocritic theatricality, on the sturdy and unwavering journey of human redemption:

We have heard
His words, his wisdom full of grace and truth.
(II, 33–34)

The levels and varieties of crisis that Milton here considered, filled all of the various usages and definitions of the Greek root *krinein,* which meant a separating and dividing things into better and worse, a meaning reinforced by a second definition: to judge and give an estimate. Judgment and separation were the twin qualities of *krisis* that Milton embraced as he sought in a lifetime of poetry to comprehend and explain the differences between love and power that animated the four dominant tropes of Renaissance English habits of thought. This notion of crisis did not disappear as the English habits of thought changed into articulations privileging power.[34]

34. The opposite theological view of fallenness and of the totally redemptive and obedient Christ can be seen in the doctrines of monophysitism, which divided the single nature of Christ into two natures instead of two *personae.* The two natures of the monophysite Christ, one human and the other divine, obliterated the mystery and majesty of sinlessness and disconnected redemption either from God or from humanity. Milton, of course, in his final commentary on fallenness and redemption, emphasized the dual and connected mysteries of sinlessness in Christ and redemption in humanity.

On the two varieties of monophysitism, that Christ was essentially divine and only appeared human (Apollinarianism) or that Christ was essentially human, only incidently divine (Nestorianism), see Norman P. Tanner, S. J., *Decrees of the Ecumenical Councils,* 2 vols.; Washington, D.C., 1990), I, 21–35, for the Council of Constantinople in 381, which condemned Apollinarianism in canon 7, (37–74); for the Council of Ephesus in 431, which condemned Nestorius in the Formula of Union, the judgment (*sententia*) against Nestorius, and in the third letter to Nestorius; and for the Council of Chalcedon in 451, which again condemned monophysitism in the *Tome* of Leo the Great, and the Definition of Faith (75–103). See also C.-J. Hefele and Dom H. Leclercq, *Histoire des conciles d'apres les documents originaux* (11 vols.; Paris, 1907–52), II, Pt. 1, 1–48, on the Council of Constantinople, and 219–377, on Nestorius and the Coun-

Samson Agonistes, professedly closet drama, stands as Milton's ultimate critique of power-theatricalism. Even the Messenger re-presents the catastrophe to a little audience, inspiring Manoa to project fatuous masques of commemoration. *Paradise Lost* and *Paradise Regain'd* stand with Donne's sermons as among the most massive explorations in the English language of the trope of journey and stand by themselves as the profoundest. We would at this juncture add one particular and one general point.[35]

The final three books of *Paradise Lost,* together with *Samson Agonistes,* strike us as Milton's final retrospect and prospect on the phenomenology of fallenness: retrospective because biblically historical, prospective because focused on mindscapes and terrene cities implicated in power-lust yet implicated in hopeful newness. Milton divided this vision into a complementarity: interior and psychological in *Paradise Lost,* X, and the public and political in *Paradise Lost,* XI and XII. The psychology of Adam and Eve appears in their outward manifestations of speech and demeanor, and the vividness of the metamorphosis to serpents and of the compulsive eating of forbidden fruit (among much else) dramatizes the essentially psychospiritual nature of Milton's hell. But, always, there is with the fallen angels, as with Adam and Eve, a recirculatory reciprocity between outer and inner; the two aspects cannot be indefinitely separated, any more than can the political positions manifested by main currents of hellish thought, first in speakers and then in rivers, in *Paradise Lost,* II. Epiphany in hell is degraded to theatrical technique with *Paradise Lost,* X, when Satan blazes forth to his following like a special effect by Inigo Jones and moments later Pentecost and prophecy are degraded to a proleptic Babel of forked tongues.[36]

---

cil of Ephesus; II, Pt. II, 649–855, on the Council of Chalcedon and the papal position there taken. The monophysites were not the only issue addressed here by Milton. There was also the long Christian tradition of the inner struggle in which good and evil contended for domination of the journey. On this, see Aurelius Prudentius, *Psychomachia,* in J. P. Migne, ed., *Patrologiae cursus completus . . . series Latina,* (221 vols.; Paris, 1844–64), LX, cols. 19–89.

35. We have long believed that Milton's pastoral and systematic theology was Catholic, though, of course, his Eucharistic theology, biblicism, and ecclesiology were Calvinist. See, for example, *Paradise Lost,* V, 117–20, II, 559–65, I, 713–21, III, 478–96. John Shawcross, explicating *covenant,* coincidentally alerted us to the force of Milton's Latin, muted by the Columbia and Yale translations; see his *John Milton: The Self and the World* (Lexington, Ky., 1993), 129–37 (a characteristic instance of his critically wide-ranging but always judicious care).

36. Compare T. S. Eliot's famous lines in "The Hollow Men" on the shadow falling between the motion and the act. If the motion is power, the shadow is that of Babel. The Pentecostal point we owe to our student Adolfo Rodriguez.

For Adam and Eve, however, there was, now in history, the hopeful newness of their graced hermeneutic dialogue. Beyond the selfish breakdown in dialogue early in *Paradise Lost,* IX, or bickering at the end of *Paradise Lost,* IX, their discourse now had a mutually and successively supplementary nature that was new, signaled by the openness of penitent prayer, ratified by divine response.

In Book X the damaged pair acquired the now-essential virtue of repentance, thus traversing the crisis of moral choice on a personal level and embarking on the general journey toward God. This particular personal choice would not, Milton judged, be made by all, or even most, as humanity expanded into flawed community (before Babel) and several subcommunities (afterward). A series of vignettes, from both sacred and profane history, illustrated the varieties of moral choice to be made, as in agriculture (XI, 429–35), peace (XI, 556–97), vice (XI, 607–27), or war (XI, 638–59), and those actually made, as by Enoch (XI, 665–71) or Nimrod (XII, 24–63). The poetry was emblematic, only incidentally literal in the Augustinian sense, but not metaphorical, as these sorts of choices would literally be made as the result of fallenness. In the last three books of *Paradise Lost,* Milton presented the four tropes of journey, moment, theater, and ambassadorship in narrative form and as the very fabric of human history.

"Upon Appleton House" was Marvell's analogously serious attempt at anatomizing fallenness: what may be done, firmaments of vulnerable excellence, descents into psychospiritual underworlds, secularized and even militarized worldscapes. But Marvell differed in his progresses in making gardens of the curse. Milton differed more generally, in his *personalizing* of all he knew and believed on behalf of his nation. Milton may be said to have a retrospect toward the old dispensation of old priests and a prospect toward the rising age of individualist priestly believers. The publication of *Paradise Regain'd* with *Samson Agonistes* in 1671, *Poems* in 1673, and the second edition of *Paradise Lost* in 1674 should be taken to complete Milton's calling to be his own liturgist, a uniquely personal, distinctly non-Parliamentary Book of Commonwithal private Prayer.

Further, and in summary, there is a matter of degree. Our *Milton and the Hermeneutic Journey* construes Milton as one of the preeminent love poets in English, the most *philosophical,* given the physical, the temporal, and above all the hermeneutic implications of his dominant, biblical, and Augustinian trope of journey. Much as he intensifies virtually every epic convention to an extreme degree, he also aggrandizes each trope. Journey becomes epistemological and ontological and eschatological for John Milton in history and in his *officium* as Bard, for certain other figures in the poetry, and for the reader. Theater is perhaps the most obvious case. What larger conception of the trope can be imagined than a Producer-Director God who presides over all action within and beyond time acted by an ontologically all-inclusive cast who can "play it" diversely: as farce, such as conspiracy (pretended secret, "justly" had "in derision"); as poignant comedy, in faithful Abdiel's supposition of bringing news or in solitary Adam's discontent or in the graced inner stage of Lord President's castle bounded by the wood temporarily Comus'; as tragedy, in the lethal presumption of Eve and Adam to become "as gods." Obviously, too, Satan, like Comus, was presented as a compulsive scenarist, the guises and disguises of his sterile productions failing ("driven in" or "visage drawn to sharp and spare") and to be overborne At Last by the creative Producer.

The trope of calling is manifest in sonnets on time as "subtle theef of youth," on his blindness (but not *really* on his blindness, as the Shawcross note rightly says), in the famous autobiographical moments in the prose, and in "Lycidas," where one is called to be a faithful ambassador from the *civitas Dei* in the *civitas terrena* but is simultaneously critically stricken with the sense of potential ambush on the way to fulfilling that calling. But the "swain," rescued by Michael somewhat as the Lady was by Sabrina, comes to understand the issue is only secondarily doing or not doing, is primarily *fidelity.*

Fidelity, as we have argued, is the essence of *Paradise Regain'd,* the profoundest meditation in English on calling. It is the whole constellation of questions about and challenges to and would-be subversions of calling: for the Son, certainly; for the Bard (here as in *Paradise Lost;* we follow Martz in this); and optionally for the reader. The Son fulfills his calling by standing, complementarily to journeying, in repeated confession of the Father, which is to say, in loving obedience. "He said, and stood": The climactic moment of Jesus' stand on the temple spire (and Satan's fall from it) is the quintessentially tropic moment for the Son, who has journeyed step by step, thought by meditative thought, led on by the spirit for more than forty days and assailed, even whirled aloft, by Satan.

That tropic, decisive moment in a larger sense concluded the very long train of Miltonic reflections, alert now to ambiguously careering days and races to be run "not without dust and heat" or prompted age, now to the service of those "who only stand and wait." Standing, in Miltonic construal, condenses the tropes of journey, moment, and calling and rejects the trope of theater. The Bible, for example, gave him God saying: "Thou shalt not eat of it; for in the day that thou eatest thereof thou shalt surely die" (Gen. 2:17; Eve, similarly, at Gen. 3:2–3). "Now, lest he put forth his hand, and take also of the tree of life . . . God sent him forth . . . drove out the man" (Gen. 3:22–24). Somewhat like the Bard of *Paradise Regain'd* reimagining the temptations, the Expositor of *Christian Doctrine* wrote, "si steteris, manebis, non steteris, eiicere" (I, iii; "If you stand, you remain; if you don't stand, you will be expelled"). Hence the Redeemer fulfills his calling at an emblematically critical moment on his journey, on the spire, as by implication on the cross, by a stand.

Contrastively, Milton's Samson, though greatly aware of his calling, has "run wrong" (like the mercurial character in Donne's "Satire Three"). Conceiving the calling as coming from a God too exclusively of power, the agonistic Samson, as if wrestling with an angel, has presumed to argue God down (in "reasoning" from "she of Timna" to marry Dalila). And Samson confessed in language of earthy suggestiveness his failure to stand firm against seductive assaults on his "capital secret."

Finally, as the action of the play itself was scripted to unfold in the *relatively* inviolate theater of the reader's mind, weary and tormented Samson was described as eventually standing. Perhaps he should be imagined to stand to refuse Manoa's regressive offer of lounging at home, more probably to stand to refuse Dalila's analogously seductive offer, most probably to vanquish Harapha's swagger. Finally, the messenger's report has invited readers to imagine Samson's last and most agonistic stand between the pillars. It is tragic for the usual complex of reasons: heroically serious because of his sense of a transcendent God; tragic because he can imagine his calling as providing no better fulfillment, being from a God of war; tragic because by the precedents of Samson's life and Milton's own era violent force might be necessary but could not be sufficient. The multiple physiological suggestions of the play, so many of them sexual, intimate the tragic question "How could he not fail, made so?" (unless of course *redeemed* from failing strength, as he ultimately is by a *very* severe grace).

Perhaps that is the moment of reflective recognition to which the ironically "rousing motions" of Samson, the stunning reports, the poignant conjectures of Chorus and Manoa all invite. More surely, the egregious showiness of court masque, chastened and sobered by Milton nearly a whole poetic career earlier for the devout Egertons, is here further discredited in the example, the fatal indulgence, of the Dagon festival, filtered to fit audience through the book—filtered from what Milton saw as the increasingly idolatrous outer world—into private study, where even any music would formally be of the inner ear only, in the relatively legitimate theater and private liturgy of the mind. That *Samson Agonistes* has been done into grand opera would presumably strike Milton as ironic, like (we suggest) Fortinbras putting on the theatrical funeral ostensibly for Hamlet but more appositely for himself. Milton, in Sonnet 22, had dismissed the "vain mask" of this world.

Thus, in the context of the ending era, we emphasize Milton's powerful engagement with the trope of moment. As early as the mid-1630s, in "On Time," he had posited an "individual kiss" to deliver each believer from the vicissitude of the merely mundane into the beatitude of eternal divine presence. *Paradise Lost* turns on ontologically originary moments: Satan's rebellious turn engenders Sin and Death, presumably in an instant, though it cannot without "process of speech" be told. So, too, the Son's choice and commissioning engender the world of redemption. The Eve and Adam two-step engenders the world of human history.

But one may return to the literal and dramatic falling action ending *Paradise Regain'd.* Every reply by the Son to each speech by Satan, we have argued, represented a moment of fidelity under pressure, a symbolic stand, with the final response atop the tower of the temple only the most literal and spectacular. We infer that the Son's years following of active ministry (not literally mentioned by the Bard) were for Milton an extension in the scale of human history analogous to the faithful responses to Satanic occasions. The descent with angels to mother earth mirrors an ascent with angels from mother earth. "Mother's house," in biblical literalness in Nazareth, would in Milton's imagination be for Mary, as for his own mother (and for Lycidas), a heavenly mansion. In heaven, moment would be fulfilled, infinitely expanded by perfect love and joy, the Miltonic sense of eternity. In Milton's hell, conversely, moment is literally subverted, forever indecisive because forever narcissistic, as emblematized by the circular arguments about free will and foreknowledge and by the compulsive eating of the ashen fruit each return of the time ("some say"). Marvell, complementarily, heralded the rising secular world: Some moments are more important than others but more because of worldly considerations than spiritual ones.

By the seventies, the psychopolitical world had quietly begun to change. New values and standards of judgment that could be called the crisis of European consciousness, so brilliantly described in 1935 by Paul Hazard, were still largely obscured behind the facade of divine right.[37] But underground streams flow as strongly as those on the surface, and the overwhelming psychological presence, power, immediacy, and terror of formal religion as the general and cultural mode of political judgment was on the ebb. Still as universally subscribed to, though not as fervently felt, religion had gradually begun to seep away from formal public life in an essential way, even when not yet in a symbolic way. The chapel at Versailles was built near the end of the Sun King's life and was off to the side, not at the center as were the king's apartments.[38] The Reformation, and the psychological and political centrality of denomination and doctrine that characterized that period, began to fade into the past, to lose presence.

Presence is essentially a function of care, not of visual or physical togetherness or of institutional obligation. Of course, care is not necessarily *agape.* Whose daily journey is not furnished with physically absent but real presences, whether immanent or transcendent? But care and the presence it creates need constant renewal, and as the seventeenth century waned, the care needed to maintain a presence of the divine within daily life began to fade. What had variously been *agape* (Milton's or Donne's) or the doctrinal self-righteousness of those who would define their antagonists' liturgy as bad theater (whether "Popery" or "wretched enthusiasm") drifted toward *bienfaisance.*

The Friends with their quiet attendance on the presence of the Spirit were the Restoration style of reform, rather than Congregationalists, Presbyterians, Baptists, and assorted Levellers and Diggers and Fifth Monarchy saints arrayed in bloody quasi-cosmic combat to bring in the new Jerusalem. As reli-

37. Hazard, *The European Mind,* esp. Pt. I. See also Richard F. Hardin, *Civil Idolatry: Desacralizing and Monarchy in Spenser, Shakespeare, and Milton* (Newark, Del., 1992), esp. 207. We agree in general with him that at the end of the century imagery needed to be less allegorical or mythic, more literal or realistic, than at the beginning. Accordingly, even Henry Purcell's *Dido and Aeneas* was taken to be nonpolitical.

38. Rouvroy, Louis de, duc de St. Simon, *Memoires* (41 vols.; Paris, 1879–1928).

gion gradually became more a private matter between one's soul and one's God, the public tension aroused by the existence or threat of formal heterodoxy slowly dwindled. With the increase of historical knowledge and the perfusion of a mechanical world picture, each tick of the clock became less a moment for choice or step on a tropic journey than a quasi-spatial interpolation, thrusting biblical incident farther off.[39] Without formal pronouncements, standards other than religious ones by which to judge the king and Parliament suggested themselves. Those standards tended to involve the efficacy of the exercise of political power. For a time, as the Test Act and the Popish Plot indicated, the old denominational / political noises were made, and as late as the Protestant Succession and the Old Pretender, religion could rally the nation. But the psychological tide was moving in another direction. What was later and tendentiously to be called the Enlightenment had almost arrived, though quietly, unexpectedly, unattended by stars or other portents. When John Bunyan published *The Pilgrim's Progress* in 1675, it was already the old-time religion, and the journey of faith had become suspiciously allegorical (compared, say, to Donne's "Good Friday, 1613. Riding Westward"). And it seems like another eon from Bunyan and Titus Oates to John Locke and Isaac Newton. But it was a decade.

The end of one "climate of opinion," or (better) the prevalence of one set of public habits of thought yielding to the prevalence of another, cannot be so precisely dated as a war or an election. The old and new attitudes of thought simply mix and mingle until contemporaries (and cultural historians) become aware that the old, once popular orthodoxy has gone quaintly out of date and the new, once radical, is now respectable and ordinary, appearing "natural," if not inevitable, to politicians, suburban rectors, and insurance salesmen. Of course this took time, in the case of the Enlightenment, a long generation, in

39. Prelapsarean and postlapsarean language in *Paradise Lost* is thoughtfully and provocatively analyzed (along somewhat different lines) by John Leonard, *Naming in Paradise: Milton and the Language of Adam and Eve* (New York, 1990). See also Knoppers, *Historicizing Milton,* 159–60: in *Of True Religion,* the English, like the Chorus in *Samson Agonistes,* are finally not punished and thereby moved from idolatry but rather left to it. With David Loewenstein, *Milton and the Drama of History,* we disagree on some points but concur on the Miltonic notion of profane or sacred theater (see esp. 136–43); Milton might excoriate new Babels or temples of Dagon and prophesy their fall while Marvell chided or satirized, but for others, like the Kircher of our frontispiece, such projection was handsome urban development.

the case of civil rights, a decade, of the Beatles, seven minutes on Ed Sullivan. When dealing with large shifts in the general cultural focus, precision is the enemy of accuracy. In 1914 T. S. Eliot published "The Love Song of J. Alfred Prufrock," and this has often been regarded as the beginning of modern poetry. But in Paris Guillaume Apollinaire had been publishing modernist *poesis* for years before 1914, and after that date Robert Frost, Siegfried Sassoon, and W. H. Auden wrote very traditional poetry. In 1798 William Wordsworth and Samuel Taylor Coleridge published the *Lyrical Ballads,* often seen as the opening volley of high Romanticism, but *The Sorrows of Young Werther* had come a quarter century earlier and seemed romantic enough in its time. No date and no event can be claimed as explanatory (though it may be emblematic and even influential) of so substantial a cultural change as a permanent alteration in habits of thought. There are only the odd signposts that were symptomatic or prophetic of change, at least as seen with hindsight, and that often for contemporaries meant much less. We have chosen two such signposts from among many, the first a throwaway paragraph by Andrew Marvell from his 1672 / 73 prose work *The Rehearsal Transpros'd:*

> Whether it be a war of religion or of liberty, it is not worth the labor to enquire. Whichsoever was at the top, the other was at the bottom; but upon considering all, I think the cause was too good to have been fought for. Men ought to have trusted God; they ought and might have trusted the King, with that whole matter. The "arms of the Church are prayers and tears"; the arms of the subjects are patience and petitions. The King himself, being of so accurate and piercing a judgment, would soon have felt where it stuck. For men may spare their pains where nature is at work, and the world will not go faster for our driving.[40]

"Nature" there seems to be the ultimate power mode, or perhaps *medium,* of (presumably) divine will. This was written twelve years before Locke's first *Letter on Toleration,* published anonymously in Latin in Holland in 1685.[41] It was not the first essay to suggest that religion was not an appropriate cause for

40. Andrew Marvell, *The Rehearsal Transpros'd,* Pt. 1 (1672 / 73), in *Andrew Marvell,* ed. Frank Kermode and Keith Waller (Oxford, 1990), 265.

41. John Locke, *Treatise of Civil Government and A Letter Concerning Toleration,* ed. Charles Sherman (New York, 1937), 167–224 for the letter.

persecution and civil war; Sebastien Castillio had made the same proposal in 1560, though to a less receptive audience.[42] And in England, Marvell was certainly far behind Milton in espousing a decent obscurity and general freedom when it came to men's souls.[43]

Nor were Milton and Marvell alone in defending religious freedom. In 1621, on Christmas Day at St. Paul's, Dean Donne had remarked:

> The *reformation of abuses* in *State* or *Church,* is a holy purpose, there is that drop of the dew of heaven in it; but if it be *unseasonably attempted,* and have not a farther concoction, then the *first motions of our owne zeale,* it becomes ineffectuall. . . . Actions precious in the acceptation of God, are purposes conceived by his Spirit, and executed in his time *to his Glory,* not conceived out of *Ambition,* nor executed out of *sedition.*[44]

The two passages make a suggestive diptych. With Donne, heavenly grace or the workings of the Holy Spirit in human projects of reformation were imaged as a "drop of dew." We take the primary association to be fertility and benignity in nature, followed probably by poetically conventional associations of dewdrops with jewel-like aesthetic loveliness, and ecclesiastical associations with the purifying waters of baptism. With theological orthodoxy but inventive representation, the absence of love for God—love responsive to the graced inspiration—could be thought to yield only something like a failed alchemy or a defective gear-train slipping ineffectually or clashing in

42. On Sebastien Castillio, who debated with Calvin and argued that religious doctrine was so doubtful that it was improper and immoral to kill over these inconclusive issues, see John T. McNeill, *The History and Character of Calvinism* (London, 1954), 168–69, 176. Castillio's book *On Heretics* maintained his view that toleration was the only proper position for a Christian. Calvin ran him out of Geneva. See the modern edition of *On Heretics* (New York, 1935).

43. Milton was never more emblematic on freedom of soul than in "On the Forcers of Conscience" (1647) and Sonnet 16, on Cromwell (1652). See the elegant distillation of decades of Perez Zagorin's historical scholarship and reflection, *Milton, Aristocrat and Rebel: The Poet and His Politics* (Rochester, N. Y., 1992); he is judicious on the issues (among many) of Milton's relation to Machiavelli (limited, essentially, to *Discourses*) and to Hobbes (antipathetic, 156–58), but Zagorin's sense of politics reasonably enough limits his treatment of Milton and love to Milton's lifelong "concern with moral or ethical action" and heroic championing "of freedom of conscience" (149, 158–59).

44. *The Sermons of John Donne,* ed. George R. Potter and Evelyn Simpson (10 vols.; Berkeley, 1953–62), III, S17, 922–30.

power conflicts of ambition or sedition. There hovered also about conceptions "out of *Ambition*" the suggestion of misconceived and self-aggrandizing roles in the *theatrum mundi;* and there was about executions "out of *sedition*" suggestions of double-agent ambassadorship (even more sinisterly theatrical) or ambassadorship from some idolatrous kingdom. Donne's sermon remark is glossed by Milton's angry survey in 1647, a dual epitome of revolutionary fervor ineffectual or corrupted or betrayed by degeneration into power fetishism: "New Presbyter is but old Preist writt large."

Andrew Marvell's soberly judicious retrospect belongs in the same line, but it betokened less a crisis of moment or revolutionary decade, more the obscurer cultural transformation under way. He was evidently implicated in that transformation, quite possibly in ways deeper than he recognized. The "religion" and the "liberty" that could be one "at the top, the other . . . at the bottom" were not utterly static, taxonomic, abstract intellectual counters. But neither were they the all-embracing dynamisms of Milton's universe of love. Marvell did suggest a domestic *saeculum* by the final "Let's in" at the end of "Upon Appleton House"—"in" to the *philios* of domestic nurture of mind and generation. Here, in *The Rehearsal Transpros'd,* something akin to that was conceived for the *domus* of church and state: Prayers, tears, patience, and petitions are fundamentally genres of love, though all can be abused, and the last can degenerate into the unlove of nonnegotiable demands (as veterans of the American sixties recall).

But the ambiguity remained. Was it the armamentarium of tears and petitions Charles I would have felt to have stuck in his own judgment? Would his judgment have felt (with those helps) the wrongs complained of? And the more stunning and momentous ambiguity: The cultural change under way was accounted *nature,* not to be speeded (or impeded?) "for our driving," which would seem to derogate the freedom of human will to a degree Milton would have deplored and might seem to make *driving* the mode of choice. Yet how much latitude of choice was there as the meanings of the very tropes of culture changed? Journey would endure as a popular trope but usually horizontalized to emphatically secular itineraries. Theater could be reduced to grammar and called analytic philosophy. Moment would be reduced to the secularity of *coup de théâtre* or *coup d'état* or further degraded to tychastic time or event time in a power train ("T minus thirty, and counting"). Ambassadorship would be reduced to something between *langue* and *parole,* to "discourse"; ambassadors themselves disappear in any "agentless semantics of action." The eighteenth century with its more secular climate of opinion approached.

Marvell was a cautious elected politician, however, one who had served in the Protectorate, had lauded Cromwell albeit ambiguously, and now represented Hull on a permanent basis. He evidently did not believe, as Philip Larkin was to believe in this century, that "Hull is other people." So he made a cautious remark, buried in a tedious treatise, though one praised by contemporaries as witty. But Marvell made it nonetheless. The old poet's insight was still true. The old habits of thought were being abandoned to be replaced by a new secularism, with power the fundamental business of government (and *parties* of more or less, federal or local), with religion a private matter, and with reason, power, and representation increasingly divorced from love. Through the eighteenth and nineteenth centuries many of the fighting words of earlier sectarian differences dwindled to comedy of manners. The tropes have subsided to common cultural metaphors: They have become more and more often detached from any transcendent reference. The English Renaissance and Reformation were slipping swiftly and almost silently away.

A Note on Shakespeare

Our intention to scrutinize some major Renaissance texts with regard to love, power, and the tropes has here seemed to suggest relatively brief treatment of the gigantic case of Milton because we have supplemented this attention to him with a separate book. Attention to Shakespeare has been even more drastically abbreviated because on these matters (as on innumerable others) he deserves a book to himself. But the economy of this book may admit a frame to the scattered references above, as well as a short overture to such a book.

This, then, is a short parallel to our general historical argument in this volume. With regard to Shakespeare as to others, one of the most obvious ways New Criticism (never in its diversity to be called *the* New Criticism) was historical was to emphasize traditional rhetoric, especially of "figures" such as metaphor and irony, as well as to give attention to the tradition of larger rhetorical structures such as genre. But occluded if not ignored have been the ancient tropes of theater, journey, calling, and moment, pervasive in the Renaissance. They merit attention now because they thrive today in torqued or alternate forms but then were regarded as connecting earth and heaven, *media,* indeed, of what earlier scholarship (a bit too ambitiously) called "world view" at large and the terms in which myriad cultural transactions were construed locally. These tropes of journey, moment, calling, and theater were the terms of expression through which the religious culture of the English Renaissance understood both its duty and its end.

Nowhere is the duality and connection between heaven and earth more poignantly expressed than in formal Renaissance theater. Consider *Hamlet,* a play seemingly encountered everywhere, even in high school, and when without notice taken of "the play-within-the-play"? How many teachers must have reassured students with the confirmation that "catching the conscience of the King" suggests more generally the idea of theater as device to illumine obscure truth, only to make thoughtful students uneasy with the suggestion of an Aristotelian proportional metaphor: "The Mousetrap" is to stage audience as *Hamlet* is to world of the greater audience? But there are *numerous* plays-within-the-play. Most of them are conspicuously detached from any transcendent orientation of the trope. They slight or ignore connection with the producership and spectatorship of God, who was sufficiently (for a Renaissance audience) introduced to the discourse by references to Christmas, Cain, failing prayers, divinity shaping ends, and the like. Hamlet's "solemn black" and "actions that a man might play" are, he *complains,* a kind of conventional and appropriate theater, representative of and guilty by association with a fallen world of meretricious theatricalism. Laertes, in contrast, would demand more theater, a larger show of "formal ostentation" than had been made for his father's funeral. He would similarly theatricalize his sister's death and has "a speech o' fire," but his expressive tear "drowns it," and Hamlet has occasion at the grave to scorn his "rant." Laertes is as compulsive a theatricalizer as his father and his king. Of course, the king was supposed to traffic in theater: It was part of the *officium* of royalty, but that theater was properly to be Godly and honest rather than manipulative and deceitful.

Polonius as well scripts meretricious street-theater that would take the "carp of truth" about Laertes, scripts his daughter's responses to the supposed theatricalizing of Hamlet, then her behavior as bait to diagnose Hamlet's madness, and finally scripts (albeit more loosely) the audition of which he himself dies. A dangerous thing, theater. Similarly, Claudius calls Rosencrantz and Guildenstern "to use" them as shrewdly cast instruments in the first playlet for Hamlet's death. Later, Laertes will be cast in a scene designed as well for his own death as Hamlet's. Meanwhile, Claudius routinely abuses the ears of Gertrude and Denmark with palliative theater. He acknowledges, in a rueful moment, his own "plast'ring art" and "painted word." But that *moment* is tropic for no one on stage, any more than is Hamlet's acknowledgment, in rehearsal to himself before the closet scene with his mother, that his "tongue and soul [will] in this be hypocrites."

Characteristically, Hamlet's own theatricalism seeks discovery rather than masking, seeks scenario to find truth, not deception (or at worst seeks self-defense, as when aboard ship: "Or I could make a prologue to my brains / They had begun the play"). Hamlet, in viewing as a spectator "The Mouse-trap" and his own "cause," sees there that of Laertes as well. In Claudius' sword-play, Hamlet is the only character who would connect theatricality with any transcendent ground, with the "divinity that shapes our ends." The military state funeral ordered by Fortinbras (like that ordered by Octavius Caesar at the end of *Antony and Cleopatra*) is a regression to cynical statism: a masque equating "most royal" with worldly and militant show.

Those "rites of war" and the impending masque of election (and coronation) of Fortinbras constitute a darkly ironic reversal, for Hamlet has undergone a journey of calling, punctuated by moments less and more salvific. He goes from *cursing* the spite of "the time" that calls him to "set it right" to somberly acknowledging commission from the heavens to be "scourge and minister" to accepting some part in divine shaping of ends. That journey is marked by conversive and aversive *moments* for decision: He struggled with unsatisfactory alternatives of revenge on earth or in heaven, scorned secular "honor" imperiling more soldiers than fit on the ground they fight for, struggled to connect life and calling in a union of his own truth and the public recognition (and voice for Fortinbras).

Even in this play so richly diverse in Judaeo-Christian allusion, Hamlet's aversions from love to power or conversions from power to love do not always have a clear transcendent orientation. Clearly the turn from Claudius seemingly at prayer is the turn of a beguiled fallen man who would judge Claudius' eternity as if godlike. The moments of turning in the last act, in faith toward the rough-hewn ends, toward oneness, toward Laertes, toward Horatio, are arguably turns toward truth. And that, in "Denmark" 's Christian dispensation, might at least make one free.

In some contrast, the decisive moments in Antony's journey through Mediterranean environs more starkly involve secular power or love. So it is with the fatal turn to wed Octavia, one of *numerous* royal masques and would-be masques in this play of statism. So it is with Antony's turn from land-fight to sea-fight at Actium, his turn in erotic love from military responsibility in battle to follow Cleopatra's ship, or his turn in philadelphic love to send after Enobarbus the latter's goods. And Cleopatra turns, at the last, away from some Caesarean masque of power to a fantasy (to the English) of love in Elysium.

The more daring Shakespearean *coup de théâtre* is the thirty-seven-line scene beginning Act III: the Parthian King's slain son "borne before" the Roman troops. "Thy [son] Pacorus, Orodes, / Pays this for [our officer] Marcus Crassus," remarks Ventidius, who proposes to find and flatter Antony. Interminable vicissitudes of revenge and narcissism are formulated as a moment *for the theater audience,* implying the choice, the only Roman choice, between the pageant of Octavian absolutism and that of carnality and carnage.

In another of the illuminating contrasts fostered by the tropic perspective, one easily notes how the trope of moment appears in comedy. Shakespeare's comedies regularly feature moments of more-or-less laboriously achieved trothplight. But weddings or wedding celebrations in numerous fifth acts have routinely been taken as so conventional as to obscure how the trope is amplified by Shakespeare (and occluded in other ways by Middleton and Jonson). The ring subplot in *Merchant of Venice,* the "taming" plot in *Taming of the Shrew,* the year of trials prescribed at the end of *Love's Labors Lost* all, in their mini-theaters-of-instruction, enforce on resistant learners, male except for Kate, that the moment of trothplight is a radical turn to new life, a "world without end bargain," not just an eddy in the flow. So, more darkly, with Benedick's "I am engaged" in response to Beatrice's "Kill Claudio" and the besieged women's ostensible "yeses" in the bed-trick plays within *Measure for Measure* and *All's Well That Ends Well:* False or feeble troth is tested and defined by ostensible breach or threatened excess.

Such testing or defining of tropic moment notable in the comedies may be construed as stretched and complemented in the romances: the notorious sixteen-year interval that both does and does not break *The Winter's Tale* in two; the onerous journeys into exile or exoticism or danger (never quite the savage heath of Lear) in *The Winter's Tale, Pericles, The Tempest.* The ministry of time amplified or materialized in journey seems essential to enable protagonists to find home and know it in some sufficiently profound sense, even if not always in explicitly heavenly terms. In the half-romance *All's Well,* Bertram flees from home and trothplight to a feckless war and supposed carnal opportunity, while his rejected bride, called to be her healer-father's healing daughter, ostensibly repairs to an abbey. The reluctantly chastened Bertram at the end swears he will "love her dearly, ever dearly," and we may all wonder. But can any fail to note that the king, who stayed home, ignorantly continues to make marriages by fiat.

In the greater *Henriad,* journey tends to express calling more than moment. The many, many more and less secular theatricalizings and moments tend to be subordinate to the journey toward calling. Consider: "The King hath thrown his warder down," *i.e.,* God's vicegerent Richard has aborted the divinely sanctioned trial-by-combat (itself a long journey, Mowbray has ironically said); "I do, I will" banish Falstaff and all the world, Hal promises in a tavern playlet, because he acknowledges himself called to do what the best-intentioned prince cannot by fiat do, "redeem the time," at least of the realm's vicissitude, even if he can redeem his own feckless years. Richard II, legitimate king, had led the realm no closer to accommodation with the City of God but only to Ireland, thence to "sit upon the ground and talk of death of kings," thence "down like glistring Phaethon," thence finally (minus the realm) to Pomfret and into his own reflective mind. Henry IV, with more acrid irony, led not the projected pilgrimage to Jerusalem but rather multiple sorties to stem insurrection, ending at last in a tavern side-parlor.

Henry V, conventionally considered as the climactic element of the *Henriad,* repays consideration as an early case in a series on ambiguous callings and journeys. In the spectrum of that context, it would take a middling position. On the one side, there are dramas such as *As You Like It, The Tempest, Pericles,* and *The Winter's Tale,* in which a dethroned monarch or faithful dependent undergoes a journey of exile (or flight), profound and often therapeutic contact with nature, and ultimate renewal of familial love, with the state's power largely *attending* and reinforcing the significance of that renewal. There are associations or intimations of grace in those renewals. But King Hal is acknowledgedly a usurper's son. Called ambiguously to "redeem the time," called implicitly to legitimize the monarchy or, failing that, to rehabilitate it or, failing that, to regularize it, he undertakes what is ambiguously a journey of redemption or distraction to France. Some, we are assured, go to France like horse leeches, "the very blood to suck"; the whole enterprise is ironically sanctioned by a black masque of venal ecclesiastics whose disbelief in miracles makes questionable their belief in grace and hence their callings. After the ambiguous miracle of Agincourt (power of God or power of longbows?), Katherine the spoil-of-war is accorded the impromptu masque of courtship (theater as time out from the march of time) to be wooed and (like Theseus' Hippolyta) perhaps more than physically won, as if a domesticated political idyll of love. The Epilogue, however, formally reminds us of what everyone knew: Whatever the French project's pretensions to grace or to Jerusalem, it had failed as *policy.*

On the other side in this spectrum, darker callings and journeys familiar especially in the tragedies marshal themselves. Macbeth is called to faithful thaneship and its rewards by a king in grace but called by his wife to a tendentiously defined manhood and called with darkest ambiguity by the witches. His responsive actions are lightly marked as a tropic journey: a literal movement to coronation at Scone; a partly figurative river of blood "waded deep"; the terrible emptiness of days as "petty pace" and fools' "way"; life as theatrical strut and fret—absurd movement killing time. Lear, called to fulfill his imperfectly fulfilled kingship, and Othello, called to discharge his newly augmented commission (the latter against the so-defined enemies of Christendom), not altogether unlike Macbeth, are beset by demonic figures without and (we are invited to understand) demons within. Their enacted journeys, to stormy heath as to stormy sea and ambiguously civil Cypress, give evidence that "that way madness lies," though ultimately both Lear and Othello come through madness to humility. But in the very essence of these tropes' tragic possibilities, repatriation of exiles will mostly fail, renewals of familial love (if any) and repairs of state will be ironically disjunctive, and learning the truth of self and "what our seemers be" sets protagonists ironically free from life itself.

That phrase of Vincentio's, as he temporarily deposes himself from the ducal throne of Vienna, leaving Angelo in charge, can serve to remind us in summary that *Measure for Measure,* like *Henry V,* invokes from a middling position multiple contrasting possibilities in all four tropes. The Duke has flagged in his calling to just administration (presumably as God's vicegerent, in this conspicuously ecclesiastical play), though perhaps we should understand he has heeded a potentially competing calling to study and know himself. He avows dislike at "staging" himself to his people's eyes but does so (as a monk) and produces playlets that test every character in the play. His announced monastic retreat to still and spiritual ascent is a busy round of discoveries, whereon most fail his tests, some in a bad moment (Mariana, Escalus, and the jailer are notable exceptions). Order in the state and domestic affections are certainly reaffirmed at the final theatricalized trial scene at the city gates, and they are affirmed as not altogether disjunctive. But their consonance surely varies in the marriages now to be public and social (in supplement to *diverse* earlier, private professions): Claudio and Juliet, Mariana and

Angelo, Lucio and his whore, and (will it be a marriage?) Isabella and the Duke. What seems implicit is that love and power cohere in the state only by the agency of one as intimately present as a confessor, as theatrically inventive as Shakespeare himself, and nearly as omnipresent to the society and potent with regard to the flow of time itself as Shakespeare's God.

These sample variations may suggest the study we intend on the Shakespearean corpus as an inexhaustibly rich set of explorations of love and power primarily (far from exclusively) in the *media* of the four tropes of theater, journey, moment, and calling.

Index